LISTENING

Attitudes, Principles, and Skills

JUDI BROWNELL
Cornell University

PEARSON
and

Boston ▪ New York ▪ San Francisco
Mexico City ▪ Montreal ▪ Toronto ▪ London ▪ Madrid ▪ Munich ▪ Paris
Hong Kong ▪ Singapore ▪ Tokyo ▪ Cape Town ▪ Sydney

For the people who have always listened with me:
my parents, my partner, and my children.

Executive Editor: Karon Bowers
Series Editor: Brian Wheel
Editorial Assistant: Heather Hawkins
Senior Marketing Manager: Mandee Eckerslee
Editorial-Production Service: Whitney Acres Editorial
Manufacturing Buyer: JoAnne Sweeney
Electronic Composition: Modern Graphics, Inc.
Cover Administrator: Joel Gendron

For related titles and support materials, visit our online catalog at www.ablongman.com

Between the time Website information is gathered and then published, it is not unusual for
some sites to have closed. Also, the transcription of URLs can result in typographical errors.
The publisher would appreciate notification where these occur so that they may be corrected
in subsequent editions.

Library of Congress Cataloging-in-Publication Data

Brownell, Judi
    Listening: attitudes, principles, and skills / Judi Brownell.—3rd ed.
        p.   cm.
    Includes bibliographical references and index.
    ISBN 0-205-45356-2 (pbk.)
    1. Listening.   2. Listening—Problems, exercises, etc.   I. Title.

    BF323.L5B663 2005
    153.6′8—dc22   2004066162
                                                                         CIP

Printed in the United States of America
10 9 8 7 6 5 4 3 2 1   09 08 07 06 05

Photos on pages 3, 35, 71, 103, 139, 173, 224, 267, 307, 357 are reprinted with permission of Gary
Brownell. © Gary Brownell.

CONTENTS

CHAPTER TWO
Listening Theory and Research   37

PART II: Listening: Principles and Applications   69

CHAPTER THREE
The Process of Hearing   71

CHAPTER FOUR
The Process of Understanding   105

CHAPTER FIVE

The Process of Remembering   141

CHAPTER SEVEN

The Process of Evaluating   228

CHAPTER EIGHT

The Process of Responding   270

CHAPTER TEN

Listening Challenges   361

PREFACE

Effective communicators are, first and foremost, effective listeners. Only when you listen to your partners and understand their perspectives can you make informed choices about what to say or do. Whether you're listening to your instructor in class, or to persuasive messages through the media, or to a friend who needs your help and support, listening is one of your most essential skills.

Listening: Attitudes, Principles, and Skills introduces you to the HURIER model, a behavioral approach to listening improvement that serves as a unifying framework for understanding and developing your listening ability. This model suggests that listening is a system of interrelated components that include both mental processes and observable behaviors. The six skill areas, or components, include: hearing, understanding, remembering, interpreting, evaluating, and responding.

Listening improvement in each component of the process requires:

1. *Appropriate attitudes toward listening*—Attitude plays a key role in your ability to listen well. Unless you believe that listening is essential for your personal development, it will be difficult to devote the necessary energy to improving your competence. In addition, effective listening requires an attitude of openness and interest in others.
2. *Knowledge of principles about listening*—Listening theory and research lends important insight into how your listening can be improved. Key principles guide your efforts as you work to become more effective and more consistent in meeting your listening challenges.
3. *Acquisition of fundamental listening skills*—Ultimately, the development of appropriate *attitudes* and the application of listening *principles* will result in *improved performance*. The primary goal of this text is to change your behavior—to help you become a better listener.
4. *Development of listening strategies*—As you will discover, listening requirements vary according to both your purpose and the listening context. Making informed choices about how and when and under what circumstances to apply your listening skills is one of your most important tasks.

In addition to learning about listening and practicing effective listening behaviors, it is also important to think about listening and its broader implications. Throughout this book you will be asked questions, such as: Is empathy, completely understanding another person's perspective, really possible? How does your personality influence your listening improvement? and, Is it ethical to behave like a good listener when you are really disinterested or bored? Your thoughtful reflections on these and other questions are part of becoming a better listener.

ORGANIZATION OF THE TEXT

This text is organized into three parts: An Introduction to Listening, Listening: Principles and Applications, and Listening: Relationships and Challenges. There are ten chapters, each followed by an applications section that encourages you to think about and apply what you have learned. Through self-assessments, cases, and individual and group exercises, applications provide opportunities for you to practice and discuss the ideas presented in each chapter.

Chapter 1 introduces you to the HURIER model and emphasizes the importance of listening in your increasingly global, fast-paced environment. Listening improvement requires motivation. Unless you are ready to work at increasing your effectiveness, it will be difficult to realize significant changes in your performance. At the end of the chapter is a self-assessment inventory that you can use to individualize your listening instruction. A set of questions corresponds to each component of the HURIER model. By analyzing the results of this assessment and by creating a personal listening profile, you can quickly identify the areas in which you feel most comfortable as well as those that may need improvement.

The second chapter places listening within the larger context of what is called relational communication. Both the communication process, and the individual listener, are viewed as systems of interrelated components. Although this text focuses on the individual listener, an understanding of relational communication is prerequisite to appreciating the central role listening plays in human communication. An overview of listening research, and the underlying assumptions of the HURIER model, are also discussed.

Each of the six chapters in Part II, Principles and Applications, presents principles and skills related to one component of the HURIER model. An extended case highlights the main points of each chapter and is used to clarify key concepts as they are discussed. Applications sections begin with a review of the relevant questions from the listening self-assessment instrument so that you can identify areas of particular concern. Although the six components are interrelated, by identifying your specific listening needs you will be able to focus your attention on the most relevant topics and activities. You will find that the third edition incorporates new material on appreciative listening (Chapter 3) and on emotional intelligence (Chapter 6).

The final component of the listening process, responding, places responsibility on you as a listener to indicate the extent of your listening effectiveness. In relational listening situations, the quality of your listening is judged by the appropriateness of your response. In determining the nature of this response, two considerations are key—communication purpose and the communication context.

Effective listening requires more than the simple acquisition of attitudes, knowledge, and skill. It also implies that your newly acquired behaviors will be applied wisely—at the right time and in the right situation. Responsible listeners use sound judgment in deciding *what* skills to apply to various listening situations. A model has been added in the third edition that draws attention to the importance of listening purpose and context in developing your specific listening strategy. In addition, the final part of your text examines a variety of listening relationships and provides guidelines suggesting the most appropriate listening behaviors for each situation. Listening in the family, in school, and in organizations is discussed.

The last chapter introduces issues that arise for listeners as they confront continuous change, globalization, and high-technology environments. The listening challenges created by gender are also discussed. Finally, you are asked to consider the challenge of ethical listening and the extent of your responsibility, as a listener, to ensure that communication is consistently ethical. Each chapter begins with an extended case, and applications sections once again provide exercises and activities to strengthen your skills.

Your journey into listening will be an exciting one. Few skills have more potential for facilitating so many important outcomes—better relationships, increased enjoyment of your surroundings, and personal and professional effectiveness. Spend some time improving your listening. It makes a difference.

ACKNOWLEDGMENTS

The International Listening Association, founded in 1979, has done much to stimulate listening research and to make the applications of what we know about listening accessible to educators and practitioners. Through both its annual conventions and its journal, this organization serves as a forum for study and for conversation (www.listen.org). The many listeners of ILA have been a constant source of inspiration for me, and I thank all of them.

Others who made this third edition possible include Brian Wheel, my editor at Allyn and Bacon and Heather Hawkins, his editorial assistant. Thanks also goes to Faye Whitney, my production editor. The following reviewers for this third edition—Lisa Abraham, Western Oregon University; Mary Bozik, University of Northern Iowa; and Thomas Marshall, Robert Morris University provided valuable insights into how we could create a text that readers would find timely, relevant, and compelling. My sincere gratitude goes also to members of the editorial staff at Allyn and Bacon, especially my executive editor, Karon Bowers. My administrative assistant, Diane Craig helped immensely by handling all the planned and unplanned tasks that allowed me to devote time to this project.

I hope my family already knows how much I appreciate their constant support and encouragement, and how lost I would be without them. Thank you, Gary, for always being there and thank you, Conor and Cody, for helping me to listen and to learn along the way.

PART I

AN INTRODUCTION
TO LISTENING

PEANUTS Reprinted by permission of United Features Syndicate, Inc.

CHAPTER 1

IMPROVING LISTENING
EFFECTIVENESS

A good listener is not only popular everywhere but,
after a while he knows something.

—WILSON MIZNER

OUTLINE

CHAPTER OBJECTIVES

After completing this chapter, you will:

Become more aware of:

- the importance and benefits of effective listening
- the usefulness of the HURIER model in developing listening skills
- the value of a behavioral approach to listening
- the importance of understanding yourself as a listener

Better understand:

- the components of the HURIER model
- the development and advantages of the HURIER model

- the principles of self-monitoring
- the principles of constructive feedback

Develop skills in:

- identifying listening tasks and opportunities
- identifying factors that influence your listening effectiveness
- using the HURIER model to assess your listening behavior
- self-monitoring
- providing constructive feedback

THE IMPORTANCE OF LISTENING

Somewhere in the attic, or in the back of a drawer, there's a book that tells about a child's first years. Her parents have recorded the day she first rolled over, the moment she first smiled, the first time she took a step. There's an entry that reads, "Jane said 'maa' today. February 8, 1986." A few pages further, there's a torn, rumpled piece of yellow paper where the child scribbled her first word. A section at the very back has a space to record her favorite book and the date she learned to read. But nowhere in this book of a child's growth, of her first magic years of learning and exploring and discovery, is there any mention of listening. Could it be true? Did the child never learn to listen?

> How do you determine what to listen to?

Like many others, you probably grew up believing that it was important to do as much talking as possible. "Let's all be quiet. It's Mary's turn to speak," your first grade teacher might say, and everyone's attention would dutifully turn to Mary. Sometimes she would have an interesting story to tell or an important piece of information to share. Usually, however, Mary talked about Mary, and everyone else waited impatiently for her to finish so that they, too, could have a turn in the spotlight. Think about it. Was anyone *really listening* to Mary during those early experiences? And, if they had wanted to listen, did anyone know how?

Think about the number of times that you have misunderstood a homework assignment, misinterpreted a friend's tone of voice, or forgotten someone's name at a party. While such instances influence your individual effectiveness, the consequences of poor listening can be even more far-reaching as we communicate regularly over thousands of miles and interact with people from diverse cultures.

As technology increases the number of messages and the speed with which they are delivered, listeners must confront a constantly changing and increasingly complex listening environment. They must be able to scan the information that they receive, determine where to focus their attention, and make sense of what they hear.

Often, a response is also required. Something can go wrong at any stage of this process. Millions of dollars and thousands of personal relationships could be saved every day if people were better listeners. Consider these examples:

- You are director of marketing for a large company. You receive a voice mail from a foreign client and, while you begin to address the problem, you do not call back. The client becomes offended and your company loses a multimillion dollar account.
- A hotel reservationist becomes confused and enters the wrong date for a large banquet; she discovers, too late, that the date the caller intended has also been booked and both parties show up for their events.
- Equipment is used improperly because employees were distracted and didn't hear essential instructions during an orientation program on safety procedures. Three people are seriously injured as a result.
- A teenager displays subtle warning signs of an emotional problem. No one listens. A suicide note testifies to her feelings of alienation and despair.

Do you have a responsibility to listen all the time? Is that even possible?

Why was no one listening? There are any number of reasons. For one thing, until recently, no one knew very much about listening (Box 1.1). The emphasis in school was almost entirely on how to be an effective speaker—how to be clear and persuasive, whether your audience was sitting next to you or across the ocean. Listeners were viewed as objects; speakers were taught to analyze audience members as if they were scientists examining a chemical compound. Was equal time spent on the role and techniques of effective listening? Probably not.

Since no one was sure what it meant to listen well, even teachers who were interested in helping you improve your listening ability didn't know exactly where to begin. In fact, one observer reported that when a class listened poorly on an important test, a well-meaning but frustrated teacher simply shouted out as loudly as

---

BOX 1.1

COMMUNICATION SKILLS AND FORMAL INSTRUCTION

COMMUNICATION SKILL	WHEN LEARNED	EXTENT USED	EXTENT TAUGHT
Listening	1st	1st	4th
Speaking	2nd	2nd	3rd
Reading	3rd	3rd	2nd
Writing	4th	4th	1st

he could, "Listen! This is important material. You've got to listen!" It was obvious that he associated the power of his voice with the effectiveness of his message.

Perhaps one reason why many people never learned to listen is that listening takes time. You have to make listening a high priority—you need to *choose* to listen. In some cases you'll be frustrated by circumstances that make it difficult to listen as carefully as you would like. Your roommate has a problem, but you've got to go to class. Your brother called to tell you about his new job, but you have an important soccer game. You face numerous decisions every day.

When you think about it, however, the way we've always approached communication—by focusing on the speaker—is really upside down. Unless you listen first, you have no way of knowing what to say. Effective communication begins with listening, not speaking. Think of the listener as carrying 80 percent of the responsibility for effective communication (Figure 1.1). You'll soon see how this principle not only makes a lot of sense, it also makes a significant difference in the quality and effectiveness of your interactions.

THE WORLD OF LISTENING

The turn of the century has brought with it changes of a magnitude and force that affect, and will continue to define, the nature of all human interaction. The first significant change is the increase in our dependence on technology as a communication media. As one study concluded, "information and the capacity of the technology required to store, transmit, and retrieve it are increasing at virtually an exponential rate" (Bowman

How were you taught to listen?

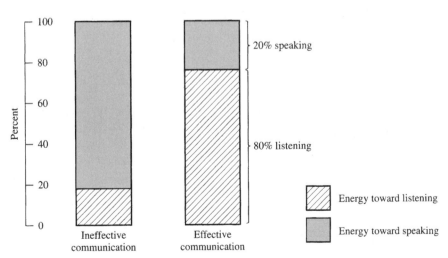

FIGURE 1.1   **Listener Responsibility**

& Klopping, 1999, p. 83). For most of human history, the amount of information shared among individuals was determined by what could be spoken, heard, and remembered. Today, electronic mail is quickly replacing memos and phone calls; presentation software, video and electronic conferencing, and the wide range of Web applications are commonplace ways of sharing information. Technology has made possible unprecedented convenience, flexibility, and choice with regard to the information that we seek (Walther, 1996; Pedersen-Pietersen, 1999; Rea, Hoger, & Rooney, 1999; Tapscott, Ticoll, & Lowy, 2000).

This *knowledge economy*, a direct result of the revolution in communication technologies, has a profound impact on you as a listener. Today, virtually no knowledge is without competition for your attention. Communication technologies revolutionize the way that organizations operate because they facilitate all global business activities. Knowledge, and how effectively and ethically it is used, will determine the quality of our futures. From your home, nothing is beyond your reach—regardless of how far away it may be.

> What are the ethical considerations created by the knowledge economy?

Accompanying this knowledge revolution, then, is the globalization that comes with the ability to increase our reach worldwide. Shell, for instance, has developed a massive global knowledge base and deployed its employees separated, as one author put it, "by a million miles and a million mindsets" (Hulnick, 2000, p. 34). A vital factor in the success of globalization is the effectiveness of communicators—those individuals responsible for the selection, transmission, and reception of information across time and space. Multilingual communicators will be in demand as individuals from different countries regularly interact. An understanding of cultural dimensions and how they affect an individual's perceptions, values, attitudes, and communication practices is essential to both organizational and individual effectiveness. The challenges ahead are considerable, and the speed of continuous change and development will require individuals who constantly learn and adapt; such change will require that individuals listen well.

REASONS TO LISTEN

There also are numerous personal reasons to improve your listening. Reading through this section, and thinking about the three topics that follow, may help you to identify additional ways in which better listening can have a significant impact on your work, your relationships, and your overall well-being.

Accomplish Tasks and Build Relationships: The China Affair

Matt felt a knot in his stomach as he heard his name called. "Not again," he thought to himself. He had been assigned to a history project group with Nancy and Bill twice now, and it was time for a change. "Please move into your groups," Dr. Schaffer said as he put the roll book back down on his desk.

When all group members had gathered, Bill was the first to speak. "Let's just divide up the work. Each of us can report on a separate country. I'll take China." Nancy glared at him. "First of all," she countered, "we're supposed to work together. Our topics need to be integrated. Second," she sighed and leaned toward Bill even further, "maybe someone else would like China. You can't just grab the piece you want and leave the rest of us to take the leftovers."

"That's fine for you to say," Bill shot back, "all you do is go to classes. I work and I don't even have access to the web in my apartment. My time is limited. I want to make this project as simple as possible."

There was a long silence before Matt spoke up. "Dr. Schaffer said we had to work together. That means that we do each topic together, as a group. I'm with Nancy. After last week's exam, I need a good grade on this project. We have to work as a team. It's going to be hard, but we have three weeks so we should be able to get together."

Nancy looked down at her calendar. "Where do you get three weeks? The projects are due November 6. That's ten days from now."

"Didn't Dr. Schaffer say that the project reports were due on the 6th, but that we had until the 20th to submit the final projects?" Matt asked.

"Look," Bill stood up and pushed back his chair. "I'm taking China. I'm not going to sit here and listen to you argue over dates. I'm doing all of my work this weekend. You can do whatever you please."

Every time you communicate, two things happen. First, your behavior either contributes to or hinders the accomplishment of your task. Second, your relationship with the other person is either strengthened or harmed. Your listening ability, as you can see from the China Affair, affects both of these dimensions (Box 1.2).

Listen to Accomplish Tasks.   Your listening skills affect your ability to get work accomplished. Perhaps, like Matt, you've been a member of a small group project team. The quality of your finished product was likely related to the quality of your listening. Ineffective listening often results in misunderstandings and mistakes. Notice that Matt's history project group can hardly function because no one really listened to Dr. Schaffer's initial guidelines. Although everyone heard the same message, disagreements occurred regarding such essential points as project requirements and due dates.

> In a group, are you more likely to pay attention to task-related or relationship-related information?

This scenario is far too typical. In fact, one study suggested that over 60 percent of errors made in business can be attributed to poor listening (Cooper, 1997). And, while 80 percent of executives rated listening as the most vital skill for accomplishing tasks in the workplace, nearly 30 percent also admitted that listening skills were most lacking (Salopek, 1999).

Highly effective work organizations recognize the importance of listening to improving performance and quality. In addition to the key role listening plays in managerial practice (Johnson & Bechler, 1998; Boyle, 1999), the need for effective

■ ■ ■ ■ ■

BOX 1.2

TASK AND RELATIONSHIP FUNCTIONS IN LISTENING

Task Functions Promote
- Accurate understanding
- Responsiveness to change and/or novel situations
- Timely feedback
- More direct and frequent communication
- More accurate recall
- Better decision-making
- Collaborative problem-solving and decision-making

Relationship Functions Promote
- Attention to emotional aspects of communication
- Understanding of person's unique needs, values, interests
- Greater accuracy in self-assessment
- Increased information-sharing
- Less stressful encounters
- Authentic communication and trust
- Valuing of diversity and respect for others

listening also has been recognized in health care (Bentley, 1998), the military (Anderson, 2000), sales (Goby & Lewis, 2000; Kemp, 2000; Feiertag, 2002), marketing (Render, 2000), and numerous other organizational settings.

Peters and Austin (1985) distinguish excellent companies as those that value listening. Sperry Rand, a manufacturing company, was one of the first to promote itself as a "listening organization." Listening training was provided at all organizational levels, and employees began to think of themselves as people who listened. Organizations concerned with quality listen to employees and to customers as part of their overall competitive strategy; they listen to improve their products and adapt to new market demands. The link between listening and leadership effectiveness also has been well-established (Steil & Brommelje, 2004).

Lifelong learning has now become a necessity. The more you know, the better prepared you will be to understand accurately new ideas and adjust to the changes around you. "I must be getting old" is no longer an excuse—not for anyone. When new computer systems are introduced, you need to understand how they operate. When your doctor suggests a battery of new tests, insist that she explain their purposes and potential risks. When you listen to the media, make sure you identify and understand the facts.

Listen to Develop Relationships.   Listening also connects you to other people. True understanding often requires listening over time; you need to make a personal commitment and investment of energy. It's difficult not to like and feel closer to people who listen to you, who show that they value your thoughts and ideas.

Listening is critical to the development of professional as well as personal relationships. Notice how the poor relationships in Matt's group disrupted its ability to function. No one was listening. Bill feels misunderstood and resents the fact that his time is more limited than his classmates'. Rather than showing concern for his situation, other group members focus on their own goals. Matt wants to get a good grade, Nancy wants to make sure they do the project "right." If group members had heard Bill's frustration and anxiety as well as his words, they might have approached the problem from a different perspective.

Effective listening often goes even further than building a single relationship. The practice of sincere and consistent listening contributes to the development of a unique atmosphere or climate that makes further information-sharing possible. It's called trust. The development of trust allows for greater risk-taking. In the last chapters you will see how physicians, health care providers, clergy, service employees, and counselors are among those who must build trust and positive relationships in order to be effective in their work (Elias, 2003). Such environments can develop in families, organizations, or any on-going group. Even sales training has moved from "this is what you tell a prospective buyer" to "listen—find out what is important to your customer." When you make important purchases, your trust in the sales representatives translates into trust in their products (Brownell & Reynolds, 2002). Think about the groups to which you belong and the way in which listening affects levels of trust among members.

> How is trust developed over the Internet, in chat rooms, auctions, and other online exchanges?

A central concern of this text, and one that is related to trust, is the awareness and development of ethical listening practices. Ethical listening is discussed in Chapter 10, but it really touches all aspects of human communication. Therefore, it will be addressed throughout your reading as it relates to various topics of discussion. Integrity and character are not something that you are born with; they are developed through the choices that you make. What you know is important, but what you do with what you learn is equally as important. As technology explodes and as globalization brings together individuals from diverse cultures and value systems, you have an increasing responsibility to be concerned with the ethical dimension of your communication choices, as well as with their effectiveness.

> How have you built or harmed trust in your relationships through your listening behavior?

The importance of listening in building strong relationships is nowhere better expressed than in the arts. Much of our poetry speaks eloquently to the delicacy of human relationships. Every person needs to feel connected in some meaningful way to fellow human beings. Our music, movies, literature, and art suggest that building relationships is a fundamental human need.

Make Wise Decisions: The Selection Process

"I don't know what to do," Sally complained as she and Marge sat down at a table in the employee cafeteria. "I talked with all three candidates this morning. They seem equally well-qualified, and I just can't decide whom to hire."

"Well, what are you looking for?" Marge asked. "What specific skills or traits are essential for the job?"

"Pat Reynolds is clearly the most experienced," Sally reflected as she sipped her coffee. "Pat has had six years in engineering and holds a graduate degree from a very prestigious school. Still, he didn't seem to know our company very well. He wasn't sure about our mission, didn't recognize Mr. Tanner's name, and couldn't talk specifically about the contributions he could make. It was as if he came in off the street and just happened to be in the right field!"

"And the others?" Marge probed.

"I was impressed with George Garison's interest and the way he had prepared himself for the interview. It was clear he wanted a job with us, not just any job. He outlined exactly what he felt we needed, and how he could help us reach our goals. He seemed to be very motivated and focused. The recommendations we have from his current employer are excellent. They say he is hard-working and self-motivated. But," Sally hesitated, "but he's just so dull! When he speaks, it's like talking to a computer!"

Marge laughed. "Remember, his job is not to entertain you!"

"Yes," Sally smiled, "but I really liked Sara Miller. She would definitely be easy to work with and would fit in well with others in the department. She's outgoing and friendly, and I know she'd be a great team member. We have the same astrological sign and read the same books; she and I really clicked. Although at first I was troubled that she talked so negatively about her former employer, I decided it was just that we had hit it off so well. It's important to like the people in your department. I think Sara would really fit in here."

Sally's listening, and her interpretation of what she heard, will influence her hiring decision. In order to make the best decision, she must recognize that her personal preference for Sara may be the most compelling, but not necessarily the wisest, reason to hire her. Sally will have to weigh George's interest and commitment against the difficulties he may present as a member of a work group. Such decisions are never easy, but they arise every day. Effective listening skills ensure that you will make the best possible choices under difficult or changing circumstances.

The information age ushered in an explosion of knowledge and resources; the speed with which information travels has increased the complexity of decision-making at all levels. Decision-makers must determine who to listen to, what to listen to, and how much information to consider before making their choice. Those in leadership positions have come to realize the consequences of poor listening and are quick to identify listening as a key competence for success in fast-changing, competitive organizations (Brownell, 1994).

Appreciate and Enjoy What You Hear: A Second Chance

Peter closed the door of his apartment. He looked down the road in the direction of the university where he was a second-year English major. He must have traveled this short route from his home to class a million times. Today, however, it all seemed very different. It was the first day he was able to attend classes after a near-fatal automobile accident. The details of the crash are all still vivid in his memory. Although the experience was frightening, it increased his awareness of the little things he often missed, the things he had always taken for granted.

Today Peter experiences a world of sights and sounds that he had too often pushed into the background as he focused on his own thoughts and problems. It's a world that now gives him great pleasure. As he walks toward the tall university buildings, he hears the sounds of a lawn mower in the distance, too faint to overpower the chirping of sparrows on the telephone line above his head. A wagon rumbles over the sidewalk as its occupant, a blonde four-year old, squeals with joy. Neighbors talk quietly as they wait for the local bus, while music from an open window drifts through the nearby streets. Peter stops for a moment and takes a deep breath, wondering how he could have missed out on so much that was going on around him.

You often listen for simple enjoyment. As you will learn in Chapter 3, appreciative listening plays an important role in your daily activities. From poetry readings, theater presentations and music, to the sounds of close friends laughing, there are good reasons to take pleasure in your sensory environment. Listening is critical to language development and to your appreciation of the world around you. With technology making more and more sophisticated media available, your entertainment options are increasing rapidly. Many of them require active listening.

Consider Peter's awakening and think about all of the sounds you've learned to ignore, sounds that provide a backdrop and rich context for your daily activities. What sounds do you listen to for enjoyment? Music? Birds? Water? Listening can help you to relax; it can bring you satisfaction and pleasure. You may discover that listening becomes an important part of your daily routine.

Much of what we have just discussed may seem obvious. You may think it's largely common sense, and you're right. Listening is important. You knew that. The consequences of not listening can be devastating. You knew that. Effective listening has many benefits. You knew that. Why, then, spend time reviewing these points? Because it's important for you to think about listening *a lot*. It's important for you to think about your listening all of the time.

We're suggesting a different *focus* in your communications, a different *attitude* in your daily interactions. When you begin to *think like a listener* instead of a speaker, you'll seek out listening opportunities and recognize how essential they are to both your personal and professional development. You'll discover that there's nothing superficial about listening—it's a dynamic, complex process that will provide you with frustrations and challenges throughout your entire life. Understanding its nature is your first step.

THE HURIER APPROACH TO LISTENING

Four goals direct our journey into listening:

1. to recognize the importance and pervasiveness of listening so that you will be highly motivated to listen well;
2. to learn the principles of effective listening so that you know what to do to improve your effectiveness;
3. to acquire a range of listening skills so that you can practice effective listening behavior;
4. to analyze each listening situation so that you can choose the most appropriate listening strategies for your particular purpose and context.

Components of the HURIER Model

We begin by examining the six-component HURIER listening model, which serves as a framework for building your listening skills. Competence in each component is developed by acquiring appropriate attitudes, learning relevant principles, and demonstrating specific behaviors.

   The letters in HURIER represent six interrelated listening processes: hearing, understanding, remembering, interpreting, evaluating, and responding (Figure 1.2). Each chapter in Part II of your text introduces you to one of these components, identifying the attitudes, outlining the principles, and describing the behaviors associated with each skill area.

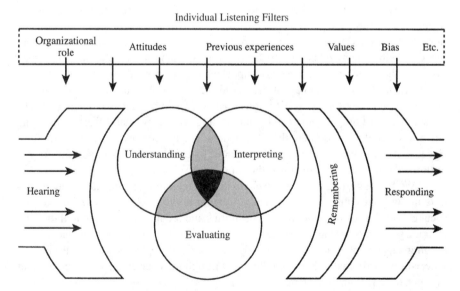

FIGURE 1.2   A Model of the Six-Component HURIER Listening Process

Chapter 3: Hearing.   Hearing involves the accurate reception of sounds. To hear, you must focus your attention on the speaker, discriminate among sounds, and concentrate. This chapter introduces the physiological aspects of hearing and the principles that govern attention. In addition to learning techniques that improve your concentration, you will also be introduced to the effects of listener apprehension and the importance of nonverbal attending behaviors.

Hearing, as you know, takes place even when you are alone. The ability to appreciate music, to enjoy nature, and to recognize other sounds in your environment depends upon the sensitivity and discrimination developed through your hearing.

> Why is it more difficult to discriminate the sounds of a foreign language?

Chapter 4: Understanding.   The ability to understand what you hear, listening comprehension, improves with practice. A number of processes involved in comprehension are intrapersonal; that is, they take place inside your head. This section familiarizes you with the nature of human information processing and the concept of inner speech. You learn guidelines to help you improve your understanding of messages as you develop strategies to build your vocabulary, ask appropriate questions, and take efficient notes.

Chapter 5: Remembering.   There has been a great deal of research on memory. Remembering is essential if you intend to apply what you have heard in future situations. This chapter acquaints you with the three basic memory systems and the work that has been done in listening training and assessment with regard to the memory process. You will learn key techniques for retaining and recalling information as well as the obstacles that inhibit memory. Creative approaches to problemsolving are also addressed.

Chapter 6: Interpreting.   When you interpret messages you do two things. First, you take into account the total communication context so that you are better able to understand the meaning of what is said from the speaker's point of view. Your ability to empathize, or to see a situation from the other person's perspective, requires that you pay attention to emotional meaning and to the communication context. Second, effective listeners let their partners know that they have been

> How do your personal experiences affect the way you interpret messages?

understood. This chapter, then, introduces you to topics related to nonverbal communication such as facial expression, body posture, eye behavior, silence, and vocal cues so that you can develop greater sensitivity to these important dimensions of the communication context.

Chapter 7: Evaluating.   You listen from a unique point of view and are influenced by your perceptual filters—your past experiences, attitudes, personal values, and predispositions. It is therefore impossible not to evaluate, to some extent, everything you hear. Understanding the principles of logic and reasoning, and recognizing bias, stereotyping, propaganda, and other factors that may influence the conclusions you draw, is essential. Effective listeners, as you might suspect, deliberately reduce the influence of their own viewpoint until they have first understood the speaker's ideas. Objectivity, in this sense, is prerequisite to making wise evaluations. This unit sensitizes you to language and propaganda, and provides guidelines for assessing speaker credibility.

Chapter 8: Responding.   Your partner makes judgments regarding the quality of your listening based largely on the nature of your response. As you will learn in Chapter 2, our approach to communication views each participant as both speaker and listener. The HURIER model incorporates your response as an integral part of the listening process. This approach suggests that effective listeners analyze the communication situation and purpose, and then choose an appropriate response from among alternatives.

Personal Listening Filters

The HURIER model also recognizes that you are constantly influenced by both internal and external factors that color your perceptions and subsequent interpretations. The nature of these personal filters, and the degree of impact each has on your listening, varies from one situation to the next. In some cases you may be influenced by speaker characteristics such as mannerisms, or by environmental factors such as the seating arrangement or the temperature of the room. In other instances, anxiety or fatigue may make it difficult for you to concentrate. Effective listeners realize that they are always subject to influences that may distort their perceptions.

Keep in mind that any model is only useful to the extent that it helps to increase your understanding of the listening process and provides a strategy for improving your effectiveness. No model can capture completely a process as complex and dynamic as listening. Because you will be applying the HURIER model in a wide range of contexts, it is also important to recognize the interaction between your listening processes and the broader context in which communication occurs.

Listening Purpose and Context

As you will soon discover, the extent to which each of the skills in the HURIER model becomes important to your listening success varies according to both your purpose and the nature of the communication context. Listeners often approach a communication situation with a particular purpose in mind. It may be to relax, to provide support, or to build a stronger relationship. While you may listen in class to learn, you listen to a salesperson in order to make a purchase decision. Understanding the influence of communication context on your listening requirements is another of the keys to becoming a truly effective listener. Regardless of the situation, you are always affected by the dynamics created by other communicators as well as by the on-going flow of events that surround each unique listening encounter. While your ability to listen is influenced by these situational variables, the nature and quality of your listening also has an impact on the listening environment. That is, while contextual features beyond your control contribute to shaping your listening response, you are not simply a pawn in the process. By developing listening effectiveness, you also influence the "listening environment" (Brownell, 1994). The enhanced HURIER model (Figure 1.3), recognizes the impact of purpose and context on the listening process.

> Do you agree that the nature and quality of listening can influence the communication context? Provide examples.

Chapter 2 further emphasizes the need for what we call listening strategy—a listening response that is adapted to meet the needs of the particular purpose and context. To emphasize this link, each of the chapters that address a component of the HURIER model (Chapters 3–8) begins by acknowledging the impact of these two variables on the listener.

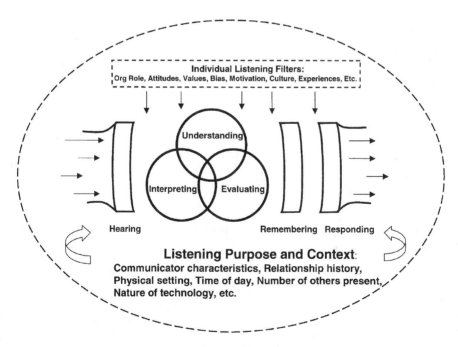

FIGURE 1.3   The HURIER Listening Model: Purpose and Context

J. Brownell 2004

Applying the HURIER Model

A major advantage to using the HURIER model is that when listening is presented as separate but interrelated skill areas, you have a clear method of assessing and improving your listening on an *individualized* basis (Figure 1.4). You can readily:

1. assess your current performance in each of the six skill areas;
2. set personal goals by identifying the component(s) you would like to improve;
3. learn relevant principles and acquire specific skills;
4. practice your new listening behaviors;
5. be assessed on exactly what you have learned and practiced.

The self-assessment instrument at the end of this chapter is a starting point for improving your listening behaviors. Each question on the instrument is related to one of the six components of the HURIER model. After taking this self-assessment, you can readily establish personal goals and identify areas of particular interest. Each chapter, then, addresses selected items from the assessment instrument. Application activities at the end of each chapter directly correspond to questions on the assessment, providing opportunities for you to practice specific skills. This approach enables you to focus your efforts and work on one skill area at a time.

The more thought you give to identifying your personal interests and needs, the more benefit you will derive from the content and activities of this text. In keeping with the emphasis on individualized learning, the next section discusses the importance of understanding yourself as a listener and presents some of the tools you will need as you begin developing your listening skills.

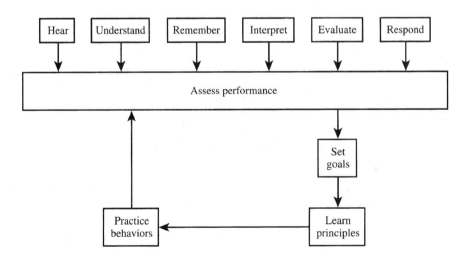

FIGURE 1.4 The Process of Listening Improvement

UNDERSTAND YOURSELF AS A LISTENER

Listening begins with you. You communicate with yourself when you think, when you make decisions, when you engage in any type of communication activity. The most effective listeners understand themselves and are sensitive to their own needs and values.

Self-listening, therefore, influences all other relationships. The process of listening to oneself is integrally linked to the process of listening to others. This involves listening to our self-images as well as our thoughts and feelings. Only when we listen well to ourselves and recognize our values, beliefs, prejudices, and needs can we listen to others with insight and sensitivity.

Lundsteen (1993, pp. 107–108) suggests that awareness of your own thinking process is prerequisite to changing or improving your behavior. Deliberate self-reflection guides you in monitoring those mental listening processes that are inaccessible to others, and enables you to select appropriate strategies as you pursue a specific listening goal.

Internal monologues, however, can also inhibit effective interaction. Listening well to others may require quieting your inner as well as your outer voice. "We cannot fill a full cup," Purdy (1991, p. 25) cautions. If you talk to yourself too much—if you focus entirely on your own agenda and feelings—it is difficult or impossible for you to accept what another person has to say. Any time you become emotional or preoccupied with your own needs, your listening behavior is affected. The most productive approach to take in this class, then, is to concentrate on helping your classmates—on listening to their interests and ideas.

> What self-messages interfere with effective communication?

Two of the most potent ways in which your learning in this course can be facilitated is through (1) continuous self-monitoring, and (2) constructive feedback from your classmates and instructor. Since you will be depending upon your peers to assist you in this learning process, the communication of accurate and constructive feedback becomes a shared responsibility. First, however, we examine the role self-monitoring plays in facilitating your listening development.

Self-monitoring

Self-monitoring is a special kind of social sensitivity. It refers to your awareness of how your behavior affects another person within the context of a specific interaction and, importantly, the degree to which you choose to modify your response based on that knowledge. High self-monitoring—the ability to assess a situation accurately, determine an appropriate response, and then modify your behavior in light of that knowledge—has been suggested as prerequisite to effective communication.

Snyder (1974) defines self-monitoring as "self observation and self control guided by situational cues to social appropriateness" (p. 526). You and your classmates may vary dramatically in your ability and your interest in self-monitoring. Clearly, however, self-monitoring has significant implications for listening.

If you are a high self-monitor, you are concerned with social appropriateness and are particularly sensitive to the expressions and self-presentations of others a characteristic that you will learn more about in Chapter 6 called "Emotional Intelligence" (Goleman, 1998). Nonverbal cues such as voice quality, body posture, touch, and the use of space play an important role in shaping the high self-monitor's impressions. Information about an individual's status, feelings, attitudes, and the nature of the interaction, expressed through nonverbal behavior, is used by the high self-monitor as a guide for modifying her own behavior. High self-monitors adjust their own responses and nonverbal behaviors according to the demands of the particular situation.

As you can imagine, high self-monitors, because they are concerned with the appropriateness of their responses, may vary their communication behaviors significantly from one interaction to the next. When they are uncertain about the appropriateness of their emotional reactions, high self-monitors look to the behavior of others for guidance. If, for instance, a high self-monitor went to a movie with a group of friends, she would be likely to laugh when her friends laugh, even though she may not have found the episodes particularly funny. In other words, high self-monitors model the emotional states of others who are in the same situation and who appear to be behaving appropriately (Haferkamp, 1989).

Low self-monitors, in contrast, rely more heavily on their own values and feelings as guides in managing their behavior. Conse-

> In what ways does culture affect self-monitoring?

quently, their communication is relatively consistent from one person or one situation to the next. In fact, low self-monitors are three times more likely to demonstrate consistency between their attitudes and their actual behaviors than the more situationally responsive high self-monitors. We might expect a low self-monitor to experience less stress in social situations as well, since this person is likely to place less emphasis on social appropriateness and on maintaining the goodwill of others.

Although staying true to your personal values and beliefs is essential to authentic listening, low self-monitors may have some difficulty recognizing others' viewpoints and collaborating with those from different cultural orientations.

Snyder's (1974) interest in self-monitoring led him to develop a Self-Monitoring Scale, an 18-item true–false inventory that measures the following:

1. Concern for social appropriateness
2. Expressive self-control
3. Other-directed self-presentation
4. Cross-situational variety of behavior

A similar but somewhat broader-based scale was developed by Daly, Vangelista, and Daughton (1987) to measure what they called conversational sensitivity, or the degree to which people attend to and interpret what occurs in conversations. Their inventory assesses the ability to make high-order inferences about verbal and non-verbal messages, to detect power and affinity relationships in conversation, and to self-monitor. As might be expected, the issue of skill development is also relevant. Some people with a high need for approval may closely monitor their environment, yet may lack the skill to respond appropriately.

> Is it ethical to *manage* your true feelings and thoughts according to the situation?

Such inventories emphasize that communication is an important element in relationships. Even the personality characteristics you perceive in your friends may depend upon the characteristics they perceive in you. If you appear warm and friendly, your friends will behave in ways that encourage you to feel comfortable and perhaps continue interacting with them. If, however, you look repeatedly at your watch, your partner may interpret your behavior as impatience and may in turn become nervous and distracted.

Keep in mind that your objective is not to take self-monitoring to an extreme, but to acknowledge that effective listening may require you to modify your response in light of your partner's expectations and the constraints of the specific listening situation. This type of behavioral flexibility is necessary in order to communicate effectively across a wide range of situations.

Howell's Dimensions

Howell (1982) has developed a model that illustrates the problems that can arise for those who are particularly low on the self-monitoring scale. He identifies five levels of communication competence based upon your communication ability and the accuracy of your self-assessment.

Howell's dimensions address the often intangible, intuitive aspects of communication and the importance of accurately assessing your own abilities in order to improve your performance. Although the categories and descriptions below may at first appear humorous, these levels have been adapted to illustrate listening situations and will provide useful insight as you consider your own listening behavior.

1. Unconscious incompetence: This individual is a poor listener and has no sensitivity whatsoever. Unfortunately, he thinks things are just fine.
2. Conscious incompetence: This individual does not listen well and knows it, but has no idea what to do about it. He might try hard to improve, but seems always to say or do the wrong thing.
3. Conscious competence: This person may learn and demonstrate all the right listening skills, but he is so robot-like and analytical that the behavior appears awkward and unnatural.
4. Unconscious competence: This person trusts his spontaneous responses, which are usually right on target. He learns new skills and applies them appropriately.

The authentic listening behavior that we are striving for is generated by a sincere interest in others. It can be distinguished from behavior that is forced or repeated so often that it becomes what we call scripted (Miller, 1996). When listeners depend upon their scripts, they don't respond appropriately to new, incoming information. Scripted behavior might be displayed by poorly selected service employees whose greetings are uninspired and forced, or by a student who has over-rehearsed for an interview and asks questions that have already been answered.

You can see that effective listening requires an attitude of openness and genuine concern. Individuals who focus on their own agendas find it difficult to listen well to others. Truly effective listening cannot be forced or faked; it arises from a sincere desire to understand, to share, to help, or simply to appreciate. One of the most powerful, although deceivingly difficult, ways to facilitate more effective listening is through constructive feedback.

Constructive Feedback

Although communication sensitivity is essential to effective listening, your best guesses regarding how your behavior is perceived or what your partner is feeling may not always be accurate. As Wilmot (1987, p. 144) explains, "Our perceptions of the other are grounded in permanent uncertainty." This is particularly true when you communicate through distance technologies and with individuals whose background and experiences are very different from your own. If you are really interested in improving your listening behavior, clear and direct feedback is essential. Information sharing with your classmates provides everyone with opportunities to check their personal perceptions against their partner's impressions.

Through constructive feedback, you facilitate listening improvement by providing information to your partner in a thoughtful, planned, and straightforward manner. A recent survey of Fortune 500 companies revealed that poor feedback accounts for a large percentage of internal communication breakdowns. Why? Because giving constructive feedback isn't easy. It's tempting to resort to indirect cues which are easily misinterpreted or to make judgments which quickly arouse defensiveness.

You have learned to expect feedback from those of higher status or with greater expertise. In this class, however, your most valuable and frequent feedback will come from your peers—others who, like you, are interested in improving their listening behavior. Following the guidelines below will increase the likelihood that the feedback you give and receive in this class will be helpful and appreciated (Box 1.3).

Rules of Constructive Feedback

1. Constructive feedback is descriptive, not evaluative. When you evaluate, you tell people that their listening is "good" or "bad," that their competence is "terrific" or "terrible." This type of information does not provide direction; they are not likely to change because they don't know exactly which behaviors need modification. Instead, be descriptive. Tell individuals that you are troubled because they did not remember your name after you introduced yourself, or that when you began to talk

BOX 1.3

RULES OF CONSTRUCTIVE FEEDBACK

1. *It is descriptive . . .*

Tim, I liked your report. The style was clear and concise and your ideas were organized logically. The documentation you used made the problem credible and vivid.

> *. . . not evaluative.*

Tim, that was a terrific report.

2. *It focuses on behavior . . .*

Tim, slow down a little bit, and I think you can reduce the number of errors.

> *. . . not on personal characteristics.*

Tim, you could be a lot faster on that machine if you were better coordinated.

3. *It is specific . . .*

Tim, I couldn't hear you from where I was sitting.

> *. . . not general.*

Tim, your voice isn't effective.

4. *It is timed appropriately . . .*

Tim, let's get together around 2:00 p.m. and talk about your progress on the AMF.

> *. . . not delayed or left to chance.*

Let's get together sometime.

5. *It is offered . . .*

Tim, perhaps my reactions to your report would help you in preparing for next week's meeting. Would you like to get together sometime this afternoon?

> *. . . not imposed.*

Tim, I've got talk with you about that report before you give it at our meeting next week.

---

about your experiences in China, they interrupted to describe a recent stay as a foreign student in India.

2. Helpful comments focus on those aspects of behavior that people can change and that are relevant to the situation at hand. Telling your cousin that you're so intrigued by the color of her eyes that you can't pay attention to what she says, or that she could concentrate better if she just stopped worrying about her sick cat, may not be useful.

3. Own your opinions by phrasing them appropriately. Acknowledge that your comments are made from your point of view—others may have a different opinion. Appropriate phrases include "to me," "as far as I know," "from what I've observed during the past week," or simply "I think."

4. Feedback must be given as soon after the behavior occurs as possible. If you observe a classmate in a situation where feedback is appropriate, don't wait to tell her. It will be much more meaningful if you provide information immediately after your observation. Be careful, however, to avoid embarrassing someone by giving her constructive criticism in an inappropriate setting.

5. Information is more readily acknowledged and acted on if it is seen as useful. Ideally, the person you direct your comments to has a strong desire to know what you think of her performance. Unwanted information will seldom be appreciated or acted on. It is likely, instead, to make the person upset and defensive. Your relationship with the person, and her motivation to improve, are both influencing factors.

If you turn this guideline around, you can see how useful it is if you make a habit of requesting feedback from your classmates. In that way, you will be encouraging your friends to practice important communication skills while helping you improve your listening behaviors. Constructive feedback is the most appropriate and useful way to provide individuals with information about their behavior— knowledge that they may not be able to obtain in any other way. Once informed, they are in a position to either act on the information or not, depending on their own assessment of the situation.

Assessing Your Listening Behavior

Throughout this text you will be asked continuously to reflect on your listening. There are a variety of ways in which you can keep track, and subsequently keep thinking about, your listening challenges. As Rhodes, Watson, and Barker (1990) explain:

> An individual who has competency can demonstrate both the cognitive and the behavioral aspects . . . . Competent listening cannot be defined only as possession of knowledge; effective . . . listening is a behavioral act and, like any other behavioral acts, listening can be improved with practice and feedback (p. 64)

In the following chapters you will be asked to think about your listening goals and to challenge yourself to reach them. To begin, the inventory at the end of this chapter asks you questions about your listening behavior. You will then be shown how to use this information to personalize your program for listening improvement.

As you know, the HURIER model enables you to assess and improve your listening on each of six dimensions. You will be encouraged to observe your own behaviors, to consider feedback from your peers, and to participate in a variety of in- and out-of-class activities. You will keep diaries and logs and complete personal inventories. Through work in small groups, you will receive the maximum amount of constructive feedback and generate solutions to common listening problems.

SUMMARY

Effective communication begins with effective listening. Unless you listen well, you cannot hope to communicate effectively. Listening may be the single most important skill in facilitating your personal and professional development. Although competence in written and oral communication has long been recognized, the benefits of effective listening—and the consequences of poor listening—are only now beginning to be fully explored. New developments of the 21st century make listening effectiveness more necessary than ever before. As the number of messages increases due to technological advances, effective listeners must be able to make wise decisions about what to listen to and develop skill in understanding and evaluating what they hear. In addition, globalization has resulted in the need for listeners to develop greater empathy and sensitivity to those whose life experiences and values are different from their own. As the world becomes increasingly interconnected, the need for effective listening becomes ever more essential. There also are significant personal benefits to effective listening. Among other things, listening facilitates (1) the accomplishment of task and relationship functions, (2) wise decision making, and (3) appreciation and enjoyment of the sounds in your environment.

The HURIER model presents a behavioral approach that focuses on the development of six interrelated skills: Hearing, Understanding, Remembering, Interpreting, Evaluating, and Responding. These skills are applied in light of the listener's particular purpose and within a larger listening context. Purpose and context, then, affect the relative importance of each of the six listening components.

To consistently demonstrate appropriate listening behaviors, it is essential for you to listen to yourself and to become a high self-monitor. In addition, the skills of constructive feedback are essential as you learn more about your listening by sharing perceptions with your classmates. The importance of constant self-assessment, and the usefulness of the HURIER model in accomplishing this task, is a recurring theme of this text.

APPLICATIONS

Application 1: Understand the Importance and Benefits of Listening
Application 2: Understand the Components of the HURIER Model
Application 3: Understand Yourself as a Listener

Application 1: Understand the Importance and Benefits of Listening

Participating in the following activities will make you more aware of how important listening is in accomplishing your daily activities, and help you think about the many benefits of effective listening.

Remember that *motivation* plays a key role in listening improvement. Think carefully about the questions and exercises in this chapter—you have to want to become a better listener before any behavioral changes will occur.

Activities

1. It's easy to see how we can benefit from improved listening, but what about its impact on those around us? Think for a moment about how your increased listening

effectiveness can benefit *others*. Try to give at least three benefits to others in each of the following contexts:

> My improved listening ability benefits others—family, friends, colleagues:

a. At school:

b. At home:

c. With friends and colleagues:

2. Self-motivation is a key to improved listening. Try to identify at least four of what you consider to be your primary "motivators." What would really make you work hard at developing your listening competence?

3. What help do you need to solicit from your instructor, your friends, or your family as you work to improve your listening?

Group Activities

Form a small group of four to six people. You may want to keep the same group for all activities, or you may find it more interesting to change groups so that you get to hear the opinions and ideas of a greater number of your classmates.

1. Read each of the situations described below. Discuss relevant examples of each with your group members. Then, choose an example from one of the categories to role-play. Discuss how poor listening contributed to the specific problem, and what might have been done to promote more effective communication.

    a. Someone doesn't listen and then finds the information was necessary (safety procedures, first aid, changing a flat tire, following directions, etc.).
    b. A misunderstanding results from poor listening and leads to a major interpersonal conflict.
    c. A good listener is seen by his or her supervisor as competent and likable; a poor listener appears egocentric and less credible.
    d. An individual helps a colleague feel better about himself through effective listening (or use another relationship—supervisor–subordinate, parent–child, friend–friend).

2. Determine how costly ineffective listening is to you by answering yes or no to the statements below. Think of *related examples* if the ones provided don't fit your experiences.

    a. When I leave my dentist's office I am still not clear why I need to have a root canal instead of another filling.
    b. When the doctor explains what to do for my illness I understand, but a few hours later I can't really remember what I was asked to do.
    c. When I'm unhappy with my grade on a term paper, I make an appointment with my teacher to discuss the evaluation. I often leave her office still confused about what I did wrong.
    d. When I'm nervous, I have a hard time following instructions or directions.

In each of the above cases, how might you have prepared yourself to listen? Discuss your responses with the rest of your group. What seem to be common, recurring listening problems? Determine an appropriate listening response in each case.

3. How early should listening instruction begin? With your group, create some innovative ways in which elementary school teachers might make children more aware of the importance of listening and help them to begin developing their listening skills. After thirty minutes of discussion, share your thoughts with the rest of the class.

Application 2: Understand the Components of the HURIER Model

The HURIER model provides a framework for better understanding the listening process and for developing specific listening skills. To get started, make sure that you are very clear on how each of the six components is defined.

Activities

1. Take the self-assessment inventory at the end of this chapter.

Group Activities

Form a small group of four to six people. You may want to keep the same group for all activities, or you may find it more interesting to change groups so that you get to hear the opinions and ideas of a greater number of your classmates.

1. Read this short case and identify each component of the HURIER model as it is illustrated in the scene below.

> *"Hi everyone!" The door slammed as Sheri came in from her morning class.*
>
> *"Sheri, before you get carried away with something else, please pick up in the kitchen. It's your week to do dishes and I can't even find a clean spoon. I thought you agreed to take care of it when we talked Friday night."*
>
> *Marge was trying not to sound like her mother as she approached what had become an increasingly tense situation between the two women.*
>
> *"Guess what!" Sheri threw down her books and sprawled on the couch. "Sam is coming to visit in two weeks! He didn't think he could get away until Thanksgiving break, but he called this morning to say he got a day off and he's driving down."*
>
> *"Good," Marge managed a brief smile in recognition of Sheri's excitement. It was impossible for her to be enthusiastic when she was so angry at her housemate. "Before he comes, I hope you'll straighten this place up. It's a pigpen."*
>
> *Sheri laughed. "Living with a perfectionist isn't easy, but somebody has to do it," she teased as she threw a pillow across the room at Marge. "You are worse than my mother."*
>
> *"So what's your problem, kid?" Sheri just noticed that her other housemate, Brenda, was sitting in the corner of the room reading a magazine. "Did you hear my news?"*

Brenda looked up and took out her earphones. "What are you doing back so soon? I thought you had classes all morning."

"I came back to tell you two that Sam got some time off and will be here in a couple of weeks. Great news, huh?"

"Great news," Brenda said as she and Marge exchanged glances.

"Excuse me," Marge began again, "but what about the kitchen? I can't find anything. The garbage is overflowing. You said you were going to keep it clean this time. It's disgusting."

"It's comfortable," Sheri replied and headed for the stairs. "I know exactly where everything is. You never have anyone over anyway, so what difference does it make to you?"

Marge felt her blood pressure rise. She was almost relieved that Sheri disappeared into her room or she would certainly have said something she might later regret.

Case Questions

1. a. What role did hearing play in the interaction above? Were there things said that were not heard by one or more of the parties involved? Why?
    b. How did memory influence the relationship between Sheri and Marge?
    c. Give examples of how interpretation affected the way in which messages were perceived. Around what issues were there different points of view? Pay particular attention to tone of voice and other subtle aspects of the conversation.
    d. Cite instances where listeners were evaluative or judgmental. How did that affect the interaction and the relationship?
    e. Discuss the appropriateness of various responses that are made throughout the situation. Give particular attention to:

    - Marge's response when Sheri first came in the door.
    - Sheri's initial response to Marge.
    - Brenda's response to Sheri.
    - Sheri's final response after Marge outlines various problems with the kitchen.

    f. Identify some of the main communication problems that resulted from ineffective listening. Discuss how each housemate might have handled the situation more appropriately.

2. Listening is defined as a skill. Some skills, however, are a combination of learned behaviors and innate tendencies. Generate a list of activities that can be learned by anyone, another that requires some innate abilities (coordination, courage, flexibility, etc.), and a third one with activities that depend to a large extent on innate ability. Now, review each component of the HURIER model, and discuss the extent to which behaviors in each component are either completely learned or completely innate or intuitive. Note any areas of disagreement among group members. Compare your results with findings from other groups.

3. Consider the listening contexts described in the list below. For each situation, determine which of the six components of the HURIER model would be most important and which would be least important for communication effectiveness.

Indicate your assessment by placing a "V," "I," or "N" on the appropriate line for each skill cluster. See if members of your group can reach consensus. Discuss why it may be more difficult to single out the most relevant skills for some contexts than for others.

V = very important
I = important/somewhat important
N = not very important

	H	U	R	I	E	R
a) listening to a car radio	__	__	__	__	__	__
b) listening to an elderly woman with dementia	__	__	__	__	__	__
c) listening to the details of your best friend's night at the prom—you did not attend	__	__	__	__	__	__
d) listening to someone who is speaking with disrespect about a topic that is important to you	__	__	__	__	__	__
e) listening to the ocean and boats anchored in a harbor	__	__	__	__	__	__
f) listening to a fellow passenger who has been delayed at an airport	__	__	__	__	__	__
g) listening to an instructor in a large lecture course with which you are having difficulty	__	__	__	__	__	__
h) listening to a non-native European speaker who has just arrived in the United States	__	__	__	__	__	__
i) listening to someone with whom you have had numerous disagreements	__	__	__	__	__	__
j) listening to your roommate who has just gotten back to your apartment and awoken you from a sound sleep	__	__	__	__	__	__

Application 3: Understand Yourself as a Listener

Self-assessment of your listening behavior is on-going. In addition to developing self-monitoring skills, take advantage of the classroom context to solicit as much feedback as possible from your friends and share as much information as seems appropriate regarding your perceptions of both your own listening behaviors and those of others.

Activities

1. Keep a journal for at least two weeks. Note the types of listening you are required to do and any misunderstandings or confusion that result from ineffective listening. At the end of two weeks, take a good look at your observations and set some personal goals for listening improvement. As you move through this text, you will gain the knowledge necessary to develop a specific action plan to accomplish each objective.

a. When do most of your listening difficulties occur?

b. Do you seem to have trouble listening to particular people?

c. In what settings do you find it difficult to listen?

Set three goals for yourself. Be as specific as possible.

2. Try to think deliberately about your thinking. It might be easiest to identify the process you go through when you need to make a decision. How does increased awareness of this activity help you as a listener? Under what circumstances are you most aware of your thinking? Why is that the case?

3. In what situations are you called upon to provide feedback? How effective do you feel you are when you need to communicate information to someone about his performance or habits? How does he respond?

Group Activities

Form a small group of four to six people. You may want to keep the same group for all activities, or you may find it more interesting to change groups so that you get to hear the opinions and ideas of a greater number of your classmates.

1. Consider how your personality influences your listening behavior. What characteristics work to your benefit? Which ones create listening problems?

    Ralph Nichols (1948) has identified characteristics of effective and ineffective listeners. Look at the list below and circle five traits you believe to be *most* characteristic of your personal style. Then check to see which have been designated as typical of good listeners and which are more characteristic of poor listeners.

    a. interested   g. inattentive
    b. curious   h. defensive
    c. impatient   i. quick to evaluate
    d. understanding   j. alert
    e. emotional   k. empathetic
    f. responsive   l. caring

    Poor Listeners: c, e, g, h, i
    Good Listeners: a, b, d, f, j, k, l

2. In this class, it is important to get to know one another well. This activity provides an opportunity for you to learn about your classmates and to think more seriously about your personal listening characteristics.

    Imagine that a group has just formed and you want very much to be a member. Existing group members, however, know that they can be very particular about whom they invite to join them since it is a cohesive and high-performing team. They have decided to make the selection based upon the applicant's listening ability.

    Group members have decided to be creative and to ask all applicants to fill out a "Buyers Guide" that will give them the information they need to make a selection decision. The form you fill out will be reviewed by the group, after which members will ask you questions about how your responses might affect your listening behavior. Remember that you are in competition with at least three other people for one open position in the group.

Buyer's Guide

a. My standard features are:

b. Additional options, at some extra cost:

c. My performance record:

d. Maintenance requirements:

e. Direct benefits of ownership:

f. Comparison to competitor's models:

3. This exercise is designed to help you get to know members of your group and to get some feedback on how you're perceived.

    Take turns in the role of "focus person." When you are the focus person, others in the group randomly share their assumptions about you in "I imagine" statements. They may say things like, "I imagine that you come from a big family," or "I imagine that you like to listen to classical music." It's very important that statements be made by individuals who don't know if they are correct or not. Members who know you well should refrain from participating. When the focus person has received five "I imagine" statements, he then responds to each by providing the correct information. Each group member takes a turn as focus person. When everyone has finished, discuss the experience. How accurate were members' guesses? What cues were used to make the "I imagine" statements?

4. Practice the skills of constructive feedback. In groups of three, assign each person to (a) share information about themselves, (b) serve as communication partner, or (c) observe the process and provide feedback to the participants.

    Once roles have been established, the person who will be sharing information selects one of the topics listed below. For five minutes, the person talks about the topic with his or her partner. When this dialogue has ended, the observer responds by summarizing his or her perceptions of the process and of the listening behaviors of each participant.

Topics

The listening situation that frustrates me the most is . . .

I would like to improve my listening skills because . . .

A person I admire for his/her listening ability is . . .

When I feel no one is listening to me, I . . .

Past problems that have resulted because of ineffective listening include . . .

I think businesses should listen more effectively because . . .

Educators can demonstrate effective listening by . . .

The ways in which listening will be important to me at work include . . .

Feedback

Apply the rules of constructive feedback as you provide information to the participants in this exercise. After each person has received feedback, allow several minutes for them to react to what was said about their behaviors.

a. What nonverbal behaviors did each participant demonstrate?

b. How did each person indicate to the other that he/she understood what was said?

c. Were any inappropriate behaviors evident?

d. Was there "noise" in any part of the communication process? If so, what was it and how did it influence the communication process?

e. Did both participants focus their full attention on the conversation?

f. In what aspects of the encounter did most self-disclosure occur?

g. Was any feedback provided by either participant?

YOUR HURIER LISTENING PROFILE

Complete the listening questionnaire on the following pages. Each question corresponds with one of the six listening components you learned about in Chapter 1 Hearing, Understanding, Remembering, Interpreting, Evaluating, and Responding.

It might be fun, before you go any further, to guess how you will do.

I think I will score highest on the component of _____

I will probably score lowest on the component of _____

Now, respond to each of the following questions concerning *your perception* of your listening behavior. Write the appropriate number in the blank to your left, using the key below. Unless your instructor gives you other directions, *choose one specific listening context* and answer all questions with that situation in mind. This will help you be more consistent in your responses.

Key: 5 = almost always
       4 = usually
       3 = sometimes
       2 = infrequently
       1 = almost never

_____ 1. I am constantly aware that people and circumstances change over time.

_____ 2. I take into account the speaker's personal and cultural perspective when listening to him.

_____ 3. I pay attention to the most important things going on around me.

_____ 4. I accurately hear what is said to me.

_____ 5. I understand my partner's vocabulary and recognize that my understanding of a word is likely to be somewhat different from the speaker's.

_____ 6. I adapt my response according to the needs of the particular situation.

_____ 7. I easily follow conversations and can accurately recall which member contributed which ideas in small group discussions.

_____ 8. I consider my partner's personal expertise on the subject when she tries to convince me to do something.

_____ 9. I do not let my emotions interfere with my listening or decision-making.

_____ 10. I can remember what the instructor has said in class even when it's not in the book.

_____ 11. I recognize my "hot buttons," and don't let them influence my listening.

_____ 12. I take into account the person's motives, expectations, and needs when determining the meaning of the message.

_____ 13. I provide clear and direct feedback to others.

_____ 14. I let the speaker know immediately that he has been understood.

_____ 15. I overcome distractions such as the conversation of others, background noises, and telephones, when someone is speaking.

_____ 16. I enter communication situations with a positive attitude.

_____ 17. I am sensitive to the speaker's tone of voice in communication situations.

_____ 18. I listen to and accurately remember what my partner says, even when I strongly disagree with her viewpoint.

Your HURIER Listening Profile   *Continued*

_____ 19. I encourage information sharing by creating a climate of trust and support.

_____ 20. I concentrate on what the speaker is saying, even when the information is complicated.

_____ 21. I consider how the speaker's facial expressions, body posture, and other nonverbal behaviors relate to the verbal message.

_____ 22. I weigh all evidence before making a decision.

_____ 23. I take time to analyze the validity of my partner's reasoning before arriving at my own conclusions.

_____ 24. I am relaxed and focused in important communication situations.

_____ 25. I listen to the entire message without interrupting.

_____ 26. I make sure that the physical environment encourages effective listening.

_____ 27. I recognize and take into account personal and cultural differences in the use of time and space that may influence listening effectiveness.

_____ 28. I ask relevant questions and restate my perceptions to make sure I have understood the speaker correctly.

_____ 29. I listen carefully to determine whether the speaker has solid facts and evidence or whether he is relying on emotional appeals.

_____ 30. I am sensitive to my partner's feelings in communication situations.

_____ 31. I have a wide variety of interests which helps me approach tasks creatively.

_____ 32. I distinguish between main ideas and supporting evidence when I listen.

_____ 33. I am ready to focus my attention when a presenter begins her talk.

_____ 34. I readily consider new evidence and circumstances that might prompt me to reevaluate my previous position.

_____ 35. I can recall what I have heard, even when I am in stressful situations.

_____ 36. I take notes effectively when I believe it will enhance my listening.

After completing all questions, you can figure out your score.

Identifying Your Listening Profile

Transfer your self-ratings for each question to the corresponding question numbers below.

For instance, if you gave yourself a 4 on question 1, you would find question 1, under Evaluating, and would put a 4 on the appropriate line. Continue for all thirty-six questions.

Total the points you assigned for each of the six sets of questions.

Place your total for each component in the *Total* space.

HEARING	UNDERSTANDING	REMEMBERING
4 ___	5 ___	3 ___
15 ___	11 ___	7 ___
16 ___	25 ___	10 ___
20 ___	28 ___	18 ___
24 ___	32 ___	31 ___
33 ___	36 ___	35 ___
___ Total	___ Total	___ Total

Your HURIER Listening Profile   *Continued*

INTERPRETING	EVALUATING	RESPONDING
2 ___	1 ___	6 ___
12 ___	8 ___	9 ___
14 ___	22 ___	13 ___
17 ___	23 ___	19 ___
21 ___	29 ___	26 ___
30 ___	34 ___	27 ___
___ Total	___ Total	___ Total

Let's look at what this information tells you about your self-perceptions regarding your listening behavior. Transfer your totals for each component to the *Total Points* column below. Rank order each of the six components according to your totals.

		Total Points	Rank
COMPONENT I:	Hearing	_____	_____
COMPONENT II:	Understanding	_____	_____
COMPONENT III:	Remembering	_____	_____
COMPONENT IV:	Interpreting	_____	_____
COMPONENT V:	Evaluating	_____	_____
COMPONENT VI:	Responding	_____	_____

Use the following guide to assess each skill area:

25–30 points: you see yourself as an excellent listener
20–25 points: you believe you are a good listener
15–20 points: you consider your listening skills adequate
10–15 points: you perceive some problems in your listening behavior

Now consider:

- In what skill area are you high?
- Which one do you see as a potential problem?
- How did your actual ranking compare with your earlier guess?
- Is there a particular component with a significantly different total—either much higher or much lower than the others?
- How do you think someone else would rank your listening behaviors? Take the role of your roommate, your parent, or some other person who knows you well and answer the questionnaire from that person's perspective. How did you do?

Keep these results in mind as you cover the specific listening skills throughout this text.

BIBLIOGRAPHY

Anderson, D. A. (2000). Effective communicative and listening skills revisited. *Marine Corps Gazette, 84*(3), 60–61.

Bowman, J., & Klopping, I. (1999). Bandstands, bandwidth, and business communication: Technology and the sanctity of writing. *Business Communication Quarterly, 62*(1), 82–90.

Bentley, S. C. (1998). Listening better. *Nursing Homes, 47*(2), 56–60.

Boyle, R. C. (1999). A manager's guide to effective listening. *Manage, 51*(1), 6–7.

Brownell, J. (1990). Perceptions of effective listeners: A management study. *The Journal of Business Communication, 27*(4), 401–416.

Brownell, J. (1994). Listening and career development in the hospitality industry. *Journal of the International Listening Association, 8*, 31–49.

Brownell, J. (1994). Creating strong listening environments: A key hospitality management task. *The International Journal of Contemporary Hospitality Management, 6*(3), 3–10.

Brownell, J., & Reynolds, D. (2002). Strengthening the food and beverage purchaser-supplier partnership: Actions that make a difference. *Cornell Hotel & Restaurant Administration Quarterly, 42*(4), 1–13.

Cooper, L. O. (1997). Listening competency in the workplace: A model for training. *Business Communication Quarterly, 60*(4), 75–84.

Daly, J. A., Vangelista, A. L., & Daughton, S. M. (1987). *The nature and correlates of conversational sensitivity.* Paper presented at the annual meeting of the Speech Communication Association Convention, Boston, MA.

Elias, M. (September 23, 2003). *USA Today,* p. D.09.

Feiertag, H. (2002). Listening skills, enthusiasm top list of salespeople's best traits. *Hotel & Motel Management, 217*(13), 20.

Goby, J., & Lewis, H. (2000). The key role of listening in business: A study of the Singapore insurance industry. *Business Communication Quarterly, 63*(2), 41–51.

Goleman, D. (1998). *Working with emotional intelligence.* New York: Bantam Books.

Haferkamp, C. J. (1989). Implications of self-monitoring theory for counseling supervision. *Counselor Education and Supervision, 28*(4), 290–298.

Howell, W. S. (1982). *The empathic communicator.* Belmont, CA: Wadsworth Publishers.

Johnson, S. D., & Bechler, C. (1998). Examining the relationship between listening effectiveness and leadership emergence: Perceptions, behaviors, and recall. *Small Group Research, 29*(4), 452–471.

Kemp, M. (2000). Listening skill saves time, increases effectiveness. *The American Salesman, 45*(9), 3–8.

Lundsteen, S. (1993). Metacognitive listening. In A. D. Wolvin and C. G. Coakley (Eds.), *Perspectives on Listening,* pp. 106–123. Norwood, NJ: Ablex Publishing.

Miller, A. (1996). Using probing skills to uncover customer needs. *Telemarketing and Call Center Solutions, 15*(5), 72–75.

Nichols, R. (1948). Factors in listening comprehension. *Speech Monographs, 15,* 154–163.

Pedersen-Pietersen, L. (1999). Reworking education in a virtual schoolhouse, *New York Times, Late Edition,* (3), 13.

Peters, T., & Austin, N. (1985). *A passion for excellence.* New York: Warner Books.

Purdy, M. (1991). Intrapersonal and interpersonal listening. In D. Borisoff and M. Purdy (Eds.), *Listening in Everyday Life: A Personal and Professional Approach,* pp. 21–58. New York: University Press of America.

Rea, A., Hoger, B., & Rooney, P. (1999). Communication and technology: Building bridges across the chasm. *Business Communication Quarterly, 62*(2), 92–96.

Render, M. (2000). Better listening makes for a better marketing message. *Marketing News, 34*(19), 22.

Rhodes, S., Watson, K. W., & Barker, L. L. (1990). Listening assessment: Trends and influencing factors in the 1980s. *Journal of the International Listening Association, 4*, 62–82.

Salopek, J. (1999). Is anyone listening? *Training & Development, 53*(9), 58–59.

Snyder, M. (1974). Self-monitoring of expressive behavior. *Journal of Personality and Social Psychology, 30*, 526–637.

Steil, L. K., & Brommelje, R. K. (2004). *Listening leaders: The ten golden rules to listen, lead, and succeed.* St. Paul, MN: Beaver's Pond Press.

Tapscott, D., Ticoll, D., & Lowy, A. (2000). *Digital capital: Harnessing the power of business webs.* Boston: Harvard Business School Press.

Walther, J. (1996). Computer-mediated communication: Impersonal, interpersonal, and hyperpersonal interaction. *Communication Research, 23*(1), 3–11.

Wilmot, W. W. (1987). *Perception of the other: Dyadic communication.* New York: McGraw-Hill.

LISTENING THEORY AND RESEARCH

I have a task and that is talking to you. You have a task and that is listening to me. I hope you do not finish before I do.

—AUTHOR UNKNOWN

OUTLINE

CHAPTER OBJECTIVES

After completing this chapter, you will

Become more aware of:

- the central role listening plays in the communication process
- the importance of individual perception in the listening process
- the complexity of the listening process
- the variety of listening definitions
- factors that influence your listening

Better understand:

- the systems perspective
- the key concepts of relational listening

- problems encountered by listening researchers
- issues related to listening assessment
- how models of listening contribute to understanding the process
- the assumptions of the HURIER model
- how your listening is influenced by purpose and situation

Develop skills in:

- identifying individual differences in perception
- defining the situation
- identifying specific contexts and purposes to determine appropriate listening strategies

THEORETICAL PERSPECTIVES

A systems view of human communication is one of the most useful approaches for examining both the role of listening in the communication process as well as the interrelationships among the six components of the HURIER model.

A systems perspective implies that elements of a process are interrelated and interdependent (Littlejohn, 1989). When you adopt a systems approach, you view each part of the whole as it relates to and is affected by all other parts. We talk about systems with regard to the solar system, the weather, and even our government. This idea of interrelatedness, however, is particularly useful when examining listening. In our study of listening we are concerned with understanding systems at two levels: (1) the relational level in which you communicate with another person, and (2) the individual level where the listener functions as an independent system.

The broadest system, relational communication, focuses on face-to-face human interaction (Figure 2.1) where listening and speaking functions occur simultaneously (Eisenberg & Goodall, 1993, p. 107). Not all of your listening, however, occurs in face-to-face settings. An increasing amount of listening now takes place independent of another person's immediate presence, in situations where you and your partner are physically separated. Listening, as discussed in Chapter 1, now takes place over great distances and is mediated by a wide range of new technologies. In addition to television, CD-ROMs, and DVDs, the widespread use of videoconferencing, voice mail, and other electronic communication systems extends the opportunities for and challenges to effective listening. Researchers suggest that some people spend well over a quarter of the time that they are awake listening to some form of mediated communication (Louhils-Salminen, 1999; Trevino & Webster, 1992; Walther, 1992).

> What distance technologies do you regularly use to communicate?

While our first view captured both communication partners, our second lens, the one with which we are most concerned, *frames* the individual listener as an

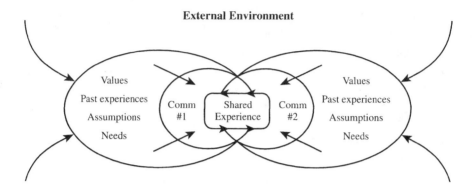

FIGURE 2.1   A Systems Perspective: The Relational Communication Process

independent system so that we can examine what goes on both mentally and physically during the listening process. Through the HURIER behavioral model, we view one individual's listening behavior as a system of six interrelated elements—hearing, understanding, remembering, interpreting, evaluating, and responding. Before we move to examine these components in detail, however, it is helpful to better understand just how listening functions within the larger context of human communication.

Early Perspectives on Communication

In early models of communication, senders and receivers played very different roles. Emphasis was on how the speaker made decisions about language, organization, and delivery factors in order to accomplish a specific purpose. From this perspective, called the *arrow approach,* the speaker's task was to shoot a carefully constructed message at passive listeners. Success was determined by the extent to which the message listeners received matched the one the speaker had in mind. As you can see, this approach assumes that listeners' responses to a speaker's message can be predicted in advance of the communication experience itself (Figure 2.2).

While the arrow approach was the basic framework for understanding public communication, more interactive encounters were viewed in terms of stimulus and

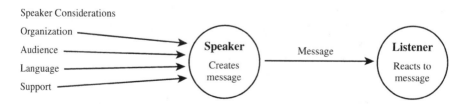

FIGURE 2.2   Arrow Approach to Communication

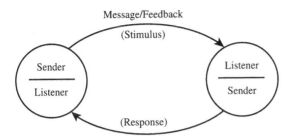

External environment

Message/Feedback
(Stimulus)

Sender
———
Listener

Listener
———
Sender

(Response)

FIGURE 2.3   Stimulus–Response Model of Communication

response—two communicators shooting arrows at each other (Figure 2.3). Terms like sender, receiver, noise, feedback, channel, and message appeared in descriptions of the communication process (Box 2.1).

Common communication models were circular and sequential. The sender created and delivered messages. Listeners processed the information and, depending upon their interpretations, provided feedback. Senders subsequently used this feedback to adjust their messages. Noise in the system was anything that interfered with the communication process. Noise could be overcome through modifications to the message, the setting, the channel, or the sender's behavior. The goals of effective communication continued to be clarity and accuracy.

Both the arrow and stimulus–response approaches are inadequate if you want to truly understand the dynamics of human communication. As one author noted (Howell, 1982, p. 28), if your interaction goes just the way you plan, it has probably failed, because you have not fully considered the other person's unique characteristics and perceptions. Unless you continue to listen during the entire communication process, you are likely to miss essential information that will help you to tailor your response.

Recognizing the importance of communication variables, theorists began to develop models that took into account not only overt behaviors, but also the less visible, psychological aspects of communication. Such considerations were essential to understanding how communication takes place between individuals who have different values, assumptions, and world views. These new models also recognized the importance of the ongoing communication event itself in perceptions of the message. One such approach, what we have referred to as relational communication, is described below. The relational view focuses on *meanings* rather than *messages* and proposes that listening and

When did you last have a conversation where listening to your partner's *attitude* was essential?

BOX 2.1

ELEMENTS OF TRADITIONAL COMMUNICATION MODELS

Sender
The person who originates and transmits a message.

Encode
The activity of choosing words and other symbols to express the ideas that the sender wants to convey.

Message
The verbal and/or nonverbal symbols that convey the sender's intentions and that are transmitted to a receiver.

Channel
The medium through which the message travels. Channels can be verbal, nonverbal, or mediated—e-mail, radio, television, and the like.

Receiver
The individual(s) who receive the speaker's message.

Decode
The receiver interprets or assigns meaning to the words and symbols in the sender's message.

Feedback
The response a receiver makes to the sender's message. Feedback can be verbal or nonverbal, direct or indirect, intentional or unintentional.

Noise
Factors that interfere with the accurate exchange of messages. Noise can be internal or external, and can originate from any of the variables in the communication process. Examples of noise include distracting mannerisms of the speaker, inappropriate language in the message, literal noise in the conference room, or listener fatigue.

Communication Effectiveness
The extent to which the interpretations of the receiver match the intentions of the sender.

---

speaking occur *simultaneously*. Listening, not speaking, becomes the central feature of effective face-to-face, or interpersonal, communication.

The Relational Perspective

Imagine that you are in the computer lab, telling a friend about your new Web design for your home page. As you speak, you watch her reactions closely to determine whether she is really interested, whether she is entertained by your stories or impressed by descriptions of your animated graphics. Although you seem to be doing most of the talking, it is apparent that you are doing quite a bit of "listening" as well. You listen to determine her attitude toward technology and her knowledge of Web design and to judge how she feels about the fact, that while she holds an after-school job, you are spending hours each evening on line.

Recognition that communicators speak while they're listening and listen while they're speaking is relatively recent. Listening isn't a function that communicators turn on and off at will, but an integral part of a larger process, or system, in which you strive to share meanings with your friends.

> Under what circumstances would a speaker intentionally distort her message?

The relational approach differs in very fundamental ways from earlier perspectives. For a start, communication does not always take place to accomplish a specific purpose, and accurate understanding is not always a necessary outcome of the encounter. Communicators may intentionally distort messages. They may try to remain ambiguous or even mislead listeners. They may develop their purpose as they speak, or shift purposes in the course of their conversation, or speak without any predetermined agenda at all.

While the relational perspective can be applied to all communication situations, its greatest practical application is to interpersonal, face-to-face situations. Recall that the most effective communicators listen effectively *as they speak* and adapt their behaviors to their perceptions of how the communication event is changing. Participants simultaneously create and interpret cues, and each person is affected by the presence of the other. Howell (1982) aptly calls this process a "joint venture interaction" (p. 30). Think of the joint ventures you've participated in recently and how your interactions might be viewed from a relational perspective.

The relational approach also emphasizes your mental as well as physical activity. We become interested in what goes on in the *minds* of participants. Words are not meaningful apart from the specific content of the interaction *as perceived by the participants*. Even then, complete understanding is not expected since, as you well know, no two individuals experience the world in exactly the same way. You really come to your understanding

> When listening, are you comfortable thinking of yourself as a "good guesser"?

of what your partner means through "an infinite series of successive approximations" (Broome, 1991, p. 240). Think of effective listeners as "good guessers."

Relational models emphasize what goes on *between* people communicating rather than on the process of creating and sending messages. Focus is not on the speaker's content and delivery, but *on the way in which listeners' minds construct meanings from what a speaker has said*. Emphasis has shifted from choices the sender makes to your interpretive process as a listener (Eisenberg & Goodall, 1993, p. 24). You can see that the listener plays the central role. Effective communication becomes a listener-defined activity; that is, a message means whatever you, the listener, thinks it means.

Senders of messages, therefore, are at the mercy of the receivers who interpret what they hear (Clampitt, 1991, p. 42). You are the one, as a listener, who determines the meaning of what you hear, regardless of what the sender intends. As you well know, meanings can be assigned without any message having been sent at all! You may be communicating even if you are *not* responding; meanings are

What are some practical implications of listening as a *receiver-defined activity*?

produced in the listener's mind as soon as there is even the *assumption of intent* on the part of the listener. Put another way, meanings are *elicited* as listeners perceive and interpret what they hear. I cannot force you to understand me, or to do what I ask. My challenge is to put together words and behaviors in ways that will bring forth in you experiences and associations that provide glimpses of the images I hold, the images I'm trying to communicate. Let's look at a couple of examples:

- An Asian friend has just received oral feedback from your communication instructor immediately after delivering an oral presentation in class. She indicated that he needs "considerable work on vocal variety, especially volume." While your instructor views her comments as relevant and constructive, your friend is upset and interprets the message as a personal attack. He vows to drop the course, even though your instructor assures him that he is doing well.
- You and your roommates are engaged in a lively discussion regarding possible vacation destinations. You look over and see that one of your friends is paying no attention to what is going on. She's looking out the window and is not reacting to what is said. You immediately interpret her behavior as poor sportsmanship. You assume that she is annoyed because earlier she suggested that you drive to Vermont, but no one liked the idea and told her exactly what they thought.

How do the speaker's *intentions* become part of the message that you hear?

As we examine the components of the HURIER model more closely, you'll see how this interpretive process takes place and the impact it has on your listening behavior.

At first, this relational view may seem a bit overwhelming, even discouraging. You're probably wondering, "What's the point of giving a lot of thought to a process that's so complicated and seemingly impossible to control?" A clearer understanding of the complexities of communication doesn't *make* it more difficult— it simply gives you, as a listener, a clearer sense of the challenges involved and increases the likelihood that you will handle your communication encounters in productive ways.

Let's take a closer look at three key elements of the relational system that we're exploring. The relational perspective is best understood by examining *perceptual differences*, the *negotiation of meanings*, and the *communication framework* (Figure 2.4).

Perceptual Differences.   Think about this: From the other person's point of view, she is probably right. Each of us has a unique framework for viewing the world, a special set of crayons to color our visions. This uniqueness becomes apparent in many simple ways every day. You may get up looking forward to morning

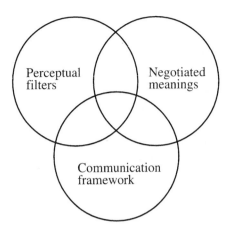

FIGURE 2.4   Elements of Relational Communication

exercise while your roommate dreads becoming sweaty and tired. You and your date leave a party; you were impressed with the music, the decorations, the graciousness of your host. Your friend is annoyed. There wasn't enough wine cooler, the music was too loud, the room was stuffy. Our predispositions, expectations, and individual preferences all contribute to shaping perceptions of our experiences and these experiences, in turn, influence the way we will view tomorrow's events (Figure 2.5).

To a large extent, you also hear what you expect to hear. You create your own reality through the stimuli you consciously or unconsciously choose. No two people pay attention to all of the same cues, nor do they assign the same meanings to their perceptions. Think of it this way. Whenever you hear a message, you're not passively taking in information but, rather, you are actively participating in a *creative process*. You control the type and amount of information you receive and, on occasion, you may even hear things that were never said.

By the same token, you may be selective and not hear important pieces of information. Your previous experiences and expectations may inhibit you from recognizing ideas that don't "fit" with the current image you hold. Thus, no matter what you say or do, you cannot completely control the impression you make on another person. You can deliberately smile, shake hands, initiate a conversation, and maintain eye contact. If your partner, however, decides that you are faking and that you are really dull, insincere, and disinterested, whatever you do will be interpreted within that framework. Perceptual factors have a profound impact on your listening; yet, because they are internal, they are also difficult to recognize.

> What are the ethical implications of listening as a *creative process*?

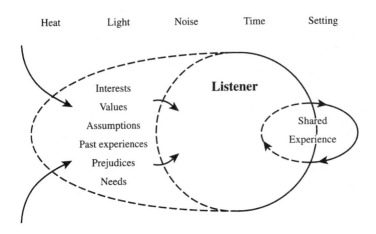

FIGURE 2.5   Unique Personal and Cultural Filters

In addition, what you hear is meaningful only to the extent that you perceive some structure and stability in the situation. Once you have accumulated a reservoir of past experiences, you have a basis on which to "make sense" of new information. Another person's behavior or words are understandable to the extent that you can put them into a context, connect them to things with which you are familiar. In fact, people often become angry when others violate their expectations about how to behave or what to say. Predictable people tend to be better liked than unpredictable ones (Wilmot, 1987). Imagine, for instance, that you are about to meet a new classmate. If, instead of saying, "Hi, I'm Fred," he asks loudly, "What color is your underwear?" you would likely experience at least a moment of confusion and discomfort.

> How might the concept of selective perception influence cross-generational communication?

When you begin to recognize the tremendous influence past experiences and expectations have on your perceptions and subsequent interpretations, you can easily understand the complexities of the listening process. It's really amazing that we coordinate our language and behavior, that we "get things to work," so much of the time.

If you begin with the premise that no two people can ever have exactly the same experience and, therefore, meanings are never identical for any two individuals, then the next step is to consider the process by which we try to overcome this lack of common experience by *negotiating* meanings.

Negotiated Meanings and Sense Making.   The notion of *meaning* is central to relational listening. Imagine being in a room where everyone is talking, but you can't hear anything that is being said. How would you know what to say? How would you "fit into" the conversation? What if the group is discussing a friend's recent illness and you blurt out, "That sure was a great party last night." Unless you first hear what is being said in a situation, you have no way to align your thoughts with your partner's. It is difficult to say something that makes sense in a specific context unless you first listen.

The concept of negotiated meaning emphasizes the role listening plays as you come to better understand other people and to align your behavior based on a process of constant listening and subsequent adjustment. This is what scholars mean when they say that reality is "socially constructed." If, for instance, your meaning for "getting in at a decent hour" is midnight while your parents' meaning is ten o'clock, you are likely to find yourselves miscommunicating. Cultural differences make the possible miscommunications even more striking. An American woman visiting friends in Paris, for instance, is likely to imagine an "early dinner" at five; only through experience does she discover that early in France is closer to seven o'clock.

Consider another example. Your friend waves to you from across the parking lot and shouts, "Five days!" What does she mean? Perhaps no one else knows but you. How can you assign a particular meaning to her words while no one else has any idea why someone would shout "five days"? It's because of a specific shared past experience which has given you the additional information needed to interpret what she has said. You don't require the full message; it's not essential for her to say, "On September 5 we are going to Bermuda and I'm excited because now there are only five days left before we leave!"

Shared meanings may be cultural as well as personal. Imagine that as you enter your political science class, your friend whispers quietly, "Get out those toothpicks!" What common understandings is she assuming in order for you to assign a meaning similar to what she intends? First, you have to know that she is referring to the imagery of using toothpicks to hold up your eyelids. This is a cultural expression; she is assuming that you share an understanding of the phrase generally. Then, she further assumes that you think as she does and find Professor Jones boring. If you thought of him as dynamic and engaging, her comment may still confuse you. You would think, "Toothpicks? What is she talking about?"

It should be clear that differences in background and experiences result in a situation where meanings are never completely shared. Over time, however, you become familiar with other people and begin to *anticipate* their probable responses. The process of predicting how another person will respond to a given idea or event has been called "defining the situation." If you accurately define the situation, your behavior is more likely to be appropriate because you have figured out how the other person expects you to respond.

As you can see, the more effective your listening—the more you pay attention to the other person—the more likely you are to reach your goal of shared meanings. Those who don't listen well, who discount perceptual differences, or who ignore

What specific actions do you take when you have to define a *new* situation?

important verbal and nonverbal cues, cannot hope to coordinate effectively their actions. Keep in mind, however, that the best you can do is to *approximate* your partner's meanings—to become a good guesser. Regardless of how well you think you understand your friends, you can never completely duplicate their experiences or share their feelings.

Meanings are strongly influenced, then, both by the communicator's past experiences and by the specific communication context. This context, or what we call the communication framework, is the final element of our relational system.

Communication Framework. The communication framework is the larger image of a situation that you use to make sense of what is going on. This "framing" is dynamic and often has such a strong influence on the way you perceive the world that your interpretations of what you hear become severely limited.

Although you may be able to predict someone's behavior with greater accuracy after you have had frequent interactions with them, you also run the risk of becoming so familiar with a particular person that you no longer really listen; consequently, you miss important cues.

Clampitt (1991) provides an interesting example of the power of framing and how it affects your interpretations. He recounts the following dialogue between two men who meet in a city park. One man has a dog on a leash. Looking over at the dog, the first man asks, "Does your dog bite?" The second man assures him that his dog does not bite. The first man then reaches down to pet the dog and is immediately bitten. "I thought you said your dog didn't bite," the man shouts, holding his injured hand. "This isn't my dog," the second man calmly replies.

Here, the communication framework was a major factor in what most of us would call a misunderstanding. You can clearly see how meanings are the product of both content—which appeared to be understood by both parties—and the context or framework, which led the first man to some incorrect assumptions. Listeners often look to the context of the situation for additional cues to make sense of what they hear. In this case, the first man made an assumption. He had past experiences that led him to believe that a person walking a dog is very likely the owner. This framework went unquestioned and was subsequently used to make sense of the event. Obviously, assumptions can be incorrect.

You can readily see how difficult it is to ensure that your interpretive framework is accurate. One person can never expect to hear or see everything that is going on in a situation. Key questions for effective listeners become, "Am I paying attention to the *right* cues in this setting?" "Are there other ways of thinking about this situation that I've been missing that would help me make sense of what I'm hearing?" "How do my background and culture restrict or bias my view?"

Constructing meanings, as you can see, is a dynamic process that takes place in your mind as the message content interacts with your unique interpretive framework. Remember, effective listeners strive to *predict* their partner's response by recognizing the impact of perceptual differences and the significance of both what is said and the context in which it occurs.

Listening-Centered Communication

It should now be clear that in our relational system, listening plays a central role. Speaking and listening functions are integrated; cues from your environment are continuously being processed as you work to share meanings with your partner. As Bostrom (1990) asks, how can you say that a certain percent of your time is spent "just listening"? Research that attempts to identify the proportion of time you devote to listening implies that when you are engaged in another communication activity, listening stops. This is clearly not the case.

> What are the *disadvantages* and/or *challenges* of a communication model that is listening centered?

Notice that the listener's focus has also shifted. Rather than attempting to reproduce what is inside a speaker's head—a task we have described as virtually impossible—the emphasis is on negotiating shared meanings. Although one-way communication situations may tempt you to assume the arrow or stimulus–response perspectives, the relational view encourages you to always think like a listener.

We now step back to examine listening as a separate system. The next section provides an overview of what we know about listening behavior and presents some of the key findings listening researchers have discovered about the process. With this background, you will be prepared to move on to Chapter 3 and to explore each of the six components that make up an individual's listening "system."

WHAT WE KNOW ABOUT LISTENING BEHAVIOR

Although researchers are confident that listening is a discrete activity, separate from such closely related processes as memory and reading comprehension (Caffrey, 1955; Hanley, 1956; Spearritt, 1962), agreement about the nature of listening ends here. As you might imagine, throughout the years researchers have produced numerous definitions of listening, each attempting to capture the essence of the process (Box 2.2). Scholars are mystified that one concept could have generated such a wide variety of variables and

> Why do you think definitions of listening vary so widely?

approaches. The lists compiled by Wolvin and Coakley (1992) and by Glenn (1989) provide striking examples of the wide range of listening definitions currently in use. When Glenn (1989) analyzed fifty of these definitions, she determined that similarities and differences among various approaches depended largely on the presence or absence of seven independent dimensions: attention, perception, interpretation, memory, response, spoken sounds, and visual cues.

■ ■ ■ ■ ■ ▬▬▬▬▬▬▬▬▬▬▬▬▬▬▬▬▬▬▬▬▬▬▬▬

BOX 2.2

DEFINITIONS OF LISTENING

A representative sample of listening definitions includes:

. . . the ability to understand spoken language (Rankin, 1926, p. 847)

. . . a definite, usually voluntary, effort to apprehend acoustically (Barbara, 1957, p. 12)

. . . the composite process by which oral language communicated by some source is received, critically and purposefully attended to, recognized, and interpreted in terms of past experiences and future expectancies (Petrie, 1961, p. 329)

. . . a process of taking what you hear and organizing it into verbal units to which you can apply meaning (Goss, 1982, p. 304)

. . . a process that includes hearing, attending to, evaluating, and responding to spoken messages (Floyd, 1985, p. 9)

The component of interpretation was present most frequently, occurring in 72 percent of the definitions. The next most common dimensions were perception, appearing in 64 percent of the cases, and attention, occurring 44 percent of the time. Response (32 percent) and memory (13 percent) trailed behind. A related finding makes the state of confusion even clearer. When Barker and Fitch-Hauser (1986) reviewed the listening literature two decades ago, they discovered over 315 variables associated with listening.

As you know, the HURIER model suggests that there are six interrelated components in the listening process. The model was created in response to employees' perceived need for greater managerial listening effectiveness. Organizational leaders had asked their associates to identify the problems they were experiencing on the job. Repeatedly, employees complained that their managers "didn't listen." While some reported that their supervisor "doesn't look at me when I talk," others were dissatisfied because, when their supervisor heard about a problem, they didn't take action and later forgot their promises. When all behaviors associated with perceptions of listening effectiveness were collected and a factor analysis performed, six discrete components emerged (Brownell, 1990; Brownell, 1994).

> When was the last time you accused someone of "not listening"? What exactly did you mean?

Recognizing the pressing need for a common framework, a group of scholars from the International Listening Association met with the goal of reaching consensus on a single definition of listening. Their efforts produced the following: *Listening is the process of receiving, constructing meaning from, and responding to spoken and/or nonverbal messages* (Emmert, 1994). Nearly every year this definition is revisited to ensure its continuing relevance to listening scholars and practitioners throughout the world. Note that the HURIER model incorporates these three components in its more comprehensive system.

Challenges in Listening Research

Not surprisingly, scholars have been frustrated by the lack of clarity regarding which variables should be included, which dimensions are central, and whether listening is a unitary or multidimensional process. This uncertainty complicates research, assessment, and teaching of the subject. Three major concerns have emerged from the literature to date:

1. *Lack of a theoretical framework:*   A recurring criticism of listening research has been its lack of a theoretical framework. The HURIER model seeks to address this problem by providing a clear theoretical base from which listening can be examined as a multifaceted, integrated process.

2. *Covert nature of the listening process:*   Most definitions of listening, as we have seen, focus on cognitive processes that are impossible to observe directly or to measure. How, for instance, do we know if someone "assigns meaning" or correctly "interprets" a behavior? Conclusions about listening competence must often be based on observable indicators of unobservable processes. Researchers have consequently begun to develop more behaviorally anchored paradigms, like the HURIER model. The behaviors that are associated with judgments of listening effectiveness, however, are still only *indicators* of the quality and nature of processes taking place on an intrapersonal level in the listener's mind.

3. *Lack of information sharing across disciplinary boundaries:*   The academic discipline which guides listening research also influences the methodology that is applied and the conclusions that are drawn. Concepts such as memory or listening comprehension may lend themselves to quantitative approaches while other topics, like empathy, may best be examined through qualitative studies. Listening becomes the elephant around which scholars from many disciplines gather, each grasping a different part of the whole and believing that what they have discovered represents the entire animal. Insights gained in any discipline have the potential to advance research across disciplinary borders, and must be systematically shared.

FACTORS THAT INFLUENCE LISTENING

This confusion and disagreement may seem to suggest that little progress has been made, but a growing number of scholars have contributed significantly to our understanding of listening behavior through their research into specific topics. In answer to some of the first questions that might come to your mind about listening, a few of their findings are summarized below.

1.   What are the characteristics of an effective listener? Are some people just born good listeners?   The answer is yes, and no. Personal style does affect your listening ability. If you are impatient, high-energy, and anxious—your tendency will be to seek information that comes in neat packages. A more patient, reflective person takes more time to listen and, consequently, may be perceived as listening more effectively.

Effective listeners are open-minded and interested in a wide variety of subjects. They tend to like people and have a generally positive attitude. Keep in mind, however, that there is a wide range of listening purposes and situations. Individuals who may be very effective listening to disturbed children may panic if they have to work as an interpreter in a highly charged political arena.

2. I'm just an average student—Is it still possible for me to improve my listening skills significantly? Even the earliest studies linked listening competence to intelligence. Over half a century ago, Nichols (1948) realized that the best predictor of effective listening was cognitive ability. Yet, much of this research focused on listening comprehension in lecture situations. Certainly, you know of individuals who are highly intelligent but who don't demonstrate effective listening behaviors. That is because intelligence, as a listening variable, interacts with a number of other factors such as personality, motivation, attitude, and interest in the subject (Kelly, 1963).

It's also important to keep in mind that different people have different listening strengths and weaknesses. While intelligence may be a significant factor in listening to difficult lecture material, listening and participating effectively in conversations or group discussions takes a different set of abilities (Bostrom, 1990).

3. Why is it that when the information is really important, or when I'm nervous about the communication situation, I find it more difficult to listen? Anxiety and stress have a profound effect on your ability to listen well. Your attitude toward communicating in general affects your stress level and consequently your overall listening ability. Stress can make it difficult to follow a discussion or to participate in a relevant manner. High anxiety in listening situations may lead to asking questions that have already been answered or making statements unrelated to the current topic of discussion.

While the fear of speaking is probably related to social approval, the anxiety you experience as a listener is more likely a consequence of your fear of misinterpreting or misunderstanding the speaker. Wheeless developed an assessment instrument, called the RAT test (1975), which measures listening apprehension. Fortunately, listening anxiety can be reduced as you learn strategies for listening effectiveness and as you become more confident of your listening ability. Such practice, of course, requires that you regularly expose yourself to a wide range of listening situations.

4. If I start out with a negative attitude, will that interfere with my ability to listen? Your attitude almost certainly influences your listening, as it affects both the selection and perception of stimuli. Even under the best of circumstances, you tend to listen selectively. If you dislike a speaker and anticipate that she will have nothing of value to say, it is likely that what you hear will confirm your expectations.

In addition, "willingness" to listen—a basic interest in other people and their ideas—is key to concentration and accurate interpretation (Cegala, 1981; Daly &

McCroskey, 1984). Most people can improve their listening effectiveness simply by devoting more effort and energy to the activity, and by connecting what the speaker says to their personal needs and interests. As you will learn in later chapters, unless you are open-minded and sincerely interested in your partner, you are likely to block and distort information.

5. How does gender influence the listening process? The question of gender differences in listening has attracted considerable attention (Emmert, Emmert, & Brandt, 1993; Marsnik, 1993). Goleman (1978) was among the first to suggest that females perform better on tasks that involve verbal ability, while men perform best when visual skills are involved. Women are also thought to be more sensitive to nonverbal cues, suggesting that they are more likely to take these variables into account in listening situations (Tannen, 1990; Borisoff & Merrill, 1991). Although some differences are attributed to socialization or to learned behavior, others are believed to have a biological link.

6. Can I expect my friends from other cultures to listen differently than I do? An individual's culture, background, role, and other variables determine his unique perspective. This world view influences both perceptual processes and information processing. As your school and workplace become more diverse, it becomes essential for you to recognize and value individual differences in perception and view-point. Taking multiple perspectives in-to account will enrich your communication and decision-making; ignoring them will create conflict and misunderstandings (Ostermeier, 1993). The cultural dimension, as you might imagine, also affects listening expectations as well as definitions of effectiveness.

> As a culture, how much do we value listening? What leads you to that conclusion?

7. If the speaker is disorganized or distracting, is it more difficult for me to listen well? Message and speaker variables both affect your listening. The clarity of the organization has a significant impact on your ability to comprehend and recall the information you hear. Speakers who use clear organizational strategies are easier to follow than those who present ideas randomly.

A speaker's mannerisms and delivery have an impact on her credibility and affect your attention, comprehension, and retention (Beatty & Payne, 1984). As you will discover in the following chapters, focusing your attention for any length of time on a message that is either poorly designed or poorly delivered takes a tremendous amount of energy and self-discipline.

8. Do I listen differently to the television than I do to a CD or to a live speaker? Definitely. You listen differently to a CD-Rom than you do to a video-tape, and listening to a live speaker presents yet a different set of challenges. Listening retention and concentration improves, for instance, when you receive information from a live speaker, rather than a DVD or other mediated communication. This is due to an interesting concept called "social presence," which means that the physical presence of another human being is in itself stimulating (Short, Williams, & Christie, 1976). Although we know that the addition of visual stimuli improves some listening behaviors, the accuracy of comprehension may decrease with the added stimuli of background music, visual effects, and the like. In addition, when verbal and visual messages conflict, most people will choose the visual channel (Leathers, 1979).

> What is your preference for listening channels? How does it change according to your purpose?

Study of channel choices and other variables has, as you might suspect, advanced our understanding of the nature of the listening process (Karr & Vogelsang, 1990; Schnapp, 1991). As the importance of listening has become more widely recognized, educators and trainers have been challenged to document the effectiveness of their efforts. This, in turn, has prompted researchers to explore various means of assessing listening behavior.

RESEARCH ON LISTENING ASSESSMENT

You might ask yourself: How do I know when I'm listening *effectively*? A review of several key issues related to evaluating your listening ability provides a background as you work to increase your listening competence.

Types of Assessment Instruments

In the appendix of Rankin's (1926) doctoral thesis is the text of the first unpublished listening test. This and other early measurement instruments, many of which were developed during the 1950s and 1960s, focused almost exclusively on listening in presentational speaking situations. Listeners' ability to comprehend and recall messages was determined by paper and pencil measures in a format similar to that used to measure reading comprehension. Two standardized tests from this period which are still in use are the Brown–Carlson Listening Comprehension Test (Brown & Carlson, 1995) and the Sequential Test of Educational Progress (1957). As mentioned earlier in this chapter, the results of these and other listening comprehension tests are highly correlated with measures of general intelligence.

During the late 1970s and early 1980s, the interpersonal or interactive aspects of listening began drawing increased attention. Researchers moved from assessing listening in one-way communication situations to examining the more complicated dynamics of two-way interaction. Tests such as the Watson–Barker (1984b) and the Kentucky Comprehensive Listening Tests (Bostrom & Waldhart, 1983) were developed to measure dimensions such as interpreting nonverbal and vocal, or paralinguistic, cues. Other tests produced during this period include the

Listening Comprehensive Test (1974), the Jones–Mohr Listening Test (1976), and the Michigan Listening Test (Michigan Department of Education, 1979). As technology made more adequate means of recording events available, audiotapes were used with increasing frequency to capture the unique aspects of oral language and the dynamics of two-way communication. Due to the success of these efforts, many assessment instruments continued to be revised and improved throughout the 1990s (Watson–Barker Listening Test, 1991; Brown & Carlson, 1995).

This renewed interest in assessment led to studies that explored the validity of existing instruments (Rubin, Daly, McCroskey, & Mead, 1982; Applegate & Jackson, 1986; Roberts, C., 1986; Fitch-Hauser & Hughes, 1987; Plattor, 1988; Rhodes, Watson, & Barker, 1990; Villaume & Weaver, 1996; Bentley, 1997; McKenzie & Clark, 1995) as well as efforts that resulted in the creation of additional measures (Steinbrecher–Wilmington Listening Test, 1997; Stein, 1999). Guidelines were also developed to assist in test construction (Backlund, Brown, Gurry, & Jandt, 1982).

Assessment Concerns

No one said that assessing listening was easy. Although efforts to measure your listening ability have increased, a number of important concerns remain. These include:

1. *Lack of clarity regarding the constructs of listening:*   The confusion previously described regarding both the nature of the listening process and what is being measured has made the development of valid and reliable tests difficult. As C. V. Roberts (1988) commented, "It would seem prudent to first discover what it is that we should be studying before deciding how we should measure it" (p. 3).

2. *Lack of correspondence between behaviors being assessed and those being taught:*   Assessment measures must be chosen with consideration as to how instructional goals match the dimensions being evaluated (Brown & Carlson, 1955; Watson & Barker, 1984a; Bostrom & Waldhart, 1988). In this regard, the HURIER model provides a clear blueprint for skill development and subsequent testing.

3. *Use of written measures to assess behavioral dimensions:*   The results of listening tests may be dependent on your reading and writing abilities (Faires, 1980; Rubin, Daly, McCroskey, & Mead, 1982); consequently, deficiencies in these skills adversely affect the results of your listening test. The written response you make on a listening test is not the same as listening. Recent research has confirmed that not only is oral-based prose easier to understand, but it also takes less cognitive effort than reading (Rubun, Hafer, & Arata, 2000).

Importantly, tests can be biased by language ability or cultural orientation. If, after hearing a speaker say, "And I never want to see you again," you are asked to determine whether the person was feeling (a) angry, (b) resentful, or (c) annoyed, you must first be able to distinguish subtle differences in the meanings of the choices provided before you can respond appropriately. As you now know, such meanings may be culturally determined.

4. *Difficulties in skill transfer:*   It would be nice to assume that because you demonstrate appropriate behaviors in the classroom, you will practice your newly acquired skills once you are on your own. Of course, such is not always the case. If doing well on a listening assessment instrument is important to you, you may try hard—and thereby improve your score. Such incentives may be missing in your daily communication contexts. Specialists have therefore become wary of the results reported in studies that have used undergraduate classes to support claims of listening improvement in non-academic settings.

Even when you leave the classroom highly motivated and with good intentions, there is speculation that newly acquired listening behaviors may not persist in less supportive environments. Little concrete evidence has been gathered regarding the long-term effect of listening instruction on your performance. If you score significantly better on a standardized listening test after listening instruction, does this mean that your listening has permanently improved? We hope so, but can we be sure? Too few longitudinal studies have been conducted to document the impact of training on performance.

5. *Role of motivation and listening improvement:*   Individuals vary significantly in their listening behavior; yet, the causes of these differences are poorly understood. We do know, however, that there is a strong link between motivation to listen and listening effectiveness. Motivation has been recognized as a major factor in determining the level and persistence of newly acquired listening behaviors.

Although you may "mobilize" your listening energy when you are highly motivated, such as in a test situation, it does not follow that you necessarily will listen as well at home, at work, or in other situations. Steil et al. (1983) recognized the influence of motivation and subsequently suggested the LAW of listening. Listening, he noted, is dependent not only upon ability (A) but also upon your willingness (W). Steil's LAW of listening, Listening = Ability plus Willingness, is a useful device to remind us of the importance of attitudes as well as behaviors in our pursuit of greater listening effectiveness.

THE HURIER MODEL: A BEHAVIORAL APPROACH

The HURIER model, as you know, provides a framework for the systematic development of your listening skills. You should now have an understanding of the central role listening plays in the relational communication process and be familiar with several of the issues listening researchers confront. As we move on to examine the elements of the HURIER model more carefully, it is important to clarify the basic assumptions of this approach. One way to proceed is by responding to several key questions (Wolvin & Coakley, 1996).

1. *Is listening a unitary function or a cluster of related processes?* The HURIER model views listening as a system comprised of six interrelated processes. Although the six processes function together and all are involved to some degree in every listening encounter, *different purposes and types of listening require emphasis on different listening behaviors.*

2. *Should listening involve reception of both verbal and nonverbal symbols?* Yes. Listening involves both hearing and seeing. Participants are profoundly affected by context, or communication framework, which may involve a visual as well as an aural dimension. Aspects of voice, or paralanguage, and nonverbal cues influence the way a perceptive listener interprets meanings (Bostrom, 1990; Purdy, 1991).

> Under what circumstances do you listen to yourself? How is this different from listening to others?

3. *Can listening occur only in face-to-face situations?* No. The most useful definitions of listening are broad enough to include situations in which individuals listen to the media, to music, to themselves, and to a variety of messages and sounds where others may or may not be present. The nature of listening and the importance of various components vary according to whether listeners are involved in small groups, attending a lecture, engaging in a solitary activity, and so forth.

4. *Does listening always require conscious effort?* Yes. Although individuals can hear when they are passive, effective listening is active and mindful.

5. *Is response a necessary component of listening? Must it be overt?* Yes. Your response is an essential component of listening and can take many forms. When engaged in the relational communication process, participants judge the quality of the exchange based largely on the listener's response (Rhodes, Watson, & Barker, 1990). The HURIER model suggests that in face-to-face listening in particular, an overt response facilitates shared meanings. In other settings, the listener's response may be delayed or it may be unobservable.

6. *Is listening always purposeful?* No. Although listening requires conscious effort, it is not always intentional and planned. In fact, much of the communicating you do is spontaneous and unplanned. Even when you have a specific reason to listen, purposes are constantly changing. You may expect to be entertained and discover that you have learned a great deal, or you may be persuaded by a message that you had assumed was strictly informational. Recall that meanings are *elicited* and shaped by your previous experiences, expectations, and other individual variables. You have no way of predicting in advance exactly what the message will be or exactly how you will respond to it.

■ ■ ■ ■ ■ ■

BOX 2.3

Intrapersonal

Intrapersonal communication is a covert, mental activity that occurs when an individual communicates with himself or herself. Information processing takes place at this level; the individual is aware of his or her reflection and self-talk, which serves a variety of functions.

Interpersonal

Interpersonal communication is generally characterized as an interaction that takes place between two or three people who are in relatively close proximity. Participants are physically oriented toward one another, and nonverbal cues play an important role in the accurate interpretation of meanings. Two communicators are referred to as a dyad; a three-person interaction is a triad. Interpersonal communication may be either formal (an interview) or informal (friends talking).

Small Group

When four to eight individuals interact face-to-face, they are generally designated as a small group. An important characteristic of small group communication is that all parties readily can see one another and are aware of one another's verbal and nonverbal behavior. The interaction occurs in a face-to-face setting; each member has an equal opportunity to actively participate in the exchange. Due to the dynamics of small group interaction, individual differences become a particularly important variable in the process.

Public

Public communication, often referred to as presentational, is more formal than either interpersonal or small group and is often referred to as "one way." The individual designated as the speaker is often physically distant, and always distinct, from his or her listeners. The message is generally created in advance of the communication occasion. While extended dialogue is seldom possible in public communication contexts, listeners continuously provide nonverbal cues in response to the speaker's message. Effective speakers continuously modify their messages in response to this feedback. It is common for question and answer sessions to follow presentations.

Mediated

Communication that takes place through, or is facilitated by, some form of technology is called mediated communication. In such situations, individual communicators may not be in physical proximity but may be separated by hundreds or thousands of miles. This distance creates a distinctive situation in which fewer cues are available to understand and accurately interpret messages. The communication is necessarily influenced by the nature of the medium through which it is transmitted. Examples of mediated communication include videoconferencing, television, radio, and telephone.

DEVELOPING LISTENING STRATEGY

Traditionally, scholars have approached the study of speech communication in one of two ways. Many view communication in terms of the specific situation or context—interpersonal, small group, presentational speaking, or mediated communication (Box 2.3). A second fruitful approach has been to examine the process in terms of the individual's purpose. Studies of persuasion are perhaps the most obvious example of how purpose has guided our exploration of communication variables. With regard to listening, Wolvin and Coakley (1996) made purpose a dominant theme by distinguishing five listening goals; discriminative, comprehensive, therapeutic, critical, and appreciative.

As discussed at length in Chapter 1, purpose and context significantly influence listening requirements. Effective listeners not only display appropriate attitudes, understand relevant principles, and develop specific skills, they also adapt their listening behavior to meet the needs of the particular situation. As the model

---

BOX 2.4

LISTENING STRATEGY IS DETERMINED BY CONTEXT AND PURPOSE

Listening Context

Intrapersonal: *within one person;*

Dyadic/Interpersonal: *between two people;*

Small group: *three to eight people face-to-face;*
Public: *over eight people;*
Mediated: *communication that takes through, or is facilitated by, some form of media*

Relative Importance of Components in the HURIER MODEL

Listening Component	Strategy (H, M, L)
Hearing	Moderate
Understanding	Moderate
Remembering	Low
Interpreting	High
Evaluating	Low
Responding	High

Listening Purpose

Discriminative: *to distinguish and identify sounds;*
Comprehensive: *to understand and learn;*
Critical: *to evaluate and judge;*

Therapeutic: *to identify feelings and to empathize;*

Appreciative: *to enjoy*

in Chapter 1 suggests (Figure 1.3), the relative importance of each of the six components of the HURIER model is determined by the listener's goals and other aspects of the communication context.

You will see that effective listening is achieved by focusing to a greater or lesser degree to each of the six essential components, or skill areas, presented in the HURIER model. Excellent listeners adjust their strategies to each new set of listening requirements (Box 2.4). A political speech, for instance, may require considerable skill in evaluative listening while a lecture class calls upon your ability to understand and remember what you hear. By demonstrating appropriate, situation-specific listening behaviors, you are likely to accomplish your tasks with fewer misunderstandings and establish healthy, positive relationships with family, friends, and coworkers.

SUMMARY

Listening is appropriately viewed from a systems perspective, whether as part of the larger communication process or at the level of the individual listener. Early arrow and stimulus–response approaches to communication did not capture the central role listening plays in this complex process. From a more recent relational perspective, listening is prerequisite to effective communication; listening and speaking are viewed as simultaneous processes. Relational listening is characterized by a concern for three dimensions: individuals' perceptual orientations, the negotiation of shared meanings, and participants' unique communication framework.

Research in listening has increased substantially during the past decade. Listening is a complex, largely covert activity that has been defined in a variety of ways. A review of listening definitions illustrates the variety of approaches that have been taken to the subject.

Researchers have also examined variables that potentially affect listening behavior. Motivation, attitude, gender, age, anxiety, channel, and characteristics of the message all influence listening effectiveness. Another relevant area of research is listening assessment, since measuring the effectiveness of listening behavior is prerequisite to improving performance.

Underlying assumptions of the HURIER model are presented. The extent to which each of the six components is relevant depends upon both the listening situation and the listening purpose. In addition to developing appropriate attitudes, acquiring relevant knowledge, and learning essential behaviors, those interested in improving their listening effectiveness must develop a listening strategy by making wise choices about the skills that are brought to bear in each listening situation.

APPLICATIONS

Application 1: Understand Relational Communication
Application 2: Understand Research in Listening
Application 3: Understand Listening Assessment
Application 4: Recognize How Situation and Purpose Influence Listening Strategy

Application 1: Understand Relational Communication

The discussion questions and activities in this application will help you to better understand the principles of relational communication as they apply to practical listening situations. Remember that our relational model suggests that listening is the key skill for effective communication.

Activities

1. Talk with several individuals who have had extensive experience in another country. Ask them for examples of the ways in which they went about sense-making; that is, what did they take for granted that may have been perceived differently in another culture? Record your findings so that you can share them with your class.

2. How much responsibility does the listener have for ensuring that effective communication takes place? Use the following list to generate a discussion of the role listeners play in each situation:

   a. a lecture course
   b. a play
   c. a business meeting
   d. a casual conversation at home
   e. an employment interview

   Think of other situations and add to the above list.

3. Read news magazines, watch movies, and consider novels that have examples of perceptual differences that had a profound impact on individuals, decisions, or events. Select one or two of the best examples, and bring these in to discuss with your group.

   a. What was the listening problem?
   b. What impact did it have?
   c. What could have been done to improve listening effectiveness?

4. Make a list of words that are "emotional triggers" for you. Describe your "semantic reaction." How do you explain this response? What might you do to reduce your strong emotional reaction?

Group Activities

Form a small group of four to six people. You may want to keep the same group for all activities, or you may find it more interesting to change groups so that you get to hear the opinions and ideas of a greater number of your classmates.

1. Listening has been described as a system of six interrelated components. Generate some examples of other systems and make as many parallels or analogies as possible between the listening process and other processes.

   Be creative! For example, how is listening like photosynthesis? The solar system? Electricity?

2. Share examples of situations in which you entered a new group—a club, an organization, a team—and had a different understanding of the meaning of a particular word or event. Discuss how you began to "make sense" of what was going on.

   Example: When you made the basketball team you knew that you were expected to go to "a lot" of practices. You didn't realize, however, that practices were every evening and that it was unacceptable to miss any of them.

3. Recall an example where you engaged in the process of negotiating the meaning of some concept, either with your parents or a friend. Share your example with the rest of the group.

   Example: Perhaps your parents wanted you home from an event at a "reasonable hour." How did you go about determining what that meant?

4. We have proposed that listening is the central communication function. What changes would take place if everyone became listening-centered in their communication? List both positive and negative consequences.

5. How can you apply the relational, listening-centered model of communication to traditionally one-way communication situations like public presentations? Generate a list of suggestions, and then share them with the rest of the class.

6. Read the short case below and then answer the accompanying case questions.

   Jamie almost ran into him as she approached the doorway to the auditorium, her bookbag in one hand and a coke in the other. As she took an awkward step backwards, he laughed and gently grabbed her arm, swinging her back against the wall. Jamie's friend, Christy, stopped next to her.

   "Well," Shawn said as he grinned at Jamie's obvious embarrassment, "I can't think of anyone I'd rather run into. But I don't know if I'd choose a classroom hallway for such a close encounter!" He laughed again and then noticed Christy. "Hey Chrissy, are you here to keep Jamie from misbehaving?" Shawn winked.

   "It's not Jamie who's misbehaving," Christy countered.

   "Aw, come on, so many women, so little time . . ." Shawn began when Jamie abruptly pulled her arm free.

   "Excuse me," she said without looking at him, and headed into the large lecture hall. Christy and Shawn exchanged looks, shrugged, and then Christy followed Jamie into the crowded room.

   "What is the matter with you?" Christy asked. "He's only teasing. Shawn's a good guy. He makes me laugh. And besides, he's got a really cute smile. Did you notice the way he calls me 'Chrissy' all the time?"

"He makes me ill," Jamie said flatly. "He can't keep his hands off me, and he's obnoxious. Every time I see him he teases me, and I don't like it."

"Jamie, honestly, he's absolutely harmless. Don't you remember Bob telling us that he has a girlfriend at Kentucky State? He doesn't even date anyone around here. You've got to loosen up and not take men so seriously. You'll never have any fun if you're always on the defensive."

Case Questions

1. How did Jamie's and Christy's perceptual orientations affect how they interpreted Shawn's actions? What accounted for the differences in their orientations and the way each defined the situation?

2. Describe the communication framework Christy used to interpret events.

3. Consider the case in terms of listening purposes. What was Christy's purpose? Jamie's? Shawn's?

Application 2: Understand Research in Listening

The more we learn about listening, the better able educators will be to help you improve your listening effectiveness. By considering the questions below, you will more fully appreciate the issues that must be addressed as we work to better understand this complex process.

Activities

1. After reading this chapter, what do you believe are the most serious problems confronting listening researchers?

2. Identify someone whom you believe is an exceptionally good listener. Identify the characteristics of the person which led you to this conclusion. Are some people good listeners in some situations and not in others? With some individuals and not with others? What accounts for these differences?

3. Have you experienced differences in listening behavior among the people you know or work with that you can attribute to gender or age? Provide some examples. What guidelines might individuals keep in mind to avoid stereotyping on this basis?

4. Reflect on other classes you have taken, perhaps in science or psychology. What models have you learned that have been particularly helpful in explaining important concepts? List some of the models that you recall, and summarize their usefulness.

5. Do some research and generate five or ten models of communication. Almost all speech communication textbooks present a model somewhere in the first few chapters. Examine each closely to determine how listening is positioned within each framework. Compare the way in which listening is treated in each case. Be prepared to share your findings with the rest of the class.

Group Activities

Form a small group of four to six people. You may want to keep the same group for all activities, or you may find it more interesting to change groups so that you get to hear the opinions and ideas of a greater number of your classmates.

1. Why do you think it has been so difficult for scholars to agree on a definition of listening? If you were charged with this task, what process would you use to come to a common definition? In reviewing the seven most commonly used variables in listening definitions, which ones do you feel are most essential? Support your decision and be ready to present your conclusions to the rest of the class.

2. Now that you are familiar with a number of listening definitions, generate one of your own. Make sure it includes all of the aspects of listening you believe are important. As a group, create a visual model to accompany your verbal definition. Share your conclusions and your model with other groups.

3. How would members of the following disciplines define listening? (Feel free to add to the list below.) Compare and contrast the approaches you imagine each would take:

   a. Anthropology
   b. English Literature
   c. Political Science
   d. Physics

   e. Music
   f. Theatre
   g. Business
   h. Psychology

4. Discuss how the communication channel (oral, written, media, and so forth) influences your perceptions of the message. There has been some criticism of television, which provides a high degree of sensory stimulation without requiring the participant to do much independent thinking. Do you believe that there is any danger in watching too much television? Does it harm or help listening ability? Share your thoughts with the rest of the class.

5. Review the listening models described in the chapter. As a group, you will either choose or be assigned to *one* of the models to use in analyzing a communication situation. First, generate some examples of specific communication breakdowns that have occurred as a result of poor listening. After describing the problem, identify where the breakdown occurred in terms of the model you have selected. Share your analysis with the rest of your classmates. Discuss whether the model you used influenced what you paid attention to in the situation.

Application 3: Understand Listening Assessment

You now have a general background on listening assessment and are familiar with some of the issues listening researchers confront as they work to develop reliable and valid assessment instruments. Since the feedback you receive from assessment is invaluable in improving your listening behaviors, it is important to consider ways in which you might take greater responsibility for this process.

Activities

1. What assessment instruments have you taken? These might be personal style, conflict management, critical thinking, or other measures. Did you feel the results were accurate? Why or why not?

2. You know that motivation plays a key role in developing listening skills. What can be done to ensure that you and your classmates stay motivated to work on your listening skills after this class is over?

Group Activities

Form a small group of four to six people. You may want to keep the same group for all activities, or you may find it more interesting to change groups so that you get to hear the opinions and ideas of a greater number of your classmates.

1. Discuss the problems involved in applying skills you have learned in the classroom to outside-of-class situations. How can you, as a student, facilitate this transfer process? Share your ideas with the rest of the class.

2. Do you agree that many tests are "contaminated" because they require reading and writing skills in order to make judgments about other behaviors? Give some examples of tests you have taken that may put non-native students or other minority groups at a disadvantage. Is there anything that can be done to offset such problems?

3. In addition to formal assessment instruments, what other ways might you assess your listening? How valid are these measures? Propose as many methods as possible for judging listening improvement (keeping journals, self-reports, and so forth). Present your ideas to the rest of the class for discussion.

Application 4: Recognize How Situation and Purpose Influence Listening Strategy

Listening behavior is modified according to specific situational requirements. While you may have no problem listening to your friend in an informal setting, you find paying attention during Chemistry is almost impossible. Perhaps there's a television personality who annoys you and makes it difficult for you to concentrate—or one you find stimulating and provocative. Every time you listen, both the situation and the purpose influence your behavior.

Activities

1. To what extent do the changes required by context and purpose obstruct efforts to formulate one listening definition? How does your listening change in the following situations? Explain in terms of both context and purpose.

    a. At a party
    b. In class
    c. In an interview
    d. At the dinner table with your family
    e. At a sports event
    f. At a concert

2. Purpose and context can affect your motivation to listen.

   How does your listening vary depending upon your purpose for listening?

   Do you find some types of listening more difficult than others? Why might this be the case?

   Does the specific situation affect your ability to listen?

   Make a list of listening purposes to which you devote the most energy, and another list of the situations in which you are highly motivated to listen. Each list should have at least four items.

   What do these lists tell you about your listening needs?

Group Activities

Form a small group of four to six people. You may want to keep the same group for all activities, or you may find it more interesting to change groups so that you get to hear the opinions and ideas of a greater number of your classmates.

1. Recall examples of situations in which your listening was dramatically influenced by either the situation or your purpose. Share this experience with members of your group.

2. Which component of the HURIER model was most affected?

BIBLIOGRAPHY

Applegate, J. S., & Jackson, J. (1986). *The measurement of the listening construct: Review and synthesis*. Paper presented at the annual meeting of the International Listening Association, San Diego, CA.

Backlund, P. M., Brown, K. L., Gurry, J., & Jandt, F. (1982). Recommendations for assessing speaking and listening skills. *Communication Education, 31*, 9–17.

Barker, D. R., & Fitch-Hauser, M. (1986). *Variables related to the processing and reception of information as published in ten selected psychology journals*. Paper presented at the Research Task Force of the International Listening Association, San Diego, CA.

Beatty, M. J., & Payne, S. K. (1984). Listening comprehension as a function of cognitive complexity: A research note. *Communication Monographs, 51*, 85–89.

Bentley, S. (1997). Benchmarking listening behaviors: Is effective listening what the speaker says it is? *International Journal of Listening, 11*, 51–68.

Borisoff, D., & Merrill, L. (1991). Gender issues and listening. In D. Borisoff and M. Purdy (Eds.), *Listening in Everyday Life: A Personal and Professional Approach*, 59–86. New York: University Press of America.

Bostrom, R. (1990). *Listening behavior: Measurement & application*. New York: The Guilford Press.

Bostrom, R. N., & Waldhart, E. S. (1983). *Kentucky comprehensive listening test*. Lexington, KY: The Kentucky Listening Research Center.

Bostrom, R. N., & Waldhart, E. (1988). Memory models and the measurement of listening. *Communication Education, 37*, 1–18.

Broome, B. J. (1991). Building shared meaning: Implications of a relational approach to empathy. *Communication Education, 40*(3), 235–249.

Brown, D. P. (1950). Teaching aural English. *English Journal, 39*, 128.

Brown, J. I., & Carlson, G. R. (1995). *Brown-Carlsen listening comprehension test*. New York: Harcourt, Brace and World.

Brownell, J. (1990). Perceptions of effective listeners: A management study. *The Journal of Business Communication, 27*(4), 401–416.

Brownell, J. (1994). Teaching listening: Some thoughts on the behavioral approach. *Business Communication Quarterly, 57*(4), 19–26.

Caffrey, J. (1955). Auding ability at the secondary school level. *Education, 75,* 303–310.

Cegala, D. (1981). Interaction involvement: A cognitive dimension of communication competence. *Communication Education, 30,* 109–121.

Clampitt, P. G. (1991). *Communicating for managerial effectiveness.* Newbury Park, CA: Sage Publications.

Daley, J., & McCroskey, J. (1984). *Avoiding communication.* Beverly Hills, CA: Sage Publications.

Eisenberg, E. M., & Goodall, H. L., Jr. (1993). *Organizational communication: Balancing creativity and constraint.* New York: St. Martin's Press.

Emmert, P. (1994). A definition of listening. *Listening Post, 51,* 6.

Emmert, P., Emmert, V., & Brandt, J. (1993). An analysis of male-female differences on the listening practices feedback report. *Journal of the International Listening Association,* special issue, 43–55.

Faires, C. L. (1980). *The development of listening tests.* Paper presented at the annual meeting of the Mid-South Educational Research Association, New Orleans, LA.

Fitch-Hauser, M., & Hughes, M. A. (1987). A factor analytic study of four listening tests. *Journal of the International Listening Association, 1,* 129–147.

Furness, E. L. (1957). Listening: A case of terminological confusion. *Journal of Educational Psychology, 48,* 481.

Glenn, E. C. (1989). A content analysis of fifty definitions of listening. *Journal of the International Listening Association, 3,* 21–31.

Goleman, D. (1978). Special abilities of the sexes. *Psychology Today, 12,* 48–49.

Hanley, C. H. (1956). Factorial analysis of speech perception. *Journal of Speech and Hearing Disorders, 21,* 76–87.

Horrworth, G. L. (1966). Listening: A fact of oral language. *Elementary English, 43,* 857–858.

Howell, W. S. (1982). *The empathic communicator.* Belmont, CA: Wadsworth Publishers.

Jones-Mohr Listening Test (1976). LaJolla, CA: University Associates.

Karr, M., & Vogelsang, R. W. (1990). A comparison of the audio and video versions of the Watson-Barker listening test: Form A and B. *Journal of the International Listening Association, 4,* 165–179.

Kelly, C. M. (1963). Mental ability and personality factors in listening. *Quarterly Journal of Speech, 49,* 152–156.

Kelly, C. M. (1970). Empathic listening? *Small Group Communication: A Reader.* In R. S. Cathcart and L. A. Samavar (Eds.), pp. 251–259. Dubuque, Iowa: Wm. C. Brown Company.

Leathers, D. (1979). The impact of multichannel message inconsistency on verbal and non-verbal decoding behaviors. *Communication Monographs, 46,* 88–100.

Littlejohn, S. W. (1989). *Theories of human communication.* Belmont, CA: Wadsworth Publishers.

Louhils-Salminen, L. (1999). "Was there life before them?": Fax and e-mail in business communication. *Journal of Language for International Business, 10*(1), 24–42.

Marsnik, N. (1993). The impact of gender on communication. *Journal of the International Listening Association,* special issue, 32–42.

McKenzie, N. J., & Clark, A. J. (1995). The all-in-one concept: How much must listening research include? *International Journal of Listening, 9,* 29–43.

Michigan Department of Education. (1979). *MEAP listening test.* Michigan: Michigan Department of Education.

Nichols, R. (1948). Factors in listening comprehension. *Speech Monographs, 15,* 154–163.

Ostermeier, T. H. (1993). Perception of nonverbal cues in dialogic listening in an intercultural interview. *Journal of the International Listening Association,* special issue, 64–75.

Plattor, E. (1988). Assessing listening in elementary and junior high schools: An examination of four listening tests. *Journal of the International Listening Association, 2,* 20–31.

Purdy, M. (1991). What is listening? In D. Borisoff and M. Purdy (Eds.), *Listening in Everyday Life: A Personal and Professional Approach,* pp. 3–20. New York: University Press of America.

Rankin, P. T. (1926). The measurement of the ability to understand spoken language. *Dissertation Abstracts, 12.* University of Michigan.

Rhodes, S., Watson, K. W., & Barker, L. L. (1990). Listening assessment: Trends and influencing factors in the 1980s. *Journal of the International Listening Association, 4,* 62–82.

Roberts, C. (1986). A validation of the Watson-Barker Listening Test. *Communication Research Reports, 3,* 115–119.

Roberts, C. V. (1988). The validation of listening tests: Cutting of the Gordian Knot. *Journal of the International Listening Association, 2,* 1–19.

Rubin, D., Daly, J., McCroskey, J., & Mead, N. (1982). A review and critique of procedures for assessing speaking and listening skills among preschool through grade twelve students. *Communication Education, 31,* 285–304.

Rubun, D., Hafer, T., & Arata, K. (2000). Reading and listening to oral-based discourse *Communication Education, 49*(2), 121–133.

Schnapp, D. C. (1991). The effects of channel on assigning meaning in the listening process. *Journal of the International Listening Association, 5,* 93–107.

Short, J., Williams., E., & Christie, B. (1976). *The social psychology of telecommunications.* New York: Wiley and Son, Publishers.

Spearritt, D. (1962). *Listening comprehension.* Melbourne, Australia: Australian Council for Educational Research.

Steil, L. K., Barker, L. L., & Watson, K. W. (1983). *Effective listening: Key to your success.* Reading, MA: Random House.

Stein, S. K. (1999). Uncovering listening strategies: Protocol analysis as a means to investigate student listening in the basic communication course. Unpublished PhD dissertation, University of Maryland, College Park, MD.

Steinbrecher, M. M., & Wilmington, S. C. (1997). Steinbrecher-Wilmington Listening Test. Oshkosh, WI: University of Wisconsin Oshkosh.

Tannen, D. (1990). *You just don't understand: Men and women in conversation.* New York: Ballantine Books, Inc.

Trevino, L. K., & Webster, J. (1992). Flow in computer-mediated communication: Electronic mail and voice mail evaluation and impacts. *Communication Research, 19*(5), 539–547.

Villaume, W. A., & Weaver, J. B., III. (1996). A factorial approach to establishing reliable listening measures from the WBLT and the KCLT: Full information factor analysis of dichotomous data. *International Journal of Listening, 10,* 10–20.

Walther, J. (1992). Interpersonal effects in computer-mediated interaction: A relational perspective. *Communication Research, 19*(1), 52–61.

Watson, K. W., & Barker, L. L. (1984a). Listening behavior: Definition and measurement. In R. N. Bostrom (Ed.), *Communication Yearbook Eight,* pp. 83–97. Beverly Hills, CA: Sage Publications.

Watson, K. W., & Barker, L. L. (1984b, 1991). *Watson-Barker Listening Test.* New Orleans, LA: Spectra Incorporated, Publishers.

Wheeless, L. (1975). An investigation of receiver apprehension and social context dimensions of communication apprehension. *Communication Education, 24,* 261–268.

Wilmot, W. W. (1987). *Perception of the other: Dyadic communication.* New York; McGraw-Hill.

Wolff, F., & Marsnik, N. (1992). *Perceptive listening.* Fort Worth, TX: Harcourt Brace Jovanovich.

Wolvin, A. D., & Coakley, C. G. (1996). *Listening* (5th ed.). Dubuque, IA: William C. Brown.

PART II

LISTENING: PRINCIPLES
AND APPLICATIONS

PEANUTS Reprinted by permission of United Features Syndicate, Inc.

CHAPTER 3

THE PROCESS OF HEARING

*If we had a keen vision and feeling of all ordinary human life, it
would be like hearing the grass grow and the squirrel's heart
beat, and we should die of that roar which lies
on the other side of silence.*
—GEORGE ELIOT, *MIDDLEMARCH*

OUTLINE

CHAPTER OBJECTIVES

After completing this chapter, you will

Become more aware of:

- the importance of hearing to the listening process
- the ways in which you can influence the hearing process
- the complexity of the processes associated with hearing
- the types of research that are being conducted on the hearing process
- the daily opportunities for appreciative listening

Better understand:

- the mechanics of hearing
- the relationships between attention and hearing

- the processes of auditory discrimination and selective attention
- the ways you can learn to focus your attention by using the thought–speech differential
- how anxiety influences listening
- appreciative listening

Develop skills in:

- improving your concentration
- applying the vocalized listening technique
- identifying and reducing distractions
- recognizing and reducing stress

Individual Listening Filters

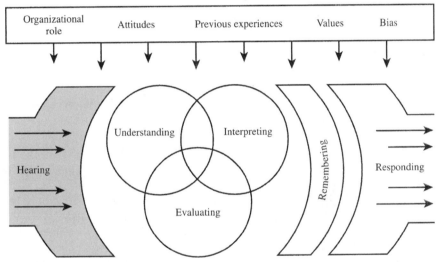

A Model of the Six-Component HURIER Listening Process

HEARING: SITUATION AND PURPOSE

Hearing is prerequisite to all listening that involves vocal communication, regardless of the purpose. It may be more difficult to hear and to focus attention, however, in lecture or one-way communication situations where you are physically farther from the speaker and less actively involved in the communication event. In such situations, both internal and external distractions are more likely to affect your concentration.

Hearing is often the key component in appreciative listening situations or situations where no other person is present. In such settings, the ability to hear and discriminate sounds is prerequisite to your enjoyment. Whether listening to music, nature, or poetry, your ability to hear and enjoy a wide range of sounds is an important human ability.

CASE: THE HOME FRONT

It was 7:00 p.m. when Matt and Josh finally pulled away from Josh's trailer and into the heavy Friday night traffic. It was 7:18 p.m. when they entered the crowded lecture hall and found two of the few seats left, immediately in back of a panel that had been set up for the high tech, multi-media show displaying Dr. Plack's photography.

As Dean Plack began to speak, it was clear that getting any useful information from the presentation was going to take a lot of effort. It was hot and crowded. Sitting in back of the display panel, neither Josh nor Matt could see all of the speaker at one time. "Give it a chance," Josh said to himself as he took off his coat and tried to get comfortable on the folding chair.

Soon Josh became very conscious of a woman in front of him. She was trying her best to eat a boxed dinner without drawing undue attention to the activity but who was, for all of her efforts, attracting a great deal of attention. Josh noticed, in fact, that most of the people seated near him were also watching her systematically unwrap her sandwich. Ten minutes later all that remained of the dinner was several crumpled wrappers.

It was almost 8:00 p.m. when the audio system failed. Dean Plack's assistant began immediately to adjust the controls. When he looked up at her, she smiled and gave a quick shrug, as if to excuse herself from any responsibility for the added distraction. She quickly finished her job and gracefully made her way back up to the front of the room. Watching her, Josh began to think about his wife, Jill, who was in San Diego. He wondered what it was like out there on the west coast. He imagined himself on the beach, under a clear blue sky, with boats sailing in the harbor and a cold drink in his hand.

It was 8:52 p.m., and Dean Plack was answering the last question from the audience. As they left the auditorium, Josh began to feel guilty for leaving his two young daughters home with a sitter just so that he could get out of the trailer. Later that night, as Josh opened the trailer door, he paused to listen to the nighttime sounds he so seldom appreciated. How could he have known that sitting on his patio with the crickets and windchimes would have been profoundly more enjoyable than attending Dean Plack's lecture?

The next morning Josh tried hard to be patient with his daughters, but it had been a difficult night. Both girls were up for what seemed liked hours; even when he got back in bed Josh had trouble going to sleep. He was sure he heard a soft whimper coming from Jesse's crib, or the creak of the floor as four-year-old Tanya got up to get herself a drink. Every sound in the trailer was exaggerated. He lay on his back, staring into the dark bedroom. Whenever he closed his eyes, the intermittent sounds would take on a life of their own.

Jill had gone back to her job as a sales representative a week after Jesse was born, while he had taken a six-month leave to be home with the two little girls. Jill traveled a lot, and this week she would be in San Diego until Wednesday. Lost in his own thoughts, Josh was stacking the breakfast dishes when a loud crash startled him. The sound seemed to shake the entire trailer with its intensity. Jesse, who was in her seat, immediately began to cry. Jesse's cry was almost a scream; her small body stiffened and her eyes shut tightly.

Josh had noticed how even the ring of their telephone would startle Jesse and set off a crying spell. Tanya came running from the next room and threw her arms around her father's legs. "It's okay," Josh reassured Tanya. He put Jesse's musical bear next to her in the chair. She loved to pat her bear's worn fur, and when it was playing "Rock-a-Bye Baby," her eyes would follow it as Tanya moved it to different positions in her crib. Now the bear seemed to be working its magic once again. Jesse was quieting and Tanya seemed to feel safe just hanging on to her father's leg.

The doorbell rang. It was their neighbor, Rolf, who had just moved with his family from Europe a few months ago. They were nice people, Josh thought, but they had come to depend too heavily on him for support. The family's biggest obstacle was that, although Rolf's company had provided intensive English language courses for them, their grasp of English was still minimal. Josh felt somewhat guilty thinking back on the times he had deliberately avoided running into Rolf because he found their encounters so stressful.

"Hi, Rolf," Josh said enthusiastically as he opened the door. "Come on in."

"Can't stay," Rolf replied in a now-familiar manner. After that abrupt opening, Josh was once again lost. Try as he might, he just couldn't seem to figure out what Rolf was saying. He'd catch a word now and then, but basically he found himself smiling and nodding at whatever he heard. Although Josh responded with enthusiastic head nods and interjected "um; un-huh," he felt completely helpless and anxious whenever Rolf started talking.

As Rolf spoke, the door swung open again and in bounded his five-year-old daughter, Gretchen. After just five months in an American school, Josh found Gretchen easier to understand than her dad. She loved visiting Jesse, and would sing to her in her own language, banging a spoon or stick in time to the music she was creating. The sounds of their language were strange to Josh; he had trouble distinguishing where one word stopped and another began. Gretchen badly wanted to teach him some of the words, but he always laughed and found a reason not to try. Secretly, he was afraid that he wouldn't be able to make the strange sounds. Tanya, on the other hand, was an avid pupil and could now sing right along with Gretchen.

The banging and singing that had begun in the next room made it particularly difficult for Josh to follow Rolf's conversation. His mind would wander as he wondered whether the banging was only on the floor, or whether the girls had begun to find more interesting objects for their band. Although Josh tried hard to maintain eye contact and to continue his encouraging nods, his thoughts were clearly elsewhere.

Fifteen minutes later Rolf had rounded up Gretchen and the two were standing in front of the door, engaged in what had become a prolonged goodbye, when the kitchen phone began ringing. "Oh, now, so long Josh! We go," Rolf said as he motioned Josh to get the phone. "Thanks, Rolf. See you soon," Josh replied, stumbling over the toys Gretchen and Tanya had dragged into the living room as he made his way to catch the phone.

"Hello," Josh began, then immediately shouted to Tanya, "it's mommy!"

"Mommy!" Tanya repeated and rushed to stand next to Josh, grabbing at the receiver and chanting "mommy, mommy, mommy."

"Please, Tanya, just a minute," Josh said more firmly as he turned his back to Tanya and held the receiver close to his ear. The phone had awakened Jesse, who was now crying loudly from the nursery.

"Mommy, mommy, mommy," Tanya continued.

"Tanya, I can't hear," Josh said impatiently. "Just stop please. You can talk to her in a minute. If you're quiet, I'll tell you what she says."

Tanya became quiet and intent as Josh repeated Jill's words: "It's been very warm and sunny . . . and I've been working hard but I think I've made a lot of progress on the Peters' project . . ."

"Well, honey, it sounds wonderful. We'll talk some more in a minute, but I have this cute blonde standing next to me who is anxious to say hi to her mom. What do you think, should you talk to her?"

"There," Josh handed Tanya the phone. "Now it's your turn." He untwisted the cord and headed to the next room to see if he could quiet Jesse.

THE PROCESS OF HEARING: PRINCIPLES

Deaf children find it difficult to master oral language because they have no model of correct speech. Often, those who hear well take this critical process for granted. Yet, hearing is a necessary—although insufficient—condition for effective listening. Look back at the definitions of listening that were presented in Chapter 2. You will find phrases like, "a process that includes hearing . . . ," "a process of taking what you hear. . . ." If you reexamine the listening definitions, you'll find that hearing recurs as a fundamental component.

> What are the consequences of not controlling your attention?

This emphasis on hearing should come as no surprise. We live in a rich auditory world—just review "The Home Front" and notice the number of times Josh was aware of and influenced by sounds in his environment. Of all the dimensions of the listening process, hearing is the most fundamental.

This chapter introduces principles that you will find helpful as you work to improve this component of the HURIER model. Since hearing involves the reception and processing of sound, it often requires the ability to attend and to concentrate. As a listener, your goal is to exercise as much control as possible over what you hear. It would be encouraging to think that you could decide to focus your attention on key aspects of a situation and fully concentrate on whatever stimuli you chose, ignoring distractions and irrelevant messages. Obviously, controlling your attention and concentration is not that easy.

Topics related to attention and concentration, therefore, are part of this component because they affect your ability to control and therefore to improve your hearing. You will learn about auditory selectivity and discrimination as well as the factors involved in attending to aural messages. Appreciative listening is discussed as it depends upon your ability to focus on and derive personal satisfaction from what you hear. To begin, essential background information on the mechanics and levels of hearing is presented so that you will have a general understanding of the physiological principles that may affect your listening behavior.

The Mechanics of Hearing

Hearing involves three interrelated stages: reception of sound waves, perception of sound in the brain, and auditory association. The importance of this process is clear; only when you accurately perceive what is said can you focus on the critical matter of assigning meaning to the speaker's words. Although your goal isn't to become an expert on the principles of hearing or on the physics of sound, a basic knowledge of these processes is essential.

First, recall that sound travels in waves as it moves through the air. These waves bump into air molecules and create either positive or negative pressure. When air molecules are pushed together, positive pressure is created; sound waves may then pass through the air at up to 760 miles per hour. It is actually the sound waves that you "hear."

> How often is your listening affected by difficulties in hearing?

How useful is your outer ear—that piece of cartilage and skin sticking out from the side of your head? Although it serves an important function, there's much more to your hearing apparatus than the portion you can see (Figure 3.1). Your outer ear catches the sound

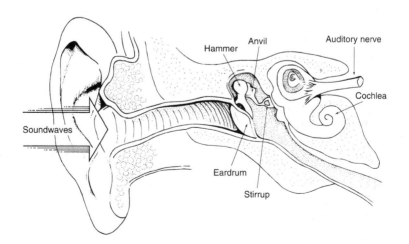

FIGURE 3.1   Parts of the Ear

From *Building Active Listening* Skills, by Brownell, Judi, © 1986. Reprinted by permission of Prentice Hall, Inc., Upper Saddle River, NJ.

waves and channels them through the auditory canal to the eardrum. The sound waves then cause the drum membrane to vibrate. Three small bones on the other side of the drum—the hammer, stirrup, and anvil—amplify these vibrations.

Next, sound waves reach your inner ear. Here the cochlea, a snail-shaped structure filled with liquid, takes over. Inside the cochlea are hairlike nerve cells that change pressure vibrations to nerve impulses. These, in turn, are transmitted to the auditory nerve and then to the brain. Finally, you perceive sound.

Understanding the mechanics is only the first step. As Josh discovered in "The Home Front," there are times when you want to hear something and can't, and other times when you would like to ignore a sound that seems to attract all of your attention instead. Although several factors influence your hearing, the characteristics of the sound itself can make focusing your attention either automatic or almost impossible.

Levels of Hearing

Establishing control over the listening situation is an important goal for anyone interested in improving his or her hearing. There are times, however, when characteristics of the sound override your voluntary selection and cause what we call switching—a change of focus from one sound to another.

Switching often occurs because there are three different "levels" or types of hearing. At the *primary* level, hearing is voluntary. You select the information you want to concentrate on, deliberately tuning in to certain sounds while ignoring others. In a crowded cafeteria you are able to hear what your friend is saying in spite of the background noise going on around you because you are devoting concentrated effort to that task. You know, for instance, that if you sit at the back of a large class you will have to work harder to hear the lecture. When you concentrate on the primary message, all other sounds usually fade into the background.

Recall Josh's experience when he tried to listen to Dean Plack, however. Why do you suppose he was so distracted by the woman who was eating and by adjustments that were being made to the control panel? Did he choose to listen to these sounds?

At the *secondary* level, your involuntary or autonomic nervous system is also at work. You may be focusing on one task, such as talking on the telephone, and still be conscious of a housemate coming into the dining room and opening a box of cereal. Likewise, you can be absorbed in a discussion yet still be somewhat distracted by an infant crying or a child playing nearby. You may notice individual differences in the degree to which your friends attend to secondary sounds. While you would want a preschool teacher to be aware of the activity going on around him, this may not be the case when a pilot is depending on the person in the control tower to guide her to a safe landing.

What were some of the instances from "The Home Front" that illustrated listening at the secondary level? When Josh and Rolf were talking, Josh was very much aware of the banging going on in Tanya's room. What other situations illustrate this level of hearing?

Finally, on the *tertiary* level, you have little or no control over what you hear; the central nervous system is not involved in processing the stimuli. Rather, the autonomic system responds to a sound simply because of its intensity. A fire alarm ringing in the middle of a conversation, a lamp that crashes to the floor as you tip back your chair—such sudden sounds are loud enough to startle you so that it is impossible to avoid hearing and responding to them.

Again, illustrations from "The Home Front" should help you distinguish this level. The loud bangs that were so upsetting to Jesse disrupted Josh and Tanya as well. Both Rolf and Josh were distracted by the telephone ringing; the sound was loud enough that they had no choice but to pay attention to it.

Characteristics of Sound

We have seen that an intense stimulus, one at the tertiary level, demands greater attention than one that is softer, dimmer, or smaller. Other dimensions of sound that affect your ability to concentrate include: repetition, change, novelty, and intensity. Each of these aspects is described briefly below. These characteristics should become easy to identify in a wide range of listening situations. Often, they are presented as speaking strategies, techniques designed to keep listeners focused when delivering formal presentations or conducting meetings and seminars.

1. *Repetition:* Listeners attend more readily to a sound that is repeated than to one that occurs only once. Often, after hearing a sound once, you consciously wait for it to be repeated in order to confirm your impression. Prolonged repetition, however, may cause you to become indifferent and tune out the stimulus. If telephones are always ringing or buzzers are sounding all day long, you learn to ignore those particular stimuli.

To illustrate, an example is given of the lighthouse keeper who lived for twenty years hearing his warning cannon fire automatically on the hour every hour all night long, steering ships away from the dangerous rocks. One night the cannon failed to fire. The keeper awoke with a start and shouted, "What was that?"

You may recall from "The Home Front" that Tanya repeated "mommy" over and over. Although the word itself became meaningless, Josh responded with annoyance to the distraction Tanya was creating. Since oral communication, unlike the printed word, is fleeting, speakers often use redundancy or repetition to reinforce their point. The Martin Luther King (1960) speech "I Have a Dream" remains one of the most outstanding examples of the impact of this technique as King repeats, "I have a dream . . . ," each time building the emotional pitch of his message still further. You can probably think of songs, commercials, and other media that provide examples of the effectiveness of repetition as an attention-getting device.

2. *Change:* A significant element in securing attention is change. Speakers use vocal variety—particularly variation in pitch, volume, and rate—to command attention and provide emphasis. When speeches are long, presenters may use a number of instructional methods, from videotapes to group discussion, simply for variety. Unfortunately, from what we know of Dean Plack's presentation, he failed to take advantage of this technique for gaining and maintaining attention. Josh describes the talk as "boring" on the basis of delivery as well as content.

3. *Novelty:* Although most adults attend to messages in 8- to 15-second intervals, novelty may extend this focus of attention. If a communicator does the unexpected, he or she is likely to hold attention better than if a listener correctly anticipates the speaker's behavior. When speakers raise our interest and curiosity, they also increase our attention.

Generally, you concentrate most when circumstances are unfamiliar and established patterns of interaction do not work. As Weick comments, "Words may count most when it is impossible to be mindless" (1983, p. 25); that is, when you are consciously thinking about what you're hearing, your attention improves. When you already know what someone is going to say—or when you assume you know—your full attention may not be devoted to the speaker, and you consequently become less attentive. Consider a typical situation where an individual's expectations are so firmly planted that listening no longer occurs.

One student routinely asks, "How are you?" to which the second student responds, "My best friend died last night." The first student then smiles and replies, "That's good. Have a nice day."

4. *Intensity:* The intensity of sound is yet another dimension that influences the likelihood that you will hear a particular stimulus. As you already know, an intense sound commands attention because it is perceived at the tertiary level; you respond automatically. Recall that you have no choice when the intensity is high—your reaction is as much physical as mental. If you've enjoyed a fireworks display or responded to the ring of a bedside telephone in the middle of the night, you likely have a clear understanding of how intensity affects your listening.

Auditory Discrimination

Beyond the reception of sound, your job also involves distinguishing different sounds and then identifying *what* you have heard. Otherwise, sounds would have no meaning for you. When you perceive sound accurately, you know more than just the fact that you heard something—you know *what* sound it was. Perhaps you have a friend who can identify bird calls, or know of parents who can pick out their child's laughter from among all of the voices on the playground. This process is called *auditory discrimination*.

In what situation(s) do you have a particularly high level of auditory discrimination?

Much of your ability to discriminate—to isolate and identify sounds—is based upon your past experiences and familiarity with the specific sounds you hear. This part of the process is largely developmental and experiential. Auditory discrimination improves naturally with age, but you can also deliberately work to cultivate discriminatory skills that will improve your listening effectiveness. In addition, your ability to localize a sound source is a critical aspect of this process since it permits certain sounds to be attended to in the presence of other competing sounds.

Some of the most useful research on auditory discrimination has been conducted by Weaver and Rutherford (1974), who developed a hierarchy of the auditory skills that are developed during early childhood. Selected items from their framework are presented (Box 3.1) so that you can see in greater detail how this process unfolds.

Sophisticated discriminatory skills involve such activities as recognizing the sound structure of a language. Your success in identifying words within a foreign language, for instance, is dependent upon your knowledge of the vocabulary of that language. If you're unfamiliar with French, an audiotape of a conversation won't make any sense; you won't know where one word stops and another begins. That's because incoming nerve impulses are compared to a memory file of whatever you have heard in the past. During information processing, the new stimulus is matched to previously learned sounds. This process is called *auditory association*. There are several theories of auditory association. One common explanation is that the mind sorts data into categories. Auditory association, then, is a matter of finding the specific category into which the incoming information fits so that it "makes sense." This sense-making is taking on new meaning as computers translate almost any kind of information into patterns of pitch, rhythm, and volume. Called *sonification,* this

■ ■ ■ ■ ■ ▬▬▬▬▬▬▬▬▬▬▬▬▬▬▬▬▬▬▬▬▬▬▬▬▬▬▬▬▬▬▬

BOX 3.1

DISCRIMINATION SKILLS

Prenatal
Fetus moves in response to sound

Infancy
Responds differently to each unique sound
Imitates speech sounds
Is quieted by sounds
Searches for sounds
Responds to sudden loud noises

Preschool
Focuses on distinct sounds and screens out background sounds
Matches identical sounds

Repeats a sequence of sounds
Names sounds
Associates sounds with people or objects
Can match same sound

Kindergarten to Grade 3
Recognizes that sounds differ in intensity, pitch, pattern, and duration
Recognizes differences in initial, medial, and final sounds in words
Recognizes distinct words within a sentence
Recognizes rhyming words
Identifies accented syllable with a word

Adapted from the National Council of Teachers of English (1974).

method can flag suspicious travel activity or assist doctors in identifying cancerous cells (Roush, 2003).

Why do you suppose Josh had so much trouble understanding Rolf? Had he known more about Rolf's language, he might have been able to isolate specific sounds that he could then identify. Children seem much better able to adjust to new languages and to reproduce unfamiliar sounds than do adults. Recall that Tanya readily learned to sing along with her new friend by imitating the sounds she heard.

Another key discriminatory skill involves detecting the vocal or paralinguistic cues that are essential for the accurate interpretation of messages. These cues are generally communicated through various aspects of your voice, including pitch, volume, and rate. You will learn more about the activities involved in interpreting vocal cues in a later chapter. For now, we examine the process of attention as it influences what you hear.

HEARING AND ATTENTION

To hear a message, you need to pay attention to it. Attention is a selective process that controls our awareness of events in the environment. Every day there are literally hundreds of sounds all around you that you never notice because you aren't paying attention to them. Although theories of attention remain incomplete, what is known about attention with regard to listening behavior can be useful as you work to improve your personal effectiveness.

Attention determines which auditory or visual stimuli are processed. If you don't pay attention to something, it's as if it never existed. Attending to a stimulus, whether auditory or visual, involves following its pattern over time against a background of on-going activity in the same medium. Hearing the trumpets in a particular symphony, for instance, requires that you learn what sounds to listen for and discriminate among a variety of sound patterns.

Visual and auditory processing use different nerve pathways and therefore interference from one mode is not as distracting as if the two messages were present in the same medium. In other words, Josh's focus on the speaker would have been more affected by the sound of the woman eating than by watching Dean Plank's assistant make her way back to the front of the room. In humans, a visual stimulus is often dominant over an auditory one (Witkin, 1993), although other factors, such as intensity, play a key role in determining which sounds ultimately capture your attention.

Several additional concepts will help you realize the complexity of this process. As you read about subjects like perceptual readiness and selective attention, try to relate the ideas presented both to your own listening experiences and to situations from "The Home Front."

Perceptual Readiness

The term *set* refers to those specific factors that influence which stimuli you select. As you might imagine, our set prepares us to perceive stimuli of a particular class or to perceive events in a particular manner. When listening for a child's voice or the sound of your mother's footsteps, your perpetual set, or readiness, increases the likelihood that you will hear what you are prepared to hear and decreases the chances of noticing other sounds. Josh kept thinking that he heard Jesse and Tanya throughout the night because he was, in a sense, "set" to hear their voices. The way your expectations structure your perceptions can be illustrated by a simple exercise.

> In what situations do you have a *readiness* to hear a specific sound?

Pronounce each of the following words in sequence: Mactavish, Macdonald, Macbeth, machinery. What happened? If you pronounced *machinery as mac-hinery* before realizing that it didn't fit the pattern established by the first three words, then your mental set got the best of you!

This preattentive process can work to your advantage or it can interfere with effective listening by predisposing you to perceive in a particular manner. This predisposition, as we noted in our discussion of communication frameworks in Chapter 2, also constrains your choices. Langer (1989) has written eloquently about the harmful effects of what she calls chronic mindlessness, a state in which individuals rely so heavily on preconceived notions that they fail to be mindful or to hear what is really going on.

Selective Attention

You can only focus on a few stimuli at any given time. When you attend to an auditory or visual cue, it is drawn out from the background and becomes vivid. Other sounds and objects are then perceived more dimly and remain in what listening researchers call the margin. There is always a tradeoff between depth and breadth of information processing. Clearly, no one can attend to even a fraction of the stimuli available to the senses at any one time. As you climb up on some rocks overlooking the ocean, you may be exposed to the sound of the waves, the sea gulls, the wind, the ship's whistles, the beachcombers below. What do you hear? It depends. Recall that attention is partly a developmental process; you discipline yourself to focus and then shift your focus as the situation demands. You learn what's important in different contexts and then you hear what you've learned to hear.

Interest is a key factor in focusing attention. A stimulus is selected on the basis of such things as its immediate importance, your related past experiences, and your present motivations. Once you become interested in something, your attention is almost automatic. If you don't develop an interest, however, you will always have to work hard at attending to that particular stimulus. Focusing on some topics or speakers may always require intensive effort; that is, extra energy will always be required to sustain attention. A good example is Josh's struggle to focus on Dean Plack's presentation. Periodically, other sounds replaced the speaker's voice as the primary stimulus. Had Josh been more interested in the speech, he would not have had to work so hard at focusing his attention.

Recall that, in our discussion of communication framework, effective listening also requires attending to the "right" things in order to better understand what's

▬ ▬ ▬ ▬ ▬▬▬▬▬▬

In any given situation, how do you determine the *right things* to listen to?

▬▬▬▬▬▬▬▬▬▬

going on. The significance of selective attention, what you choose to hear from a wide range of possibilities, is a recurring theme throughout this text.

Imagine, for instance, that you are at a meeting that is running late and a friend is waiting for you out in the car. In such a situation, you will be highly interested in and sensitive to any "closing" cues sent by other members of the group. You will hear the scraping of chairs being pushed back from the table, the deep sighs as participants close their notebooks, and the sounds of briefcases popping shut.

Selective listening, as you can imagine, has posed a variety of challenges as researchers attempt to study the process. Two paths that have been particularly productive are studies in dichotic listening and speech shadowing.

Dichotic Listening.   Dichotic listening occurs when you receive two messages simultaneously—one in one ear and one in the other. Whenever there is noise around you, it is almost inevitable that you will be distracted—that you will hear at least part of a second message. Familiar voices and emotionally-laden words are especially powerful in drawing our attention away from the primary message. As Ann Landers notes in a recent column, nothing improves your listening faster than when someone mentions your name. Dichotic listening, however, requires attention to a complete message rather than isolated words.

Although you may have been told repeatedly to concentrate on the message at hand, in some situations you may choose to listen dichotically. A skilled dichotic listener is aware of what is going on around her and is therefore less likely to miss an important secondary stimulus. Dichotic listeners have a sense of the entire situation and are particularly effective as child care providers, service employees, or in performing other jobs where they can't afford to turn off stimuli created by the multiple activities going on around them.

Shadowing.   Shadowing occurs when you repeat a continuous verbal message as you hear it (Moray, 1969). Most people can learn to accurately track a verbal message at rates up to 150 words per minute. While you may not see much point in verbal tracking, researchers have found it an important tool in their investigations of hearing and attention. Clearly, when you are successfully shadowing a message, it's guaranteed that you're paying attention to it. When Josh repeated Jill's words to Tanya during his telephone conversation, he was shadowing what his wife was saying.

Through studies in dichotic listening and shadowing, researchers have explored aspects of selective attention that affect listening ability. Although hearing is easy to take for granted, a great many misunderstandings occur just because someone didn't hear accurately, heard only part of the information, or didn't attend to the most essential aspects of the message.

LEARN TO FOCUS YOUR ATTENTION

You've likely heard friends complain, "I wanted to listen to what she was saying, but I just couldn't concentrate!" Repeatedly, you have been asked to think of yourself as having control over your environment and the ability to direct your attention to the messages that are important to you (Box 3.2). In fact, several studies suggest that people aren't very good at determining when they are being distracted or what is distracting them!

Many jobs require an intense and often sustained focus of attention. Recent research has confirmed that service employees' degree of attention drives guest satisfaction (Ruyter & Wetzels, 2000). Those who work crisis hot lines in airport control towers or in emergency rooms provide just a few examples. In these and other situations, one of your many listening challenges is to control your focus of attention—to concentrate on the things that you determine are most important.

Some troublesome distractions, however, result not from external noise, but from *internal stimuli* which compete with the verbal message. As you well know, important appointments, an upcoming exam, or a recent conflict with a friend may prevent you from focusing your full attention on the message at hand.

Imagine, for instance, that you're sitting in a political science class. Next period you have an exam in British literature. Your instructor indicated that she was interested in your application of the material and wanted you to cite direct quotations to support your conclusions. She suggested that you have your textbook readily available. You have just realized that you left your book in your apartment, and there is no way you have time before the exam to go back and get it. How can you possibly concentrate on political science under these circumstances?

There are several things you can do to improve your concentration. Four strategies that will help you better manage this process are: capitalizing on the thought–speech differential, reducing your anxiety, developing a positive attitude, and preparing to listen.

BOX 3.2

REDUCE DISTRACTIONS

- Eliminate external distractions by shutting off a radio, moving to a quiet area, or taking some other appropriate action.
- Sit toward the front of the room where it is easier to hear.
- Pay attention to your physical environment; don't let the room get too cold or too hot. Make sure you are comfortable and that there is enough light.
- Have a paper and pencil handy so that as you think of things you need to do you can write them down and get them off of your mind.

The Thought–Speech Differential

First, notice how fast people speak. It's probably somewhere between 120 and 180 words a minute. Now, how fast can you mentally process incoming information? The average person can understand up to 400 to 500 words a minute—almost three times more than what is required by the rate at which most people speak. This difference is referred to as the thought–speech differential, and it lends insight into why you might have difficulty concentrating.

Since a speaker's words occupy only a small portion of your mental capacity, you are tempted to entertain thoughts unrelated to the oral message. When you use this "bonus" time to daydream, to worry, or to reflect on unrelated items of business, listening problems result (Box 3.3). Half of your attention may be on the speaker's message, but half is on your personal concerns. Recall that Josh immediately began thinking of his wife when he became bored at the lecture.

> How is the concept of *bonus time* helpful to you?

The vocalized listening technique, a method recommended to overcome distractions resulting from the thought-speech differential, suggests that you use this bonus time to mentally restate, review, and process the oral message. Think of vocalized listening as a form of self-talk. You keep your attention on the communication at hand by creating a specific mental task that takes up the lag time and prevents your mind from wandering to other topics (Box 3.4).

Studies related to the thought–speech differential have relied on speech compressors (Witkin, 1993; Beatty & Payne, 1984), tape recorderlike machines that increase the rate of speech without changing the pitch. Speech compressors enable researchers to determine the effect of increased rate on various aspects of listening. Although practice enables most individuals to improve their comprehension at significantly higher than normal rates of presentation, there is a threshold in rate beyond which comprehension drops rapidly. Research suggests that after listening regularly to faster paced speech it is difficult to sustain attention at normal speaking rates.

BOX 3.3

THE WOLFF AND MARSNICK ONE PROCESS BRAIN CONCEPT

The one process brain concept is simple. If you are listening well, you can't be doing anything else. Not anything. The D Formula is easy to remember. When you're listening:

DDOT	Don't do other tasks
DMP	Don't make plans
DD	Don't daydream

(Wolff & Marsnick, 1992, p. 78)

■ ■ ■ ■ ■

BOX 3.4

VOCALIZED LISTENING

Apply the following principles:

1. Repeat portions of the speaker's message to yourself silently. This will help you reinforce ideas and store them in your memory. It forces you to think about what the speaker is saying rather than your own agenda.
2. Ask yourself questions concerning the ideas presented. Try to "make sense" of what it said.
3. Relate the information to your personal needs.
4. Repeat key ideas. Make mental summaries so that you are sure you follow the speaker's purpose and main points. With practice, you will be able to use the speaker's natural pauses to mentally highlight what was said.
5. Stay mentally involved and physically alert.

In addition to rate of presentation, your ability to concentrate is affected by your age, intelligence, health, and other variables. As you know, listening is also influenced by characteristics of the source, channel, message content, and speaker. Personal style, too, affects your concentration. Research into learner styles suggests that different message channels (visual, print, oral, electronic) are appropriate for different individual needs (Emmert, Emmert, & Brandt, 1993).

Listener Apprehension

Listener anxiety has a significant impact on your concentration. This anxiety can be caused in a variety of ways. You may be responding to events outside of the immediate situation, or to factors of the listening experience itself. Apprehension is frequently created by the fear of misinterpreting, inadequately processing, or not being able to adjust psychologically to what you hear. The increased anxiety this fear of poor listening causes often results in further reduction of your listening ability (Wheeless, 1975; Clark, 1989).

Listening may deteriorate during the communication event as you realize that the material is difficult or confusing. Information that is difficult to process tends to accumulate as "cognitive backlog" and subsequently creates additional anxiety and mental blocking. This can happen in combination with ineffective use of the thought-speech differential; you daydream, and when you try to refocus your attention on the immediate event, you realize that you have lost the speaker's point. The anxiety created by the awareness that you are "behind" causes further stress and results in greatly reduced ability to process

■ ■ ■ ■

What are your major physical and psychological reactions when you experience high anxiety?

information. Learning to relax and stay focused are among the best ways to improve your concentration. A variety of physical and mental exercises will help you to sustain attention.

1. *Muscle relaxation:* Relax your muscles, one group at a time. Tighten a single muscle group—your neck, your lower arm, your foot—for 5 or 6 seconds, and then completely relax it. Begin at the extremities of your body and work inward. Don't forget the muscles of your face, particularly your tongue. As your muscles relax, you'll realize that you were experiencing significant muscle stress as normal.

2. *Imagery and fantasy:* Vividly recall a positive experience; relive all of the associated sensations—sights, smells, and sounds. Your mind will relax as it focuses on these memories. A similar effect can be obtained through fantasy as you call up imaginary events or images. In both instances, stress is temporarily reduced as your mind focuses on more pleasant experiences.

3. *Mental rehearsal:* Try out various alternatives to a stressful situation in a safe environment—your mind. When athletes have rehearsed mentally and seen themselves breaking a record or winning a race, they have gone on to be highly successful. Job applicants have found that mental rehearsal in preparation for interviews is a valuable technique. See yourself impressing that interviewer or socializing with that difficult relative. Then do it.

4. *Deep breathing:* Focusing on your breathing clears your mind and enables you to relax. Try this technique before any stressful listening event.

For better or for worse, stress is largely a mental construct (Box 3.5). You interpret a given situation as either threatening and difficult, or manageable. When you imagine a stressful situation, your body behaves as if the event is really stressful regardless of how it might be objectively perceived. Stress, then, is increased by worrying and negative thinking and reduced by a positive attitude.

■ ■ ■ ■ ■

BOX 3.5

RECOGNIZE SIGNS OF LISTENING APPREHENSION

Physical Signs	*Emotional Signs*
Elevated blood pressure	Anxiety
Elevated heart rate	Depression
Difficult breathing	Fatigue
Tight muscles	Frustration
Back and head pain	Irritability
Sweating	Tension
	Worry

Maintain an Appropriate Mental Attitude

Reducing listening apprehension requires an appropriate mental attitude as well as specific skills. The following suggestions will help you to identify attitudes that may be blocking your ability to concentrate.

1. *Take a sincere interest in people and ideas:* In our increasingly global society, it becomes important for each person to make an effort to understand and appreciate the ideas and values of others. Individuals differ in their natural interest in other people. If you have a lot of patience and enjoy interaction, you'll cultivate your interest in others with little difficulty. If, however, your ideal day would be to spend hours in front of a keyboard or in a laboratory, then you know you'll have to devote additional effort to concentrate when people talk with you.

On what topics would cultural differences likely affect listening attitudes?

The inquisitive, curious person who asks a lot of questions is called a *scopic listener*. Scopic listeners have developed an interest in many topics and have not limited their exposure to preconceived notions about what is "useful" or "important." They do not let a predetermined listening set prevent them from accurately hearing what their friends or classmates have to say.

In fact, topics that at first may seem irrelevant take on greater meaning as you consider their usefulness. Although you've probably been told that the burden for creating and maintaining interest rests with the speaker, you can take the initiative yourself by finding good reasons to listen.

2. *Listen to difficult material:* What topics do you find difficult? A particular science class? Your brother's new software package (the one he talks about endlessly)? Dull is often associated with difficult. You may not like to hear about a subject because you don't understand it and therefore it has no real meaning for you. If you avoid difficult or "dull" listening situations, you're not alone. Far too many people listen only to what they find easy to understand. Think about the long-term implications if young people only listen to things that are easy.

Seek opportunities to expose yourself to more difficult material so that you can practice your listening skills. Just because a subject is in your "dull and difficult" category doesn't mean it has to stay there. We tell children to try foods they have previously disliked—we know that tastes change. So, too, can your interests. The knowledge you gain is well worth the effort.

Be Physically Prepared to Concentrate

Focused concentration requires a certain physical as well as mental readiness. Researchers have discovered that attentive nonverbal behaviors are associated with listener involvement, a dimension directly related to concentration (Cegala, 1984). In other words, if you behave like an attentive listener, your concentration will almost automatically improve.

The attentive behaviors that have been identified include eye contact, forward trunk lean, physical proximity, and verbal following (O'Heren & Arnold, 1991). When your partner perceives that you're listening, there is often a corresponding improvement in his or her delivery factors as well. This makes it even easier for you to concentrate and begins a positive communication cycle. You will learn more about the importance of nonverbal communication in other chapters. For now, keep in mind that physical alertness and readiness to listen help you stay focused in difficult listening situations.

Develop Your Appreciative Listening

Given the stress of college life, you may be tempted to suppress your initial curiosity in favor of more "efficient" time management practices. Someone is playing your favorite music on a street corner, but you have groceries to pick up. You can hear the faint sounds of seagulls as you walk back to your apartment, but your focus is on making a decision about when to schedule your doctor's appointment. You have a lot to do—it's easy to become impatient and preoccupied. Hearing often necessitates slowing down and refocusing your priorities. Although it is important to get things done, it is equally important to maintain a well-balanced interest in the world of sound that is going on all around you.

> Since appreciative listening is a personal experience, would you define it as a type of communication? Explain.

Wolvin and Coakley (1996) define appreciative listening as a "process of listening in order to obtain sensory stimulation or enjoyment through the works and experiences of others" (p. 321). In some cases you come upon appreciative listening opportunities by accident; in other cases, you may seek them out. The point is that by paying attention to music, to the sounds of nature, and to other relaxing and enjoyable aural stimuli, you are likely to derive more pleasure from your day-to-day activities. This type of mental stimulation, and the subsequent emotional satisfaction you are likely to derive, increases your creativity and potential to make meaningful contributions in your various activities.

Keep in mind that appreciative listening is an individualized, largely emotional response to what you hear. The personal listening filters identified in the HURIER model, such as your background, expectations, and attitudes, suggest that these dimensions combine with the quality of the stimuli itself to determine your appreciative level. While you might think that better understanding the components or context of the event would increase appreciation, such knowledge is just as likely to diminish the pure enjoyment that comes from abandoning yourself to the total listening experience. As soon as you begin to analyze what you hear, appreciative listening stops and you become a critical listener (see Chapter 7). There are other cases, however, where your enjoyment is enhanced by having a "trained ear."

Taking time to enjoy the sounds around you may require some initial refocusing. Remember that appreciative listening is not defined by the source of your listening but by your listening "frame of mind" and the nature of your response. The source may be an individual sitting next to you, a film or television show, a tape, or sounds from your environment.

In an age of sound bites and satellites, it may be worthwhile to enhance your ability to listen appreciatively. You can begin to do this by:

> What messages does your culture send regarding the value of appreciative listening?

1. **Identifying the specific things that give you listening pleasure.** While you could stumble randomly into appreciative listening opportunities, your experiences would be enhanced—and more frequent—if you give thought to the sounds and situations that bring you pleasure. Once identified, you can then create opportunities to hear the sounds you enjoy, whether country western music or a waterfall.
2. **Deliberately searching for ways to expand the focus of your appreciative listening.** Many listening experiences are pleasurable because of the associations we have with past events. A song may remind you of a first trip to Europe, or the call of loons may elicit memories of your family cottage on the lake. While each of us may draw on past listening experiences to make choices about future appreciative listening opportunities, there is also a good rationale for exploring new appreciative listening situations and expanding the scope of our listening experiences. Try listening to books on tape, go to a Celtic concert, or attend with greater appreciation to the sounds that surround your daily activities. Curiosity is a healthy thing, especially for the appreciative listener.
3. **Developing a positive attitude and willingness to spend time listening appreciatively.** Increasing your appreciative listening is not only likely to require trade offs in your time, it also takes additional energy. Sounds that have been perceived as part of the background need to be brought into focus with greater clarity. Rather than passively letting sounds "happen" around you, the appreciative listener expends energy and concentrates fully on the listening experience.

You can increase your listening enjoyment, reduce stress, and enrich the quality of your life simply by recognizing appreciative listening opportunities and reflecting on the types of experiences that are most meaningful.

SUMMARY

Hearing is the first stage in effective listening. In order to hear accurately, listeners must attend to aural stimuli and concentrate on a particular message. The first step to improving your hearing is to know something about how your ears work, and to learn basic principles regarding the mechanics of hearing. A number of variables affect the hearing process, such as the level of the sound and characteristics of the sound itself.

More complex cognitive processes, such as auditory discrimination and selective attention, also influence what we hear. Studies conducted on dichotic listening and shadowing reveal useful information that can be applied to improve your hearing process.

As you work to improve your concentration, keep in mind the thought-speech differential—the difference between average speaking rate and the time it takes to process incoming information. Discovering ways to effectively use this bonus time is likely to improve concentration dramatically. In addition, reducing your anxiety, maintaining a positive attitude, and remaining physically alert also increase the likelihood that you can sustain your attention, thereby hearing more of the message. Finally, those who take time for appreciative listening will increase their enjoyment of what they hear.

APPLICATIONS

Application 1: Focus on Your Hearing
Application 2: Identify and Reduce Distractions
Application 3: Adopt an Appropriate Listening Attitude
Application 4: Apply The Vocalized Listening Technique
Application 5: Overcome Listener Apprehension
Application 6: Behave Like a Good Listener
Application 7: Become an Appreciative Listener

_____I accurately hear what is said when someone speaks to me.
Application 1: Focus on Your Hearing

_____I overcome distractions such as the conversation of others, background noises, and telephones when someone is speaking to me.
Application 2: Identify and Reduce Distractions

_____I enter a situation with a positive listening attitude.
Application 3: Adopt an Appropriate Listening Attitude

_____I concentrate on what the speaker is saying.
Application 4: Apply The Vocalized Listening Technique

_____I am relaxed and focused in important listening situations.
Application 5: Overcome Listener Apprehension

_____I am ready to focus my attention when a speaker begins to talk.
Application 6: Behave Like a Good Listener

Application 1: Focus on Your Hearing

Your first step in becoming a better listener is to make sure that you hear what is said. Becoming more aware of your discriminative listening skills can sensitize you to the hearing process. Remember that listening takes energy. The saying "perk up your ears" is almost literal—your entire body responds when you are listening actively.

Activities

1. Wear a pair of ear plugs for three or four hours during the day. How is life different for the deaf or hearing impaired? What difficulties did you have? What aspects of communication did you miss the most?

2. Listen to a tape of a foreign language with which you are unfamiliar. Take a sentence or reasonable unit of speech, and try to repeat it. Were you successful? What problems did you encounter? Were some of the sounds difficult for you to make?

3. Notice what sounds and words attract your attention. Identify examples of sounds at the tertiary level.

Group Activities

Form a small group of four to six people. You may want to keep the same group for all activities, or you may find it more interesting to change groups so that you get to hear the opinions and ideas of a greater number of your classmates.

1. In small groups, select one of the following tongue twisters. Take several minutes and practice repeating it as a group. Then, say the tongue twister together, four times fast. Were you successful? What sounds were particularly difficult to articulate? How does articulation affect hearing?

    1. Sweet silly Sally sells silly sea shells.
    2. Carrol's colossal collection of classic comics for Christmas.
    3. Peter Piper picked a peck of pickled peppers peppering pieces as he progressed.
    4. Rubber baby buggy bumpers.
    5. The big black bug bit the big black bear.
    6. Fanny Finch fried five floundering fish for Francis' father.
    7. The sixth sheik's sixth sheep's sick.
    8. She stood at the door of Burgess's fish sauce shop welcoming him in.
    9. The seething seas ceaseth and thus sufficeth us.
    10. The Chinese chieftain chastised Ching for leaving chopsticks in Chang's chop suey.

2. Select one of the following topics. Choose a member of your group to begin talking about the topic. After two or three minutes, the person to his or her left takes over and continues speaking. Repeat this process until everyone has had a turn.

    Who was easiest to hear and understand? Why?

    Americans are known for their poor articulation. What words tend to be mispronounced?

    What final consonant sounds are often dropped? Did anyone have an accent or regionalism? What was it?

Suggested Topics

   a. Things that distract my attention
   b. Sounds I love to hear
   c. People who drive me crazy
   d. Listening to members of my family
   e. Listening to the television

3. Talk with a classmate from another country, or invite a foreign student to your class. Ask him or her to share personal experiences related to hearing. What sounds in the English language does this person find difficult to distinguish or reproduce?

   Identify classmates who have traveled recently to a foreign country. What language problems did they experience?

4. Meet with members of your group outside of class, and make a tape of common sounds—a vacuum cleaner, a garbage truck, a computer, and so on. Play the tape for the rest of the class and ask members to identify the various sounds. How accurate were the identifications? What might account for differences in perception?

5. Choose a member of your group to be the speaker. The speaker opens to any page in the text and begins to read. Other members of the group, one at a time, practice vocal tracking. As soon as the tracker loses his or her place three times, move on to another person.

   a. Were there significant differences in tracking ability from one person to the next?
   b. What made it difficult to track?
   c. What speaker characteristics helped or hindered the tracking process?

6. Participate in the "Just a Minute" listening exercise. Its purpose is to practice skills of hearing and concentration. Begin by identifying six participants who each try to speak for one minute without breaking a rule, and a judge who determines when rules have been broken. As soon as one of the participants hears a rule being broken, he or she hits the table and calls out the rule that was broken. If the judge agrees, the person who hit the table takes over where the speaker left off and tries to finish out his/her minute on the *same topic*. The new speaker is again subject to the same rules, and may be stopped by another participant who hears a rule broken. As soon as 1 minute is up, the next participant begins again with his or her topic. The winner is the participant with the most points after all six topics have been presented.

Rules

   a. Speak on the assigned subject
   b. Do not repeat any nouns (objects, people, etc.) or verbs except the verb to be (am, is, are, etc.) and words written on your topic card
   c. Do not pause for more than *two seconds*
   d. Do not use any "nonfluencies" such as "um," "er," "like," "ah," etc.
   e. Use correct English grammar and sentence structure at all times

Points

   +2   Speaking at the end of the minute
   +1   Hitting the table and making a correct call
   −1   Hitting the table and making an incorrect call

Topics

Topics appear on topic cards, which are distributed randomly to the six participants. Sample topics might include:

Animals of the jungle
The problem with computers
Things that make me really nervous
What to do when your homework is finished

Application 2: Identify and Reduce Distractions

As you now know, there are potentially both internal and external distractions in any listening situation. You may have stayed up most of the night to study for a difficult exam and found it nearly impossible to concentrate in class, or taken a seat in a restaurant next to a man with four young children. In one case, fatigue will reduce your ability to concentrate; in the other, the noise and irregular movement of the youngsters may distract you.

Regardless of what the specific distraction may be, our premise is that you can deliberately manage many elements of the environment so that *you* control your focus of attention.

Activities

1. Keep a diary or log for a week, noting specific internal and external distractions. Include the things you worry about, people who occupy your thoughts, and external stimuli—noise and distractions in the environment. Review your log and make a list of what you consider to be the major distractions you encounter.

    What can you do to reduce or eliminate each? Be creative in your problem-solving, and make your action plan as concrete as possible. Consider discussing your findings in small groups so that you can help one another generate a list of solutions.

2. Describe a situation in which you exercised a great deal of self-discipline in order to concentrate and overcome distractions. What were the characteristics of the situation? What motivated you to work hard at listening? How can this determination be transferred to other listening situations?

Group Activities

Form a small group of four to six people. You may want to keep the same group for all activities, or you may find it more interesting to change groups so that you get to hear the opinions and ideas of a greater number of your classmates.

1. While listening to a speaker discuss a complex subject, write down elements of the presentation, speaker, or the environment that you find distracting. In small groups, compare your lists. Did different individuals generate different lists, or was everyone in close agreement?

2. Discuss the value and application of dichotic listening. In what situations is it appropriate? Inappropriate?

3. Rate each of the listed sound situations for its level of distraction, using the following scale:

   4 = very distracting
   3 = moderately distracting
   2 = slightly distracting
   1 = not distracting

   a. telephone ringing (yours)_____
   b. telephone ringing (someone else's)_____
   c. conversations near you_____
   d. laughter near you_____
   e. radio/music_____
   f. radio/news_____
   g. television_____

   Compare your ratings with those of other group members. What are some possible causes of discrepancies? In what situations do distractions bother you the most? Why do you feel that's the case?

4. Generate a list of 10 to 15 words that sound alike or have tricky prefixes or suffixes. Examples are *metal, entangle, borough*. Sit back-to-back with a partner. Person A is the speaker, Person B, the listener.
   Round 1: A reads the list of words while B writes down what he or she hears.
   Round 2: Change roles and repeat.
       Work with at least three different partners. In each case, make sure to check the accuracy of your list before moving on. In a large group of people, this exercise should generate noise and movement.

   Was it difficult for you to concentrate?
   Did you improve as you went along?
   How much difference did the speaker make in your ability to hear?
   How well did your listeners score?

Application 3: Adopt an Appropriate Listening Attitude

Focusing your attention requires not only self-discipline, but an appropriate attitude as well. Recall that you can improve your concentration by taking a sincere interest in people, listening to difficult material, and listening once in a while just to appreciate and enjoy the sounds in your environment.

Activities

1. Are you generally curious? List ten things that you'd like to learn more about this year. Take four or five items on your list, and note specific actions you can take to find out more information on each. If you had a hard time coming up with ten ideas, it should be an indication that perhaps your focus has become more narrow than you'd like it to be.

2. Try the following exercise. List six topics that you enjoy. List six others that you find "dull" or "boring." For each item indicate:

   a. Your degree of knowledge about it
   b. Your judgment of how difficult it is

I LIKE TO HEAR ABOUT:	know a little		know a lot			difficult			easy	
1._____	1	2	3	4	5	1	2	3	4	5
2._____	1	2	3	4	5	1	2	3	4	5
3._____	1	2	3	4	5	1	2	3	4	5
4._____	1	2	3	4	5	1	2	3	4	5
5._____	1	2	3	4	5	1	2	3	4	5
6._____	1	2	3	4	5	1	2	3	4	5

I AM NOT INTERESTED IN:	know a little		know a lot			difficult			easy	
1._____	1	2	3	4	5	1	2	3	4	5
2._____	1	2	3	4	5	1	2	3	4	5
3._____	1	2	3	4	5	1	2	3	4	5
4._____	1	2	3	4	5	1	2	3	4	5
5._____	1	2	3	4	5	1	2	3	4	5
6._____	1	2	3	4	5	1	2	3	4	5

   Now total your score for each question. If No. 1 under "I like to hear about" was "Baseball," and you gave your knowledge about baseball a "4" and its difficulty a "5," then the score for baseball would be "9."

   Do you notice any difference in your scores between the two categories—what you enjoy listening to and what you are interested in? Is it true that those topics you are not interested in tend to be those you perceive as more difficult or those you know less about?

3. Take a 10-minute walk. Notice all the sounds that you hear along your path. Sit in your backyard or on a porch. Stay silent for ten minutes and just listen. What do you hear?

4. What are your favorite listening experiences? How often to do you take time to experience these listening pleasures? Make a list of the barriers you would have to overcome to take advantage of these listening situations more frequently.

Group Activities

Form a small group of four to six people. You may want to keep the same group for all activities, or you may find it more interesting to change groups so that you get to hear the opinions and ideas of a greater number of your classmates.

1. Bring in an article you find uninteresting. In your group, discuss how the material could be made more relevant and useful to you. Rewrite the material or explain how it could be adapted. Share your "before" and "after" articles with the larger group. Identify another audience and repeat these steps.

2. Make a list of specific individuals you believe are excellent speakers. In small groups, discuss the characteristics of these individuals and record your responses.

   What mannerisms do they have?
   What do they do to hold audience attention?
   What do they do to develop rapport?

What does each do to generate audience interest?

Generally, how well do you like each of these people?

Examine your findings. What conclusions can you make regarding concentration and speaker variables?

3. Discuss your earliest listening experiences. What things did you enjoy listening to as a child? How did these experiences change as you got older?

Application 4: Apply the Vocalized Listening Technique

Poor concentration often results from misuse of your "bonus time," that interval resulting from the difference between speaking and information-processing rates. The key to concentration, then, is learning to use this time effectively.

Vocalized listening, as you know, is based on the premise that you can *control* how you spend your bonus time. You can *choose* to concentrate on the speaker's ideas, or you can choose to let other elements in the situation distract you.

Activities

1. Make a list of the listening situations you regularly encounter in which the vocalized listening technique might be useful. How long is your list?

2. Next time you listen to a presentation, try the vocalized listening technique. Restate the speaker's ideas to yourself, mentally ask yourself questions about the content, try to "stay with" the speaker. Practice the vocalized listening technique three or four more times. Keep notes to yourself concerning any problems you encounter. Does vocalized listening seem to get easier with practice?

3. Practice the vocalized listening technique. Whenever you become distracted, write down the nature of the distraction. Do you notice any patterns?

Group Activities

Form a small group of four to six people. You may want to keep the same group for all activities, or you may find it more interesting to change groups so that you get to hear the opinions and ideas of a greater number of your classmates.

1. Create a list of well-known personalities from the media who speak relatively fast and those who speak more slowly. They can be entertainers, talk-show hosts, political figures, actors, or anyone else likely to be familiar to members of your group. Discuss the effectiveness of each person. Do there seem to be common perceptions related to speaking rate, or does rate appear to be insignificant?

2. Select three individuals to prepare a four-minute presentation independently. Appropriate topics include: interesting vacations, hobbies, descriptions of recent movies, and so forth. Form four random groups.

Group 1 listens to speaker 1; Group 2 listens to speaker 2, and Group 3 is asked to listen to speaker 3. Group 4 is told to listen to whomever they want. Groups 1, 2, and 3 are instructed to use the vocalized listening technique. (*Variation:* Ask just one or two groups to use the vocalized listening technique.)

Listeners are positioned randomly throughout the room. Speakers all stand in the front of the room, separated by five to ten feet. When a signal is given, all three individuals begin talking simultaneously. Each speaker strives to gain and maintain the listeners' attention to "win" over the two competitors by attracting the most attention. At the end of four minutes, the speakers are stopped.

Take several minutes to answer the *What Did You Hear* questions below. Then, join with other members of your group and discuss the following questions:

a. What did you hear? Why?
b. What did each speaker do to gain your attention? Was it effective?
c. Why did different people hear and recall different information?
d. What speakers were distracting? What else distracted your attention?
e. Are the messages you hear always the most "important" ones?
f. Were there differences in the amount of recall between groups that applied the vocalized listening technique and those that did not?
g. What were the advantages and disadvantages of the vocalized technique?

As a group, share your findings with the entire class. What conclusions can be drawn from the results of this exercise?

What Did You Hear?

Three individuals will be speaking to you simultaneously. After 2 or 3 minutes, you will be asked to record what you remember hearing on a separate piece of paper.

Speaker.1:
What did you hear?

Speaker 2:
What did you hear?

Speaker 3:
What did you hear?

Application 5: Overcome Listener Apprehension

Printed messages are relatively permanent. You can go back, check facts, and think about the ideas presented. Oral messages, by comparison, are fleeting. You must hear words as they are spoken. Often, you don't hear what is said simply because you are anxious about your ability to remember.

Activities

1. Keep a datebook for two weeks in which you note all meetings, oral communication events, appointments. Work on your organizational and time-management skills, paying particular attention to your ability to plan wisely. Note any problems that arise: instances when you were late and the reason, occasions when you did not hear the first part of a speaker's message, times when you got lost because you didn't have enough background on the subject, or other similar situations. Review your recordings and create an action plan to improve your personal effectiveness.

2. Describe two situations that you dread. When you know you have to be in one of those environments, how do you prepare yourself? Is there physical preparation? Mental preparation? What do you find effective? Ineffective?

3. Practice deep breathing. Lay on the floor or assume a relaxed posture in your chair. Inhale slowly and deeply through your nose. Put your hand on your abdomen. You should be able to feel your abdomen move. Establish a pattern of deep breathing—breath in through your nose and out through your mouth. Continue for 3 minutes.

4. Practice visualization to relax. Close your eyes and put the palms of your hands over them. Block out all light and visualize just the color black. Use a mental image of something you know is very black and focus on the color for two minutes. Remove your hands and open your eyes very slowly. Notice how relaxed your eyes feel.

5. Visualize an image you associate with tension. Slowly replace it with an image you associate with relaxation. Use all of your senses to make each image as vivid as possible. Examples might be:

   A loud siren changes into a music box.
   A dark cave opens into a green meadow.
   A haunted house turns into a summer cottage.
   An angry, screaming child begins to dance in a flower garden.

Group Activities

Form a small group of four to six people. You may want to keep the same group for all activities, or you may find it more interesting to change groups so that you get to hear the opinions and ideas of a greater number of your classmates.

1. List the specific listening situations that you find stressful. Try to determine what causes your apprehension. Are there any similarities? Share your conclusions with group members. Are the situations you generated similar or different? How? What might account for any differences?

2. Discuss what you could do to prepare, psychologically and physically, for each of the following situations:

   a. A business meeting
   b. A long persuasive presentation
   c. An evaluation interview where you are the interviewer
   d. Criticism from your supervisor
   e. A play, movie, or other entertainment
   f. An employee discussing his or her personal problems
   g. An angry employee with a complaint
   h. Complicated directions

Application 6: Behave Like a Good Listener

If you want to become an excellent listener, the first thing to do is to begin acting like one. In a real sense, your physical behavior influences your listening. Our interest here is only on those activities that you deliberately undertake to maintain the degree of alertness and concentration necessary to hear the speaker's message.

Activities

1. List several listening situations in which you invest a great deal of energy. Do you decide ahead of time how much effort you're going to put into listening? How is this effort reflected in your physical posture? In your mental attitude?

2. Do you believe that it is more likely that you'll listen well if you "behave" like a good listener? Why?

3. What are some of your "bad habits" that may make it difficult for you to remain attentive in difficult listening situations?

Group Activities

Form a small group of four to six people. You may want to keep the same group for all activities, or you may find it more interesting to change groups so that you get to hear the opinions and ideas of a greater number of your classmates.

1. Write down any eight numbers in a row. Pair up with a classmate and sit back-to-back. Read the numbers to your partner. Make sure he or she does not take any notes or write anything down while listening. Then, ask your partner three questions about the numbers, such as:

   a. What was the third (or fourth, or second) number?
   b. What number came just before 23 (any number in your list)?
   c. What was the second to the last number?

   Keep track of how many of your questions your partner answered correctly. When you have finished, change roles.

   Discuss the physical changes that occurred when someone knew he or she was going to have to listen intently for a short period of time. Was more energy invested in the listening when it was purposeful? What are the implications for other, more extended, listening situations?

2. You will be assigned a classmate to observe for the next few days. This person will not know who you are. Keep a record of the nonverbal behaviors you notice while this person is in classroom listening situations. Include such things as:

   a. body posture
   b. eye contact
   c. movement, fidgeting
   d. position of legs, arms

   After you have sufficient data, you will be asked to share your observations with the person you were observing. Discuss how his or her nonverbal behavior contributes to or hinders effective listening. Make a list of the variables that might influence this person's behavior such as stress, fatigue, interest in the subject, and so forth. Provide an opportunity for the person who was observed to respond to your feedback.

Application 7: Become an Appreciative Listener

Appreciative listeners take pleasure in listening to the sounds that surround them, whether they are in a natural environment listening to wildlife or in a laboratory listening to sounds created by new technologies. Their focus on enjoying the immediate experience helps to reduce anxiety and improve attention and concentration.

Activities

1. List the types of appreciative listening you do on a regular basis. Which would you like to increase? What types of listening would you like to add to this list?

2. What actions could you take to increase the amount of time you spend on appreciative listening? What are the benefits of engaging in appreciative listening more frequently?

3. Appreciative listening has been identified as one of the major listening purposes. Do you believe appreciative listening is always deliberately undertaken—that it is always purposeful? Under what circumstances might appreciative listening take place spontaneously? How might the personal outcomes be different depending on whether the appreciative listening was planned or unplanned?

Group Activities

Form a small group of four to six people. You may want to keep the same group for all activities, or you may find it more interesting to change groups so that you get to hear the opinions and ideas of a greater number of your classmates.

1. How do the types of listening activities that constitute appreciative listening change over the years? Interview someone in their 70s or 80s to learn more about their listening experiences. Other classmates might talk with young children about their favorite listening situations. Share what you learned with members of your group. In addition to age, what other factors affect listening enjoyment?

2. You have a busy schedule and often have difficulty just finding time to meet your daily commitments. What specific strategies can you implement to increase appreciative listening under these circumstances? For instance, you might walk to your classes along a different route where you are more likely to hear pleasant sounds. Create a list of suggestions to share with the rest of the class. You might go a step further and select one or two ideas to implement for a few weeks, reporting back to the class at the end of the period.

HEARING MESSAGES: SHORT CASE

Jim felt irritable, anxious. He only had a few hours to get his report in shape before the 2:00 p.m. meeting. As he leaned over the figures on his desk, he heard someone in the doorway. Jim looked up to see his supervisor, Ben, leaning against the door frame with a cup of coffee in his hand.

"Hey, Jim. Got some news for you. You know that truck you've been looking at over at Carmen's? Well, Paul says he knows a guy down the road from him who has one just like it. Sell it for a good price."

"Did I hear something about a good price?" Jack poked his head around the corner and stepped inside Jim's office. He sank down in a chair and gave a big sigh. "What a day! I'm glad someone's got some good news around here."

Just then Jim's phone rang. He picked it up. Marketing. They needed some information by the end of the day.

When Jim put the phone down, he looked up to see Marge standing in the doorway behind Ben. "Phil wants to see a couple of reports. If you pull them from your file now, I can take them back down with me."

Jim felt like he was in a daze. He couldn't concentrate on what was going on around him. All he wanted was to be left alone so that he could finish his report.

1. What, really, is Jim's problem?

2. What are the external distractions?

3. What are the internal distractions?

4. What would you recommend that Jim do in order to accomplish his goals while maintaining effective interpersonal relations?

THE HOME FRONT: CASE QUESTIONS

1. Illustrate the principles presented in the chapter with examples from the case:

    - Poor use of the thought–speech differential
    - Dichotic listening
    - Auditory discrimination
    - Listener apprehension
    - Perceptual readiness

2. What could Josh have done to have made Dean Plack's lecture more worthwhile? In other words, what were some of the distractions he experienced, their causes, and what could he have done to reduce them?

3. What can listeners do to ensure the most effective communication possible when there is a language barrier, as there was between Josh and Rolf?

4. Anxiety was a factor in several different listening situations. Identify these occasions and discuss how the anxiety was or could have been reduced.

5. Why do you think Gretchen was able to teach Tanya more successfully than Josh? What could have been done to more effectively introduce Josh to the foreign language?

6. How was listening affected by purpose and context in the case? Identify several different communication situations presented in the case, and discuss how the specific context influenced Josh's listening behavior.

7. Imagine that Josh is determined to make more progress in his encounters with Rolf and to reduce the stress he now feels whenever they meet. Create a situation of your choice and role play an encounter between Josh and Rolf as Josh begins his new approach. Possible situations include:

a. Josh has Rolf and Gretchen over for dinner.
b. Josh takes Rolf a few tools he has asked to borrow.
c. Josh and Rolf go to a ballgame together.

BIBLIOGRAPHY

Beatty, M. J., & Payne, S. K. (1984). Listening comprehension as a function of cognitive complexity: A research note. *Communication Monographs, 51,* 85–89.

Cegala, D. J. (1984). Affective and cognitive manifestations of interaction involvement during unstructured and competitive interactions. *Communication Monographs, 51,* 320–338.

Clark, A. J. (1989). Communication confidence and listening competence: An investigation of the relationships of willingness to communicate, communication apprehension, and receiver apprehension to comprehension of content and emotional meaning in spoken messages. *Communication Education, 38,* 237–248.

Emmert, P., Emmert, V., & Brandt, J. (1993). An analysis of male-female differences on the listening practices feedback report. *Journal of the International Listening Association,* special issue, 43–55.

Jaffe, D. T., & Scott, C. D. (1984). *Self-renewal: A workbook for achieving high performance and health in a high-stress environment.* New York: Simon & Schuster.

Langer, E. J. (1989). *Mindfulness.* Reading, MA: Addison-Wesley Publishing.

Marttila, J. (2004). Listening technologies for individuals and the classroom. *Topics in Language Disorders, 24*(1), 31–51.

Moray, N. (1969). *Listening and attention.* Baltimore, MD: Penguin Books.

O'Heren, L., & Arnold, W. E. (1991). Nonverbal attentive behavior and listening comprehension. *Journal of the International Listening Association, 5,* 86–92.

Roush, W. (2003). Listening to the data. *Technology Review, 106*(9), 26.

Ruyter, K., & Wetzels, M. (2000). The impact of perceived listening behavior in voice-to-voice service encounters. *Journal of Service Research, 2*(3), 276–284.

Weaver, S., & Rutherford, W. (1974). A hierarchy of listening skills. *Elementary English, 51,* 1148–1149.

Weick, K. E. (1983). Organizational communication: Toward a research agenda. In Linda L. Putnam and Michael E. Pacanowsky (Eds.), *Communication and Organization: An Interpretative Approach,* pp. 13–29. Newbury Park, CA: Sage Publications.

Wheeless, L. (1975). An investigation of receiver apprehension and social context dimensions of communication apprehension. *Communication Education, 24,* 261–268.

Witkin, B. R. (1993). Human information processing. In A. D. Wolvin and C. G. Coakley (Eds.), *Perspectives on Listening,* pp. 23–59. Norwood, NJ: Ablex Publishing.

Wolff, F. I., & Marsnick, N. C. (1992). *Perceptive listening.* Fort Worth, TX: Harcourt Brace Jovanovich.

Wolvin, A. D., & Coakley, C. W. (1996). *Listening.* Dubuque, IA: Wm. C. Brown Publishers.

CHAPTER 4

THE PROCESS OF
UNDERSTANDING

I know you believe you understand what you think I said,
but I'm not sure you realize that what you heard
is not what I meant.
—ANONYMOUS

OUTLINE

CHAPTER OBJECTIVES

After completing this chapter, you will

Become more aware of:

- the mental processes involved in listening comprehension
- the function of inner speech in listening comprehension
- the ways in which listeners can positively influence the creation of shared meanings
- the ways in which listeners can improve their comprehension

Better understand:

- the relationship between language and thought
- how language influences listening
- the process of relational listening
- the types of questions that assist in listening comprehension
- the organizational systems speakers use
- how note-taking methods can improve listening comprehension

Develop skills in:

- Recognizing inner speech
- Identifying relationships between language and thought
- Increasing vocabulary
- Asking questions
- Listening to the entire message
- Distinguishing main from supporting ideas
- Taking notes

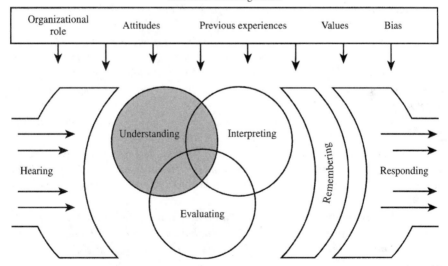

A Model of the Six-Component HURIER Listening Process

■ ■ ■ ■ ■ ▬▬▬▬▬▬▬

UNDERSTANDING: SITUATION AND PURPOSE

Understanding is almost always a key element of listening. It is of primary importance in high-task situations where the consequences of misunderstanding are serious. Following directions is one of the most frequent applications of this component. As a student, you are continuously in listening situations where understanding is your primary goal.

In some instances, understanding may not be immediate. In other cases, a communicator may deliberately frame his message in ways that lead to a variety of conclusions, so that different listeners have different understandings. In situations where the intent is to appreciate, or when there is no language involved, understanding may be secondary or even irrelevant.

In situations where you need to make decisions, understanding is also essential. When listening to persuasive messages, for instance, it is important to first thoroughly understand the speaker's ideas before evaluating them.

CASE: FIRST-SEMESTER FRESHMAN: PART I

Nikki had been looking forward to this day for over a year. She was finally settled in the dorm, and tomorrow she would participate in a day-long orientation program before classes began on Tuesday. Right now she was off to see her adviser, Dr. Gregg, who would help set up her first semester schedule. Nikki leafed through the large packet of materials she had received in the mail. She was glad she had been assigned an adviser to help her make sense of all these forms. She had studied the web pages that described the registration process, but that hadn't helped either. It all seemed so complicated.

The campus was still new to her; as she walked along the path, the buildings all seemed farther apart than they had looked driving in with her parents. By the time she got to Randolph Hall and found Room 533, she knew she was running a bit late. Dr. Gregg's door was open, so she stepped in and threw her backpack down on the floor next to a chair by the door.

"Sorry I'm late," Nikki said as she sat down and kicked her pack beneath her. Dr. Gregg looked up at her, then looked at the large clock over his desk.

"Don't get too comfortable," he said in an even and somewhat disinterested tone. "My next appointment is due in six minutes." He set down the pen he had been holding and leaned back in his chair. "How would you like to spend the time you have left?"

Nikki was confused for a second. Not only did the news of another appointment come as a surprise, but she had expected that Dr. Gregg would have the entire session planned out for her. She had assumed he would give her advice and tell her what classes to take.

"Well, uh, I'm not sure," Nikki began. "I don't know of any questions, really." She was wishing she had at least looked over some of the materials in her packet. Maybe then she would have something to say.

"All right, then," Dr. Gregg leaned forward again and reached out his hand. *"Your schedule?"* Nikki couldn't believe the predicament she had gotten herself into. *What schedule? She hadn't completed any schedule. She didn't even know what was in the packet.* Nikki was accustomed to making a good first impression. She could almost always think of something clever and interesting to say, and she was often told that she would do well because of her outgoing, bubbly personality. It certainly didn't seem to be serving her well now.

"My schedule," Nikki repeated as she searched aimlessly through the folder of papers she had in her lap. *"My schedule."* There was a long silence as she continued to rummage through her packet of registration materials.

"I'll be with you in one moment," Nikki heard Dr. Gregg say to another Freshmen who suddenly appeared at his door. She felt even more rushed and confused.

"I guess I must have misplaced my schedule," she finally concluded, looking up helplessly at Dr. Gregg.

"Well, I have to sign it before you take it to the registrar, Nikki," Dr. Gregg told her in his even, dry voice. *"I'm seeing advisees all afternoon but,"* he reached over and pulled his desk calendar closer, *"it looks like I may have a few minutes around 4:15 p.m. Now my next appointment is waiting."*

Nikki got her backpack from underneath the chair and apologized again to Dr. Gregg, who seemed to hardly acknowledge the fact that she was terribly upset and on the verge of tears. After all, no one had made anything clear. She had every reason to think an appointment for advisement was an appointment to get some advice. How could she have known she had to prepare? As Nikki left the office she resolved not to let this incident affect her enthusiasm for her new life as a college student.

The rest of the day, in fact, did improve and Nikki felt herself relaxing and enjoying the new and exciting aspects of dorm life. By that evening she had regained her confidence and was ready to tackle the classes that were to begin the next morning.

"So this is what it's like to be a Freshman," Nikki thought to herself as she walked into the first session of Introduction to Psychology, a required course for all majors. She and her classmates were alphabetized and assigned seats so that attendance could be taken more easily. After psychology, she had two hours free for lunch, followed by English Composition, Bowling, and Physical Sciences. All day she thought about what fun dorm life was and how anxious she was to get back to her room.

CASE: FIRST-SEMESTER FRESHMAN: PART II

By the fifth week of classes Nikki had pretty much adjusted to her schedule and she felt much more comfortable with her daily routines. Still, living with a roommate was an experience for which she hadn't been fully prepared. She and Sunmee seemed to be getting along okay, but there was a tension to their relationship that she couldn't quite put her finger on. No matter, she thought. They got along just fine. In fact, in just a few minutes they would be studying physical science together, an event that had become a regular part of their schedules. Nikki reflected on how lucky she was to be rooming with Sunmee, who was conscientious and dependable—and smart.

Nikki threw open the door of their room to find Sunmee already busy at her desk. She instinctively looked at her watch. Well, only a few minutes late. What else did Sunmee have to do? She'd be studying anyway.

Nikki hurried to get out her books. She arranged them in a pile and then sat cross-legged on the floor, waiting for Sunmee to begin their session.

"We've got to talk," Sunmee said as she turned to face Nikki.

"Sure," Nikki replied, puzzled that things had turned so serious.

"I can't keep doing all your work for you," Sunmee said with a tone of finality. "You seem to think it's no big deal to just sit there while I figure out the answers to all of the questions. I've been getting more and more upset about it, and I thought it was time to discuss the situation."

Nikki couldn't believe what she was hearing. Sunmee doing all the work? Hardly. She knew she contributed her share. She just didn't have a very good background in science and math, and that made it much more difficult for her. But Sunmee didn't seem to care about that.

"Are you saying I'm taking a free ride on this? That I couldn't do this stuff without you?" Nikki snapped back. She could feel her heart beating faster and the blood rushing to her face.

"Nikki," Sunmee countered, "I want to be able to discuss this situation rationally."

"So now I'm irrational, too?" Nikki shot back. "You think I'm stupid and irrational?"

"I didn't say you were taking a free ride. I don't think you're stupid and I didn't say you were irrational. I said I feel like I'm doing much more than my share of the work. I don't notice that you're helping me a lot, but I think I'm helping you in very important ways." Sunmee stopped to see how Nikki was taking all of this. Nikki remained silent.

"Studying together," Sunmee continued, "implies to me that we both contribute. I would feel better if you prepared some of the answers to the review problems. Then we could discuss them and I wouldn't be starting from the beginning every time."

"Is that what it means to study together? That I prepare the answers and then you tell me if they're okay? Like you're my stupid teacher or something?" Nikki was getting increasingly upset and confused about why things weren't working out. "That's what studying together means to you?"

"Studying together means," Sunmee paused and then continued, "that we both offer each other something. I think I've been offering you the answers to the review questions. What have you been offering me?"

"I'm out of here," Nikki said as she got up from the floor. "I don't need to take this from you or anybody else."

"Nikki," Sunmee said, "Did you know that I worked for five years before I came here to school in the States? I've had a lot of experience in the business world and I know why I need this education. My dream is to go back to China and help

others learn about the magic of physical therapy. My parents have spent their life's savings helping me get here to America. They are far away, so I am really on my own. Perhaps that's why I see things differently."

Nikki stopped and slowly sat back down. "My parents just told me to go to college, and to pick some place they could afford. I guess it's not that way for you."

"No," Sunmee replied softly. "It's not that way for me at all. A college education is very important to me personally. I've been thinking about it for as long as I can remember, and you know I'm still holding a part-time job. To me, college is a doorway, an opportunity not only to improve myself but also to help my family and my community to advance. I came here to Lehman because it has one of the very best programs in the country for physical therapy."

"We are so different, *" Nikki found herself saying as she shook her head.*

There was a long silence. "So," Sunmee finally spoke up, "being your friend is important to me too. I don't want this situation to cause a problem between us. That's why I said something."

"I think I understand," Nikki replied. "I'd like to keep on studying together, but tomorrow I'll try to do some of the problems myself. Then we can work together on them and," she paused for a moment and tried to smile, "and then you can tell me all the mistakes I've made."

"It's a deal," Sunmee responded.

Nikki found it hard to sleep, and even harder to stay awake in class the next day. She had promised Sunmee that she would try to work on some of the review questions, and to do that she needed to follow Dr. Perry's lecture closely. Everything about this class was dull and difficult. It didn't help, she reflected, that she sat in the last row where it was a challenge to even see Dr. Perry over the heads of seventy other students. Another problem was that he kept using words that were totally unfamiliar to her. He also rambled constantly. She could never tell when something was important, and when it was just one of Dr. Perry's many tangents. Those students who ventured to ask questions were often interrupted. Dr. Perry seemed to think he knew the question before they even had a chance to make their point. Consequently, class participation had decreased significantly over the weeks until now it was just Dr. Perry talking.

As Nikki sat doodling, she thought about her first days at Lehman and how many experiences she had since then. Suddenly she caught herself daydreaming, and resolved to focus on the lecture. "I've got to concentrate," she thought to herself. "This is silly. I can do it." Five minutes later, however, her mind was on her mom and dad and how long it had been since she had seen them. Nikki decided she would call her parents as soon as she got back to the dorm. And she thought about Sunmee and how committed her roommate was to getting an education. She was glad that she and Sunmee had been able to talk things out.

"Got to concentrate," she thought to herself as she realized, once again, that she had let her mind wander. As she summoned all of her energy in an effort to focus on Dr. Perry, she suddenly remembered a study skills session she had taken during Freshman orientation. Her teacher had suggested taking notes as one way to focus

attention on the speaker. She had never really tried any of the note-taking systems her teacher had recommended, but now seemed as good a time as any. She looked down at her doodles and turned to a clean page. Certainly couldn't hurt.

When the class ended, Nikki stayed in her seat and began working on the review questions. "Just wait until Sunmee quizzes me tonight," she thought. Sunmee would be in for a big surprise.

THE PROCESS OF UNDERSTANDING: PRINCIPLES

Every day you are exposed to a wide range of messages from friends and classmates. Each person represents a particular viewpoint and holds a unique set of expectations, values, and attitudes. Perhaps the person sitting next to you is from Chicago while you grew up in a small rural community in France. It's likely that you know a native American, or someone from eastern Europe or South America or Australia. Your effectiveness in diverse environments depends largely upon the quality of your listening and your ability to understand how others see the world, to recognize how they define a situation.

This chapter focuses on the principles and practices of understanding others. Although thinking in terms of each component of the HURIER model is helpful in

▬ ▬ ▬ ▬ ▬▬▬▬▬▬▬▬

Can you ever completely understand another person?

identifying and fine-tuning your skills, keep in mind that all components are interrelated. This is nowhere more obvious than when you study listening comprehension. Comprehension involves the attention and concentration that you read about in the last chapter as well as skills we have yet to cover, such as memory.

Recall that the earliest listening research focused almost exclusively on listening comprehension and the degree of understanding individuals demonstrated when presented with extended lecture material. More recently, studies have examined interactive settings. In Bostrom's search for a reliable way to measure listening, for instance, he concluded that the notion of understanding was particularly problematic. He argued that not only can you listen well to something you don't understand, but there are frequent occasions when understanding is not immediate; rather, the meaning of what you have heard is revealed over time (Bostrom, 1990).

▬ ▬ ▬ ▬ ▬▬▬▬▬▬▬▬

What visual images come to mind when you hear the words *romantic, high tech,* or *global?*

All of us, like Nikki, have had that "ah ha" feeling, of suddenly realizing that pieces of information we may have discounted are in fact very meaningful.

These approaches make it apparent that your role as a listener in dyadic and interpersonal settings may be quite different than when you are listening to lectures or listening in one-way communication situations. These differences must be taken into account when considering the principles and skills required for understanding messages. In this chapter, our focus is first on understanding how individuals make sense of what they hear. Then, we move to the business of how you can improve your comprehension when listening in interactive settings. Finally, we examine ways in which you can improve your comprehension of longer, largely one-way messages.

Understanding What You Hear

Prerequisite to listening comprehension is word recognition. You must be able to form tentative images from the sound cues you hear. Due to differences in past experiences and associations, each person imposes her own internal meaning on what she hears. As a listener, you have literally thousands of possible images that have been formed over years of accumulated experience. When you hear a sequence of sounds you scan through information in your long-term memory, a virtual warehouse full of past experiences and associations, values, assumptions, and language-related impressions. Since words derive their impact from the past associations and expectations they elicit, no word is without what we refer to as connotative meaning. Song lyrics are a good example, since they often take on special significance because of the experiences you associate with them. As we have repeatedly stressed, the challenge of really understanding another person involves guesswork; your challenge is to determine how your guesswork can be improved.

In addition to recognizing sound cues, you must also put incoming data into some kind of framework to make it meaningful; you must become "author of your own version of the context" (Minnick, 1968, p. 191). A listener compares incoming information to previous knowledge, forms relationships between new and old ideas, and creates a personalized memory file. Individuals who have difficulty scanning through their information warehouse often have difficulty making use of previous knowledge and so have trouble with listening comprehension. Here you can appreciate the close ties between comprehension and memory. Meaning, it becomes clear, is never really "literal."

> In what specific ways are you *author of your own version of the context*?

Symbols and Meanings.   Precise and concrete language facilitates shared meanings. Yet, regardless of the symbols used to express ideas, your meanings for a particular word are never replicated exactly in someone else's mind. Even under the best of circumstances, each person's filtering system and past experiences make the verbal transmission of an exact idea virtually impossible. Some theorists propose that only when individuals have shared similar experiences can they ever really understand the meaning of the language used to describe that experience. You may, for example, have read stories about soldiers who returned from war and realized that only those who were there in the trenches together could ever understand what the concepts associated with war meant.

> What experiences have you had that you don't talk about with some people because you know they wouldn't understand?

Complete understanding between two individuals, as you know, is an elusive goal; not only are meanings personal and unique, but there is also the possibility that senders are purposely unclear or receivers purposely misunderstand what is said to them (Eisenberg, 1984; Clampitt, 1991, p. 30). Look back at Nikki's situation when she met with her adviser. Was there purposeful misunderstanding? Think of your own communication encounters. You may be able to generate several examples of occasions where you have been guilty of creatively shaping impressions.

Given additional processes like selective attention, you realize that understanding is relative at best. The meanings we assign are approximate, especially when individuals' perceptual worlds are very different. Several basic concepts provide a foundation for better understanding and explaining a variety of listening situations. Two of these are the relationship between language and thought and inner speech.

> In what ways does your language shape your thinking?

Language and Thought.   Over seventy-five years ago two researchers presented a theory of language that has fascinated generations and become commonly known as the Sapir–Whorf Hypothesis (Whorf, 1926). Their findings were based on studies of individuals from different cultures. After years of research, they concluded that the language people use to describe their world is directly related to their patterns of thought about that world. Language not only develops as a result of cultural needs, it also determines the way in which a group of people perceives their environment. Language, Sapir and Whorf proposed, exerts a tremendous influence over how we think and what we think about. The implications for listening are profound.

*"I **told** you not to make things perfectly clear!"*

Numerous examples support this premise. The fact that the Eskimos have many different words for *snow,* a central concept in their experience, is one indication of how the needs of a people determine the development of its vocabulary. Wet snow, dry snow, falling snow—all "mean" something different to those who must travel, hunt, and live in that environment. Asian languages differ from those in western cultures not only in structure but also in the way in which concepts

> How does your vocabulary expand or constrain your thinking?

are expressed. The contrast is readily apparent between the high-technology languages of countries like the United States and the personification of inanimate objects and high regard for natural forces apparent in such cultures as China or Japan.

Advances in technology have extended our reach such that communicating across continents can be accomplished with the push of a button. The ease and frequency with which cross-cultural communication occurs, however, can be misleading; just because we are engaging in global communication more frequently does not necessarily mean that we are communicating effectively. Keep in mind that speed and distance may also compound the impact of conflict and misunderstanding. Our challenge is to remain sensitive to and respectful of differences in perceptions, values, and experiences.

If you accept the Sapir–Whorf hypothesis, you'll conclude that the words you use influence the way in which ideas take shape in your mind. As you expand your vocabulary, you'll not only become more articulate, but the number of associations you make will increase. In addition, you'll be able to think about the world with greater precision and clarity. We return to the importance of vocabulary-building a bit later. First, it is helpful to understand more about the uniqueness of individual meanings. The implications of this notion are nowhere more vividly demonstrated than through inner speech.

Inner Speech

Although most of us don't like to admit it, we all carry on a stream of internal conversation with ourselves. One very specialized form of self-talk is called inner speech. Inner speech serves a variety of functions in the listening process, and has been used to develop a theoretical perspective to explain how we assign or generate meanings while listening (Dance, 1979; Vygotsky, 1986; Korba, 1989).

Knowledge of inner speech will help you monitor your listening behavior and understand the process of listening comprehension so that you can better select and implement specific strategies to accomplish your listening goals. Inner speech facilitates symbolic thought as you create personal meanings for the words you hear. In other words, to a large extent, inner speech shapes how you think about things. Johnson (1993) proposes four characteristics of inner speech:

1. *Inner speech is egocentric:*   This does not mean an individual is selfish or self-centered, only that her attention is directed inward, not outward. When you are engaged in inner speech, your energy is focused on identifying past associations and clarifying your personal response to what you have heard. Because inner speech is egocentric, the meanings you assign to words are also extremely idiosyncratic (Johnson, 1993, p. 178). If, for instance, you were once kicked by a cow, your meaning upon hearing the word *cow* would be different from the meanings your friend, who grew up in London, associates with the word.

2. *Silent:*   As soon as you verbalize your thoughts, the activity is no longer inner speech. Inner speech is silent and private.

3. *Compressed syntax:*   Inner speech is not constructed in the same manner as spoken language, nor does it use the same grammar. In fact, the way in which the syntax of messages is reduced as the ideas we hear are processed contributes to the difference between speaking and listening rates. As you know, most listeners can accommodate information at three times the normal speaking rate because, as language is processed, it is also edited. If you've taken a speed reading course, you may recall that emphasis is on making sense of key pieces of information rather than on processing each discrete word. Inner speech follows much the same pattern.

4. *Semantic embeddedness:*   Due to your accumulated experiences, a word elicited in inner speech can signify or refer to much more than it does in interpersonal communication. The more first hand knowledge you have of the object or concept, the richer your resources (Johnson, 1993, pp. 172–174). Your background, as you know, provides a frame of reference that is used to "make sense" of what you hear. It becomes clear that if your experiences are significantly different from your partner's, sharing meanings will require a great deal of effort. If you have been kicked by a cow, the word *cow* is embedded in numerous semantic reactions associated with the event. Consider your immediate responses to words like *family* or *cigarette*. Do you believe your meanings are completely shared by others in your class?

Inner speech serves a variety of functions, some of which are very similar to the functions of communication generally. You can see how it helps you relate or link what you hear to your previous experiences. It also serves to regulate or control your behavior as you reflect on the wisdom of your choices. Imagine the inner speech Nikki must have had as she tried to figure out how to respond at the meeting with Professor Gregg. Her understanding of "advisement" undoubtedly shifted as a result of this encounter.

Similarly, what do you suppose was going through Professor Gregg's mind during the process? "Another freshman," "kids . . . helpless—want everything," "rude, self-centered girl—from wealthy family," "Let suffer—good lesson." The nature of an individual's inner speech, as you can see, reflects her attitudes, assumptions, and thought processes as well as the nature and content of subsequent communications.

Semantic Reactions

As the concept of inner speech makes clear, each person has complex associations with any given symbol that, for him, generate unique meanings. Even a single, very simple word is likely to have meanings for a particular individual that range far beyond those found in spoken language.

Some people react so strongly to words that they have difficulty distinguishing between what is real—out there in the environment—and the mental images elicited by words used to describe these objects and events. These are what are called semantic reactions: You respond to the word as if it were the thing described. Although some of our semantic reactions (such as jumping when we hear the word *fire* rather than waiting to witness the smoke and flames) can be useful, most only move you further away from mental objectivity and sound judgment.

> What words elicit strong semantic reactions from you?

You encountered a good example of a semantic reaction when you read about the conflict Sunmee and Nikki had over their study sessions. Words like *stupid* obviously elicited a strong emotional response and prevented further communication from taking place.

COMPREHENSION IN TWO-WAY SETTINGS

Opportunities to share meanings are greatest in two-way communication situations. Through the continuous exchange of ideas and information, you and your partner can move closer to a common understanding, a shared definition of the situation. The success of your efforts depends on a number of things. First, you need an appreciation of the impact language, or vocabulary, can have on achieving your goal. In addition, your ability to ask appropriate questions and to check perceptions affects the outcome of your interactions.

Sharing and Building Vocabulary

Perhaps you have had the feeling that you knew exactly what ideas you wanted to convey but couldn't bring the right word to mind. You may have substituted another word, but chances are you remained frustrated because you knew somehow it just wasn't "right." Those who have command of a language are often able to bring new insight to others simply through their sensitive use of words. Think about your favorite poet or author and the lines you can read again and again. Articulate speakers also tend to be more effective in their careers. An American Management Association brochure announces that the size of your vocabulary is directly related to your career development and ultimate earning power.

Developing your vocabulary doesn't take magic, it only takes determination. The following suggestions will help you to increase your knowledge of words and how to use them.

1. *Keep a dictionary handy:*   The thought of using a dictionary has probably never been exciting to you. Think for a moment, however, of situations where you cannot afford to misunderstand the speaker and her intention. Consider the times when you heard a word and stopped listening because it didn't make sense. In school, you are well aware of the specialized vocabularies associated with your different courses—biology, political science, literature, theater. In the workplace, your vocabulary is constantly expanding as each functional area creates new terms. It's only been in the last few decades, for example, that technology has introduced terms like *real time, GPS receiver, palm pilot, and megapixel.* Many have became part of our everyday vocabulary.

2. *Write down new words:* Another aid to mastering new vocabulary is to write down each word as you look it up. This gives you a concrete way of assessing how you're progressing and enables you to determine whether you are putting yourself in challenging listening situations. A periodic review of your list will help you integrate new vocabulary into your "mental file."

3. *Use new words:* Now you've got a lot of high-powered words floating around in your head—use them! Don't be afraid of your new words *if* they are more accurate and precise. Using obscure words just for effect does nothing to improve your communication or interpersonal relations. Nor does loading your speech with jargon. The correct, appropriate use of language is an art, and the more accurately you express your thoughts the better you will feel about your communication. Keep in mind, too, that your expanded vocabulary may subtly reflect your personal interests and further shape how you view ideas and events. It therefore has the potential to bring you closer to others or to exaggerate differences.

Numerous miscommunications created by language-related behavior occur every day. The story is told of a man who brought a book on the game of bridge with him on a short flight from Philadelphia to Baltimore. As the flight attendant moved down the aisle, she glanced over the man's shoulder and commented, "That must be a fascinating love story you're reading." Looking down, the man saw the chapter title: "Free Response after the Original Pass."

Similarly, children often have private interpretations—especially when the vocabulary is inaccessible to them. Six-year-olds from a New York City school, for example, were reciting the Lord's Prayer. They were heard to say, ". . . and give us this day our jelly bread, . . . and lead us not into Penn Station. . . ."

You can imagine the frustrations experienced by those from different cultures who must not only learn a new language but must also understand figures of speech and idiomatic expressions. In these and other cases, the ability to ask appropriate questions becomes essential as our world becomes smaller and as we interact more frequently with those whose language was developed to describe a different world view.

Asking Appropriate Questions

One way to facilitate understanding is through asking appropriate questions. Questions serve a variety of purposes. They can be used to request clarification, to probe, or to control the direction of the conversation. One of the most productive types of questions are those used to confirm that your understanding of your partner's message is correct. We call this type of question a perception check.

Perception Checking.   Perception-checking is a specific response that (1) provides information to your partner regarding what you understood her to say, and then (2) allows your partner to modify or further clarify her original intent.

Review the dialogue between Nikki and Sunmee regarding their understanding of what "studying together" means. Although the situation was tense, perception checking helped the women move closer to a common understanding. Nikki's responses were emotional, but her restatement left no doubt in Sunmee's mind that further dialogue was needed to come to a shared definition of the situation.

Perception checking is particularly useful when accuracy is essential, such as when a task has just been delegated to you or when an agreement has been reached. Restating procedures, dates, and final outcomes makes it less likely that misunderstandings will occur. In our everyday encounters, it is often difficult to avoid jumping to conclusions. We are in a hurry, and we seldom stop to confirm our understandings. As a result, many unnecessary mistakes are made. Imagine a typical work situation:

> When would perception checking have prevented you from making a mistake?

> Your supervisor comes over to your desk and begins to explain what he needs done during the week he'll be out of town. You're not familiar with some of the names of his associates or the terms he's using, but you hesitate to interrupt. He seems in a hurry, and the information is obviously important to him. You don't want him to think that you're slow to catch on or that you're not familiar with some of the people you probably should know by now. You decide to remain quiet, thinking that you'll be able to put the pieces together once he leaves. Finally, he's finished. As he shuts the door your phone rings. You pick it up and discover that there's a family problem that requires your immediate attention. You put down the phone, thinking about the message you just received about your brother. By the time you get a chance to reflect on your earlier conversation with your supervisor, you have forgotten much of the information. Suddenly, you wish you had done a better job of listening.

In this case, perception checking would have been appropriate. Whenever you are focusing on the accomplishment of a task, perception checking can ensure the highest possible correspondence between your understanding and the communicator's intent. Repeating the message not only enables your partner to confirm your understanding, but the act of repeating information also reinforces the content of the message itself.

Questions.   Questions are used both for clarification and to obtain additional information from your partner. Often, a communicator makes inaccurate assumptions about what you already know or neglects to provide important details. Since she is familiar with her subject and purpose, it is often difficult for her to make wise choices about what to communicate to you. Consequently, you end up with gaps in your information.

Questions for clarification let your partner know how your background compares with her assumptions about your level of knowledge. By asking thoughtful questions, you can obtain clarification on points that seem vague or ambiguous. Questions prevent you from making inaccurate assumptions when you try to act on incomplete information. Don't be discouraged by speakers who seem annoyed or impatient with your questions. Your goal is effective listening, and your ability to carry out directions will be proof of the importance of getting all the facts.

There are many types of questions; each serves a slightly different purpose (Box 4.1). Closed questions require a short, concise response: Did you bring your DVD player? What section of E-commerce are you in? Do you live in this country? These are closed questions because one or two words are all that is required to respond.

If your purpose is to have your partner provide a more complete explanation, open-ended questions are more appropriate. Dr. Gregg's first question to Nikki was open-ended: "How would you like to spend the time you have left?"

In your efforts to increase understanding, you may choose to use a variety of "probes." Probes are helpful when you don't feel you are getting adequate information to understand your partner's point of view thoroughly. Probing questions do not suggest a new topic; rather, you ask the speaker to expand on a particular issue. Imagine, for example, that your good friend said, "That course really upsets me." You might probe with a question such as, "What is it about the course that's mak-

---

BOX 4.1

TYPES OF QUESTIONS

Closed

Ask closed questions when you want a short, direct, and specific response.

"Who did you vote for in the election?"

Open

Open questions allow your partner alternatives in how he or she responds; there is more than one way of answering.

"What did you think of the candidates for senior class president?"

Leading

Your partner can tell from the way you ask the question what you expect as his or her response. These questions bias the information you receive.

"Wasn't that a stupid looking web page Marisa put together for her campaign?"

Probes

There are many kinds of probes, questions that encourage your partner to elaborate on a particular topic. Probes are often useful after your partner has made an initial incomplete or superficial response.

"How did you come to that conclusion about Peter's position?"

ing you feel that way?" You might also probe for further details when you believe the response you got was deliberately superficial.

You know from our discussion of inner speech that communication is necessarily self-centered. Your personal needs are, simply, foremost in your mind most of the time. Yet egocentricity is directly related to listening effectiveness. Objective, other-centered tendencies are positively correlated with listening effectiveness. Individuals who are disinterested in the ideas and feelings of others will find it difficult to improve their listening comprehension, since understanding another person takes effort and energy. They may also have to pay particular attention to the types of questions they ask, since not all questions facilitate understanding.

Listen to the Entire Message

While questions are necessary as you seek clarification and check your understanding, there are many instances when comprehension suffers because you have been paying more attention to personal voices than to your partner's concerns. One way you can promote comprehension is to listen completely to your partner's ideas before interrupting, even if you believe your questions are important ones (Box 4.2). Keep

■ ■ ■ ■ ■

BOX 4.2

LET THE SPEAKER FINISH

1. *Monitor your behavior.* Analyze the situations in which you are most likely to interrupt. Is it when you are speaking with a particular person? When you are in a hurry? On certain issues or subjects? Notice, over the course of a week, when you interrupt and identify some of the situational factors involved. Increased awareness alone will decrease the frequency of your interruptions. If you can substitute a checkmark in a notebook for every potential interruption, you've taken another step toward breaking this habit.

2. *Listen to understand, not to refute.* Win–win listening is as much an attitude as a skill. It's a sincere concern for the other person and a spontaneous interest in what he or she has to say. Such listening is particularly appropriate in situations where individual differences make communication particularly problematic and additional commitment is required to create shared meanings. Remember that your first responsibility is to understand your partner. Only then can you determine the value of his or her ideas.

3. *Solicit help from your friends.* Ask friends to tell you whenever you interrupt so that you can become more aware of your behavior. Establish a signal others can use to let you know when you have broken into a conversation inappropriately. This immediate feedback will prove invaluable and increase your consciousness of a habit that is relatively easy to break.

in mind that whenever you ask a question you are redirecting your partner's thoughts; she may never be able to completely reconstruct the ideas that were on her mind.

Some people interrupt out of a need for recognition, to let others know what they think. This is called shifting the focus. Your sister might begin telling you what a stressful day she's had, and you immediately interrupt to describe the pressures you're under. At other times, interruptions occur because something the speaker says inspires an idea that you don't want to forget. Even these interruptions, however, sidetrack the speaker, who is stopped in the middle of a thought.

A large percentage of interruptions occur in conflict situations, or when disagreements arise. As soon as you disagree, your first impulse may be to break into the speaker's message with your own ideas. The urge to interrupt is the greatest when you have strong opinions and are listening to someone who also appears certain of his viewpoint. *As soon as emotions heighten, neither individual is listening effectively.*

A number of variables come into play in determining when interruptions are appropriate. Long-winded communicators, for instance, make the exchange of information difficult. Interruptions to manage the free flow of ideas may be entirely appropriate. Stopping a speaker to check the accuracy of your understanding when you are confused or uncertain is usually, as mentioned earlier, a desirable listening behavior.

It should be obvious that in one-on-one interactions, opportunities to clarify meanings are continuously available. The presentational speaking context, however, makes it more difficult for you to confirm that your understanding is accurate. In many cases, it may seem awkward to ask questions or request further information when a speaker is addressing a large audience. Consequently, additional principles need to be applied and strategies developed to ensure accurate comprehension in largely one-way communication situations.

> What are the challenges of providing feedback in public speaking situations?

UNDERSTANDING IN ONE-WAY COMMUNICATION SETTINGS

The significance of an idea is most readily apparent when viewed in relation to the "big picture." Making decisions, setting priorities, establishing long- and short-range goals, all are difficult if you can't put information into a meaningful perspective.

Often, you may find it difficult to make the distinction between main points and supporting details. One study, conducted to determine the reading comprehension level of 1500 Harvard and Radcliffe freshmen, was particularly revealing. After reading a chapter in their history text, the subjects were asked to write a short statement concerning what the chapter was "all about." The number of students who responded correctly? One out of 1500! The author writes, "As a demonstration of obedient purposelessness in the reading of 99 percent of freshmen we found this impressive . . . after twelve years of reading homework assignments . . . they had all settled into the habit of leaving the point of it all to someone else" (Perry, 1969).

The same students, however, scored well on a multiple-choice test based on the details presented in the material.

Improving your comprehension in lecture situations requires that you understand how presentations are organized, and that you stay actively involved in the listening process even though you may not be able to provide an immediate verbal response.

Patterns of Organization

One way to maintain focus on concepts rather than details is to identify the way in which main ideas are related to one another. This is particularly useful when listening to reports or presentations where the speaker's message is relatively long. If a speaker is well organized, the main points will be presented in a logical and recognizable pattern. If the speaker is disorganized, it is even more important for you to create some meaning out of the material presented. In both cases, listening for main ideas and specific organizational patterns will help you concentrate and stay focused.

Five common patterns of organization are (1) chronological, (2) topical, (3) spatial, (4) order of importance or order of complexity, and (5) problem–solution. There are, of course, others as well. Below are examples of each pattern as it may be applied in an informative talk.

1. *Chronological.*   One of the easiest patterns of organization to follow is to present the main ideas in a time sequence. Topics that lend themselves to a chronological pattern are:

> As a public speaker, what patterns of organization have worked well in helping listeners to better understand your ideas?

- Description of an orientation program for foreign students
- Directions on how to assemble a piece of equipment

2. *Topical.*   When the main ideas are relatively equal in importance and could be listed in any order, the organization is called topical. Topics that lend themselves to a topical pattern are:

- The benefits of three different Web sites
- The responsibilities of a teaching assistant

3. *Spatial.*   Spatial patterns are used to organize descriptive material around location or relative position. Topics that lend themselves to a spatial pattern are:

- Plan for remodeling of an office or room
- Description of a computer screen in terms of where icons are located on the desktop

4. *Order of importance, order of complexity.*   Here, the ideas are arranged according to some order which emerges from the information itself. Topics that lend themselves to order of importance or complexity are:

- Arguments for adopting a particular plan of action
- Explanation of a difficult concept, such as electricity

5. *Problem–solution.* Often, the speaker identifies a problem and then goes on to propose one or more recommendations for resolving the situation. In persuasion, he is likely to advocate taking a particular course of action. Topics that lend themselves to this pattern include:

- Business proposals
- Political presentations

Although you might like to think all speakers follow a recognizable pattern of organization, you may be dreaming. Listeners too often discover that the burden of sense-making is primarily theirs. One way to impose order on the ideas you hear is through the application of effective note-taking systems.

Note-Taking Systems

The President's Association of New York teaches executives that they can get 15 percent more out of any communication by asking questions and 20 percent more by taking notes. Numerous studies have been conducted to determine the effect of note-taking on comprehension and on memory (Aiken, Thomas, & Shennum, 1975; Carter & Van Matre, 1975; Lashbrook, 1976; DiVesta & Gray, 1982; Bostrom & Searle, 1990). When used effectively, note-taking serves not only as a means of storing information but also as a technique for making sense of the ideas presented (Howe, 1970; Fisher & Harris, 1974).

Although you may assume that note-taking always helps you to retain more of what you hear, such is not the case. The value of note-taking is determined by such factors as your personal characteristics as a listener, your purpose in listening, the type of information being presented, and your familiarity with the material. Waldhart and Bostrom (1981) propose that if individuals are skilled in a particular type of listening, what is referred to as rehearsal listening, then

> Does taking notes generally help or harm your listening comprehension?

they will actually understand less when they take notes. Another recent study concluded that while listening comprehension improved if individuals demonstrated appropriate nonverbal attending behaviors, note-taking appeared to have no effect on rates of comprehension (O'Heren & Arnold, 1991). Remember, however, this is not true for everyone. The usefulness of note-taking depends on the type of material presented and your listening purpose.

In academic environments in particular, there are numerous occasions in which note taking is helpful, particularly since the time interval between presentation of material and recall is often substantial. In addition, academic lectures tend to include important details that may not be retained unless notes are taken. Although your instructors are likely to assume that you will take notes in their classes, most students admit that they do not know how to take notes effectively and need more information on this subject. Many believe that taking notes interferes with their ability to concentrate.

There are several proven note-taking methods with which you should be familiar. Each has advantages and disadvantages. Experiment with different methods until you find the one that works best for you, or adapt a particular method to your specific note-taking requirements (Box 4.3).

Concept versus Fact Method.   This method focuses your attention on the main points of the message. To use the concept versus fact technique, draw a vertical line down the center of your paper. On the left side jot down the speaker's main points as they occur. In the right column, indicate any supporting evidence, examples, and other information used to clarify these concepts. If the rate of presentation becomes too fast to get everything recorded, you will be able to make informed decisions about what information to include in your notes.

Not only is the concept versus fact method easy to use, it also provides a quick reference when you need to recall information later on. Even when listening to material that has not been carefully organized, you still may be able to identify the main points and impose some structure on what you hear by distinguishing main ideas from supporting data (Box 4.4).

Outline Method.   An outline format serves as an effective note-taking system since it makes the relationship of ideas readily apparent. Main ideas, usually designated by Roman numerals, are noted in phrases or one-word reminders. The accompanying evidence, or support, is then indicated by capital letters, numbers, and small letters (Box 4.5). This method is particularly appropriate when the speaker's presentation is well planned and logically organized. Note takers who get caught up in making the information they hear fit into a preconceived outline format, however, may distort the speaker's intent.

When listening to your class lectures, you may find powerpoint or other computer-generated presentations particularly easy to follow when they have been

■ ■ ■ ■ ■

BOX 4.3

NOTE-TAKING REMINDERS

1. Note-taking is usually perceived as a positive action. It demonstrates that you value the communicator's ideas.

2. Note-taking is situational. It is appropriate when facts or ideas must be recalled or when it helps keep the listener focused on the speaker's message. It is not appropriate when the speaker is talking about highly personal information.

3. Note-taking is learned. Through practice, you will be able to take notes while maintaining a high level of comprehension.

4. Be prepared to take notes; keep a notebook and pencil readily available in your pocket or purse.

■ ■ ■ ■ ■

BOX 4.4

CONCEPT VERSUS FACT METHOD

Concept	*Fact*
The sun is harmful (main topic)	
Greeks' view of sun exposure— recognized only the benefits	Hippocrates—sun for health
	Herodotus—necessary for recovery
	Tan is response to solar damage
	Sun has negative cumulative effect
Today's scientific facts are different	Heat stress—causes cramps, dizziness
	Heat exhaustion—nausea, faintness
Sun viewed as harmful	Heatstroke is life threatening
	Skin and hair damage
	Skin cancer
	Stay away 10:00 a.m.–3:00 p.m.
Sun has many harmful effects	Sun is stronger at high altitudes
	Tan slowly
Damage can be prevented	Wear a sunscreen

created around one of the boiler-plate organizational patterns. These guidelines not only help the presenter to develop ideas more completely and logically, but they also help you as a listener to make sense of the information that you hear. Such boiler plates may take the form of bulleted key points or may be developed as elaborate outlines. Think about how your listening is affected by having the notes presented as a visual while the speaker is talking.

Précis. A précis is a summary, in your own words, of the important ideas presented by the speaker. Here, you listen carefully for a few minutes and, when you sense a logical break in the material, you write down the essential

━ ━ ━ ━ ━━━━━
What would explain two people generating two different précis from the same source?
━━━━━

information. This method is very much like a verbal paraphrase. One advantage of the précis form is that its effectiveness does not depend on the speaker's organization. As long as you capture the essential elements of the message, your notes will be complete (Box 4.6).

Mapping. Mapping involves organizing information visually so that the relationships among ideas become apparent. Main ideas are recorded in the center of a page, leaving room on the sides for supporting information. Generally, underlining or circling the main points further distinguishes them from significant details, which are then written on the sides of the page and connected by lines which radiate out from the ideas they support. The final visual model is generally brief, clear, and easy to review (Miccinati, 1988; Pauk, 1989).

BOX 4.5

OUTLINE METHOD

TOPIC: The Sun Is Harmful

I. Background
  A. How the Greeks Viewed Sun Exposure
    1. Hippocrates
    2. Herodotus
  B. Scientific Facts Today
    1. Tanned skin is damaged skin
    2. Solar damage has a cumulative effect
II. Harmful Effects of Sun Exposure
  A. Stages of Sunstroke
    1. Heat stress
    2. Heat exhaustion
    3. Heatstroke
  B. Skin and Hair Damage
    1. Destroys skin cells' ability to reproduce and repair themselves
    2. Skin looks old, dehydrated
    3. Damage is irreversible
    4. Dries out hair

  C. Skin Cancer
    1. Malignant melanoma strikes 15,000 people each year
    2. Incidence of malignant melanoma has increased 340% in 10 years
    3. Highest death rate from melanoma is in Australia, Arizona, Southern California—only link is sunny weather
III. Preventive Measures
  A. Don't Be Tricked by the Sun
    1. Rays strongest between 10:00 a.m. and 3:00 p.m.
    2. Sun stronger at higher altitudes
    3. Ultraviolet rays penetrate cloud cover
  B. Tan Slowly
  C. Don't Wear Clear Glasses
    1. Intensifies ultraviolet exposure
    2. Eye area particularly prone to skin cancer
  D. Wear a Sunscreen

Using Notes Effectively

Now that you have notes, what are you going to do with them? Although the process of note taking itself is valuable, what you do with your notes is often as important as how you take them. Some actions are obvious; you review your notes as soon as possible, and then look them over again carefully just before you need the information you have recorded.

BOX 4.6

PRÉCIS

The ancient Greeks viewed sun exposure as healthy, but today we realize it has many harmful effects. Among problems: sunstroke, skin and hair damage, skin cancer. Damage by the sun can be prevented; don't be tricked by the sun, tan slowly, don't wear clear glasses, and protect yourself with a sunscreen when you go out.

One system for both taking and using notes was developed by Walter Pauk. The principles he suggests, called the Cornell Note-Taking System, have been widely successful in helping listeners better understand what they hear. The basics of his approach are outlined below.

1. *Preparation:*   Begin by drawing a line down the center of your paper. At the top of the page, label the right-hand side the Record Column and the left side the Reduce Column.

2. *Note-taking:*   As you listen, write down as many facts and ideas as possible in the Record Column. Concentrate fully and get as much down on your paper as possible. Use phrases and key words. Record statistics as well as key points.

3. *Use of notes:*   As soon as possible, review what you have in your Record Column and summarize each unit of information in the Reduce Column. Write your summary directly across from where the information appears on the page. Items in the Reduce Column should be more brief than your original notes, and may include statements or questions to aid in future review (Box 4.7).

■ ■ ■ ■ ■ ▬▬▬▬▬▬▬▬▬▬▬▬▬▬▬▬▬▬▬▬▬▬

BOX 4.7

THE CORNELL NOTE-TAKING SYSTEM

Reduce Column	*Record Column*
What are the components of the HURIER model?	HURIER model represents six integrated listening skills: hearing, understanding, remembering, interpreting, evaluating, and responding.
How is the model helpful in improving listening?	Provides way to assess and teach behavior
Why is listening difficult to assess?	Listening is difficult to assess—cannot "see" listening. Must assume it is taking place if certain things happen.
Do listeners always have a specific purpose?	Listeners don't always have a deliberate purpose. They may happen to be in front of a TV, hear something while walking to class, happen to sit next to someone who knows a lot about music
Under what circumstances might communicators not want to be accurately understood?	Communicators don't always want to be accurately understood—political speakers, senior managers in organizations, family members

When you are ready to begin studying, first cover the entire Record Column and use just the notes in your Reduce Column to recall and consider the ideas that were presented. You might want to recite these points out loud and periodically check your accuracy by uncovering the Record Column.

As you work to clarify this information, it may be helpful to add another sheet of paper to record your reflections or personal reactions to the content of your notes. This step will quickly determine whether or not there are any items you don't understand.

Finally, review all notes every week or so. Just ten or fifteen minutes a session will go a long way toward aiding both your comprehension and your recall.

SUMMARY

Listening comprehension was one of the first aspects of listening to attract the attention of researchers and educators. The complicated process of assigning meaning to symbols has both individual and cultural dimensions. Suggestions that language and thought are intimately related raise additional issues and questions.

The concept of inner speech has important implications for listening effectiveness. The unique, personal associations individuals make with regard to the words they hear creates additional challenges for those who strive to create shared meanings.

After becoming familiar with the cognitive processes involved in listening comprehension, it is also helpful to explore behaviors that facilitate understanding in both two-way and one-way communication settings. Asking appropriate and well-timed questions, particularly perception-checking, is a key means of encouraging effective interpersonal communication. At the public level, you can learn to recognize organizational patterns and develop note-taking strategies to better understand a communicator's purpose and logic.

APPLICATIONS

Application 1: Increase Your Vocabulary
Application 2: Keep in Touch with Your Inner Speech
Application 3: Listen to the Entire Message
Application 4: Ask Relevant Questions
Application 5: Listen for Main Ideas
Application 6: Use Appropriate Note-Taking Methods

_____ I understand my partner's vocabulary and recognize that my understanding of a word is likely to be somewhat different from the speaker's.
Application 1: Increase Your Vocabulary

_____ I recognize my "hot buttons" and don't let them influence my listening.
Application 2: Keep in Touch with Your Inner Speech

_____ I listen to the entire message without interrupting.
Application 3: Listen to the Entire Message

_____ I ask relevant questions and restate my perceptions to make sure I have understood correctly.
Application 4: Ask Relevant Questions

_____ I distinguish between main ideas and supporting evidence when I listen.
Application 5: Listen to Distinguish Main and Supporting Ideas

_____ I take notes effectively when I believe it will enhance my listening.
Application 6: Consider Taking Notes

Application 1: Increase Your Vocabulary

Be creative in your efforts to expand your vocabulary. Consider ways in which you can involve others to achieve your goals. Make up games. Challenge yourself. Keep score. Reward yourself for meeting goals and deadlines. Before you know it, such tactics will have become a habit, one that will produce lasting benefits.

Activities

1. Attend a lecture or seminar where you know the material will be difficult. Determine what makes the subject hard to understand, and what you could do to improve your comprehension. Is the material uninteresting? Is the vocabulary unfamiliar?

2. Keep a list of words you hear but do not understand. Include the many anachronisms used by colleagues and friends. Find out what each word means and write it down. You may want to incorporate relevant words into your own speech.

3. Keep a list of difficult vocabulary from your recreational reading. At the end of each book, go back over words and make sure you know all of the meanings. Are these words you might introduce into your own conversation?

Group Activities

Form a small group of four to six people. You may want to keep the same group for all activities, or you may find it more interesting to change groups so that you get to hear the opinions and ideas of a greater number of your classmates.

1. Compile a list of words that change their meanings according to the context or the background of the speaker (words like *crack* or *square*). Share your list with other groups.

2. Bring in a written message. Read it aloud. Compare the use of vocabulary, sentence structure, and style in oral and written communications. Make notes on your findings and share them with other participants.

3. Certain ideas can be expressed in a variety of ways. Look at the following sentences and then find at least two other ways of expressing the same idea. When you've finished, take turns making a statement which other group members will then communicate, using different words.

I feel cold.   Dancing is fun.
It's been a long day.   I hope I'm chosen next.
I wonder what to do.   It's nice to have a good friend.

4. Prepare a sentence or two that includes at least one word with which other group members will be unfamiliar. Read your sentence(s), and ask your listeners to identify the unfamiliar word and guess its meaning. If someone guesses correctly, he or she explains what led to the correct answer. If no one guesses correctly, share the correct meaning and then let another group member take a turn reading his or her sentence. After completing this exercise, you might discuss:

    a. How do contextual clues help to define unknown words?
    b. Does a limited vocabulary affect listening comprehension? If so, how?
    c. What happens when you listen to someone who uses words you don't understand? Think of a recent example.
    d. How can you let a speaker know if you are confused about his message because of the vocabulary used?

5. Compile a list of words that have come into use during the past ten years. What do these words tell us about society? Talk with several senior citizens to find what words they believe have either gone out of popular use or changed in meaning. Share your lists.

6. Discuss the ways in which language influences thought and the ways in which thought influences language. How do these two interrelate? Which do you believe is the strongest force?

7. Interview two individuals, each from a different culture. Create questions that you think may draw attention to the way in which language influences how people think about certain ideas or events. Make sure that you ask these two people the same questions during your interviews. Share your findings with members of the group. Were there any differences that could be attributed to differences in language?

Application 2: Keep in Touch with Your Inner Speech

The way you communicate with yourself influences the way you communicate with others. Becoming more aware of your inner speech—how you think about your thinking—is the first step to using it productively in communication situations. Self-talk has been used in therapy with athletes and in other situations where positive self-messages are key to successful performance. Through self-talk you can also address blocks to effective listening, such as personal bias and stereotyping.

Activities

1. It may be easiest to monitor your inner speech when you are particularly conscious of the process. Next time you have a research paper or report to write, try to focus on your inner speech. How do you use inner speech to make decisions and monitor your behavior? What role does this process serve as you formulate your ideas?

2. Identify any biases that you have as you engage in inner speech. If you dislike multiple choice examinations and have just heard that you're having one the following week, what goes through your mind? Identify and list some of the words that have strong associations for you due to your past experiences.

3. How does stress affect your inner speech? Can you recall a situation where you needed to think clearly, for example in an examination situation, but you were blocked by self-messages resulting from anxiety? How did you work through this situation?

Group Activities

Form a small group of four to six people. You may want to keep the same group for all activities, or you may find it more interesting to change groups so that you get to hear the opinions and ideas of a greater number of your classmates.

1. In what ways do you use inner speech productively? Under what circumstances are you most conscious of this process? Generate a list that includes responses from all group members. Then go back through the list to determine what items everyone has in common, and which ones are unique to particular individuals.

2. Pretend that your instructor has just asked you to make an impromptu speech on your listening strengths and weaknesses. You have three minutes to prepare. Go ahead and prepare as if you were really going to deliver the presentation, focusing on your inner speech. Now, share the process you observed with other members of your group. Thinking about your thinking may not come easily at first, but the ability to monitor this process will prove valuable later on.

Application 3: Listen to the Entire Message

Perhaps you've had a hectic day and turn to a classmate sighing, "What an afternoon! For a while I didn't think I was going to make it! I had a statistics exam, and then the disk with a paper that I was writing for my composition class crashed. . . ." "Oh!" your friend exclaims, "I thought I was the only one with a miserable day. Listen to this. I was on my way out of the apartment when. . . ." Is anyone listening?

Activities

1. Keep a journal for a week. Record the number of times you catch yourself and others interrupting each day. Note who you were speaking with, the time of day, and the topic. Are there any recurring patterns? Do you interrupt some people more than others? Research indicates that males interrupt females more frequently than they do other males. Do you find this to be true?

2. Try to determine the reasons for your interruptions. Are you adding important information to the conversation? Are you relating your ideas and experiences to the topic? Do your reasons vary, or is there a "theme" to this behavior? Notice the other person's reaction to your interruptions. Do they indicate any discomfort or irritation?

   If you find that you frequently interrupt, solicit help from a friend. Try behavior modification techniques to decrease your interruptions.

3. Everyone has semantic reactions to some words.

   a. Identify the specific words or ideas that you react to emotionally (these may change over time).
   b. Try to understand why you respond so strongly to these words. What associations are you making? Are they valid?
   c. Talk about your feelings with friends and colleagues. Don't try to hide the fact that you overreact to certain language.

With increased effort you will find yourself responding less to labels and more to the objects they represent. Keep in mind that reacting to labels prevents flexible, situational thinking.

Group Activities

Form a small group of four to six people. You may want to keep the same group for all activities, or you may find it more interesting to change groups so that you get to hear the opinions and ideas of a greater number of your classmates.

Relate a personal experience to members of your group. As you speak, group members take turns interrupting and turning the focus to their own ideas and experiences. After 3 minutes, discuss the results.

a. What were your feelings as the speaker?
b. How did those who were interrupting feel in their role?
c. What suggestions do you have for curing an interrupter?

Change roles and repeat the exercise.

Application 4: Ask Relevant Questions

Appropriate, well-timed questions can greatly improve your understanding. While perception checking—restating the speaker's ideas to ensure accurate comprehension—facilitates shared meanings, other forms of questions force the speaker to adapt better to your particular background and experiences.

Questions for clarification can be either open or closed. Your responsibility as a listener is to ensure that you and your partner negotiate meanings, and that your questions serve to bring you closer to understanding your partner's perceptions.

1. Consider your strengths and weaknesses with regard to asking questions. Rate yourself on the scale below.

	Seldom	Sometimes	Usually	Always
a. I have a purpose in mind when I ask a question; I know what I want to accomplish.	_____	_____	_____	_____
b. I allow the listener time to think after asking a question.	_____	_____	_____	_____
c. I use questions to understand what someone says in greater depth.	_____	_____	_____	_____
d. I am tactful in asking questions.	_____	_____	_____	_____
e. I ask questions for constructive purposes, not to trap the other person.	_____	_____	_____	_____

After reviewing your responses, set a goal that will facilitate the development of questioning skills.

Group Activities

Form a small group of four to six people. You may want to keep the same group for all activities, or you may find it more interesting to change groups so that you get to hear the opinions and ideas of a greater number of your classmates.

1. Think of a decision you must make in the near future. There should be two fairly equal alternatives to consider. Pair up with another group member and talk through the situation. As you speak, your partner practices paraphrasing. An observer is asked to identify any inappropriate responses—advice or questions, for example. Your partner must use *only* the paraphrase.

    Discuss how you felt having your ideas paraphrased. Discuss how the other person felt providing paraphrases (the person giving the understanding response will often feel frustrated—that's okay). In what types of situation is a paraphrase helpful? In what situations should it be accompanied by other types of response? Exchange roles, and paraphrase your partner's feelings and ideas.

2. Find a help-wanted ad in a local newspaper that describes a position for which you could apply. Give it to another member of your group and ask him or her to prepare to interview you for the position. Allow ample time for the creation of questions.

    Role-play the interview for approximately ten minutes, then discuss the interaction. Were the questions appropriate? Were any probes used? If so, what did they accomplish? Did they reveal information about the candidate that could not be obtained from a resume?

3. Form a group of three. Person A chooses a subject of genuine interest and talks about the topic for 5 to 10 minutes. While he or she speaks, Person B, the listener, practices paraphrasing, perception-checking, and questioning. Person B cannot give opinions, advice, or any other type of response. Person C serves as an observer and records the type of responses Person B makes.

    Reverse roles at the end of 5 to 10 minutes. The speaker, Person A, again chooses a topic and speaks for approximately the same length of time. Person C again analyzes the listener's responses.

    At the end of the second round Person A and Person B discuss their reactions to the exercise. After the partners have shared their perceptions, the observer provides insight from his or her notes on both conversations.

    Discuss the following:

    a. Was it difficult to limit your responses to those three modes?
    b. What other responses were observed?
    c. What effect does paraphrasing have on the speaker? When might it be appropriate? Inappropriate?
    d. What type of response comes naturally to you in this situation?
    e. Did your observer agree with the perceptions of the actual participants?

4. Form groups of three. Select one person to be both timekeeper and observer. Choose a controversial topic such as:

Labor unions	Four-day work week
Flextime	Mandatory seat belts

    Individuals A and B will engage in an argument while person C keeps time.

Speaker A has approximately 30 seconds to present his side of the issue. Speaker B then has approximately 60 seconds to first summarize Speaker A's main points, then present his own arguments. Speaker A has approximately 60 seconds to re-state Speaker B's main arguments before refuting them and presenting additional support for his case. Continue this process until each speaker has had three or four turns.

Was it difficult to restate the other person's ideas?

How did the requirement affect your listening?

Did you feel that the other speaker was really listening to you?

Do most people listen in this type of situation?

If time allows, change roles and repeat the exercise.

Application 5: Listen for Main Ideas

The ability to perceive relationships among ideas can be developed with practice. The best decision makers are those who see the big picture and who are able to anticipate how changes in one area will affect other seemingly unrelated events. On a large scale, a flood in Florida may affect lumber prices in New England; the appearance of a new beetle in the Midwest may affect food prices throughout the country.

In listening to lectures or presentations, your ability to identify organizational patterns will help you focus on the ideas the speaker feels are important. Only after you are sure you know what is key in the speaker's view can you productively move to examining the facts that support his or her contentions.

Activities

1. Next time you engage in a serious discussion, check your perception of the speaker's main concepts by restating what you believe to be the intent of his message. Summarize just the main points, not the details.

   Do the same when listening to presentations. Do you notice any differences between interpersonal and presentational contexts with regard to the difficulty you have distinguishing main ideas from supporting evidence?

2. Think of two decisions you have to make. Write down all of the alternatives to each. Then list the long-range consequences each alternative might have for you, for other people, and events in the future.

Group Activities

Form a small group of four to six people. You may want to keep the same group for all activities, or you may find it more interesting to change groups so that you get to hear the opinions and ideas of a greater number of your classmates.

1. As a group member, select an activity or event from your local or national news. Share your selection with the other group members and, together, generate a list of connected events.

   a. What consequences does the result of each activity have on other people, on subsequent decisions, on the attitudes or beliefs of those involved?

   b. Who else may be affected, either directly or indirectly, by each action or event?

2. As a group, select one of the topics below. Create at least three main points using each of two different patterns of organization.

Topics	Patterns of Organization (use two)
The new BCX copy machine	Topical
A plan for reorganization of the curriculum	Spatial
Lunch hour policies	Chronological
Going home for spring break	Order of importance
Living in a dorm	Order of complexity
	Problem–solution

  a. What effect did the organizational pattern have on the content selected?
  b. What factors influence a speaker's choice of organizational pattern?

Application 6: Use Appropriate Note-Taking Methods

Your listening strengths and preferences, your listening purpose, and the nature of the material all influence the usefulness of note taking as an aid to listening comprehension. Make the decision about whether or not to take notes by considering your personal attitudes and past experiences. Often, individuals are ineffective note takers because they have misconceptions about its use and purpose, or for some reason feel embarrassed about getting out pencil and paper. In many cases, however, note-taking can aid listening comprehension significantly.

You have read about five common note-taking systems: concept/fact, outline, précis, mapping, and the Cornell system. The exercises below provide an opportunity for you to practice them.

Activities

1. Identify the psychological blocks or negative attitudes that might prevent you from taking notes. List as many responses to the following question as possible:
     I would take notes, but . . .

2. When listening, look for opportunities to take notes. When does note-taking seem to be most appropriate? Are there any guidelines to use in determining when notes will be helpful to you?

3. As you take notes, experiment with the five different note-taking methods. Determine which method works best for you, and with what types of material. (Remember, your note-taking ability will improve only with practice.)

4. If you need additional practice, try using different methods to record written material as well as oral messages. The principle is the same, and it will increase your competence for taking notes in listening situations.

Group Activities

Form a small group of four to six people. You may want to keep the same group for all activities, or you may find it more interesting to change groups so that you get to hear the opinions and ideas of a greater number of your classmates.

1. Write an outline on any topic. Make sure you have at least three main points and that you have developed each point thoroughly. Make a copy of your outline. Take the copy and cut all the phrases apart, leaving off the letter or number identifications. Scramble the words and phrases, and pass the set to one of your group members. See how long it takes them to reconstruct your original outline. Keep exchanging the scrambled strips until every group member has had a turn at reconstructing each outline.

2. As a small group, select one of the following topics and create an outline that conforms to the structured outline provided below. See which group can accurately complete the task in the least amount of time.

> Modern music
> Organizational life
> Cross-country travel
> The high-tech age
> Apartment pets

Structured Pattern for Organization of Ideas

```
    I.
        A.
            1.
            2.
        B.
        C.
    II.
        A.
        B.
            1.
                a.
                b.
            2.
    III.
        A.
            1.
            2.
        B.
            1.
            2.
            3.
        C.
        D.
```

Create additional structures and repeat the activity.

3. Bring in a passage to be tape recorded. Select material that has a clear organizational pattern and is of at least average difficulty. When the message has been put on tape, play it for the group. Each member takes notes, distinguishing main ideas from supporting points. When the tape is over, compare results and discuss. Use the following questions to focus your discussion:

   a. What note-taking system did you use? Was it useful? Were any problems encountered?
   b. What did you select as the main ideas of the passage? What differences are there between the ideas selected by various group members? What might account for these differences? Can you reach any consensus?
   c. What is the purpose of the selection?
   d. Should all listeners end up with identical notes? Why? Why not?
   e. What can the listener do to overcome comprehension problems created by a disorganized speaker? Whose responsibility is it to make sense out of the speaker's message?
   f. What did you find particularly useful or particularly difficult about the note-taking system you chose?

   Repeat this exercise using another passage. Assign each group member a different note-taking system. How were results affected? What guidelines might be generated for the appropriate use of each method?

UNDERSTANDING MESSAGES: SHORT CASE

Charon had been recommended by her supervisor for a course in systems design. Although she was presently working in production, she was very interested in management information systems, and her long-range career objective was to move in that direction.

Charon had looked forward to the course, which was given in-house on Tuesday and Thursday during the noon hour. It appeared, however, that most of the other people who had been recommended already had a great deal more background in the field than she did. Almost all of the participants were engineers who seemed to understand the terminology and grasp the course concepts much more easily than she did. In fact, each session she felt further behind until, after just two-and-a-half weeks, she was ready to quit.

In addition to finding the material difficult, Charon didn't particularly enjoy the speaker. He was knowledgeable, but she had a hard time following what he was saying. She would be trying to understand one concept while he was moving right ahead to the next, until she found herself becoming so frustrated she would quit listening entirely.

Charon wanted to do well in the course; at least, she wanted to pass it. There would be a required written examination after the twelfth session. She felt so confused and so far behind, however, that after five sessions she wondered if she should just quit.

Questions

1. What were Charon's reasons for not understanding the course material? Do you think these were true?

2. What could Charon do to increase her listening comprehension during class?

3. What could Charon do to help her listening comprehension outside of class?

4. Can you relate to Charon's situation? What self-help measures have you taken in the past that you could recommend?

5. Do you think Charon should drop the course? If not, outline an entire strategy that she might follow to increase her understanding of the material presented.

FIRST-SEMESTER FRESHMAN: CASE QUESTIONS

1. What inner speech might be going on in the following situations:

    a. When Nikki meets with Dr. Gregg?
    b. When Nikki is trying to concentrate on Dr. Perry's physical science lecture?

2. What were some of the differences between Dr. Gregg's assumptions and Nikki's? Role-play the situation when Nikki goes to Dr. Gregg for advisement as it was presented in the case.

    a. How did different assumptions affect their understanding and definition of the situation?
    b. What was the consequence for both the task and the relationship dimensions of their communication?
    c. Could anything have been done to prevent the problems that arose from this lack of common ground?

        What might Nikki have done to better prepare for the meeting and improve her understanding of the situation?

3. How did Nikki's background and Sunmee's affect their understanding of college, studying, and related concerns?

4. What were some of the obstacles to effective listening that were blocking Nikki from understanding what Sunmee was saying when she confronted Nikki with her feelings about their study sessions?

    a. What role did vocabulary play?
    b. What would Sunmee's inner speech sound like? How about Nikki's?
    c. What semantic reactions did Nikki have?

5. What were some of the listening problems Nikki experienced when she tried to focus on Dr. Perry's physical science lecture?

    a. What or who caused each of these problems?
    b. How might Nikki have worked to overcome the obstacles she confronted?

c. Nikki was confident that she could quickly improve her comprehension and be more helpful to Sunmee. Are you as confident as she is that these problems can be permanently overcome?

6. Role-play the confrontation between Sunmee and Nikki the way it was described in the case. Then role-play the same situation again making Nikki an effective listener. What differences do you notice?

7. What listening strategies would you recommend Nikki apply to Dr. Perry's lectures?

BIBLIOGRAPHY

Aiken, E., Thomas, S., & Shennum, W. (1975). Memory for a lecture: Effects of notes, lecture rate, and informational density. *Journal of Educational Psychology, 67*, 439–444.

Bostrom, R. N. (1990). *Listening behavior: Measurement & application.* New York: The Guilford Press.

Bostrom, R. N., & Searle, D. B. (1990). Encoding, media, affect, and gender. In Robert N. Bostrom (Ed.), *Listening Behavior: Measurement & Application.* pp. 25–41. New York: The Guilford Press.

Carter, J., & Van Matre, N. (1975). Note-taking vs. note-having. *Journal of Educational Psychology, 67*, 900–904.

Clampitt, P. G. (1991). *Communicating for managerial effectiveness.* Newbury Park, CA: Sage Publishers.

Dance, F. E. X. (1979). Acoustic trigger to conceptualization. *Health Communication Informatics, 5*, 203–213.

DiVesta, F., & Gray, G. (1982). Listening and notetaking. *Journal of Educational Psychology, 63*, 8–14.

Eisenberg, E. (1984). Ambiguity as strategy in organizational communication. *Communication Monographs, 51*(3), 227–242.

Fisher, J., & Harris, M. (1974). Notetaking and recall. *Journal of Educational Research, 67*, 291–292.

Howe, M. (1970). The utility of taking notes as an aid to learning. *Educational Research, 16*, 222–227.

Johnson, J. (1993). Functions and processes of inner speech in listening. In A. D. Wolvin and C. G. Coakley (Eds.), *Perspectives on Listening*, pp. 170–184. Norwood, NJ: Ablex Publishing.

Korba, R. (1989). The cognitive psychophysiology of inner speech. In C. V. Roberts and K. Watson (Eds.), *Intrapersonal Communication Processes: Original Essays.* New Orleans, LA: Spectra.

Lashbrook, V. (1976). *The effects of cueing and storage strategies on the processing of oral messages.* Unpublished doctoral dissertation, West Virginia University.

Miccinati, J. L. (1988). Mapping the terrain: Connecting reading with academic writing. *Journal of Reading, 31*, 542–552.

Minnick, W. C. (1968). *The art of persuasion.* New York: Houghton Mifflin.

O'Heren, L., & Arnold, W. E. (1991). Nonverbal attentive behavior and listening comprehension. *Journal of the International Listening Association, 5*, 86–92.

Pauk, W. (1989). *How to study in college.* Boston: Houghton Mifflin.

Perry, W. G., Jr. (1969). Students' use and misuse of reading skills: A report to the faculty. *Harvard Educational Review, 3.*

Vygotsky, L. (1986). *Thought and language.* Cambridge, MA: MIT Press.

Waldhart, E., & Bostrom, R. (1981). *Note-taking and listening skills.* Paper presented at the annual meeting of the International Listening Association, Washington, D. C.

Whorf, B. (1926). *Language, thought and reality.* Cambridge, MA: MIT Press.

CHAPTER 5

THE PROCESS OF
REMEMBERING

There is no such thing as a poor memory, only an untrained one.
—ANONYMOUS

OUTLINE

CHAPTER OBJECTIVES

After completing this chapter, you will

Become more aware of:

- the importance of memory to effective listening
- the control that you have over your memory process
- the ways in which stress affects your memory

Better understand:

- the three memory processes—immediate, short-, and long-term
- the long-term memory techniques
- the obstacles to effective memory
- the principles of active stress managers
- the ways in which increasing creativity can facilitate memory processes

Develop skills in:

- short-term memory techniques

- long-term memory techniques
- overcoming obstacles to memory
- increasing creativity
- reducing stress

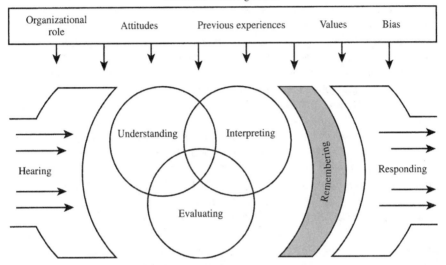

A Model of the Six-Component HURIER Listening Process

■ ■ ■ ■ ■

REMEMBERING: SITUATION AND PURPOSE

Your purpose influences not only the degree to which remembering is important, but also the type of memory involved. When listening to help someone through an emotional crisis or when listening to music, for instance, your ability to remember specific information is not as important as your general response.

Perhaps your most frequent application of memory right now is in listening to class lectures and preparing for examinations that will test your listening comprehension. Later, your memory will affect your performance in the workplace as you acquire and apply new knowledge and skills on the job. Your memory easily can be improved through practice and the application of long-term memory techniques.

The ability to remember accurately also becomes critical when listening to instructions or directions—especially in times of crisis. Researchers have concluded that the memory process required for interpersonal exchanges is different from that involved in listening and remembering lecture material. You may be able to participate effectively in group discussions or conversations, but have difficulty when listening in large lecture classes.

CASE: RUNNING LATE

Daman couldn't remember when he had gotten up in the morning and not had a million things on his mind. "Tuesday," he thought as he opened his eyes and rolled over to look at the alarm. The numbers were blurry. He shut his eyes again and pushed the snooze button. It seemed to him that he was always tired. Since he had taken on that second job last month, in anticipation of his wedding to Beth in the spring, he had felt under even more pressure than ever. In two more years he would have his degree in criminal justice and then, finally, he would be able to focus on just one thing. Until then, his classes at the local university, in addition to his two part-time jobs, kept him feeling tired and stressed.

As he got ready for class, Daman ran through all of the things he had to do and tried to figure out a master plan to get him through the day. First Astronomy, then a major test in his law class. He felt the pressure already. "Keys, books, pens, guess that's everything," he thought to himself as he started the car and headed for campus.

There was more traffic than he had figured, and by the time Daman got to his first class it was after 9:30 a.m. Dr. Barnes had already put on the projector, which displayed line after line of facts about the planets on a huge screen. His lecture went on and on—black holes, galaxies, light years, solar systems—Daman tried to take notes at first, then gave up. His friend Dora had recommended the course, assuring him that it would be an easy A. Right! Dora didn't mention that she and her dad were avid sky watchers. Daman only found out later that she had grown up with a telescope in one hand. Since he had no background in the subject, every term and every fact was new. The pieces of information floated around in his head; he had no idea how to call up the right responses.

Dr. Barnes was also known for his "pop quizzes." At the end of a lecture, it was typical for her to suddenly say, "Okay, let's see what you know." She would then throw out a series of questions: "How many light years away is Pluto?" "Explain the big bang theory in less than 20 words," and so on. Daman dreaded these episodes. He just could not remember the lecture material well enough to answer Dr. Barnes' questions, which never seemed to correspond to anything he read in the text.

Finally Astronomy ended. "Now the big one," he thought to himself as he entered the Law Building where his class met every Tuesday and Thursday. As he went to pull open the classroom door, he saw a sign that said, "Reminder. Class will meet in Sage 433 on November 11." "Oh, that's right!" Daman suddenly remembered that his instructor had told the class they'd be meeting in another room for the test. "Sage," he wondered. "Which building is that?" Since he was running late he decided to start asking anyone he met.

"Sage? Sure," a woman entering the building said when Daman stopped her on the stairs. "It's not too far, probably about a five-minute walk. Let's see. Go down to the end of the drive and turn right. You'll be on Campus Road. Walk down about three buildings and then turn left just before the chapel. You can't miss the chapel, although it's set back from the road a bit. You know, someone gets married there al-

most every week . . . But you're not interested in that! Well, you'll be taking a shortcut and crossing over in back of the buildings on Ridge Drive. When you come out to Ridge Drive, make a right on Powers Road and then an immediate left on Sunrise. It should be the second or third building on your left."

"Thanks," Daman said as he jogged off, his heart already racing. The chapel. He remembered that she had said left at the chapel. Soon he found himself crossing the grassy quad surrounded by old unfamiliar buildings. "Now what?" he thought. He came out on Ridge Drive, but that's all he could remember. It was a busy road, and Daman was lucky to find two more people who helped him find his way.

The test was being distributed as he stepped into the large lecture hall. Daman fell into a seat in the back row and took some deep breaths to calm himself. "Remember," Professor Kendle said from the podium at the front of the room, "although it says to do five of six questions, I want you to write all six. Also, I don't want to see anything on your desks except your law dictionaries. No papers, no books, nothing."

"Great," Daman thought. "The one thing I didn't bring. I wonder how much of a disadvantage that will be?" He soon found out. There were several questions that contained words he was unsure about. He could feel them spinning around in his head. "Focus," he told himself. It seemed a hopeless task. He went on to other questions. In almost every case questions began with "From our class discussions, you know that . . . ," or "Provide concrete examples from the lecture." He just couldn't think. The material didn't seem difficult, but somehow he just couldn't seem to remember what Professor Kendle had told them. He watched the hand of the clock go around. "Thank heavens we only have to do five of these," he thought to himself. As he passed in his test book, Daman had a sick feeling as he realized how poorly he must have done.

As he got back in his car he remembered that he had promised Beth he'd call her at work when he finished. Although he wasn't anxious to talk about the exam, he knew if he didn't call he'd be in trouble. He saw a pay phone on the corner and pulled over. The information operator gave him the number, 724-9771. Just then he heard a siren go off and realized he was standing right by the fire station. He looked at his watch. At least it was just the noon whistle, not an emergency. He turned back to the phone. Was it 742 or 724? He was pretty sure of the last four digits, since his own phone number began with 97 and he remembered that the last two numbers were his grandfather's age, 71. But the first three numbers? Now he could hardly remember any of them. It was too frustrating. He slammed down the phone and got back into the car. He didn't want to talk with Beth now anyway.

The last thing Daman wanted to do was to make another stop, but he knew if he didn't get to the grocery store it would be another day of crackers and orange juice. Although it was tempting to just roam the isles, looking for appealing items, Daman had made a promise to himself that he'd stick to only what was on his list. He was proud that he remembered Beth had asked him to pick up five or six things for her, too. In fact, he was going to check with her when he called after his test. So much for that idea! What was it she had asked for? Bread, for one thing. And she needed paper towels and coffee. What else? Was it lettuce? Some vegetable, he thought. He put the three items he was sure about into the cart, already mentally preparing himself for Beth's annoyance when he came back with only half of what she had asked him to buy. Well, he had other more important things on his mind than remembering a grocery list.

As Daman stood by the produce counter he felt a sudden slap on the shoulder and turned to see his good friend Conor. "How's it going?" Conor asked as he leaned against the counter. "You don't want to know," Daman said with a laugh, although he was far more serious than he would like to have been.

"Well, Debbi and I are headed out to the cheapest restaurant in town tonight," Conor continued, "and you and Beth are welcome to join us. If you find later on that you've forgotten some main ingredient here, it might just sound like a good idea."

"That just might happen," Daman replied, feeling renewed anxiety about forgetting Beth's request.

Just then a distinguished-looking woman in a business suit stopped abruptly and turned to Daman. "Daman Windham," she said with conviction, reaching out her hand. "It's so good to see you. I do hope your studies are going well, and that you're making progress on that degree."

"Sure am," Daman stammered, as he desperately tried to figure out just where he'd seen this woman.

"Well," she said, looking intently at Conor and smiling broadly, "aren't you going to introduce me to your friend? Is he in the program, too?"

"Ah, this is Conor," Daman said. It felt to him like the silence that followed lasted an hour; finally, the woman continued for him, "And I'm Margaret Fuller, Associate Dean of the Criminal Justice Program."

THE PROCESS OF REMEMBERING: PRINCIPLES

How many times have you thought to yourself, "I know I listened, but now I can't remember what she said!" Unless you capture ideas and store them for later use, you need to ask the same questions over and over. Without memory, there would be no accumulation of knowledge, no learning.

> If someone doesn't remember what you said, do you feel that she was really listening to you?

It makes little sense to develop your hearing and comprehension unless you can remember what you hear and use the information in some meaningful way.

We know that the memory function is distinct from such activities as listening comprehension. Everything that is remembered is not understood, and everything that is understood is not remembered (Ortony, 1978). Still, these two processes are fundamentally interrelated.

Nichols (1948) first defined listening as the factual recall of information. Fifty years ago, the essential measure of listening ability was an individual's recall of lecture material after a specified period of time. As you may know from our discussion of listening assessment, the Brown-Carlson Listening Test (Brown & Carlson, 1955), one of the earliest measures of listening ability, assessed both listening comprehension and memory skills. Since then, recall has been used by numerous other researchers as a basis of determining what was heard (McClendon, 1958; Thompson, 1967; Palamatier & McNinch, 1972; Rossiter, 1972; Goldhaber, 1974). More recently, Bostrom (1990) has based much of his work on memory systems and their relationship to listening. Bostrom and Waldhart's Kentucky Comprehensive Listening Skills Test (1978) focuses on memory as one of the most reliable listening measures.

The memory function takes place in the association areas of the brain's cortex. Bentley (1993) suggests that our information processing is affected, to varying degrees, by such things as:

a. self-talk
b. other information that you were exposed to at the time of input
c. characteristics of the language itself and the sequence of words
d. what you were doing while listening
e. what happened between input and recall
f. the nature of the information already stored in your memory

You will discover how some of these variables operate in the discussion that follows.

Although there is still no universally accepted theory of memory, during the last decade our understanding of memory and its relationship to listening has been significantly advanced (Bostrom, 1990; Fitch-Hauser & Hughes, 1988), and more is now known about the complexities of the memory process as it functions in communication contexts. To begin, then, this chapter will explain how memory works and how you can transform and manipulate experience in order to remember what you have heard. The impact these strategies have on listening behavior is also explored.

MEMORY SYSTEMS

To appreciate the memory process you must understand three distinct memory systems: immediate memory, short-term memory, and long-term memory. In many instances these three systems are interrelated. It is important to keep in mind, however, that not only do you depend upon different types of memory in different listening situations, but some people have more natural competence in one type of memory than in another. In addition, different types of messages have different effects on listeners. Messages that are repetitive, novel, or inconsistent may have one affect on you and another on your friend; consequently, you may recall ideas that others can't remember at all (Edwards & McDonald, 1993).

Bostrom and Waldhart (1980) emphasize that the three types of memory—immediate, short term, and long term—are also involved in listening in different ways (Figure 5.1). A familiarity with all three memory systems, and some guidelines for developing each of them, is key to improving your overall listening effectiveness.

Immediate Memory

You are always collecting and processing information. Most of what you hear, however, passes quickly through your memory system and is lost in less than a second. The saying "in one ear and out the other" is not far from the truth. Information that interests you—that draws your attention—is briefly held in your immediate memory for further contemplation. You must then decide whether to snatch it into your short-term memory or to let it fade.

It is important to remember that the components of listening are interrelated. You may recall the earlier discussion about the process of attention with regard to

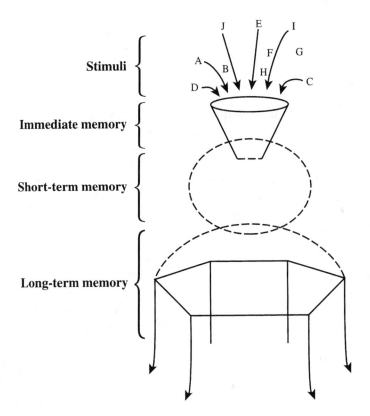

FIGURE 5.1   Types of Memory

hearing sounds. One of the reasons why paying attention to the right stimuli is so critical is that memory begins with attention. Unless a stimulus is registered as an impression, it will not be remembered and therefore cannot be used. Through focusing your attention, you select only a portion of the available stimuli and direct your energies along fairly focused paths. The Penguin Island example illustrates the wide variety of possible responses to one stimulus, each dependent upon what the receiver selected and how it was interpreted (Box 5.1). A useful way to view attention, then, is to recognize it as a process that funnels selected sensory stimuli into your short-term memory (Figure 5.2).

For example, a telephone operator uses immediate memory when she listens to a caller's request for a specific number and holds each digit just long enough to punch it on the keyboard. Much of the information you hear is held in your memory just long enough to use it; then it can no longer be recalled.

Immediate memory is an important filtering device, determining what information will be discarded and what will be kept for further processing. If information does not attract your attention, it never gets into your immediate memory system, and hence you have no opportunity to put it into short-term and long-term memory.

You improve your immediate memory simply by controlling and directing your attention. Remember to (1) focus your attention without letting it wander and (2) determine the most important facts or aspects of the message so that you will attend to and remember the right things. Since you recall only about 25 percent of what you hear, this is an important decision-point in the listening process.

BOX 5.1

PENGUIN ISLAND

In *Penguin Island,* France (1908) tells about a terrifying dragon who tormented the Penguin people. One day Orberosia, a beautiful Penguin maiden, disappeared. When she did not return her friends feared that the dragon had harmed her. When several animals disappeared soon after, the village elders met to decide what to do. They called all Penguins who had seen the dragon and asked them what they could remember. The variety of their responses is *telling:*

"He has the claws of a lion, the wings of an eagle, and the tail of a serpent."

"His back bristles with thorny crests."
"His look fascinates and confounds. He vomits flames."
"He has the head of a dragon, the claws of a lion, and the tail of a fish."

Then a woman, who was thought to be both intelligent and reasonable, responded:

"He is formed like a man. The proof is that I thought he was my husband and I said to him, 'Come to bed, you old fool.'"

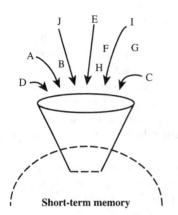

FIGURE 5.2   Process of Attention

Short-Term Memory

Short-term memory is your "working memory" and, like your immediate memory, it has a limited storage capacity. Had Daman applied short-term memory techniques, he should have had no problem recalling Beth's telephone number and dialing it seconds after the operator gave it to him.

Short-term memory is regarded as a necessary intermediate step in processing information that eventually finds its way into your long-term memory. Learning, then, only occurs when information is first maintained in your short-term memory. The longer the information persists, the more probable it is that it will be transferred into your long-term system.

Ordinarily, without rehearsal, you retain items in short-term memory for less than half a minute. It is probably to your advantage that information is forgotten so quickly, since there is no need to remember much of what you hear. From a listening perspective, short-term memory is important because it is required for appropriate interaction in conversations. In fact, there is evidence to support the hypothesis that individuals who demonstrate a high level of interpersonal competence are distinguished by their excellent short-term memories. These same communicators may or may not perform well in comprehension tests when it comes to lecture listening (Bostrom & Waldhart, 1988, 1980). While remembering lecture material appears to be related to intelligence, the successful completion of tasks that require short-term memory does not demonstrate the same strong correlation.

Once you have decided that you want to remember something, you must take an active role in processing the information. If you apply specific cognitive strategies at the time you hear the message you can, to varying degrees, determine what is remembered (Craik & Lockhart, 1972; Loftus, 1980). If your goal is to retain information in short-term memory until it can be used, three basic strategies are relevant: repetition, chunking, and the identification of logical patterns (Figure 5.3).

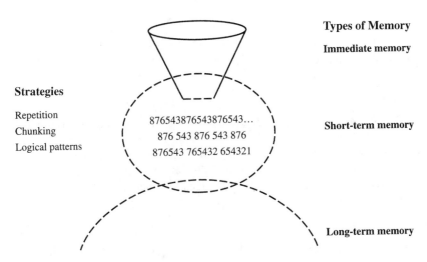

FIGURE 5.3   Short-Term Memory Strategies

1. Repetition

Nothing in short-term memory lasts for very long without constant repetition. Simply recite your list silently, over and over: "Software, books, palm pilot, tape, thumb tacks, stapler." Interference of any kind has a devastating effect on short-term memory. You've likely had a friend who, knowing you were trying to remember something, good-naturedly interrupted with irrelevant information or mixed up the sequence of items on your list. Such interruptions are effective; in fact, interference is the primary factor determining the rate of short-term memory loss.

2. Chunking

Another way to maintain information in short-term memory—and to expand its capacity—is through a process called chunking. Most people can rehearse and re-member up to seven individual pieces of information. Once your short-term memory is "full," no additional data can get in without affecting some of the original contents.

Chunking is a method of grouping items so that you have fewer units to re-member. If, for example, you had to recall eleven different tasks, you might find it difficult to keep repeating all eleven items separately. Using the principle of chunk-ing, you would group the items into a smaller number of units. If you had to repeat fifteen numbers, for instance, your chances of recalling them for immediate use would increase if, instead of taking each one separately, you chunked them into five units of three numbers each. Whatever grouping system is applied, it creates a means whereby more information can be retained and retrieved.

3. Identification of Logical Patterns

If you can identify inherent patterns in the information you hear, it is likely to be more easily retained in your short-term memory system. Numbers presented at regular intervals or in a particular sequence, words beginning with the same letter—anything that appears to fit together is easier to recall. When we recognize these inherent patterns or similarities instantly, they serve as effective short-term memory techniques. As Bent-

ley (1993) points out, memories can be available but not accessible. It is therefore helpful to listen with your recall needs in mind.

> What does it mean in your experience to say that your memory is "available but not accessible"?

When you want to retain information for future use, short-term memory is not enough. You must place information into your long-term memory, and this requires *active manipulation*. In fact, all long-term memory techniques require that you deliberately process information using methods of association that will enable you to recall it when needed.

Long-Term Memory

Think of long-term memory as a "data bank" or warehouse for all of your impressions and experiences. In long-term memory is information you heard hours, days, weeks, even years ago. It is distinguished from short-term memory in several ways. Perhaps the most important difference is that, while long-term memory (LTM) has an enormous storage capacity, input and retrieval are relatively slow. Often, long-term memory is not even activated until at least sixty seconds after presentation of the material. Short-term memory (STM), on the other hand, has a limited storage capacity but input and retrieval are relatively rapid. In addition, once in long-term memory, information does not rely on repetition for its permanence; interference, or new incoming information, is not disruptive.

One of the exciting aspects of long-term memory is its limitless capacity; in fact, the more information you have stored in long-term memory, the easier it is to remember new ideas. You might envision your long-term memory as an ever-ex-

> What are the implications of a human memory system with virtually unlimited capacity?

panding filing system where the more categories you create, the easier it becomes to find appropriate places for new information and to retrieve the old quickly. The following section on schemas discusses this concept in more detail.

Organizational Schema.   Schema theory is one of several approaches to understanding how memory works. Schema are organizational hierarchies of information established in your brain that provide blueprints for perceiving, interpreting, and remembering incoming information. These hierarchies contribute to creating the communication framework that was discussed in Chapter 2. Once established, the hierarchies influence your selection of stimuli and provide the basis upon which you make sense of new, incoming information.

The nature of this organizational hierarchy is an important predictor of your listening ability. The more elaborate the schema you have developed, the greater your capacity for understanding what you hear. When Daman realized that Dora had previous experience in astronomy, he understood why Dr. Barnes' lectures were easier for her to remember. She had many organizational schema already in place; new information could therefore be interpreted and stored in relation to existing files. When you listen to information for which you have no schema—in other words, if what you hear makes no sense—it will be very difficult to remember.

Existing schemas are often the basis upon which assumptions are made and missing details inferred. If, for instance, your friend mentions that she was given a table by the restrooms, you might infer from your past experiences—stored as schema—that the table is located in an undesirable, busy, smoky area of the dining room. Schema are constantly changing and being modified, thereby assisting in the integration of new and old information. If new messages have a strong structure, they will be integrated into your existing knowledge base. If the structure is weak, your mind will change the message to fit your previously held beliefs. Schema, then, are induced from past experiences and guide the organization of incoming information, thereby affecting future expectations (Fitch-Hauser, 1990; Paris & Upton, 1976; Edwards & McDonald, 1993).

Schema theory supports the notion that knowledge is a set of associated concepts. As organizational patterns, schema provide a kind of script that contains information about how to act in various contexts. If, for example, you are preparing for an employment interview, you know that you'll need to talk about your past experiences and your reasons for wanting the job. You expect to be told more about the organization and to be asked questions about your interests and education. You may be surprised to discover how many of your daily interactions are scripted, from placing an order at a fast-food restaurant to visiting the dentist. If you doubt that you depend heavily on schema, just imagine taking part in a ritual in a foreign country where you neither speak the language nor know the customs.

> What assumptions or information affect your schema for "used cars"? "international cuisine"?

It should be apparent that schemas are more important to your listening in interactive settings than in one-way communication contexts. In a dialogue, your response is based on information you have just heard. When you are engaged in a conversation—relational listening—the processing of incoming stimuli and the development of retrieval structures for recalling information take place simultaneously (Edwards & McDonald, 1993).

Schema theory contributes to our understanding of the memory process as it places emphasis on several important aspects of information processing. Perhaps one of the most important is that it identifies the central role existing information plays in determining how stimuli are processed. Again, you can readily see how individuals who have different backgrounds and past experiences will make different associations and generate different meanings.

As a listener, you have a great deal of control over what gets stored in your long-term memory. Memory models emphasize that the way in which you initially organize information coming into long-term memory is more important to

i   t   s retrieval than anything you do at the actual time of retrieval (Cermack, 1975; Hirst, 1988). Regardless of how much information is stored in long-term memory, it is useful only to the extent that you can get it back out again when you need to use it. Familiarity with long-term memory strategies, therefore, is essential if your goal is to remember accurately and recall readily what you have heard.

Long-Term Memory Strategies.   Learning long-term memory strategies, and selecting the appropriate method for any given listening situation, is critical. You use different techniques when listening to a speech than when you are preparing for an upcoming interview. It is well worth your while, then, to examine how long-term memory is facilitated through association, categorization, imagery, and mnemonic techniques. Keep in mind, as each strategy is explained, that these divisions are somewhat arbitrary. On many occasions, you will need to apply the techniques in combination to ensure that you remember what you've heard.

1. Association

Simple associations help you to remember what you hear. One of these is association by context. For instance, have you ever forgotten a name, but eventually recalled *where* you last saw the person? Settings provide a major cue to remembering. As you go through the mental process of trying to recall information, you search for contextual factors associated with the person or event. When Daman unexpectedly met Dean Fuller in the grocery store, he might have attempted to jog his memory by first trying to recall where he had seen her.

> If someone was afraid he would forget your name, what associations might he use to remember?

If you habitually make a mental note of the context in which important information is presented, it may well aid in your ability to recall through association. For instance, if you can remember what an individual does for a living, or what organizations she belongs to, you have established a link in the memory process. When you think of that person, you will automatically associate her with a particular company, volleyball team, or student organization.

2. Categorization

Random information can be organized into categories for greater recall. When asked to purchase ten items at a store, you may find organizing information into logical units particularly helpful. Are the items fruits and meat? Snacks? Beverages? Daman could have remembered the entire grocery list without any trouble had he taken the time to consciously organize items into several appropriate categories. Tasks, too, can be clustered according to the area in which they take place or the nature of the job—typing, telephoning, scheduling.

Any logical order that can be imposed on your information will facilitate long-term memory. In this way, information will be readily available when you need it.

3. Mediation

Meaningful units of information have a much greater chance of being remembered and recalled than unrelated pieces of data. How can you make sense out of nonsense? Try using one of several mediation techniques.

    a. Form a meaningful word (or association) out of foreign words or meaningless syllables. Imagine, for example, that you've just meet Mr. Chabador. By associating the name *Chabador* with the similar-sounding *chair-by-door,* you will aid your memory in recall. Anderson, then, would be *and-her-son.*

    b. Words can also be made out of the initial letters of the items presented. It takes practice to use this technique in your daily encounters. Some instructors, however, do the task for you. Were you taught the lines and spaces in a bar of music by remembering FACE? MADD, Mothers Against Drunk Drivers, is another example of how making sense out of items that may first appear random can improve your recall.

    c. Another mediation technique is to create a word that will link two or more words or ideas that you want to retain. If you need to remember cat, ball, and pillow, you might link them with the word "soft." This device aids in your recall as you connect the unrelated items in a structured, meaningful way.

4. Imagery: The Visual Memory System

Most information is processed into your memory through one of two channels; the visual or the auditory. Each system functions somewhat differently, and each person uses the two modalities with varying degrees of effectiveness. While visual cues only last up to 500 milliseconds (Sperling, 1960), auditory traces linger 3 to 4 seconds (Darwin, Turvey, & Crowder, 1972). Wolff and Marsnik (1992) discuss visual memory at length, and propose a strategy for taking advantage of this channel which they call the "Pictures in Mind" (PIM) technique. The authors emphasize that visualization, like other long-term memory strategies, is a deliberate technique that increases retention and recall of information.

> In what creative ways might you use your "mental theater" to help your memory?

Through visualization you use your mental theater (Wolff & Marsnik, 1992) to create visual images—pictures of objects, people, and events. The more concrete and detailed your picture, the better (Box 5.2). For example, which is easier to visualize, a young boy fishing from a riverbank or freedom of speech? Turning ideas into vivid images as you hear them aids in later recall. The ability to visualize what you hear gives you a decided advantage in tests of memory and, although some researchers suggest that the ability to visualize is innate, you can continuously improve this ability.

Recognition of the importance of visual cues to attention, comprehension, and retention has resulted in increased use of graphics and printed (often bulleted) text to supplement lecture material. In both academic and business environments, the use of visual support for presentations has become not only common, but also expected.

BOX 5.2

VISUALIZATION TIPS

- Visualize objects out of proportion, generally much larger than they really appear.
- Visualize objects in action whenever possible.
- Exaggerate the number of objects—instead of visualizing one key, look up into the sky and see thousands of keys falling like snowflakes.
- Visualize in color.
- Include emotions in your thoughts.
- Include as many senses as possible.

The ability to create your own visual cues—to create "pictures in your mind"—when none are presented can significantly increase your listening effectiveness.

5. Mnemonics

Mnemonics is a technique that combines mediation with visualization for long-term memory. Here, you create ways to make sense of the information presented and, at the same time, use visual imagery to make the impression vivid. For example, as you create the phrase *chair-by-door* in order to recall *Chabador,* you would also visualize the image described—a chair by some familiar door. Similarly, you might look closely at a person as you say her name to yourself, searching for distinctive physical characteristics. By combining the more meaningful words with a visual picture, you can recall more quickly and accurately.

Now imagine that you're at an important social gathering and have been introduced to several people: Mr. Toby, Mrs. Armstrong, and Mrs. Clipton. As you look at Mr. Toby you notice his rather large ears. Mrs. Armstrong has slender arms, but imagine that they suddenly begin expanding until muscles bulge from under her sleeves. Cement the image in your mind. Mrs. Clipton has very long hair, so you can envision several clips holding it in place. It won't be long until these kinds of associations become automatic (Box 5.3). Don't worry about how outrageous they are—no one knows what you're thinking. What associations, for instance, might Daman have made to remember Dean Fuller? Recall other situations Daman encountered and identify several of the ways in which he could have applied mnemonics to improve his memory.

Perhaps the most common mnemonic technique is the method of using loci, or location. The house schema is one example. The idea is to envision the floor plan of a familiar home and establish in your mind the location of rooms in relation to each other. Now, suppose you are presented with this list of items to memorize: a pail, a fish, a book, a monkey, a pile of snow, a computer. Begin taking a mental stroll through the house. As you enter the living room, there is a closet; the pail is hanging in the open door. Next you pass by the sofa, where the fish is reading a book. As you move into the dining room, you see the monkey dancing on the table.

BOX 5.3

HINTS FOR REMEMBERING NAMES

- Study the person's face and physical appearance as you say the name to yourself.
- Try not to think about yourself when you are being introduced.
- Repeat the name immediately after you've heard it.

- Visualize the name in printed form.
- Review the name again as soon as the person has moved on.
- Link the name with a feature of the person—"Barry" is "hairy" or "Paul" is "tall."

In the kitchen sink is the pile of snow, and in the hallway you must step over a gigantic computer. It is important to focus clearly on the impression these images make so that recalling the place in which they are located will automatically elicit the image of the item itself.

Instead of placing the items in a house, you might imagine walking down a street or driving through town. Practice placing items along your path in well-known spots. A story is told of a man who was skilled at this technique, but one day missed the object "egg" from a long list of items he was trying to remember. When he analyzed his error, he discovered that the egg was omitted not because his memory had failed him, but because he had placed it against a white wall.

Another way to recall a list is to create a story in which all items are included. The more outrageous the story, the better. If your list included radio, shoe, paint, banana, and cat, you might create the following mental scene: A lady comes home and finds her cat painting the radio. As she runs toward the cat she slips on a banana and her shoe flies off. When you need your list, just flash this mental image. You'll soon find yourself creating these wild stories almost automatically.

OBSTACLES TO EFFECTIVE MEMORY

As you might suspect, there are limitations on your memory system. These limitations account for how and why you forget. Forgetting appears to be an active process, largely conditioned by your attitudes and background (Box 5.4). Some of the most common obstacles to memory are discussed below.

Repression and Distortion

It is likely that you will remember things that support your position and forget or distort information that contradicts or is inconsistent with your current beliefs. One reason, of course, may be selective attention; you focus on things you want to hear

---

BOX 5.4

FACTORS INFLUENCING MEMORY CHANGES

1. Loss of confidence in yourself and your ability to remember
2. Fear that aging will distort your perspective
3. Sensory complications, such as impaired vision
4. Medication that produces side effects
5. Inactivity, lack of stimulating social contacts
6. Emotional situations, such as fatigue, distractions, stress, rushing, interruptions

---

As a speaker, how do you facilitate effective communication with someone who demonstrates repression and distortion?

or things you expect to hear. Distortion can also be explained, in part, through schema theory. Ideas that fit into your existing framework are stored more readily than bits of information that don't make sense in light of what you already know. In addition, threatening or unpleasant experiences are often blocked, or repressed, while positive images remain vivid.

Retroactive Inhibition

Another reason why you forget is that the information you are trying to store in long-term memory becomes intermingled with information already in your memory system. When these two information sets become confused, there is a "backward" interference of new learning on earlier stored material. This is called retroactive inhibition.

When subjects were asked to learn new information and then recall it (1) after periods of sleep and (2) after periods of normal activity, the sleeping group remembered much more information. Having less input of potentially disruptive information, there was less interference, and thus less forgetting. Retroactive inhibition increases as the similarity of the intervening material to the original information increases.

Primacy and Recency Effects

Primacy refers to the tendency to remember best the things that you heard most recently. When making a presentation, then, a speaker is wise to put strong arguments at the end. On the other hand, you also recall the material that was presented first, since the speaker probably had your full attention during the first few minutes of the presentation. This information, then, is likely to become integrated into your memory system.

Effective persuasive speakers take the primacy and recency theories into consideration when they design their messages, presenting the most important points in the beginning and at the end of their speeches. Effective listeners would do well to put more energy into remembering those ideas presented in the body of the speech.

Rigid Thinking

Have you ever had the TOT experience? This happens when a name or piece of information is on the tip of your tongue (Brown & McNeill, 1966). You know it's in your memory, but you just can't recall or retrieve it. When this happens, free association is often helpful. In fact, most people automatically initiate a process of free association when trying to recall information. The more creative you are in your thinking, the more readily you can apply association techniques that will aid in your memory and recall.

Awareness of these and other obstacles to memory enables you to reduce their impact. Then, you can move on to follow paths to a better memory.

> What inhibits you from making free associations?

PATHS TO A BETTER MEMORY

In addition to learning and practicing long-term listening strategies and recognizing the obstacles to effective memory, there are several other ways in which you can improve your memory. These include eating right, enhancing your creativity, and reducing stress.

Eat Right

Research has connected diet to levels of concentration and memory (LePoncin, 1990; Vos Savant & Fleischer, 1991; Bruschi, 1993). It is believed that foods influence the production of chemicals in your brain, thereby affecting your mood, energy level, and other aspects of your behavior. Even if you are skeptical, you have little to lose by following some basic principles of nutrition. Keep in mind, too, that modifications in your diet must be accompanied by other memory aids to have any meaningful impact on your behavior.

Basic nutritional guidelines include eating protein first at mealtimes, which will help you stay alert. Although coffee and other caffeinated beverages are generally not good in large quantities, moderate amounts don't appear to interfere with your listening. Be sure not to overdose on caffeine or high-fat foods, though, which will make it difficult for you to relax and to concentrate. While carbohydrates may help you to unwind, they also reduce your attention and may make you drowsy.

Remember, diet alone will not significantly alter your listening effectiveness; however, if you have trouble concentrating and remembering, you might examine your diet as one of many possible explanations and experiment with different types of food as one of many possible solutions.

Increase Creativity

Since many long-term listening techniques require imagination and free association, anything you do to increase your creativity will contribute, directly or indirectly, to your memory (Box 5.5). Practice incorporating more right-hemisphere thinking in all of your activities. While left-hemisphere thinking is analytical, planned, organized, and linear, the right hemisphere is concerned with synthesizing; right-brain activities are intuitive and playful. Go ahead and challenge your assumptions and stereotypes. Be receptive to new and unusual ideas. Identify your mental blocks, the "can'ts" and "shouldn'ts" that prevent you from examining the full range of possibilities in each situation. Conceptualize ideas using metaphor to make "strange things familiar and familiar things strange" (Whetten & Cameron, 1991, p. 207). Seek ways to interact with creative, stimulating people. Look for opportunities to meet and talk with people whose interests and backgrounds are unique.

> In what ways would relationships in your family be affected if everyone became significantly more creative?

When working in groups, withhold judgment until all ideas have been expressed. Encourage the greatest possible number of wild, crazy thoughts. Build on the ideas your friends suggest.

Keefe (1971) outlines the following stages in the creative process:

1. First, there is an "incubation" period where bits of information are considered and combined in various ways.
2. Next comes an active search for relationships with other information in the long-term memory warehouse.
3. Then, suddenly, the new idea appears—an "illumination" or "ah ha" feeling.
4. Finally, the new idea is tested for feasibility and desirability and then modified, accepted, or discarded accordingly (p. 69).

BOX 5.5

IDEAS FOR INCREASING CREATIVITY

- Join clubs where you can cultivate new interests.
- Go to the theater or a play.
- Play interactive games that make you think.
- Surf the Web for new ideas.

- Travel as much as possible.
- Volunteer in your community.
- Get involved with issues that you feel strongly about.
- Learn a new skill or hobby.

Listening creatively encourages others to share ideas and sets a positive tempo. Creative listeners recognize the potential in their friends and co-workers and provide opportunities for the expression of many talents. This attitude is particularly appropriate as diversity among participants increases in all group settings. In a non-threatening environment, everyone feels free to participate and to be creative.

Reduce Stress

Millions of individuals each year suffer from stress-related problems. As you know from earlier discussions of listening apprehension, the feeling that you cannot do anything about the stress you are under is particularly dangerous to your health and interferes dramatically with your listening ability (Box 5.6). Understanding the various types of stressors and learning to be an active stress manager both contribute to your mental health and, ultimately, to improving your memory.

There are four key stressors that may be affecting your listening generally and your memory in particular: time stressors, encounter stressors, situation stressors, and anticipatory stressors (Whetten & Cameron, 1991). In "Running Late," a clear example of time stressors occurred when Daman needed to find the room where his exam was being held. He became increasingly disoriented and anxious as he realized his time was limited. Encounter stressors result from difficult interpersonal interactions. Recall that Daman felt relieved when he couldn't get through to Beth on the phone; he knew the encounter with her would be difficult, and that neither of them would be listening well.

Situation stressors are also easy to identify. Daman was feeling stressed in the grocery store when an uncomfortable situation arose and he couldn't recall the Associate Dean's name. Finally, there are anticipatory stressors, or the stress Daman experienced in his astronomy class, thinking about his upcoming examination in his law class.

BOX 5.6

THOUGHTS ON LISTENING TO REDUCE STRESS

1. Just because someone is talking does not mean that you must listen. You determine what you want to listen to and when you are able to listen.
2. Listen to something just for enjoyment every day.
3. When an encounter doesn't go well, reaffirm your confidence by recalling past situations that have been effective.
4. Don't procrastinate by avoiding an unpleasant meeting. Think positively, and make that phone call or set up that date.
5. Realize that everyone is different. What may be easy for your friend may be very difficult for you. Acknowledge your personal strengths and weaknesses.

Stress, as you may recall from Chapter 3, is created largely in your mind. You interpret a given situation as either threatening or manageable according to your perceptual filters. Stress, then, can be reduced by positive thinking; you become what we call an active stress manager rather than a passive stress victim. The importance of self-talk in reducing stress cannot be underestimated. Your attitude and your perceptual filters affect perceptions of stress as they do other aspects of your communication.

> What is one of your most vivid memories? Why do you think that you recall this particular event so well?

A key to decreasing anxiety, and thereby automatically improving your memory function, is to take ownership of your stress. What happens if you say to yourself:

"I make myself frustrated when the printer breaks down."

"I make myself annoyed when I know there's a group meeting and I have a lot to do."

Contrast the strategies of an active stress manager with a passive stress victim (Box 5.7). You can readily see significant differences in the way these two groups cope with stress. It is no wonder that while members of one group are effective, those who take on the role of victim have much to learn about how to manage their behavior in productive and healthy ways.

Although becoming an active stress manager is no guarantee that all of your memory problems will be resolved, you can increase your effectiveness significantly by approaching listening situations in a balanced and calm manner.

BOX 5.7

MANAGE YOUR STRESS AND INCREASE YOUR MEMORY

ACTIVE STRESS MANAGER

1. Puts energy into areas that can be managed
2. Anticipates and plans for the future
3. Saves some time and energy for the unexpected
4. Accurate perception of challenges
5. Evaluates alternative strategies
6. Adapts a specific strategy to reduce stress
7. Takes care of health
8. Seeks support from others
9. Focuses on highest priorities

PASSIVE STRESS VICTIM

1. Leaves things to chance
2. Does not think ahead
3. Crams at the last minute
4. Does not use resources effectively
5. Little foresight
6. Lets problems accumulate
7. Takes on overwhelming tasks
8. Does not set clear priorities
9. Compulsive, stereotyped response to stress

(Adapted from Jaffe & Scott, 1984, pp. 86–87.)

SUMMARY

Listening effectiveness is greatly enhanced by excellent memory. Understanding the memory functions, and the ways in which you can increase your ability to recall, will therefore have a significant positive effect on your listening.

Memory involves three separate systems: immediate, short-term, and long-term. You cannot remember anything unless you first focus your attention on the words or event. In this way, information is available to be moved into short-term memory.

Short-term memory is required during conversations or on other occasions when you need to hold pieces of information just long enough to use them. There are three methods of retaining information in this system: repetition, chunking, and the identification of logical patterns. Since information is held on a short-term basis, interference of any sort will cause you to forget. There are many occasions, then, when your goal is to move information into your long-term memory system.

Your ability to retrieve information from your long-term memory is highly dependent upon the strategies you use to remember what you hear. One theory holds that long-term memory is dependent upon organizational systems called schema. Schema are hierarchies of information that provide categories for perceiving, interpreting, and remembering incoming information. Moving information into your long-term memory requires deliberate activity. Common long-term memory strategies include association by context and category, mediation, visual imagery, and mnemonic techniques.

Awareness of the obstacles to memory also can be helpful as you work to improve your ability to recall what you hear. Among the most common barriers are repression and distortion, retroactive inhibition, and primacy and recency effects. Rigid thinking also inhibits memory, as it blocks the free association required to recall past experiences.

Aside from mastering memory techniques and understanding what causes us to forget, there are several other ways you can improve your memory. Eating right, increasing your creativity, and reducing stress all have the potential to improve this aspect of your listening behavior.

APPLICATIONS

Application 1: Improve Your Immediate and Short-Term Memory
Application 2: Improve Your Long-Term Memory
Application 3: Reduce Obstacles To Memory
Application 4: Increase Creative Thinking
Application 5: Reduce Stress

_____I easily follow conversations and can accurately recall which member contributed which ideas in small group discussions.
Application 1: Improve your short-term memory

_____I pay attention to the important things going on around me.
Application 1: Improve your immediate memory

_____I can remember what the instructor has said in class even when it's not in the textbook.
Application 2: Improve your long-term memory

_____I listen to and accurately remember what my partner says, even when I strongly disagree with her viewpoint.
Application 3: Reduce obstacles to memory

_____I have a wide variety of interests which helps me approach tasks creatively.
Application 4: Increase creative thinking

_____I can recall what I have heard, even when I am in stressful situations.
Application 5: Reduce stress

Application 1: Improve Your Immediate and Short-Term Memory

In Chapter 4 you learned about selective attention and the importance of focusing on the key elements of your listening environment. As you know, it is difficult to keep information in your short-term memory because of interference from other stimuli in the environment. The exercises below will give you opportunities to practice the simple memory techniques associated with short-term retention. The most common of these are repetition, chunking, and the identification of organizational patterns. If effective, these techniques may automatically move information into your long-term storage.

Activities

1. Make a list of those topics that automatically get your attention. You can begin with your name, one of the most attention-getting words you'll hear.

2. Keep a journal, noting the various situations in which you use your short-term memory. Notice any interference from competing stimuli in your environment.

3. What current short-term memory techniques do you apply, and in what situations?

Group Activities

Form a small group of four to six people. You may want to keep the same group for all activities, or you may find it more interesting to change groups so that you get to hear the opinions and ideas of a greater number of your classmates.

1. Create an eight-item list (use any objects or words you can think of). Take turns reading your list to the group, pausing for two seconds between items. Then, ask group members three questions about your list. Below are some sample questions; feel free to make up your own.

    a. What was the fourth word?
    b. What word started with the letter _____?
    c. What word came just before _____?

d. How many words ended with the letter _____?

e. What was the next-to-the-last item?

Which lists were easiest for you to remember? Why? Did practice help? Did your ability to recall improve as you went from one group member to the next? What strategy were you using to keep the items in your short-term memory?

2. Make up a "history" for yourself—a new name, job title, place of employment, family, and so forth. Write down this information for later use.

Now, take turns introducing yourselves to the rest of the group (2 to 3 minutes each). All members must try to listen effectively, but cannot take any notes or write anything down.

Next, draw names randomly to form pairs. Introduce your partner to the rest of the class, including all the information you can remember about her.

After the introduction is made, check to see what was added, omitted, or distorted. How did you do?

3. Review the following lists and determine how you would use chunking as a memory aid in each case. You may form any number of categories.

a. Table, fruit, fork, milk, cup, orange, soda, apple, spoon

b. Hammer, ant, dog, nail, screwdriver, hoe, horse, wrench, wasp, pig, pick

c. Software, pencil, toothpaste, hard drive, cough syrup, monitor, ruler, bandages

Application 2: Improve Your Long-Term Memory

Only information that is stored in your long-term memory can be recalled and used at a later date. It is therefore essential to develop habits that will contribute to your ability to remember what you hear. If you are consistent in your efforts, you will discover that techniques which at first seem awkward soon become second nature. Practice is the key.

Activities

1. Look at the lists of words below and use a mediation technique to make sense out of each.

Shuttlebug	Fruitalot
Harris	Waldan
Johnson	Perry
Weller	Tailor

2. Generate a list of some of the more elaborate associations you have learned in order to recall information. How do you remember the lines and spaces of a music score? How about the number of days in each month?

3. Choose a concept that you believe is important and create a mediation device to help others remember it.

4. Are you able to visualize things easily? Practice closing your eyes and visualizing large yellow numbers. Try seeing just colors. When you are able to see colors easily, try imagining scenes. The more you practice this capacity, the easier it will be to use it as a memory tool.

Group Activities

Form a small group of four to six people. You may want to keep the same group for all activities, or you may find it more interesting to change groups so that you get to hear the opinions and ideas of a greater number of your classmates.

1. Generate a list of twelve items. Take turns reading the lists as other group members use the house schema to remember them. How did you do? Was there a difference between using repetition, as in short-term memory, and making deliberate associations?

2. Generate another list of twelve items. This time, listeners will visualize a large red number 1 as you present the first item. They should attempt to connect the item visually in some way with the number. They may place it on the number, under the number, make it a part of the number, whatever they find most vivid. Go through the numbers 1 to 12 in turn, as each is presented. Can participants recall all twelve? How effective was this technique in aiding recall? It might be fun to check the next day and see how many of the items group members can still retrieve.

3. Examine the list below and form a mental picture of each item. Which of the following are easiest for you to visualize? Rank order them individually, from 1 = easiest to visualize to 12 = most difficult to visualize. Then, rank items a second time according to: 1 = the images group members generated will be very similar; to 12 = the images group members generated will be very different.

   Share your rankings with other members of your group. Discuss why you ranked items as you did, as well as reasons for similarities or differences. Were your mental pictures similar? How do culture, past experiences, gender, or other factors influence your perceptions?

Easy to Visualize   Similarity of Images

_____	An elephant in a jungle	_____
_____	A lovable dog	_____
_____	A bank teller counting money	_____
_____	A liberal education	_____
_____	A couple doing the tango	_____
_____	English riders at a steeplechase	_____
_____	Superior transportation	_____
_____	Effective listening	_____
_____	A well being drilled	_____
_____	A graduation ceremony	_____
_____	A farm worker milking a cow	_____
_____	A hurricane	_____

4. Create a mediation technique for your own name. Then, determine a physical characteristic that you could associate with the word you identified. Take turns sharing your mnemonic device and getting additional ideas from your group members.

5. As a group, create a story that connects the items in each list below to one another in a creative and vivid manner. Share your stories with the larger group.

   a. Sun, watch, cards, apple, honey
   b. Butter, snake, tree, glass, fork, bite

    c. Book, fan, grass, towel, pencil, bug, radio

    d. Hammer, lips, blanket, nest, car, church

6. To practice your organizational skills, try this exercise. Create a large tray of random items—perhaps fifteen to twenty things like tape, a paper clip, a set of keys, and so forth. When trays are ready, exchange your tray with one another group has created. Take three minutes and, as a group, try to collectively remember all the items on the tray. When the time is up, the tray will be taken away and your group members try to remember and write down as many of the items as they can.

    One point is earned for each item that is correctly recalled; a point is deducted for items that were not on the tray. After the exercise is complete, determine the winning group. Ask these members to share their strategy for recalling items. Make a list of the ways in which individuals and the group as a team went about remembering the items.

    Do you think your team will remember these items two days later? A week later? It might be fun to see, after approximately a week, what items moved into your long-term memory.

7. Chose a partner. Your instructor will distribute a poem or passage to one person in each pair. You will then have approximately five minutes to "teach" your partner the passage. Use any method you feel is effective. At the end of five minutes, your instructor will ask for volunteers to repeat as much of the content as possible. After all volunteers have had an opportunity to demonstrate their skill, discuss the techniques each pair used to move the material into long-term memory. What worked? What didn't? What role did stress play in the memory process?

Application 3: Reduce Obstacles to Memory

You now know that distortion and repression affect your memory by causing you to forget selectively. Retroactive inhibition is much simpler to overcome than it might seem; you need to focus your attention so that new information doesn't intermingle with that which is already stored. Learning to use primacy and recency effects to your advantage will also help develop your memory skills.

    Keep in mind that motivation plays an important role in the success of your efforts toward memory improvement. It takes hard work and patience, but your payoff will be well worth the time spent.

Activities

1. Identify four unpleasant experiences you had as a child.

    Do you believe that bad experiences appear more positive to you as time passes?

    Think of past experiences that were extremely positive. How do you think your memory of these changes over time?

    Be able to support your conclusions.

2. The next time you have the TOT experience, pay particular attention to the method you use to jog your memory. Do you try to make associations? Keep a journal for a few weeks to document your mental process.

3. Keep track of the occasions when you want to remember something but can't. Could any of the barriers presented in your reading help to explain the problem? If so, what actions does this suggest you take to improve your memory?

Group Activities

Form a small group of four to six people. You may want to keep the same group for all activities, or you may find it more interesting to change groups so that you get to hear the opinions and ideas of a greater number of your classmates.

1. Recall the last time you experienced the feeling "I can't believe . . . !" What was the originally held position? What happened that was inconsistent with your previous experiences? Share examples.

2. Each group member creates a list of seven two-digit numbers. One member begins by reading the list slowly to the person on his right. After one minute of silence, the listener repeats as much as she can recall of the list. Note how many items were remembered, then move on to the next reader until all members have had a turn both as reader and as listener.

   Again, each group member creates a different list of seven two-digit numbers.

   One member begins slowly repeating the list to the person on his right. This time, the person on the reader's left provides as much interference as possible. The person who is interfering shouts out other numbers and tries to distract the listener by talking to her or asking her questions. The distracting behavior continues for two minutes after the list is read. The listener then repeats whatever she recalls from the original list. Note how much was retained, then move to the next person until everyone has had a turn as reader, listener, and detractor.

   Were there differences in the amount of information recalled?
   How does interference affect the listener?
   What can a listener do to minimize this barrier to memory?
   In what situations do you find interference a problem?

Application 4: Increase Creative Thinking

Increasing your creativity has benefits not only to your listening, but to your overall communication effectiveness. Creative individuals are generally more open and more attentive to their surroundings. They look for relationships, make associations freely, and are receptive to new ways of viewing their world.

Activities

1. How do you express your creativity? What are some recurring blocks that you notice when you need to be creative? These might be related, for example, to your environment, your specific role or situation, other individuals, your attitudes. Would it be desirable to overcome any of your blocks? How might you begin?

2. Make a promise to yourself to do at least one creative thing each day. No specific materials or tools need be involved—just your imagination!

Group Activities

Form a small group of four to six people. You may want to keep the same group for all activities, or you may find it more interesting to change groups so that you get to hear the opinions and ideas of a greater number of your classmates.

1. When might it be appropriate or necessary to form an immediate judgment on a subject? When is it appropriate to delay forming an opinion? What techniques can be used to help an individual delay his or her evaluation of an idea?

2. As a group, choose one of the items below. You will have four minutes to generate as many uses for the item as possible (*not* including its regular function). At the end of the time period, count up your responses. See how you compared to other groups. Repeat the process with another item. Remember, no ideas are evaluated.

   computer disk   suspenders   headphones
   chalk   paper clip   quarter
   pencil   cup   eraser

   Do you feel comfortable in this type of situation?
   Did you contribute to the list?
   Were you able to think of some "far-out" uses for each item?

3. Your group will be given a variety of creative materials—paper, crayons, string, cloth scraps, paste, tape, and similar items. Together, use these materials to create your own model of the creative process. You can approach this assignment in *any* way you would like. After 30 minutes, share your creations with other groups and explain your model. *Alternative Projects:* Instead of a model of the creative process, you might want to try one of the following:

   a. A representation of your group
   b. Your relationship with someone
   c. An emotion, fear, excitement, empathy

4. Think of a "process" or a "structure" that is familiar to you. Share it with the rest of the group and, together, generate analogues as they occur in other disciplines or fields. Examples include:

   A particular disease
   The operation of a machine
   The structure of an engine
   The structure of your family
   The structure of a flower
   A computer network

5. One at a time, each group member says a word. All participants then think of something they associate with the word. Perhaps the first person says *up*. Possible associations include *down, balloon, sky,* or *side*. Continue until everyone has had a chance both to present a word and to make an association with the words of all other group members. Discuss each member's reaction to this process.

6. Your group has 10 minutes to determine a creative name for itself. Share your choice with other groups. Discuss the process your group used to generate ideas and to determine which idea was most creative.

Application 5: Reduce Stress

You control your behavior, and your stress. Although some events are unavoidable, the way you approach solutions and your attitude determines how much negative impact the stress will have on your relationships and your memory. The following exercises will make you more conscious of how stress affects your listening behavior.

Activities

1. Make sure that you understand the different types of stressors by keeping a log of specific situations in which you feel stressed. Then, review your log and identify time, encounter, situation, and anticipatory stressors. Which type do you experience most often? That piece of information alone will be helpful in working to reduce your stress response.

2. What past experiences or beliefs contribute to your stress? Remember that you make yourself stressed. The way you view a situation is largely determined by your perceptual filters. Try to identify those that interfere with your listening and other communication activities.

3. Identify a particularly stressful listening situation that occurred within the past week. Write down exactly what you said to yourself—your "self-talk." What negative things were you assuming? What new things might you say that would be more positive? Decide what you will say to yourself the next time a similar situation arises.

4. In what ways are you an active stress manager? In what ways are you a passive stress victim? Can you generalize at all about your responses to situations?

Group Activities

Form a small group of four to six people. You may want to keep the same group for all activities, or you may find it more interesting to change groups so that you get to hear the opinions and ideas of a greater number of your classmates.

1. Go around your group as each person responds with the first thing that comes to *his or her* mind:
    a. One of my most common signs of stress is . . .
    b. Just before encountering a stressful situation, I calm myself by . . .
    c. Listening situations that cause me stress include . . .
    d. The last time I was in a stressful listening situation, I . . .
    e. I could become more of an active stress manager if I . . .

2. Discuss the concept of self-talk and its usefulness in stress management. As a group, address the following questions:
    Why do you think so many people engage in negative self-talk?
    How can you break this habit?
    Give an example of a stressful listening situation where positive self-talk might be particularly useful.
    What types of situations are most influenced by your assumptions and attitudes about yourself?
    How do these assumptions and attitudes affect your memory?

3. Each group member identifies one stressful listening situation and takes five minutes to respond to the following questions in writing:

   a. Is this an ongoing situation, or a single episode? In other words, do you expect to encounter this person or situation again in the near future?
   b. To what degree did you anticipate the event?
   c. To what degree can you influence the situation?
   d. To what degree are you satisfied with the way you handled the situation?

   After each person has individually responded to the questions above, group members take turns sharing their situations. After each person finishes, the group brainstorms ways in which each person could have been a more active stress manager. When the person feels *he or she* has enough ideas, move on to the next participant.

REMEMBERING MESSAGES: SHORT CASE

Riley's New Job

Ted Riley was enthusiastic about his new job. He had worked hard all through school and was known as a highly motivated person. He was interviewed by several companies, had two offers, and now found himself as assistant to the director of marketing for a large metropolitan corporation.

Although Ted was confident that eventually he could master all of the responsibilities of his new position, he found the first few days especially difficult. Once or twice he was given a series of jobs to do and forgot about something that luckily did not turn out to be crucial. Still, it was brought to his attention, and he felt badly about it. He also found it difficult to keep up with all the new people he was meeting daily. In his position, knowing names was extremely important; yet when he was asked to get one thing from one person, something from the next, and give them all to so-and-so, he would have an extremely hard time remembering what to do. Let's listen in on a typical scene.

Jim: *Ted, I'll be out of town tomorrow and Friday. Do me a favor. Salvo's report isn't quite finished because we're lacking details. Catch Joe Pirro and ask him for the latest figures on design. Give Maggie a call in purchasing and ask her if she has her portion ready. If she's not in—she may be at the national conference in El Paso this week—her secretary, Jane Stewart is super, keeps up with everything that's going on, she'll be able to help us. Tell her it's the stuff we worked on at last Wednesday's meeting. Anyway, Dave Peters and Bob McGinley also have sections they're working on, but I think those came in yesterday. Ask Sylvia to check for you. When you put it together—you shouldn't have any trouble, just ask Mary Bagley if you do, she helped me with the last one—give it all to Peter Martins. It's due Friday morning. Just a couple of other things. Give Nancy about three times that would be okay for another routine meeting. She wants to work out a permanent schedule. We need to make a quick decision on budgets for July and August. If you could draft some preliminary tables, it would help us when we get together. Make sure you do the com-*

parisons the same as Adam was doing them. File #43 has some models you can use to make sure you've got all the right information. If there's anything you need while I'm gone call 3082 and Sharon will get it for you. Oh—I told Sharon to transfer any calls I get to your office. Tell anyone who needs me immediately to call at my hotel, the Rivina between 8:00 p.m. and 11:00 p.m. Take care.

Ted: *Sure Jim. Hope I got all that.*

Jim: *No problem. Things should go pretty smoothly, and I'll see you Monday morning.*

Ted: *Fine. Have a good trip.*

As Jim closed the door behind him, Ted's stomach was tight. He "understood" everything Jim had asked him to do, but now he couldn't remember half of what Jim had said.

Case Questions: Riley's New Job

1. Why do you think Ted has a difficult time remembering? Is it him, the situation, or a combination of things?

2. How much of what Jim asked Ted to do can you remember now?

3. If you were to prioritize the jobs that were given to Ted, what would you say was the most important? Least?

4. Consider the case carefully, and then think of all the things you can that Ted might do to help remember what he hears.

   a. In this specific situation, what should he have done?
   b. In general, what techniques could he implement?

RUNNING LATE: CASE QUESTIONS

Discuss the following questions using specific examples from "Running Late" to support your points.

1. Did Daman seem to have any problems related to immediate memory—focusing his attention on the "right" things?

2. What situations involving short-term memory are illustrated in the case? How effective was Daman in accomplishing these memory tasks?

3. How did stress affect Daman memory? Was he an active stress manager?

4. Select two of the long-term memory challenges Daman encountered and, as a group, generate recommendations for the types of techniques that might be appropriate. Then create the actual memory aids. For instance, if your group decides that visualizations

would be helpful, describe examples of how the technique might be applied in Daman's situation.

5. How creative was Daman in handling the problems he encountered?

6. Apply schema theory to Daman's experience in Astronomy. What types of categories might be developed that would be helpful to him in developing his long-term memory?

7. Now that you have studied three components of the HURIER model, discuss your observations with regard to:

   a. Daman's ability to concentrate and hear what was said to him

   b. Daman's listening comprehension

      For each component, identify any problems you recognize, explain why you think the problem occurred, and recommend actions Paul could take to overcome each of his listening challenges.

BIBLIOGRAPHY

Bentley, S. C. (1993). Listening and memory. In A. D. Wolvin and C. G. Coakley (Eds.), *Perspectives on Listening,* pp. 60–77. Norwood, NJ: Ablex Publishing.

Bostrom, R. N. (1990). *Listening behavior: Measurement & application.* New York: The Guilford Press.

Bostrom, R. N., & Waldhart, E. (1978). *The Kentucky comprehensive listening skills test.* Lexington: The Kentucky Listening Research Center.

Bostrom, R. N., & Waldhart, E. (1980). Components in listening behavior: The role of short-term memory. *Human Communication Research, 6,* 211–227.

Bostrom, R. N., & Waldhart, E. (1988). Memory models and the measurement of listening. *Communication Education, 37,* 1–18.

Brown, J., & Carlsen, R. (1955). *Brown-Carlsen listening comprehension test.* New York: Harcourt, Brace, and World.

Brown, R. & McNeill, D. (1966). The "tip of your tongue" phenomenon. *Journal of Verbal Learning and Behavior, 5,* 325–337.

Bruschi, P. (1993). Mind aerobics: Releasing your personal memory power. Presented at the International Listening Association Convention, Boston, Massachusetts.

Cermack, L. S. (1975). *Improving your memory.* New York: McGraw Hill, pp. 26–40.

Craik, F. I. M., & Lockhart, R. S. (1972). Levels of processing: A framework for memory research. *Journal of Verbal Learning and Verbal Behavior, 11,* 671–684.

Darwin, C., Turvey, M., & Crowder, R. (1972). An auditory analogue of the Sperling partial report procedure. *Cognitive Behavior, 3,* 255–267.

Edwards, R., & McDonald, J. L. (1993). Schema theory and listening. In A. D. Wolvin and C. G. Coakley (Eds.), *Perspectives on Listening,* pp. 60–77, Norwood, NJ: Ablex Publishing.

Fitch-Hauser, M. (1990). Making sense of data: Constructs, schemas, and concepts. In R.N. Bostrom (Ed.), *Listening Behavior: Measurement & Application,* pp. 76–90. New York: The Guilford Press.

Fitch-Hauser, M., & Hughes, M. A. (1988). Defining the cognitive process of listening: A dream or reality? *Journal of the International Listening Association, 2,* 75–88.

France, A. (1908). *Penguin Island (L'ile des Pingouins).* Paris: Calmann-Levy.

Goldhaber, G. (1974). *Organizational communication.* Dubuque: William C. Brown.

Hirst, W. (1988). Improving memory. In M. S. Gazzaniga (Ed.), *Perspectives in Memory Research,* pp. 219–244. Cambridge, MA: MIT Press.

Jaffe, D. T., & Scott, C. D. (1984). *Self-renewal: A workbook for achieving high performance and health in a high-stress environment.* New York: Simon and Shuster.

Keefe, W. F. (1971). *Listen, management! Creative listening for better management.* New York: McGraw Hill.

LePoncin, M. (1990). *Brain fitness.* New York: Random House.

Loftus, E. (1980). *Memory: Surprising new insights into how we remember and why we forget.* New York: Addison-Wesley.

McClendon, P. (1958). An experimental study of the relationship between the note-taking practices and listening comprehension of college freshmen during expository lectures. *Speech Monographs, 25,* 222–228.

Nichols, R. (1948). Factors in listening comprehension. *Speech Monographs, 15,* 154–163.

Ortony, A. (1978). Remembering, understanding, and representation. *Cognitive Science, 2,* 53–69.

Palamatier, R., & McNinch, G. (1972). Source of gains in listening skill: Experimental or pretest experience. *Journal of Communication, 22,* 70–76.

Paris, S. G., & Upton, L. R. (1976). Children's memory for inferential relationships in prose. *Child Development, 47,* 660–668.

Rossiter, C. (1972). Sex of the speaker, sex of the listener, and listening comprehension. *Journal of Communication, 22,* 64–69.

Sperling, G. (1960). Information available in brief visual presentations. *Psychological Monographs, 74,* 1–29.

Thompson, E. (1967). Some effects of message structure on listener's comprehension. *Speech Monographs, 34,* 51–57.

Vos Savant, M., & Fleischer, L. (1991). *Brain building.* New York: Bantam Books.

Whetten, D. A., & Cameron, K. S. (1991). *Developing management skills.* New York: Harper Collins.

Wolff, F. I., & Marsnik, N. C. (1992). *Perceptive listening.* New York: Holt, Rinehart, and Winston.

CHAPTER 6

THE PROCESS OF
INTERPRETING

*Our quest for meaning in this world begins
and ends with facial expression.*
—*DALE LEATHERS*

OUTLINE

CHAPTER OBJECTIVES

After completing this chapter, you will

Become more aware of:

- the influence of your attitudes on your interpretations
- the impact of nonverbal behavior on the interpretation of meanings
- the importance of empathy to effective listening
- everyday listening problems caused by the misinterpretation of messages

Better understand:

- the role of interpreting messages within the listening process
- the nature and characteristics of empathy
- the three types of empathy
- the principles of nonverbal behavior
- the ways in which verbal and nonverbal behavior interrelate

Develop skills in:

- cognitive empathy—taking the other person's point of view
- behavioral empathy—expressing concern and understanding nonverbally
- perceived empathy—interpreting your partner's nonverbal and vocal cues

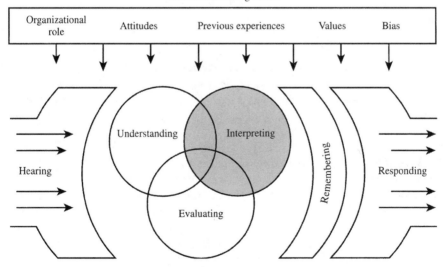

A Model of the Six-Component HURIER Listening Process

■ ■ ■ ■ ■

INTERPRETING: SITUATION AND PURPOSE

Interpretation is key when you are concerned with the *relationship* aspect of your communication. It becomes a primary factor in empathic listening, where your ability to recognize and respond appropriately to emotional meanings is critical.

Relational, face-to-face communication contexts are generally richer arenas for interpretation than settings where the speaker is less spontaneous and the message has been pre-planned. Although effective listeners are always concerned with accurate interpretation, it becomes a dominant component in cross-cultural communication settings; intergenerational situations, or other interactions where there are significant differences among communicators. Empathic listening is also a valuable skill for parents, teachers, and a wide variety of other professionals.

CASE: BURGERWORLD

Nadia flopped down hard into a chair in the living room and sighed. Her mother looked up and stared at her for a moment before venturing to ask if there was a problem. Nadia leaned her head back and watched the ceiling fan spinning around and around. She never responded directly to her mother's inquiry, but instead got up and abruptly headed toward the stairs. "What's the matter, honey?" her mom repeated, making an effort not to sound annoyed that her first question had been ignored. "I'm going to call Tina," was all Nadia offered as she disappeared into her room.

Nadia had taken a part-time summer job at a neighborhood fast-food restaurant. The money wasn't great, but it was enough to make her feel somewhat independent of her parents' good will. It was harder than she had expected to live at home again after being away at school. She knew her parents had no idea how hard the adjustment was for her. She was grateful for a break from classes, but already she had begun to count the days until fall semester. Now it was even worse, because things weren't going well at work.

Tina was one of Nadia's closest friends; from their brief phone conversation Tina could tell there was something wrong. Ten minutes later she was letting herself in the door and climbing the stairs up to Nadia's bedroom. She knocked and opened the door. "So what's up?" Tina asked as she sank down in her favorite spot, three huge lavender pillows in a corner of the room. She kicked off her shoes and stretched.

"Just work," Nadia answered. "Just my parents. Just me, I guess." She was lying across her bed, pulling at the fringe of her bedspread and swinging her legs in the air. There was a long silence. Nadia continued to pull at the fringe, placing the pieces that came out in her hand into one even pile. Tina took Nadia's cat into her lap and held up a piece of string for it to capture.

"It's everything," Nadia began. "But mostly work. I just don't like it anymore, not since the new program for the mentally disabled began last month. I used to look forward to working with my friends. We talked and fooled around, but we still got the job done. Now I work with a bunch of people who can't even speak very well, and it's no fun at all. They take too long. They can't do half as much as I can do. They live together and need transportation from the Center, so they always get the best hours. What's more, our manager doesn't even notice me any more. Part of the reason I took this stupid job was so that I could get a good recommendation. Since the new disabled employees came to work, Mark spends all of his time watching them. It's not fair. I hate it."

"Well, then quit," Tina offered as she stroked Puffy's long fur. "Quit if you don't like it. Tell Mark you got an offer to work on a cruise ship. Tell him anything, he'll believe you. You can do something else. You've only got five more weeks until classes begin." After a short pause she continued, "Besides, if you didn't work, we could hang out together."

There was a knock on the door and Nadia's mother stepped in to drop off an armload of laundry. "I hope everything's okay," she said with a worried expression as she looked intently at Nadia. "Fine," Nadia's said abruptly, avoiding her mother's gaze.

"She's upset because she has to work with those disabled people," Tina responded. "The ones that BurgerWorld hired because they had to. I wouldn't want to work with them either. It's not fair. I'd quit."

Nadia's mother paused. "Who are these people, Nadia?" she asked. "What do you think made them decide to accept such a challenge?" She waited for what seemed like a very long time without a response, then stepped out and closed the door.

When Nadia arrived at work the next day her mother's words lingered; the questions ran through her mind, try as she might to push them from her thoughts. She took her place at the grill and routinely began to put the beef patties in double rows along the back. Two of the "new" employees were working right behind her, and several of her high school classmates were putting on the condiments and wrapping the finished sandwiches. Mark, BurgerWorld's manager, stopped by just as she was finishing the first round of burgers.

"Nadia," Mark said, watching her crumple the empty wrappers and toss them across the aisle into the trash, "I've got a job for you. You know Sandy, here, is having trouble following procedures. She's always out in the dining room, never here in the kitchen when we need her." Mark put his hand on the woman's shoulder and pushed her gently in front of Nadia as he spoke. "She can't seem to get the hang of how we do things here—although heaven knows I've worked with her long enough. Every day I give her a list of what needs to be done and every day she spends all of her time sweeping the dining room. I was wondering if you could see if you could get through to her. I know you're getting your degree in education. I'm really good when it comes to working with normal people, but these guys are too much for me. It's impossible to teach them anything." He shook his head and smiled at Nadia.

"I'd consider it a favor if you'd take this little task off my hands so I can get back to my job."

"Sure," Nadia replied, a bit confused by the sudden request. "No problem." She looked past Sandy at the other employees who had all paused for a moment, listening to the conversation. Jay, who was standing in back of Sandy, made a face and then turned back to his job, laughing.

As she was cleaning up at the end of her shift, Nadia noticed that Sandy was also finished for the day. Impulsively she turned to Sandy and said, "Would you like to go over to the Fountain and have a soda with me? We could talk about the job." Sandy looked somewhat alarmed. She hesitated, then shook her head no. She turned away and hurried into the employee dressing room.

"That's what you get for trying to be friendly," Jay commented as he passed Nadia on his way back to the counter. "You go out of your way to be nice, and she doesn't even appreciate it." He made the same face again and then disappeared into the kitchen.

Nadia reflected once again on her mother's question. "Who are these people, anyway?" she wondered. "What are they thinking? Why are they working here?" Certainly not for the money, like she was. It must be a very frightening experience for them at first. Then she had a thought. Nadia walked casually into the dressing room and sat down near where Sandy was changing.

"I'll have to show you my car sometime," Nadia began, trying to seem as casual as possible. "My dad lets me drive it to work. Whenever I get the chance I go to the Fountain when I finish because it's just a couple of stores down the street. It's not a very big place, but they have eighty flavors of ice cream and the waitresses are really friendly. When I'm finished, I drive home. If you decide that you want to go for a soda with me sometime, I'd be glad to drive you back to the Center." Nadia stood up and walked closer to Sandy. She smiled and said, "Just let me know if you'd like to join me."

Sandy stared at her purse, rubbing her fingers slowly over the rough surface. Then she looked up at Nadia and said, "I like ice cream. You'll drive me home? I don't know how to get home. I take the 3:00 p.m. bus. Mr. Parker takes me home."

"I'd be glad to take you home," Nadia replied.

"I have to be home before dinner. I have to be home before 5:00 p.m.," Sandy ventured again.

"I'll have you home before 5:00 p.m. Don't worry," Nadia reassured her. "And I'll let Mr. Parker know that you'll be riding back with me."

This was a totally new experience for Nadia. Here she was, in one of her favorite hangouts, with a mentally disabled person she hardly knew. What if her friends stopped in? What if Sandy refused to get in her car when it was time to go? What if Sandy got upset and started screaming or something—what would she do?

Sandy held Nadia's arm tightly as they entered the Fountain and found a booth near the back of the dining area. "Are you ready to order?" Nadia asked a few minutes later after they had looked at the signs hanging above the counter. "Chocolate," Sandy said without hesitation. Nadia was suddenly aware it was the first time she had seen Sandy smile.

It looked like Patty would be their server. That was okay. Patty was some-times abrupt, but she was efficient and helpful. A minute later she was standing above them, pad in hand. Nadia waited. It was apparent Sandy was not going to order first, in spite of the nod Nadia had made in her direction. "I'd like a choco-late shake," Nadia said. There was a long pause. She looked at Sandy again and suddenly realized that ordering was a new experience for her. "Make that two," Nadia added.

As they sat in silence, Nadia was aware for the first time of the many sounds of the restaurant. She could hear the hum of the refrigerators, the scraping of wooden chairs against a wooden floor, and dishes being banged against each other as tables were cleared. She was also conscious of Sandy's movements across the table. Sandy's smile was now more relaxed, and she had set the napkin she had been twisting in her lap on the table next to her silverware.

"This is a nice place," Sandy said softly. "You're very nice to me." This time Nadia was at a loss for words. Before she thought of something to say, Sandy con-tinued. "Everyone at BurgerWorld is nice to me."

Nadia reflected on Jay's taunting gestures and Mark's impatience with Sandy's training needs, but decided to keep silent. Instead she said as she leaned toward Sandy, now focused completely on their conversation, "What is it that you like about working at BurgerWorld?"

"Oh, the children!" Sandy said without hesitation, smiling broadly at the thought of all the young people who regularly stopped for lunch at BurgerWorld. "I like watching the children. I make sure that everything is clean for the children when they come in to eat."

"What else do you do?" Nadia asked, surprised at her growing interest in this woman and in her view of BurgerWorld.

"Mark tells me to go to the kitchen, but I can't do that. He doesn't watch the children like I do. I've got to be there in case they spill something. They spill a lot. Their mothers like the tables to be real clean. I clean the tables for them." Nadia had never seen Sandy's face light up as it did when she spoke about her self-appointed role, and it was obvious that she took great pride in her job. "Have you seen the children?" Sandy asked. She was now looking directly at Nadia for the first time.

"Yes. Yes, I've seen the children," Nadia nodded. She knew, however, that she had never seen the children in exactly the same way that Sandy had. She knew, too, that things would have to be arranged so that Sandy could continue to take care of the children.

THE PROCESS OF INTERPRETING: PRINCIPLES

The listening component you are about to explore, interpreting messages, differs from other dimensions in that it requires not only motivation, knowledge, and skill, but also social sensitivity—an ability that is affected by differences in individual style. This makes it one of the most personal and complex components of the listening process. Effective listeners take into account the nonverbal and situational factors that influence the negotiation of meanings; in effect, they hear what is *not* said.

Imagine that you are having a coke in the student lounge as you check over some visuals you created for a term paper. A transfer student from the same class is sitting next to you and offers the following: "When I went to Rockland University last spring, I used a 760BL computer all the time and my instructor loved the graphics."

How might you interpret her meaning? By taking into account your previous interactions with this person and her personality, as well as the situational and nonverbal cues you noticed, you might conclude that she is insecure and uncertain of the impression you and your friends have of her. You interpret her underlying meanings as:

1. she went to Rockland, a highly respected university with plenty of resources;
2. she was a good student who took her work seriously and had a positive relationship with her teachers;
3. she is familiar and comfortable with computers; and
4. she is concerned and uncertain about what you think of her.

As you can see, interpreting messages is potentially risky business. You may be as likely to read in ideas that aren't there as you are to miss meanings that are essential for better understanding. That's why it's helpful to keep the relational model of communication in mind. It suggests that after you've learned all you can about your partner, that you continue to question your assumptions and modify your conclusions based upon the new information you obtain from each encounter.

This chapter begins with a discussion of empathy, the key element that enables you to go beyond the literal meaning of the words you hear and begin to consider the speaker's feelings and indirect messages. Those who are particularly skilled observers are said to have a high E.Q.; this is, they have developed their emotional intelligence. As you enhance your ability to interpret underlying meanings—to recognize unspoken messages—you will find the topic of nonverbal communication particularly useful. Relevant research on facial expression, eye behavior, gesture and posture, touch, and voice is reviewed, and you are introduced to the ways in which verbal and nonverbal behavior interrelate. Finally, suggestions are made regarding how you can apply your knowledge of nonverbal communication to become a more empathic listener. First, a discussion of empathy.

> What does it mean that interpreting messages can be "risky business"?

THE NATURE OF EMPATHY

The term empathy has been used in a wide range of contexts; still, no precise definition has yet been widely accepted (Macarov, 1978; Basch, 1983; Stewart & Thomas, 1986; Bruneau, 1989). The literature on empathy is extensive, and the ambiguity of the term has been both its appeal and its frustration. Like the construct of listening itself, empathy has been studied by scholars from a variety of fields, including social psychology, anthropology, counseling, and communication.

Types of Empathy

There appear to be three general uses of the term that provide a starting point for our discussions and which distinguish three separate but related skill categories: cognitive, perceptive, and behavioral (Figure 6.1).

How might the definition of *empathy* change from one culture to another?

1. *Cognitive Aspect*

Empathy refers to taking the role of another person and viewing the world as she sees it. Instead of thinking, "That's really a stupid thing to do," you would instead make an effort to look at the situation from your partner's perspective and think, "She comes from another culture and feels alienated and misunderstood. She thinks he was making fun of her, and her first impulse was to strike out. I understand how she must feel. Although I don't agree with her actions, when I think of it this way her behavior makes sense."

In the BurgerWorld case we have clear examples of times when Nadia demonstrated cognitive empathy. When the two women were at the Fountain and the server came over to take their order, Nadia noticed that Sandy was reluctant to speak. Nadia immediately responded by dealing with Patty rather than trying to force Sandy into an uncomfortable situation.

Later, Nadia came to understand that Sandy defined her job as looking after the children. When this was clear, it became obvious that Sandy's interpretation was in conflict with Mark's understanding and expectations. Nadia developed empathy

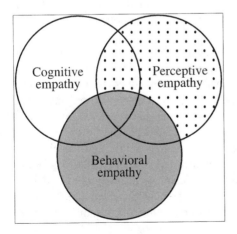

FIGURE 6.1   Three Aspects of Empathy

with Sandy on a cognitive level; she put herself in what she understood as Sandy's position so that she could see how Sandy viewed her role as an employee.

2. Perceptive Aspect

Empathy also refers to your sensitivity to nonverbal communication and your ability to interpret another person's underlying feelings by taking into account indirect, nonverbal cues and situational factors. For example, you might think to yourself, "Tom says he's not upset, but I know he just heard about the company's layoffs this morning and his dad will certainly be affected. He's tried to call home several times, and has been drinking one cup of coffee after another. Even now he's fidgeting with that napkin and unable to concentrate."

> What listener variables—age, gender, intelligence, and the like—most significantly affect perceptive empathy?

Examples of the perceptive aspect of empathy are apparent in "BurgerWorld" as well. Early in the case we are told that Nadia flops down hard in a living room chair and lets out an audible sigh. These cues were enough for her mother to recognize that Nadia had something on her mind. Knowing Nadia well helped her mother to determine that these nonverbal cues were significant.

3. Behavioral Aspect

Empathy can also refer to your ability to demonstrate verbal and nonverbal cues that indicate you are listening to and care about the other person. Such cues, or feedback, communicate that you want to understand both your partner's ideas and feelings in a nonjudgmental and helpful manner. When you project empathy, your partner might say to you, "Thanks for listening, Tom. You really seem to understand my situation."

Recall in "BurgerWorld" that Nadia not only gave Sandy plenty of time to express herself during their conversations, but she also facilitated their discussion through her strong eye contact, head nods, and by providing other nonverbal reinforcement.

An empathetic listener strives to thoroughly and accurately understand the person speaking; she does not direct the conversation, but encourages the other person to share her ideas and feelings. The empathetic listener does not impose her own opinions or values. When listening empathically, you don't evaluate; rather, you promote honest, engaged communication through total other-centered involvement in the encounter (Box 6.1).

Although anyone can develop empathic listening ability, individual differences play a significant role in determining your progress and potential. The ability to empathize varies with your maturity, attitude, personality, and motivational level. It is one of the most vital, yet troublesome, competencies for relational communication. Therefore, it may be helpful to consider briefly the role of individual differences in relation to empathic behavior.

■ ■ ■ ■ ■

BOX 6.1

QUESTIONS FOR EMPATHIC LISTENERS

Ask yourself:

- Do I understand the person speaking?
- Am I letting my personal opinions, feelings, and attitudes affect my response?

- Am I sensitive to my partner's nonverbal cues?
- Do I sincerely care about this person?
- Do my nonverbal behaviors suggest openness and interest?

Individual Differences in Empathic Listening

Young children find it almost impossible to see someone else's viewpoint; they seldom think about their own thinking process or how the other person feels as a result of what they say or do. Children's natural tendency toward egocentricity makes it difficult for them to assume the cognitive and emotional perspective of another person. It takes deliberate effort and maturity to put aside personal feelings and agendas in order to fully understand and consider another person's perspective.

Your attitude toward people, then, affects your empathic listening. As Bruneau (1993) remarks, to become an empathic listener you must be "a lover of people" and people-watching (p. 195). Establishing empathy requires a belief in the value of listening to others. It is also influenced, as you might imagine, by your past experiences and expectations.

A range of studies concludes that empathic ability may be related to personal tendencies as measured on a variety of person style inventories. Jenkins, Stephens, and Chew (1992), for instance, noted that one such instrument, the Myers–Briggs Type Inventory, indicates high correlations between the Thinking/Feeling dimension and the empathic response. High Feeling is associated with the ability to express empathy and concern for others. So, while some people effortlessly project friendliness, interest, and sincerity, others are more likely to be perceived as indifferent and aloof.

Keep in mind that personal tendencies only indicate your *comfort* with various behaviors, or your willingness to engage in the activity, not your potential *ability*. If your style indicates that you project empathy infrequently, it simply means that you must be prepared to devote more *energy* to developing these skills than someone who is higher on this dimension.

Researchers have been particularly interested in a personal style attribute called warmth, which is communicated largely through your nonverbal behavior (Reece & Whitman, 1962). Findings from research in this area are important if you are interested in developing the behavioral aspects of empathy, since expressing warmth encourages open communication (Clore, Wiggins, & Itkin, 1975). The specific nonverbal indicators of this trait are discussed in more detail later in this chapter (Box 6.2).

You are already familiar with self-monitoring and its impact on listening effectiveness. Harman (1986) puts forth a particularly interesting hypothesis. He suggests that when your empathic ability is assessed, ratings may be misleading. He proposes that high ratings on this dimension may be given to participants who, without having had an "authentic" empathic experience, are able to "assess with accuracy the extent to which their attempt merely to convey the *appearance* of having deeply understood was convincing" (p. 375). In other words, high self-monitors may project empathy on the Behavioral Aspect even when they have not actually experienced it and, in fact, are not even trying to experience it.

> Is it unethical to project concern even when you aren't really interested?

Empathy requires responsiveness to both anticipated and unexpected messages from others. It must be authentic, a concept Howell (1982) explains by contrasting what he calls "acting out," which is highly monitored behavior, with

---

BOX 6.2

COMPONENTS OF BEHAVIORAL EMPATHY

1. *Open Body Orientation:* An open posture is characterized by arms to the sides and legs uncrossed. A comfortable, relaxed, yet attentive pose lets the speaker know that you are ready to listen. Interest is also communicated by leaning forward slightly but remaining physically alert. Avoid bringing your hand to your face or covering your mouth by leaning on your elbow.

2. *Eye Contact:* Averting the eyes signals lack of interest. The most effective eye contact is not a penetrating stare, but a general focus that maintains a regular exchange of ideas and which enables you to pick up important nonverbal cues. You may look away periodically, but maintain focus on the speaker's face. This allows for effective turn-taking and communicates interest and empathy.

3. *Body Tension and Movement:* You must be physically ready to listen. Random movements and fidgeting communicate impatience, boredom, or nervousness. When it is important that your partner clearly understand your feelings, verbalize your needs; do not rely on indirect indicators. Rather than continuously glancing at your watch, tell your partner directly that you need the next few minutes to prepare for an important interview.

4. *Minimal Reinforcement:* Nonverbal communication regulates interaction, providing encouragement and feedback throughout the encounter. You also indicate your understanding through facial expressions, nodding, and tilting your head.

"working through," which is spontaneous and unmonitored. True empathy can't be forced or faked. This issue has been of particular concern to service workers, who are often called upon to project a particular attitude toward guests regardless of their personal feelings. Issues of emotional labor, the term used to distinguish jobs that require employees to express particular emotions as well as to perform relevant tasks, touch upon important questions of authenticity and ethical practice.

In addition to differences in the amount of energy individuals need to devote to projecting warmth and openness, significant individual differences in sensitivity to nonverbal behaviors also exist. These differences have a profound impact on the perceptive aspects of empathy. As you might imagine, high self-monitors are thought to be better judges of expressions in others, since they are more aware of and responsive to nonverbal cues.

Findings in this area have been advanced through the Profile of Nonverbal Sensitivity, or PONS assessment instrument. This test, developed by Rosenthal and his colleagues (1979), measures your ability to understand both tone of voice and movements of the face and body. Although a high percentage of respondents could accurately identify nonverbal cues when allowed to view the behaviors for five and one-half seconds, highly sensitive receivers were readily distinguished from poor receivers when the cues were flashed in two-second sequences (Rosenthal et al., 1979). Adding a variety of nonverbal dimensions significantly contributed to the accuracy of respondents' choices, which suggests that paying attention to a number of different nonverbal cues contributes to the accuracy of your interpretations.

> Which nonverbal indicators do you rely on most heavily to make judgments about your partner's sincerity?

Knapp (1978) reports that studies using the PONS test, and other similar measures, have been relatively consistent in indicating the following:

1. Women generally are better at interpreting nonverbal cues than men are.
2. You become progressively better at interpreting nonverbal cues until you reach your mid-twenties.
3. Accurate interpreters are characterized by their self-monitoring ability, extroversion, and general skill in interpersonal contexts.
4. There is no consistent or strong correlation between your ability to interpret nonverbal cues and either intelligence or verbal ability.

Although no completely reliable predictor of nonverbal sensitivity has been constructed, individuals who are expressive themselves tend to interpret the nonverbal behavior of others with greater accuracy. Results of assessment measures like the PONS, however, need to be processed carefully. Consensus of opinion does not necessarily mean that

> What are the potential consequences of mistaking *consensus of opinion* for the truth when interpreting messages?

the interpretation of a nonverbal behavior is accurate. Scheflen (1966) suggests that 50 million people can be wrong:

> If a particular understanding is shared by a group, it may be a doctrinal misconception rather than a private illusion; the number of people in agreement does not verify the understanding. In the past, consensual validation has been achieved about witches, a flat earth, etc. (p. 283)

You can see how important empathy is to your relational listening ability. Although you can work to increase your own sensitivity and empathic response, empathy is also unique in that it is only created through a shared experience.

Empathy Requires Reciprocity

Buber (1965) was among the first to argue that empathic listeners should not view the "other" as "object." Rather, both individuals must acknowledge that each is an interpreter, and each person must be as open and as equal as possible as they engage in the listening process. Through their interactions, both participants move to a higher level of understanding within a context which they are simultaneously and jointly creating.

What are the implications of viewing your partner as an "object"?

Traditional approaches to empathy imply that you can learn and then practice empathic listening at will. Inherent assumptions of this perspective are that (1) being a caring person automatically makes you an empathic listener, and (2) most people want to listen empathically and to better understand their partners. Buie (1981), however, suggests that this is not necessarily the case. If you think back to events in "BurgerWorld," you might conclude that Sandy would never be able to achieve the level of empathy that Nadia demonstrated. But would Mark? How about Tina?

In addition, anyone can prevent you from truly understanding him. That is, the relational nature of communication necessitates reciprocity. You may find it impossible to understand another person's perspective if he discourages the attempt by being deliberately misleading, silent, or judgmental. Empathy isn't something you can force on your partner. You can't make someone disclose her honest feelings and concerns just because you want to practice your empathic listening skills.

Does having a genuine interest in someone *automatically* improve your empathy?

Empathic listening also implies a cost-benefit ratio; that is, "being empathic . . . may cost us in terms of time, effort, and lack of positive results" (Bruneau, 1993, p. 195). Empathy arises out of mutual efforts to understand and be understood, and requires the cooperation of *both* participants. Again, as the BurgerWorld situation makes clear, Nadia could not develop empathy without Sandy's cooperation. It was only because Sandy chose to share her feelings that Nadia could empathize with her and better interpret her behavior at work.

Keep in mind, too, that empathy is not "feeling what another person feels" or putting yourself in another person's position, although for convenience we often refer to it that way. It is, rather, thinking and feeling what *you perceive* the other person thinks and feels. In "BurgerWorld," Nadia interprets Sandy's feelings from her own perspective. Empathy is productive, not reproductive; that is, you do not *reproduce* the other person's experience. Rather, you and your partner work together to *produce,* or co-create, meanings that are different from either of your individual perspectives.

Those who have studied empathy and who recognize the importance of the emotional aspect of relationships propose that *emotional intelligence* is another useful framework for improving your ability to interpret messages. An overview of this concept follows.

Emotional Intelligence

Before moving into a discussion of nonverbal behavior, one additional theory is worth mentioning as it relates to interpreting messages. Emotional intelligence is a term first proposed and defined by Salovey and Mayer as a "form of social intelligence that involves the ability to monitor one's own and others' feelings and emotions, to discriminate among them, and to use this information to guide one's thinking and action" (1990). Popularized by Goleman (1995; 1998; 2004) and others (Boyatzis & Van Oosten, 2003; Druskat & Wolff, 2001; Dawda & Hart, 2000), emotional intelligence is another way of thinking about the concepts related to self-monitoring and empathy.

Emotional intelligence, or EI, has been linked to listening effectiveness in both personal and professional contexts (Fineman, 2003; Becker, 2003). Individuals who possess a high degree of emotional intelligence have been shown to be more effective leaders and more sensitive group members due to their focus on both the cognitive and the emotional aspects of human interaction. Most researchers agree that while innate emotional intelligence varies, it can either be developed or damaged through life experiences. Particularly potent are the emotional lessons taught by parents, teachers, and other caregivers. You might think of your EI as "street smarts." While some people seem to be born with this intuitive ability, it can be developed through increased awareness and carefully planned experiences.

Several instruments have been developed to measure your emotional quotient, or E.Q. The Mayer-Salovey-Caruso Emotional Intelligence Test (MSCEIT) is an ability-based assessment that measures how well you perform tasks and solve emotional problems in four well defined branches of emotional intelligence:

1. Emotional perception, or the ability to identify emotions through facial expressions, art, music, and other stimuli.
2. Emotional facilitation of thought, or the ability to use emotion to facilitate judgment in reasoning and problem solving.

3. Understanding emotions, or the ability to solve emotional problems and to interpret complex feelings or blends of emotions such as fear and surprise.
4. Emotional management, or the ability to be open to feelings and to turn negative emotions into positive learning opportunities.

Goleman has translated this earlier work on emotional intelligence into an assessment instrument that has strong application for improving performance in work environments. The ECI-360 combines a self-report with 360 degree feedback provided by the manager's coworkers. The competencies associated with emotional intelligence are divided into four categories. Two pertain to personal dimensions—self-awareness and self-management—and two are clusters of social competencies, social awareness and relationship management. Box 6.3 lists the specific competencies in each EI cluster that are relevant to listening effectiveness.

Perhaps of most value to listeners seeking to increase the accuracy of their interpretations are the self and social awareness categories. Among the components of self-awareness is what Goleman calls "emotional self-awareness." Individuals high in this domain recognize their emotions and the effect these emotions have on others. When competency in social awareness is added (what Salovey and Mayer called "empathy"), you can expect the individual to focus on supporting and developing others. People with strong social awareness can "sense others' feelings and point of view, and . . . can anticipate and meet their needs" (Walp, 2001, p. 29).

Emotional intelligence, then, can be viewed as the ability to achieve greater listening effectiveness by allowing your emotions to guide and inform your response. Your EI, however, does not operate independent of your cognitive abilities. It is when the two systems function together that the most powerful results are achieved. As a listener, any efforts taken to strengthen your emotional intelligence will increase the likelihood that you will interpret messages accurately and communicate your understanding and support in ways that facilitate positive relationships.

BOX 6.3

EMOTIONAL INTELLIGENCE AND ASSOCIATED COMPETENCIES RELEVANT TO LISTENING EFFECTIVENESS

Personal Competence	Social Competence
Self-Awareness	Social Awareness
Emotional self-awareness	Empathy
Self-confidence	Recognizing others' needs
Self-Management	Relationship Management
Emotional self-control	Developing others
Trustworthiness	Teamwork and collaboration

Adapted from D. Goleman, 1998. *Working with emotional intelligence.* NY: Bantam Books.

It is clear that the ability to recognize and interpret nonverbal cues is essential to developing emotional intelligence. It is also key to both the cognitive and perceptive aspects of empathy. Developing an awareness of your own nonverbal communication (emotional self-awareness) is necessary to improving the behavioral aspect of empathy. The more you know about nonverbal communication, therefore, the better able you will be to work effectively toward shared meanings and satisfying relationships.

NONVERBAL COMMUNICATION

Because all language, both verbal and nonverbal, is learned, any assumptions or prescriptions provided here are necessarily culture specific. Although most readers of this text will likely be English-speaking American citizens, it is important to keep in mind that ethnocentrism—the tendency to believe that everyone thinks the same way you do—can be a major barrier to sharing and interpreting meanings. So, from a practical perspective, we will rely on the cultural norms developed in the United States to guide our discussions. From a global perspective, however, your communication will only improve to the extent that you recognize the relatively narrow range of experience and learning that keeps each of us culture bound.

> What nonverbal cues are you known for sending? How might they be misinterpreted?

Studies conducted in the United States indicate that nonverbal factors carry more than 65 percent of the meaning of an interpersonal message. When you meet someone, she does not have to speak in order for you to make assumptions about her attitude, personality, status, or emotional state. You look at the way she dresses, the way she moves, the manner in which she gestures and smiles. You observe her expressions and listen carefully to tone of voice in order to understand more fully both the person and her thoughts. Silently, a great deal of information is communicated. Silently, a great deal of information is processed and interpreted.

Determining the most authentic interpretation of nonverbal behavior is never easy. The indirect way in which individuals express their attitudes and feelings is a constant source of difficulty in interpersonal relations. Indicators that provide essential information about the speaker and his message are particularly important in contexts where emotions are high, or where the speaker's attitudes lend essential insight into both the overt and the underlying meaning of the message. Box 6.4 suggests the nonverbal behavior frequently used to make judgments about an individual's attitude. Egan (1977) has provided one of the best descriptions of the role nonverbal communication plays in the listening process:

> One does not listen with just his ears; he listens with his eyes and with his sense of touch, he listens by becoming aware of the feelings and emotions that arise within himself because of his contact with others. . . . He listens to the words of others but he also listens to the messages that are buried in the words. . . . He listens to the voice, the

■ ■ ■ ■ ■

BOX 6.4

NONVERBAL CUES COMMUNICATE ATTITUDES

Defensiveness	*Confidence*
crossed arms or legs	hands behind back
pointed finger	shoulders back
Evaluative	*Nervousness*
shaking finger	clearing throat
hands on hips	lack of eye contact
Insecurity	*Frustration*
fidgeting with jewelry, pen	short fast breath
chewing on pen	biting lip

demeanor, the vocabulary, and the gestures of the other, to the context, the verbal messages, the linguistic patterns, and the bodily movements of the other. He listens to the sounds and to the silences. (p. 228)

What does it mean, from your experience, to "listen to the silences"?

Since interpretation of nonverbal cues is often haphazard and highly dependent upon cultural orientation as well as own internal, subjective processing, it is wise to learn about this important element of the listening process (Brownell, 1994).

Basic Considerations in the Interpretation of Nonverbal Cues

Nonverbal acts occur within a particular context. Meanings must be assigned with great care since, in addition to culture, nonverbal behavior depends on such variables as role relationships, the personalities of those involved in the interaction, and each individual's past experiences and expectations. Knowing your partner, and determining whether her nonverbal behavior is intentional or unintentional, are two key elements.

Understanding the Person's Background and Culture Contexting. Even the most skilled communicator may have trouble interpreting strangers' nonverbal cues. As was demonstrated in the BurgerWorld case, knowing someone well gives you important information about what to expect and how to interpret what you hear and see. At one time or another, most people have been annoyed by a friend or family member's ability to pick up on cues they didn't realize were evident enough to be noticed.

Cross-cultural encounters, on the other hand, may result in the opposite experience. Communication with those you don't completely understand may be problematic unless you consider both your partner's background and her relationship to the specific topic. It is always important to know as much as possible about your partner and all aspects of the communication context to interpret what you hear more accurately (Box 6.5).

One powerful cultural variable that affects the way in which messages are interpreted and meanings are assigned is the nonverbal dimension called *contexting.* You may recall our earlier discussion in Chapter 2, where we emphasized the importance of using the specific situation in which a communication occurs to interpret its meaning and intent. When two communicators share a significant amount of knowledge and experience—and use it to interpret meaning—it is less important for them to provide all the details within the verbal message. Our example was when

> How does understanding the concept of contexting help you to become a more effective communicator?

your friend shouted, "Five days left!" She was working under the assumption that you would use your previous knowledge of this planned Bermuda trip to "define the situation" and understand the message.

Here, we take this concept a step further and discuss it in light of a specific communication principle—contexting. Cultures are described as being either "high" or "low" in context in terms of the balance between what is explicitly stated in the message and what is left for the listener to infer from related variables within the situation. This difference is a critical one and affects the perception and interpretation of nonverbal cues.

It is important to keep in mind that contexting is a culturally learned behavior. Members select and interpret nonverbal communication cues from a limited

---

BOX 6.5

UNDERSTAND THE CONTEXT FOR YOUR PARTNER'S RESPONSE

Your partner's past experiences

1. Who is this person? What are his or her motives?
2. Where has your partner lived?
3. What significant experiences has your partner had?
4. What is your partner's education?
5. What is your partner's past work experience?

Your partner's relation to the specific topic and event

1. What is your partner's specific purpose?
2. What is your partner's experience with the topic?
3. What other influences may be affecting your partner?
4. What is your partner's specific role in this encounter?

menu of culturally determined behaviors. The degree to which individuals depend on the context to assign meanings, as opposed to attending only to the more direct verbal message, is also culturally defined.

Communicators from high-context cultures, for instance, would assume that a great deal of information is already understood and that there is no need for exten-sive detail in the verbal message itself. Their style is often referred to as *indirect;* an important component of the message may be what is left unsaid. High-context cultures, in general, value interpersonal rela-tionships. The degree to which they know and under-stand their partners profoundly affects their ability to communicate effectively. Consequently, sharing per-sonal information becomes an important part of the communication experience. This is just as true in business as in personal settings; discussions of operations and profits are only possible after a personal relationship and a degree of trust have been established.

> Are you most comfortable with partners who are high- or low-context communicators?

Those who have a low dependence on the context and whose verbal message is more direct leave less to be interpreted from nonverbal cues. In the United States, it is common for communication textbooks to recommend a very direct approach; techniques are presented that help the communicator to organize and deliver a mes-sage that is clear and explicit. Presumably, you could close your eyes during a con-versation and not miss the main points that the speaker intended to make. Those from high-context cultures, such as Japan, Arabic countries, and Latin America, are likely to view such directness as rude and offensive.

While North Americans are generally low context, the Swiss, German, and Scandinavian cultures tend to be even more explicit and direct in their verbal mes-sages. In such cultures, focus is on gathering and presenting concrete evidence in support of points. In conversations, participants want immediately to get to the issue at hand or to get the task accomplished. It would seem that communicators often dread silence, pausing in their conversations only long enough to take a breath and appearing uncomfortable when no one is speaking. Even interpersonal conflict may be created when individuals from different cultures are unaware of the role that con-text plays in communication.

In addition to issues of background and context, the question of intentionality is also relevant.

Intentionality.   All nonverbal behaviors are *potentially* significant. It is easy, however, to assign your personal meanings to others' nonverbal cues. In other words, the meanings a behavior elicits for you—because of your personal values, agendas, or expectations—may be quite different from what your partner intended. A swinging leg could mean anticipation, boredom, frustration, a bothersome insect, or a foot that went to sleep, among others. Unconscious finger-tapping can send as strong a message as a deliberate nod of reinforcement. A puzzled expression and crossed arms provide information even though the sender may be unaware of the message. Figure 6.2 illustrates four possible sender–receiver relationships with regard to the intentionality of the speaker's nonverbal cues.

> On what basis do you determine whether a nonverbal cue is intentional or unintentional?

To improve the usefulness of your interpretations, you must first make sound and informed judgments about the intentionality of your partner's behaviors. If intentional, the behavior must be recognized as an important component of the message. If unintentional, you need to decide whether or not the behavior functions as a significant nonverbal cue, and respond accordingly. Just because your friend starts to yawn as you tell about a recent cooking experience does not *necessarily* mean that she is bored with your story. However, just because she didn't intend to yawn doesn't mean it's not a signal that she's tired of listening.

If you examine the events in "BurgerWorld," you can find examples of both unintentional and intentional behavior. Several references are made to the fact that Nadia is lying on her bed, pulling at the fringe on her bedspread. Is this repetitive behavior intentional? Probably not. Does it communicate useful information about Nadia? *Probably.* It suggests that Nadia may be feeling frustrated, confused, or uncomfortable.

The more you discover about your partner and the more you think about how her nonverbal cues can best be interpreted, the better able you will be to listen to all levels of the message and the greater the likelihood that you will accurately understand both the ideas and the feelings she is communicating. Importantly, however, you also need to know as much about each specific aspect of nonverbal communication as possible. This includes facial expression, eye contact, body movement and posture, touch, and vocal characteristics.

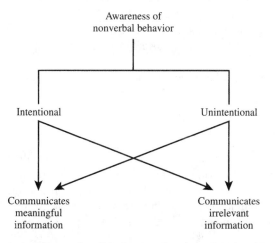

FIGURE 6.2   Possible Sender–Receiver Relationships

Facial Expression

Facial expression is one of the most reliable and accessible indicators of an individual's attitude and emotional state. It is therefore a primary indicator in interpreting emotional meaning or what is frequently referred to as affect. Some researchers suggest that as much as 55 percent of the affective component of a message is conveyed through the face alone (Mehrabian, 1971; Birdwhistell, 1970). The accurate identification of facial expressions may also help you to predict your partner's subsequent behavior. That is, if you judge him to be confused or angry or worried, this information can be used to make informed guesses about his next response.

Facial expressions convey a wide range of useful information. You rely on facial expressions to determine both your partner's attitude toward you and his feelings about the subject of conversation. Facial expressions are used to start and stop communication; on occasion, they even replace speech. You are also likely to make judgments about your partner's personality based on his face.

Most listeners look to the face to reinforce or modify the verbal message. The face, however, is relatively easy to control. There is less leakage in the face than in other parts of the body; that is, you are generally quite conscious of what you convey through your facial expressions. Yet, your ability to "fake" facial messages is often imperfect, especially if you know your partner well. Expressions may be presented at the wrong time, held for too long, or appear awkward. The unmonitored face often reveals a great deal of information of which you are largely unaware.

Ekman, Friesen, and Tomkins (1971) have designed a Facial Affect Scoring Technique (FAST), which involves the recording and scoring of facial movements. For any given emotion, a specific area of the face—eyes and forehead, nose and cheeks, or mouth and chin—carries the most important information for identification of that emotion. Most of us can accurately identify six distinct facial expressions: happiness, sadness, surprise, fear, anger, and disgust. Interest, bewilderment, and determination can also be identified with significant consistency (Leathers & Emigh, 1980). Even untrained observers can characterize faces on the dimensions of pleasant to unpleasant, active to passive, and intense to controlled, with a high degree of reliability. Experiments have also revealed affect blends, faces displaying two emotions simultaneously.

Of all the facial features, however, the aspect that plays the most vital role in listening behavior are the eyes.

Eye Behavior

Eye behavior is one of the most frequently studied nonverbal elements. Specialists from a wide range of disciplines have been fascinated with how much information can be conveyed through the direction and duration of your gaze. People in the United States use eye contact to communicate empathy, warmth, intimacy, status, and generally positive attitudes. Even pupil dilation provides clues to the level of interest and attention.

Patterns of eye behavior, like many other non-verbal behaviors, are learned (Box 6.6). Individuals from different cultures have grown up with different sets of norms governing the appropriate use of eye contact. Keep in mind that, once again, the generalizations reported here were derived from studies of people in the United States; eye contact that is inter-

In what circumstances do you become particularly conscious of your eye behavior?

preted as insufficient in one culture may be perceived as too intense in another. A closer examination of these variations, along with a review of the functions of eye behavior, should prove useful as you work to develop your empathic listening skills.

Variations in Eye Behavior.   Researchers suggest that white people in the United States exhibit nearly twice as much eye contact while listening as they do while speaking. African Americans, on the other hand, often display more eye contact while speaking than while listening (Argyle & Cook, 1972; LaFrance & Mayo, 1976). Yet, even within the same country or community, norms vary. Gender, for instance, has repeatedly been found to affect patterns of eye behavior; women generally maintain more eye contact when listening than do men.

Although eye contact is affected both by situational variables and by such factors as gender, status, age, and attraction, personal style significantly influences eye behavior. Those with a high degree of eye contact maintain it across a wide range of settings. The number of instances and the duration of eye contact correlates with a number of personality characteristics. Extroverts generally have better eye contact than introverts. Your CLEMS, or conjugate lateral eye movements, provide insight into your gaze patterns (Day, 1964; Bakan & Strayer, 1973). The direction of your gaze is a function of brain hemisphere stimulation. When the left cerebral hemisphere is stimulated, your eyes tend to move to the right and vice versa.

One research approach suggests that those who have dominant left hemispheres are generally better in science and quantitative skills, sleep less, and are more emotional. Left-movers, on the other hand, have a dominant right hemisphere.

BOX 6.6

USE OF EYE BEHAVIOR IN THE UNITED STATES

There is usually more eye contact when you are:

- discussing impersonal topics
- at a distance from your partner
- attracted to your partner

- talking with your supervisor
- extroverted
- self-confident
- female
- interested in your partner's reactions

They are described as having better verbal skills and more vivid imaginations; this group also tends to be more sociable and objective. Notice which direction your gaze moves when you pause to consider an idea before speaking. Then, apply this theory; see if these findings are true in your personal experience.

The main purpose of observing eye behavior, however, is not to determine your dominant brain hemisphere or your personal style. Eye behavior plays a key role in the listening process and is therefore of interest as you work to improve your effectiveness.

Functions of the Eyes.   For North Americans, as well as individuals from a number of other cultures, the eyes perform three primary relational communication functions: monitoring, regulating, and expressing emotions. First, you monitor and regulate conversation through eye contact cues. Although your partner may first look at you, chances are she will look away again just as you begin talking. A control phase follows where your partner glances at you periodically to obtain cues regarding how her message is being perceived. This helps her modify or adapt the message. A sequence is likely to end with a longer glance as she checks your final reaction. In this way the speaker not only gauges how her message has been received, she also lets you know that she has finished.

The absence of eye contact makes it difficult to take turns in a conversation. You may have noticed a slight discomfort when talking on the telephone or speaking to someone in another room. Without eye contact cues, individuals often speak simultaneously or experience awkward pauses. In other instances, eye contact obligates individuals to acknowledge each other; when you catch a classmate's eye as you approach her in a narrow hallway, it is almost impossible not to nod or say hello. This function is discussed more fully in a later section.

There also is a tendency to avoid eye contact when you are emotionally involved, deceitful, submissive, or embarrassed (Kalbfleisch, 1990). Similarly, eye contact can be used to produce anxiety in others. You probably know the feeling of having someone stare at you. A gaze of more than ten seconds is likely to make a Caucasian born in the United States feel threatened. In other instances, however, long periods of eye contact communicate a high degree of interest in a person or a topic.

It is apparent that the study of eye behavior is an extensive and evolving field where research is constantly providing insight into the subtle and often unconscious ways in which we use our eyes to communicate. One area of the body, however, seldom responds in isolation. Observing body movement and posture in the context of situation, culture, and other variables will provide additional cues to your partner's attitudes, feelings, and underlying meanings.

Body Movements, Posture, and Gesture

Interviewers often use body movement and posture as indicators in making judgments about an interviewee's poise and self-confidence. It takes the average recruiter just over thirty seconds to form a negative impression of a candidate. Was this impression created because of what the person said? Probably not. The interviewer was more likely responding to the way the person moved, how she sat and gestured. Accurate or not, nonverbal behaviors send strong messages about self-image and contribute to perceptions of warmth, attraction, and status.

Warmth and Attraction.   Because perceptions of warmth and degree of liking are positively correlated with such dimensions as frequency of interaction and persuasiveness, these nonverbal cues are important ones to develop. Listeners who encourage information-sharing and who communicate behavioral empathy tend to demonstrate the warm nonverbal responses summarized in Box 6.7. Although the list includes a variety of nonverbal dimensions, body posture is a key element.

Body orientation, or the degree to which your body is turned in your partner's direction, communicates interpersonal attraction or liking. A forward lean, open arms, and a relaxed posture signify a positive relationship to most people in the United States. When listening, keep in mind that your body language communicates, and consider how your partner's behaviors may reflect attitudes, emotions, or other key elements not conveyed through the verbal channel.

Your body cues, as you can imagine, are perceived as an integral part of your overall nonverbal presence. When you want approval, you are likely to gesture frequently, smile, and nod your head more often. These are also signs of inclusion; a smile and an appropriate nod will often ensure that you are accepted into social conversations.

Try it and see what happens!

Status.   Status is also communicated through body movement and posture. When you are in a high-status position, you may find your shoulder orientation is more direct; your body is more relaxed and you are more likely to keep your head raised. In addition, the higher status person often has a sideways lean when speaking.

■ ■ ■ ■ ■ ▬▬▬▬▬▬▬▬▬▬▬▬▬▬▬▬▬▬▬▬▬▬▬▬▬▬▬▬▬▬▬▬▬▬

BOX 6.7

BEHAVIORS THAT SAY, "I'LL LISTEN"

Warm Behaviors	**Cold Behaviors**
direct eye contact	stare
touching	fake yawn
smiling	looking away
nods	nervous habits, fidgeting
eyes wide open	shaking head negatively
forward lean	moving away from speaker
positive facial expression	negative facial expression

In spite of the fact that women everywhere are increasingly moving into higher status positions in the workplace, men still demonstrate a greater number of high-status behaviors than do women. Even though these indicators are often subtle, they affect your perceptions and the nature of the communication that takes place. Another nonverbal cue associated with status is touching.

Touch

Touching influences your listening behavior in a number of ways and cultural differences in touching behavior can be particularly significant. In North America, the stronger the emotions, the greater the chances of increased touching. As with all nonverbal behavior, touching may be difficult to interpret accurately. In some instances, touching communicates an individual's attitudes; on other occasions, it is used to manage the interaction itself. Henley (1977) suggests that people in the United States are more likely to touch under certain conditions:

1. when asking a favor;
2. trying to persuade;
3. communicating excitement;
4. giving information or making a request; or
5. communicating to lower status individuals.

A variety of classifications have also been developed to better understand touching behavior. One topology (Knapp, 1978) views the functions or purposes of touching as falling into categories such as professional, social, friendship, and intimate. Keep in mind that touching behavior is highly dependent on various dimensions of the listening context for its interpretation.

Research has also been conducted on gender and touching behavior (Nguyen, Heslin, & Nguyen, 1976; Henley, 1977). In the United States, men are more likely to touch women than vice versa. Increased attention to issues of harassment have made both genders conscious of touching and the potential for discrepancies in its interpretation. Perhaps this is one of the richest areas for exploring the complexities resulting from receiver-defined meanings. In addition, norms of acceptable behavior not only vary from one situation to the next, but may be modified during the interaction itself. Recognition of unique individual and cultural norms can aid in more effective communication among those with different orientations.

> What cross-cultural issues are suggested if harassment is viewed as a receiver-defined activity?

Male–female encounters, and listening generally, are also affected by your appearance.

Appearance

First impressions are critical. Your initial reaction to a person often has a powerful influence on subsequent interactions. A little frightening, perhaps, but the significance of the statement "we cannot not communicate" is obvious. Negative impressions, once formed, are difficult to overcome. They affect your attitudes and the way you listen to and interpret what you observe.

Because each listener's impressions are based, to a large extent, on her personal assumptions, expectations, and values, your final impression is a product of your unique filtering system in combination with your partner's specific attributes. In other words, the judgments you make about others reveal information about you.

It is wise, then, to learn all you can about the nonverbal variables that influence your perceptions. A significant portion of an impression is based on appearance; consequently, it is important to examine how body build and attire contribute to first impressions.

> What judgments have you made recently based primarily on appearance?

Body.   Physical attractiveness and general good looks are well-documented factors in influencing perceptions and subsequent judgments. Attractive females, in particular, are judged to be more persuasive and more credible than women described as plain or unattractive. There's a strong tendency to attribute greater success, popularity, sexuality, and even happiness to people who are perceived as generally good-looking (Singer, 1964; Mills & Aronson, 1965; Widgery, 1974).

United States culture and its stereotypes have also developed notions about what kind of personality certain individuals have based upon their body build. Cortes and Gatti (1965) developed a short self-description test which asked respondents to choose the adjectives they felt best described their personalities. The adjectives provided on the test correspond to three categories correlated with three different body types: endomorphic, ectomorphic, and mesomorphic. Endomorphs are heavy individuals who are generally perceived as easygoing, tolerant, cooperative, generous, and warm. Tall, slender ectomorphs are seen as shy, detached, anxious, sensitive, and meticulous. The muscular, athletic mesomorph projects an image of confidence, courage, dominance, and competitiveness. Results of the test provided respondents with three numbers indicating the relative proportion of adjectives chosen from each of the categories. Next time you catch yourself forming an immediate first impression, see if it conforms to this notion of body type and personality.

Attire.   Clothes, too, serve functions well beyond keeping you warm. They are used for decoration, concealment, and group identification. BurgerWorld, for instance, required employees to wear a uniform. Why do you think that might be the case?

Goffman (1974) provides numerous examples of the impact uniforms have on the nature of interpersonal encounters. He notes that police, clergy, and others in the public domain are approachable largely because of the strong identification created by their attire.

Motives for selecting a particular wardrobe vary widely. Requests of any nature are more frequently granted to those wearing higher-status clothes; those perceived to be more important generally get better results. Attention to clothes as a form of communication may help you to better understand your partner.

In addition to the nonverbal cues displayed through face and body, your voice also has a nonverbal dimension referred to as paralanguage. An examination of these vocal features provides additional insights into how emotions are conveyed nonverbally.

VOCAL CUES

What can you tell about someone just by listening to his voice? It's surprising how much voice reveals, even to the untrained ear. The following situations illustrate how people use voice cues to make judgments.

- You're expecting a call. The phone rings, you pick it up. Immediately, you realize it's not the person you expected.
- You need some information and decide to place a call. A receptionist answers and takes your message. From his voice and manner, you form a general image not only of the person, but the organization as well.
- As you come into class, you stop to say hello to one of your roommates. Although he responds appropriately to your overture, you can tell immediately something is on his mind.
- You made an appointment last week to talk to your instructor. Today, you enter her office and take a seat. She looks up and asks what she can do for you. Almost instinctively, you realize that this isn't a good time to speak with her.

Vocal dimensions account for up to a third of the meaning assigned to a given message; consequently, your listening effectiveness increases as you learn to recognize and identify these cues. The better you know someone, of course, the more accurately you can interpret her vocal cues. Still, you derive a great deal of information from the voice alone. You make inferences about your partner's mood, gender, age, education, nationality, attitude toward the subject, attitude toward you, and even her personality (Box 6.8). Because these inferences are made almost unconsciously—and because they influence the encounter to such a great degree—it is worthwhile to take a closer look at voice as a nonverbal element.

> How many inferences can you make just from listening to someone's voice?

As you are well aware, a person may say one thing but mean something very different. By examining the vocal characteristics that create these different impressions, you may make more informed judgments about the meaning your partner intends (Davitz, 1964). The accompanying chart summarizes what we know about how vocal characteristics provide cues to an individual's feelings and attitudes (Box 6.9). Recall, too, that the ability to identify paralinguistic cues varies significantly from one person to the next and does not appear to correspond with performance in other types of listening tasks (Bostrom, 1990).

BOX 6.8

PERCEPTIONS OF VOCAL CHARACTERISTICS

Vocal Cue	Gender	Perception
breathiness	female	sexy, shallow
nasal	male/female	whiny, low credibility
increased rate	male/female	nervous, anxious, extroverted
pitch variety	male/female	dynamic, enthusiastic

Characteristics of Voice

There are four main vocal characteristics over which a speaker has considerable control: volume, pitch, quality, and rate. Because each characteristic influences your response to a message, it is helpful to understand how they are produced and their impact on your interpretations.

Volume: Loud and Soft.   Volume is related to breathing. The more deeply you breathe, the louder or stronger your voice. Vocal instructors often ask their students to sit up straight, allowing their lungs to expand as they fill with air. When a speaker becomes anxious, his or her muscles tense and breathing becomes more shallow. This causes him to run out of breath when he's speaking, often in the middle of a sentence. When a speaker begins strong and trails off at the ends of sentences, or gasps for breath irregularly, it may be due to nervousness.

> In addition to differences in the actual words and sounds, in what other ways does culture influence voice?

BOX 6.9

VOCAL COMMUNICATION OF EMOTIONS

Emotion	Volume	Pitch	Rate
joy	loud	high	fast
sadness	soft	low	slow
anger	loud	high	fast
impatience	normal	normal	moderately fast
affection	soft	low	slow
apathy	moderate/low	moderate/low	moderately slow

Volume is often associated with credibility and conviction, so listeners assume that a confident speaker projects her ideas forcefully. Gender differences often put women at a disadvantage in presentational situations because their voices are generally softer than their male counterparts' and listeners tend to perceive them as less confident.

Pitch: High and Low.   When your friend says one thing but you sense he really means something else, it is often due to the *way* he uttered the message. Sarcasm is a good example of how pitch can be used to alter perceived meanings. Voice may reveal more than the person intends about feelings and emotional states. Be alert to changes in pitch and try to identify a speaker's underlying meaning without projecting your own assumptions.

Did you ever wonder how changes in pitch occur? The larynx, a protruding structure of cartilage and bone located at the top of the windpipe, houses the vocal cords. These cords are folds of elastic tissue that are attached to the inside of the larynx. When you breathe, the vocal cords rest along the walls of the larynx. As you begin to speak, the cords stretch across the larynx; the air passing out from your lungs causes the vocal cords to vibrate. This vibration creates sound, and the rate of vibration determines the pitch.

Vocal cords work on the same principles as the strings of a violin. The longer and thicker the cords, the slower they vibrate and the lower the pitch range. The shorter and tighter they are, the faster they vibrate and the higher the pitch. The lower pitch of a male voice is due, then, to the relative length and thickness of the vocal cords (Box 6.10). Once again, emotions affect this vocal dimension. If someone is upset or anxious, the vocal folds tighten and pitch automatically becomes higher.

Quality: Resonation.   If you were told that your head was hollow, to some extent it would be correct. In the front of your head are three cavities, or resonating chambers. Air waves, produced by the vibration of your vocal cords, bounce off these cavity walls. The condition of the cavity walls and the way the cavities are used determine your vocal quality.

■ ■ ■ ■ ■ ▬▬▬▬▬▬▬▬▬▬▬▬▬▬▬▬▬▬▬▬▬

BOX 6.10

ON THE LINE

"Dad," said our 16-year-old, "every time I answer the phone and someone is calling you, they think I am *you*."

"You think *that's* bad?" countered our 13-year-old boy, whose voice hadn't changed yet.

"When I answer the phone, they think I'm Mom."

Quality gives voice its unique character, and emotions affect vocal quality. Voices are perceived as harsh, nasal, denasal, breathy, strident, hoarse, or raspy, and you've likely heard expressions like "choked up" or "squeaky" used to describe voice qualities. Strong stereotypes exist for many vocal qualities. We think of a sexy woman's voice as "breathy," a con man's voice as "smooth," or an old woman's as "harsh" or "strident."

Whenever you are tense or anxious or sad, it is reflected in your voice. Recall that Nadia's mother could tell right away that something was wrong, even when Nadia said that everything was "just fine." When someone is upset, angry, or under unusual stress, he is likely to experience corresponding changes in his voice resulting from modifications either in the functioning of the resonating cavities or in the condition of the cavity walls.

Rate: Fast or Slow.   Cues to an individual's mood or emotional state can also come from the rate at which she speaks. A high-energy, nervous person, or someone who is excited or upset, is likely to speak faster than the individual who is tired, bored, or relaxed. Rate increases under conditions of high stress, excitement, or limited time constraints.

Rate becomes a problem when it interferes with your ability to mentally process a message. Some people are difficult to understand, not because they speak too fast, but because they mumble. As rate increases, the speaker must move his articulators—the tongue, teeth, lips, and palate—more rapidly to form the consonant sounds. Most United States speakers are lazy and their vocal problems are magnified when rate is increased. You do not always have enough time to guess at the word and put everything into a context before the speaker goes on to another idea.

Keep in mind that under normal conditions, rate alone does not create listening difficulties. As you know, experiments with compressed speech have demonstrated that you can maintain maximum comprehension even at rates up to three times faster than normal. What is essential is that key words be clearly articulated and easy to recognize.

Silence

What happens when there are no vocal cues, when there is only—silence? As Mark Knapp (1978) writes:

> Silence is charged with those words which have just been exchanged; words which have been exchanged in the past; words which haven't been or will not be said, but which are fantasized; words which actually may be said in the future . . . . (p. 360).

Throughout the world there are many kinds of silence (Box 6.11). Silence can show respect for another person, or indifference. We are silent when we are too angry to speak. We are silent when we listen intently. We are silent in a state of grief or depression. We are silent when we wish to gain attention, or when we wish to avoid attention (Rosenfeld & Civikly, 1976, p. 141).

■ ■ ■ ■ ■

BOX 6.11

Those tears shining on Mama's face were falling for me. When the bus started down the street,
I wanted to run back and say something to Mama.
I didn't know what.
I thought, maybe, I woulda said, "Mama, I didn't mean what I said, 'cause I really do care."

No, I wouldn'a said that. I woulda said, "Mama, button up your coat. It's cold out here."
Yea, that's what I forgot to say to Mama.

Claude Brown
Manchild in the Promised Land

Source: Reprinted with the permission of Scribner, an imprint of Simon & Schuster Adult Publishing Group, from *Manchild in the Promised Land* by Claude Brown. Copyright © 1965 by Claude Brown.

You experience silence in many ways. Take a closer look at how you use silence in your encounters and how it affects your listening behavior. Are you uncomfortable with too much silence? Since silence is an important turn-taking cue, you may find that you experience some discomfort and begin to speak as soon as your partner has stopped talking (even when you have nothing to say). Refusal to accept your turn in the conversation, on the other hand, may encourage the speaker to continue. Interviewers find this technique effective when they want to encourage greater disclosure. They simply create silence and, almost automatically, the applicant will continue to speak.

In "BurgerWorld," for instance, Nadia's mother asked a probing question regarding BurgerWorld's policy of hiring disabled employees, but received no response. What do you suppose Nadia's silence meant? How did her mother interpret Nadia's response? Regardless of the situation, your sensitivity to silence and its many meanings can only increase your overall effectiveness when you communicate.

Several final considerations are now addressed as you increase your understanding of the nonverbal dimensions of communication and develop the sensitivities that will enhance your empathic response.

VERBAL AND NONVERBAL CUES INTERRELATE

Although many nonverbal cues replace verbal messages or function independently, others can only be interpreted in conjunction with information received through the verbal channel. Illustrators (Ekman & Friesen, 1969), for instance, are learned nonverbal behaviors that accentuate, emphasize, punctuate, elaborate, or frame the verbal message. Illustrators vary dramatically from one culture to the next. What may be an innocent sign of encouragement in one culture can mean something obscene in another. Consequently, care must be taken to interpret these behaviors within their appropriate cultural context.

How was silence viewed, or used, by your family when you were growing up?

The following categories identify four of the most common ways in which verbal and nonverbal behaviors interrelate.

Contradicting

You ask your roommate if she can stay for a few minutes to help you prepare for an evening presentation. She says, "Sure," but her tone of voice indicates moderate annoyance and displeasure. "Come in, uh, good to see you," your friend says as he fidgets with his pen and glances at his watch. What messages come across?

When verbal and nonverbal messages contradict, listeners generally judge the nonverbal cues as the most reliable. Recognition of these often subtle behaviors, then, is essential to accurate interpretation.

Substituting

At times your partner many remain silent, but express important information through a nonverbal channel. These nonverbal cues are particularly significant when he has difficulty putting his ideas or feelings into words. As the poem in Box 6.12 suggests, there are numerous instances where you need to be sensitive to what is *not* said. Your ability correctly to interpret nonverbal cues can promote more open and productive communication if the information gained is confirmed and used in appropriate ways.

Complementing

Nonverbal behavior complements verbal messages by providing information about the nature of your relationship and by reinforcing the verbal message. We know, for

---

BOX 6.12

I suppose it was something you said that caused me to tighten and pull away. And when you asked, "What is it?"
I, of course, said "Nothing."
Whenever I say, "Nothing,"

You may be very certain there is something.
The something is a cold, hard lump of Nothing.

Lois Wyse
Love Poems for the Very Married

instance, that subtle nonverbal cues indicate each participant's perceptions of *his or her* relative status in the relationship. In addition, when a speaker has strong feelings about a person or idea, changes occur in his gestures, movement, and facial expression. The thoughtful use of nonverbal cues to reinforce and complement your words strengthens the impact of any oral message.

> What nonverbal cues are you likely to display when your status in the relationship is either particularly low or particularly high?

In fact, speech and movement can function as one system. This is referred to as speech–body movement synchrony. Synchrony has the potential to reveal a great deal about listening behavior as well as other aspects of interpersonal relationships. Perhaps the most common examples of synchrony are listener responses, often called minimal reinforcers, which occur at the ends of rhythmical units of speech. Typical listener behaviors include head nods and slight movements of the hands and feet.

Relating and Regulating

You are already familiar with the ways in which eye behavior serves as a regulating function in interactions. The flow of conversation is affected by other nonverbal cues as well. Rituals for greetings and goodbyes, for instance, can be complex. Kendon and Ferber (1973) studied the stages that characterized greetings individuals make when approaching each other from a distance. They describe the event from the first wave or smile through the head dip, grooming behavior, gaze, and head tilt to the final, ritualistic verbal exchange.

While speakers yield or maintain their position, listeners request or deny their turn to speak. Extensive video analyses have been done to determine exactly how such intentions are communicated. Those who don't want to take their turn speaking employ a different set of nonverbal behaviors than those who are anxious to talk. In addition to lack of eye contact, a relaxed posture and minimal reinforcers such as "uh-huh" and "oh" are used to pass up a turn to speak.

Think for a moment about how you indicate to your partner that you'd like to make a comment. One familiar method is just to speak up—to interrupt. Knapp (1978) describes this process in detail, observing that "an upraised index finger . . . accompanied by an audible inspiration of breath and a straightening and tightening of posture" (p. 360) often signals an intent to speak.

We all make judgments about our partners from their turn-taking behavior and how smoothly the interaction progresses. If you question the role of nonverbal communication in this process, just think back to some of your telephone conversations. When the nonverbal channel is missing, the probability of overlapping speech and awkward silences increases significantly. Look at the interactions described in "BurgerWorld." Notice how frequently silence affected participant's interpretations.

BECOMING AN EMPATHIC LISTENER

Even under the best of circumstances, nonverbal behavior is difficult to identify and interpret. You must ask yourself largely subjective questions:

Is the behavior intentional?
Is it linked to the speaker's personality?
Is it a reflection of his attitude?
Does it give clues to an emotional state?

Regardless of how much natural sensitivity you possess, empathy and the skills related to interpreting nonverbal messages can be learned, practiced, and improved (Blesius, 1989; Verderber & Verderber, 1989; Weaver, 1990). Individual differences, as mentioned earlier, only affect the amount of effort and energy you need to expend acquiring new behaviors and perspectives. If a skill doesn't come naturally, you must work harder at it to achieve your goals.

Although lack of clarification makes the development of an empathic response somewhat difficult to approach (Katz, 1963; Redmond, 1983; Stewart, 1983; Thomlison, 1991), a variety of recommendations have been made. There seems to be general agreement that to interpret messages effectively, you need to demonstrate high levels of competence in the following areas:

1. social perceptiveness
2. self-awareness
3. self-monitoring

Barrett-Lennard (1981) proposes that you can become more sensitive and empathic by following a five-step process, what he calls the empathy cycle (Figure 6.3). The first step requires that you assume an attitude that promotes cognitive empathy. This enables you to be receptive to your partner's unique perspective or world view.

The second step Barrett-Lennard calls empathic resonation. This involves a directed effort to understand the other person and to make her experiences clear and vivid. In step 3, you communicate your understanding to your partner through both verbal and nonverbal behavior.

Step 4 is termed received empathy. The speaker now has information regarding your degree of understanding, and this enables her to complete the cycle by providing feedback to you. Your perceptions may then be confirmed, corrected, or modified in the final stage of the cycle. Keep these stages in mind as you practice the skills identified in the following applications section and as you pursue your relationships outside of the classroom.

> Given the empathy cycle, where would you anticipate having the most personal difficulty?

Positive attitudes

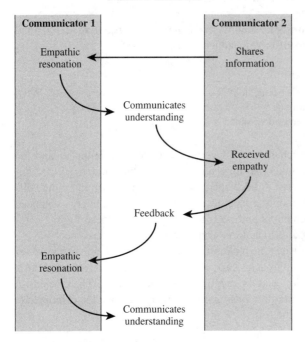

FIGURE 6.3   Empathy Cycle

SUMMARY

Interpreting messages requires knowledge, social sensitivity, and an authentic concern for others. Effectiveness in this dimension is significantly influenced both by individual differences and by cultural orientation.

Interpreting messages requires empathy, a concept that remains ambiguous in spite of substantial research efforts to better define its nature and scope. One of the most useful ways to think about empathy is to view it as three related dimensions: cognitive, perceptive, and behavioral. Remembering these categories will help to structure your efforts to improve empathic listening skills. Another useful framework for assessing and developing your ability to interpret messages is emotional intelligence.

Since interpretation relies on your sensitivity to situational and nonverbal dimensions of the communication encounter, knowledge of nonverbal behavior is essential. Aspects such as facial expression, eye behavior, body movement, posture, gestures, touch, and appearance all contribute both to perceptions of listening effectiveness and to your ability to recognize important feelings and attitudes. Vocal cues, as well as silence, also communicate important messages to the perceptive listener.

Verbal and nonverbal dimensions interrelate in providing you with information regarding your partner's attitudes, feelings, and ideas. In addition, a cluster of nonverbal behaviors are associated with the communication of warmth and openness. In your efforts to become a more empathic listener, you might also increase your social sensitivity, self-awareness, and self-monitoring skills.

APPLICATIONS

Application 1: Develop the Cognitive Aspects of Empathy
Application 2: Develop the Perceptive Aspects of Empathy
Application 3: Develop the Behavioral Aspects of Empathy
Application 4: Interpret Your Partner's Vocal Cues
Application 5: Identify the Ways in Which Verbal and Nonverbal Behaviors Interrelate

_____ I take into account the speaker's personal and cultural perspective when listening to him.

_____ I take into account the person's motives, expectations, and needs when determining the meaning of the message.
Application 1: Develop the Cognitive Aspects of Empathy

_____ I am sensitive to the speaker's feelings in communication situations.
Application 2: Develop the Perceptive Aspects of Empathy

_____ I let the speaker know immediately that she has been understood.
Application 3: Develop the Behavioral Aspects of Empathy

_____ I am sensitive to the speaker's tone of voice in communication situations.
Application 4: Interpret Your Partner's Vocal Cues

_____ I consider how the speaker's facial expressions, body posture, and other nonverbal behaviors relate to the verbal message.
Application 5: Identify the Ways in Which Verbal and Nonverbal Behaviors Interrelate

Application 1: Develop the Cognitive Aspects of Empathy

Prepare yourself for empathic listening by developing the cognitive aspects of empathy. This requires that you cultivate an attitude of openness and an appreciation of potential differences between your partner and yourself. Egocentricity is a major block to developing empathy; strive to mentally free yourself of your own biases, values, and immediate needs so that you can focus on your partner.

The first step in this process is recognizing how your life experiences form the basis of your assumptions and shape your expectations. The same is true for your partner. Taking into account your partner's past experiences and relationship to the topic at hand will help you to interpret what you hear and to negotiate shared meanings.

Activities

1. Describe a situation you've experienced which required emotional labor. Perhaps it was a wedding, a reception, or a job responsibility.

   What was your response to this experience?
   What did you learn about yourself?

2. Make a special effort to meet and interact with people you believe hold different values or come from backgrounds different from your own. Keep a journal of these interactions, noting the ways in which cognitive empathy is required for effective communication.

   Ask yourself the following questions:

   a. Do I have a fundamental respect for my partner?
   b. Have I looked at my own listening behaviors and attempted to be as open and concerned as possible?
   c. Have I assessed my own nonverbal response style and developed behaviors that communicate warmth and support?
   d. Have I taken steps so that my personal opinions, feelings, and attitudes will have a minimal affect on my response?
   e. Did I attempt to learn as much as possible about my partner?
   f. Am I sensitive to my partner's nonverbal cues?
   g. Have I worked to create a supportive listening environment?

3. Select three individuals whom you believe have very different points of view due to their values, role, or past experiences. Choose one of the topics listed below and try to predict how each would respond. What accounts for any differences among the three people? Check with each person, if possible, to see how accurately you predicted his or her response.

   a. abortion
   b. mandatory drug testing
   c. a carefree, live and let live attitude toward their work
   d. gay adoptions

4. What specific events or messages contributed to shaping your attitudes toward each of the following:

   a. health
   b. education
   c. travel
   d. gender roles
   e. drugs

5. Make a list of your five best friends.

   a. In what ways are they similar to you?
   b. In what ways are they different?
   c. What conclusions can you draw from this exercise with regard to cognitive empathy and your choice of close friends?

Group Activities

Form a small group of four to six people. You may want to keep the same group for all activities, or you may find it more interesting to change groups so that you get to hear the opinions and ideas of a greater number of your classmates.

1. Each group member identifies a famous person he or she believes demonstrates cognitive empathy. Members share their choices and discuss:
   How is this attitude conveyed?
   Would everyone agree with this choice?
   What characteristics do all the listeners who were mentioned have in common?

2. Brainstorm political situations throughout history where cognitive empathy was important in negotiations and eventual peace. What are the best examples? What situations have been provoked or have escalated as a result of participants' lack of cognitive empathy? Describe.

3. Supervisors often have to discuss employees' personal problems when these problems begin to affect their job performance. Likewise, educators often advise students in matters that may not pertain directly to their courses. In such situations, the manager or teacher may only be interested in performing *his* job and have no real interest in the person who is sharing personal information.

   a. To what extent do you believe this happens? Use personal experiences, whenever possible, to support your points.

   b. In what other contexts is it likely that individuals may project empathy without truly experiencing it? Are these situations inevitable?

   c. Are there actions either party can take to remedy this situation?

4. As a group, identify a conflict situation that could result from differences in perception due to different role relationships such as:

   student/teacher
   parent/child
   secretary/supervisor
   repairperson/home owner
   doctor/patient

   Role-play the conflict. Discuss how the conflict might have been avoided had the perspectives of the other individual been taken into consideration.

   Role-play the situation a second time, attempting to resolve the conflict through empathy and compromise. Did it work? Are there some conflicts that cannot be resolved in this way?

5. Discuss the role and importance of cognitive empathy in communication. What can you do as a listener to foster and maintain open attitudes? What role does effective listening play in creating a positive relationship? Provide examples.

6. Discuss experiences group members have had visiting:

   a. other families (dinner, overnight, parties, etc.)

   b. other parts of the United States, or

   c. other countries.

   What differences did you find most striking?
   How did you adjust to these behaviors or situations?

Application 2: Develop the Perceptive Aspects of Empathy

and

Application 3: Develop the Behavioral Aspects of Empathy

In the exercises that follow, both your sensitivity to nonverbal cues (perceptive aspects) and your nonverbal responses (behavioral aspects) are examined. As a listener, you must both interpret your partner's nonverbal cues and send nonverbal messages that facilitate shared meanings. In other words, your goal is to demonstrate a high level of emotional intelligence.

Keep in mind that your nonverbal communication may not translate across cultures in the manner you intend. Nonverbal cues must be placed into a cultural as well as a personal context. Our discussions pertain exclusively to the dominant culture of the United States; your response must be adapted when communicating with individuals from other backgrounds and orientations.

Activities

1. Note how much eye contact you use in your daily interactions.

   - When is your eye contact strongest?
   - In what situations do you have difficulty maintaining your focus?
   - Do you find it easier to look at your partner when you are speaking or listening?
   - Do you have better eye contact with your classmates and friends or with your teachers?
   - In what ways do you use eye behavior as a cue in your communication?

2. Break several eye contact norms and see what happens. Stare at people in elevators. Look intently at someone's elbow when you speak. Think of some creative ways to change your typical behaviors and see what happens.

   a. How did you feel?
   b. What was the other person's response?
   c. How did it affect your communication?

3. When do you use your sense of touch? Do you touch others easily? What influences your attitude and comfort level toward physical contact with others? Why do you think it is that many people in the United States tend to use distance receptors—eyes and ears—for most of their communication?

   What connotations does touching have for people in the United States?
   For those from other cultures?
   How does touching affect listening?

4. Identify two or three individuals whom you would describe as good listeners. Observe them "in action."
   What nonverbal cues do they provide?
   What sets them apart as a good listener?

5. Observe an extended conversation where you will not influence the participants. As you watch, take notes and try to determine:

   a. whether the nonverbal behaviors are intentional or unintentional;
   b. what emotions are being communicated through facial expressions;
   c. whether the person's body and posture provide useful cues to his or her meanings or emotional state;
   d. if eye behavior is affecting the communication encounter or if the participants are experiencing any discomfort;
   e. whether silences provide insights into the participant's meanings.

6. Turn off the volume of your television set and see how much of the meaning of the exchanges you can determine just through observing nonverbal communication. Observe the actors' facial expressions, gestures, and movements. How are they used to create meaning?

   Alternative Exercise: Complete this assignment with a partner. Compare your interpretations of the nonverbal behavior. Did you both interpret what you observed in the same way?

7. Consider the extent to which you were born with emotional intelligence and the extent to which you have made a conscious effort to develop this aspect of your listening behavior.

   What early experiences do you recall that give you clues to your innate E.Q. ability? In what ways have you tried to consciously develop and realize your E.Q. potential? Do you agree that you can increase your emotional intelligence through focused efforts?
   Which of your family members have a high E.Q.? How do they demonstrate this "intelligence"?

8. Fill out the following *Self-assessment of Nonverbal Listening Behavior.* Consider the results, and then set a concrete objective for yourself.

   At this stage, you may want to double-check your perceptions against those of your group members or several good friends. When you feel comfortable with your goals, solicit the help of a friend in carrying out your plan to use more effective nonverbal behaviors.

Self-assessment of Nonverbal Listening Behavior

	YOU AS A LISTENER		
	Need to Develop	Effective	Need to Eliminate
A. Face and head Movements			
1. Head Nods	_____	_____	_____
2. Calm, yet expressive facial movements	_____	_____	_____
B. Eye Behavior			
3. Blank stare	_____	_____	_____
4. Averting eyes when another looks at you	_____	_____	_____
5. Spontaneous eye contact when listening	_____	_____	_____

YOU AS A LISTENER

	Need to Develop	Effective	Need to Eliminate
C. Hands and Arm Movements			
6. Stiff, lack of appropriate gestures	_____	_____	_____
7. Frequent touching behavior	_____	_____	_____
8. Repetitive or distracting hand movements	_____	_____	_____
D. Body Position			
9. Slouching	_____	_____	_____
10. Relaxed but alert posture	_____	_____	_____
11. Rigid posture	_____	_____	_____
E. Body Orientation			
12. Body positioned toward other	_____	_____	_____
13. Physically distant from other	_____	_____	_____
14. Sit close to others	_____	_____	_____
15. Lean away from others	_____	_____	_____

Group Activities

Form a small group of four to six people. You may want to keep the same group for all activities, or you may find it more interesting to change groups so that you get to hear the opinions and ideas of a greater number of your classmates.

1. Summarize your eye contact habits and your comfort level with eye contact. Compare your summary with those created by other members of your group. Look for both similarities and differences. Discuss the possible reasons for the individual differences you identify.

2. As a group, discuss the following questions:

    a. What aspects of an individual's appearance do you believe are particularly significant?

    b. How do you interpret specific aspects of appearance, such as shoes, jewelry, hairstyle, dress, makeup, and other personal factors?

    c. Bring in several pictures to share with group members. Discuss them as examples of how body and attire communicate. Notice any difference among group members' perceptions, and discuss the reasons for these differences.

3. How do your clothes influence others' perceptions of you? Take a look at the inside of your closet. What colors stand out? Are there bright colors, patterns, browns and blues, solids? Do you own a variety of styles and designs, or do you stick to a couple of basics? Do you choose clothes for comfort? Cost? Style?

    Summarize your findings and share them with members of your group. What conclusions can you draw about the ways in which clothes communicate?

4. Under what circumstances do you intentionally manipulate your appearance to project a particular impression? Have you had an experience where you've been listened to (or not listened to) on the basis of how you look? Discuss the details of this experience with other group members. What are the ethical concerns related to impression management?

For instance, when you go for an employment interview, how much should you engage in "impression management" to project the image you believe the interviewer wants to see—regardless of whether or not it is characteristic of your style? Share your concerns related to this topic.

5. Form a circle. A volunteer begins by displaying any facial expression to the person to his or her right. That person must first mirror the facial expression back to the first person and then turn to the person on his or her right with a facial expression that is a reaction to the one he or she just mimicked.

The third person then mirrors the facial expression received before turning to his or her right and responding with a new expression. Continue around the circle until all participants have had an opportunity both to mirror an expression and to respond to that expression with a new one.

Discuss any difficulties involved as well as any individual differences that were noted as the activity progressed.

6. Discuss the many ways in which eye behavior is used to facilitate or block communication. Generate a list of generally accepted rules that are used in the dominant culture of the United States. Ask members of your group who are from other cultures to note how their norms differ. Share your completed list with other groups and compare. Discuss what happens when these rules are broken, and how listening is affected.

7. Your goal as a group is to create a human machine—any kind of coordinated, integrated, moving system that functions to accomplish a particular purpose. Use your imaginations. The machine must be created, however, with *no talking during any stage*. All planning and organizing must be accomplished *nonverbally*. After ten minutes, each group takes its turn performing for the rest of the class.

Following the demonstration, respond to the following questions:

a. Was it frustrating not to be able to speak?
b. In what ways did members of your group communicate nonverbally?
c. Did a leader emerge? How?
d. What were the most significant or helpful nonverbal cues?
e. Was there any conflict or disagreement within the group? If so, how was it resolved?
f. Did everyone "listen"?
g. Did any group-specific nonverbal codes or language develop? Explain.

8. Your small group will be assigned an emotion. Your goal is to demonstrate to the rest of the class, *as a group,* the nonverbal dimensions that communicate this emotion by using the following behaviors. Be creative in your presentation!

a. eye behavior
b. posture
c. gesture
d. movement
e. facial expression
f. voice

Possible emotions include sympathy, confidence, anger, embarrassment, enthusiasm, hesitation, defensiveness, and so on.

9. Sit facing a partner and stare at each other for two minutes. Don't speak. When the two minutes are up, discuss your reactions.

   a. What did you notice about your eye behavior?
   b. Were there any unintentional nonverbal behaviors demonstrated?

   Now, form a circle with your entire group. Remain in the circle for three minutes without speaking. Observe the behavior of other group members. Discuss your reactions and the nonverbal behaviors you observed.

10. Sit back-to-back with a partner and discuss a personal topic such as how you feel about an important issue, an embarrassing or emotional experience you've had recently, or some other appropriate subject. Make sure you include your feelings as well as your ideas. After four minutes, change roles. How did the absence of nonverbal cues affect your interactions?

11. Think of someone you know who projects a strong impression, either warmth or aloofness. Generate a list of nonverbal cues that this individual sends. Then, identify someone who projects the opposite impression and follow the same procedure. Compile your lists of cold and warm behaviors. How does your list compare to the one presented in the text?

    Go around to each member of the group and help that person identify two or three behaviors that are typical of his listening response. Do these behaviors suggest warmth? Can everyone in your group agree?

12. Divide into groups of three or four.

    Person A is the speaker. He chooses an interesting topic on which he can speak for two to three minutes—a vacation, a movie, a fantasy, and so on.

    Person B is a very good listener. While A speaks, B listens carefully and attentively. She provides reinforcement and shows complete interest.

    Person C is a poor listener. He is disinterested, apathetic, bored, and anxious. He indicates in many obvious ways that he would rather be elsewhere.

    Person D (optional) is trying hard to listen but is distracted by other stimuli, both internal and external. She wants to listen, but is not too successful.

    When you have completed the exercise, discuss the following:

    a. What feelings did you have as you performed your role?
    b. What nonverbal behaviors were demonstrated by each of the three (or four) role-players?
    c. Where did Person A focus his attention? How did he respond to Person C?
    d. What behaviors appear to characterize a good listener?
    e. What behaviors communicate indifference? apathy? anxiousness?

13. Choose a partner. Stand face-to-face for thirty seconds and examine the other person carefully. Then, turn so your backs are together and quickly make five "changes" in your appearance (remove a watch, unbutton a shirt, part hair differently, and so forth). Face each other again. See if you both can identify all five changes in your partner's appearance. What did you learn from this experience?

Application 4: Interpret Your Partner's Vocal Cues

Often, it's not what you say, but how you say it, that makes the critical communication difference. The more you know about the dimensions of voice, and the more aware you are of its power to communicate, the better able you will be to use voice as one source of information in interpreting messages. The following exercises will heighten your awareness of your own voice and of how vocal (paralinguistic) cues function as a form of nonverbal communication.

Activities

1. How comfortable are you with silence? Notice situations where silence occurs. How do you react? Do you tend to ooververbalize to prevent long silences? Are you more comfortable in some situations than in others? Why?

2. What voices do you find communicate a strong image? List media figures—singers, actors, politicians—whose voices are distinctive. Describe the impression they make on you, and identify the characteristics of their voices that contribute to this image.

Group Activities

Form a small group of four to six people. You may want to keep the same group for all activities, or you may find it more interesting to change groups so that you get to hear the opinions and ideas of a greater number of your classmates.

1. *Round 1:* Form groups of from ten to twenty members. A volunteer from the group selects one of the emotions listed below. After making his selection, he stands facing away from the rest of the group and counts to ten, communicating the emotion through *voice* alone. Group participants then guess which emotion was expressed. Repeat this procedure with three or four more volunteers.

   Round 2: This time, the volunteers face the group and communicate the chosen emotion using both *voice* and *facial expression.* Participants again guess the emotion being communicated.

   Round 3: Volunteers again select an emotion. This time they use *voice, facial expression,* and *gesture* to communicate. After all volunteers have had a turn, discuss the following:

   a. Was it easy to communicate through voice? Through facial expression?
   b. How accurately were participants able to identify the emotion?
   c. Which cues do you rely on most for information about the speaker's emotional state?
   d. Is it true that multiple channels help you interpret feelings more accurately?

   #### Possible Emotions

sympathy	pity	curiosity	apathy
anger	fear	sorrow	hesitation
revulsion	joy	surprise	

2. Each member of your group chooses one of the items below and determines two different meanings that could be communicated. Members then write down the meanings they will be projecting vocally.

Example: That was nice.   Meaning 1: That was a thoughtful thing to do.
                               Meaning 2: What a stupid thing to have done!
        Next, take turns saying your item twice, changing your vocal cues so that a different meaning is projected each time. After each person presents her two items, members try to guess the meanings being communicated.

a. When is it particularly important to listen for vocal cues to accurately interpret someone's meaning?
b. How do you go about improving your sensitivity to vocal cues?
c. What features of voice were modified to alter meanings?

Items for Vocal Meaning

a. She did.   d. Go ahead.
b. That's okay.   e. Too bad.
c. All right.   f. Nice job.

3. Review the *Listen for Feelings* worksheet. Select a member of your group to read the first sentence silently and determine what feeling is most appropriate to convey. Then, ask that individual to read the sentence to the group, using his or her voice to communicate a paralinguistic feature or emotion. Other members of the group each guess what feeling the speaker's voice conveyed. Move to the next sentence, and select another member of the group. Repeat the process above until all sentences have been read. How accurate were group members in identifying the various meanings?

Listen for Feelings

Read each of the following sentences carefully. Then write down several adjectives that describe how the person might be *feeling*.

1. Hey, leave that alone! It's mine!

    Feeling: _____

2. Why don't you just tell me what's wrong? All you do is mope around without even answering when I say something to you.

    Feeling: _____

3. No wonder he got the promotion. He was sitting next to his supervisor, hanging on every word he said. It's disgusting.

    Feeling: _____

4. It happened again! Just when I thought everything was going well, the boss comes in and tells me I'm still not working "up to speed." What does he expect?

    Feeling: _____

5. Hey, you won't believe this! I just got a letter of congratulations from Mr. Mackey on the job I did last month. What a surprise!

    Feeling: _____

6. Every time I go to the cabinet to get some supplies, we're out! How can I keep up with the ordering when no one ever tells me she's taken something?

    Feeling: _____

7. I came very close to staying home this morning. First the furnace went off, then Katie had hurt herself pretty badly walking up to the bus. I had a headache—nothing went right and I just wanted to go back to bed.

    Feeling: _____

8. Of course Mike was the one to get the promotion. All he does is sit around trying to figure out who to talk with, who to sit next to, who to do favors for. I just try to do a good job here. Guess I have the wrong approach.

    Feeling: _____

4. Make a tape recording of your voice (three to five minutes of normal conversation). Listen to the recording as you complete the following *Voice Self-assessment.*

    Are you generally satisfied with your voice?
    What aspects are strong?
    What aspects would you like to work on?
    Now, play the tape for members of your group. Share your responses to the *Voice Self-assessment* and determine if your group members agree with your analysis. Discuss any differences of opinion.

Voice Self-assessment

1. In terms of volume:
    _____ I am easy to hear: I project my voice well and I am quite loud.
    _____ I am generally easy to hear, although at times my voice fades.
    _____ I can be heard, but my voice is often soft and my partner has to listen closely to hear what I say.

2. In terms of pitch:
    _____ My pitch is generally very high for my gender and age.
    _____ My pitch is generally very low for my gender and age.
    _____ I don't tend to vary my pitch very much in conversation.
    _____ I vary my pitch quite a bit in conversations.

3. In terms of rate:
    _____ I have a tendency to speak fairly quickly.
    _____ I have a tendency to speak rather slowly and thoughtfully.
    _____ I have a tendency to speak quickly when I become excited or emotional.
    _____ My pace is regular and consistent.
    _____ My pace varies according to what I am talking about.

4. The quality of my voice is generally:
    _____ normal   _____ breathy
    _____ harsh   _____ hoarse
    _____ nasal   _____ other
    _____ denasal

5. When I am in the following emotional states:
    Angry   My voice tends to:
    Upset   My voice tends to:
    Excited   My voice tends to:
    Happy   My voice tends to:
    Other comments:

6. Overall:

_____ I am quite satisfied with my voice.

_____ I use adequate vocal variety when I speak.

_____ I am a bit too monotone when I speak.

_____ I convey appropriate attitudes and emotions when I speak.

_____ There are a few aspects of my voice that I need to work on before I'm satisfied with the way I sound.

7. My action plan:

Application 5: Identify the Ways in Which Verbal and Non-verbal Behaviors Interrelate

Your ability to make others comfortable in communication situations can be improved through greater attention to nonverbal cues. Observing significant nonverbal behavior gives you information that might otherwise be overlooked. Nonverbal cues can indicate that your partner is anxious, embarrassed, or bored. Remember, however, that your interpretations might be incorrect; perception-check verbally before you rely too heavily on your assumptions about the meaning of nonverbal cues.

Activities

1. What nonverbal behaviors do you use to regulate conversation? What do you do when you want a turn to speak? What do you do when you want to end the encounter?

2. Do you sometimes have trouble regulating conversations over the telephone? Why? What factors make telephone conversations more difficult to interpret accurately? The next time you have a telephone conversation, pay special attention to the ways in which you nonverbally indicate turn-taking.

3. During the next week, keep a list of the nonverbal cues you notice that you believe are unintentional.

   Indicate the circumstances in which the behavior occurred. What types of behaviors occur most frequently?

   Can you identify examples of nonverbal leakage?
   Were there occasions when the verbal and nonverbal messages were contradictory?
   Do some people appear to be more expressive nonverbally than others?

Group Activities

Form a small group of four to six people. You may want to keep the same group for all activities, or you may find it more interesting to change groups so that you get to hear the opinions and ideas of a greater number of your classmates.

1. Identify and discuss recent situations where an individual's verbal and nonverbal communication were contradictory.

   Which message was intended?
   How did you respond? Why? Were you satisfied with your response?
   Try deliberately projecting contradictory verbal and nonverbal messages.

- Pound a table with your fist as you say gently, "This is a beautiful kitten."
- Jump up and down vigorously as you say quietly, "We have to be calm now."

Use your imagination to create other mixed cues. Demonstrate one of your original "mixed messages" to the rest of the class.

2. Identify a situation in which an individual's verbal and nonverbal behavior is contradictory. How does this situation create misunderstandings?

Select one situation that has been discussed and role-play it for the rest of the class. Discuss what should be done by the listener when she perceives mixed messages. Sample Situations:

   a. Person says he's not nervous . . .
   b. Person says she's having a good time . . .
   c. Person says she's in no hurry . . .
   d. Person says he's glad to help out . . .
   e. Person says it's his favorite meal . . .

3. What nonverbal cues are you particularly sensitive to in interpersonal contexts? How do they affect your perceptions of the verbal message? Think back to when you were growing up. What mixed messages did you receive from the adults around you—parents, teachers, relatives?

4. Brainstorm nonverbal cues which are typically used to substitute for words. What ones do you use?

5. Do some research on the nonverbal cues other cultures use in various situations that are different from behaviors in the United States. Share your findings with your group.

As a group, select an appropriate example and role-play it for the rest of the class. How might these cues be misinterpreted by someone from the United States? What would an effective listener do to ensure that meanings were shared?

SHORT CASES FOR ANALYSIS AND DISCUSSION

1. The Transfer: On Tuesday Sally learned that her husband might be transferred at any time to another plant in the eastern region. The news came as a surprise, and Sally found it particularly upsetting because it would likely mean that, after having worked hard and having learned a great deal about the company she worked for, she would be forced to resign her position and start over at another firm. At work the next day she felt totally disoriented. She was still adjusting to the news—information she didn't feel as yet she could share with even her closest colleagues.

   a. What nonverbal cues might Sally be sending?
   b. Describe what Sally was feeling.
   c. Assume that a co-worker and good friend has come up to Sally and asked her what the trouble was. Write a dialogue between the two the way you would imagine the conversation going.

2. Subtle Cues: Sally had worked with John as her partner in their science class for over half of the semester. She enjoyed his company, and their working relationship seemed very good. This past weekend, however, she had been out of town and had gotten backed up on her work for the course. John was very understanding, although concerned about the pressure they were now under to get their lab work in on time.

Role-play this situation three times, communicating a slightly different meaning each time.

> Situation 1: John really doesn't mind.
> Situation 2: John is really upset, but he is trying to act polite and be understanding.
> Situation 3: John is upset and annoyed.

    a. What nonverbal differences did you notice among the three role-plays?
    b. What implications does each scenario have for the participants' listening behavior?

    3. Feeling Rejected: Sitting at her desk looking over their last lab report, Sally suddenly had the urge to talk to someone. Her father's company had just transferred him to a plant in Singapore, and the move was very much on her mind. She walked over to where John was working and looked down at the pile of papers on his desk. He glanced up at her and smiled, but kept on reviewing the papers in front of him. Sally waited for what seemed like an eternity, and still John kept his attention on his paperwork. Feeling unhappy about her family's eminent move, guilty for having tried to interrupt John, and hurt that he had ignored her, she walked slowly back to her desk.

    a. What nonverbal cues did John send that gave Sally a clear message?
    b. What information do we have about Sally that helps us interpret her behavior?
    c. What nonverbal cues was Sally sending? Which were intentional? Which were unintentional?
    d. In what other ways could Sally have handled this situation?
    e. Did John show a lack of empathy? Did Sally? Explain.

BURGERWORLD: CASE QUESTIONS

1. Give an example of how point of view influenced an individual's listening behavior and interpretation of a situation. What was at the root of Nadia's anxiety over her relationship with Sandy?

2. Consider the relationship between Nadia and Sandy, and discuss how the degree of empathy Nadia experienced changed over time.

3. Discuss each person's listening effectiveness and their level of empathy as portrayed in the case.

    a. Nadia's mother   d. Mark
    b. Tina   e. Sandy
    c. Nadia   f. Jay

4. What nonverbal indicators provided cues to how an individual was feeling? Be sure to address such aspects as touch and silence as well as other dimensions.

5. Why did Sandy turn down Nadia's offer to go to the Fountain the first time she was asked? How did Nadia modify her strategy in light of Sandy's response?

6. As a group, role-play the following encounters for the rest of the class. Pay particular attention to the nonverbal and vocal aspects of communication. Elaborate on the information provided in the case in any way that seems appropriate.

a. Nadia's mother tries to talk with her about working with the disabled. Tina quietly observes.
b. Mark asks Nadia for her help in training Sandy.
c. Nadia invites Sandy to the Fountain for a soda.
d. Patty takes the order for Sandy and Nadia at the Fountain.
e. Sandy and Nadia discuss working at BurgerWorld.

Discuss the listening behavior of the participants in each encounter. Were they listening? If not, what recommendations can you make to facilitate more effective relational communication?

7. In your text a point is made about the fact that both participants in the communication encounter must work toward empathy—it's not something that can be imposed. Discuss this point with regard to the empathy Nadia was able to establish with Sandy.

8. What responsibility do you think Mark has toward Sandy as an employee? Do you believe that part of his job entails listening to her and understanding her needs as a unique person, or is a manager's obligation just to get the job accomplished through his staff?

BIBLIOGRAPHY

Argyle, M., & Cook, M. (1972). *Gaze and mutual gaze.* New York: Cambridge University Press.
Bakan, P., & Strayer, F. F. (1973). On reliability of conjugate lateral eye movements. *Perceptual and Motor Skills, 36,* 429–430.
Barrett-Lennard, G. T. (1981). The empathy cycle: Refinement of a nuclear concept. *Journal of Counseling Psychology, 28,* 91–100.
Basch, M. F. (1983). Empathic understanding: A review of the concept and some theoretical considerations. *American Psychoanalytic Association Journal, 31,* 101–126.
Becker, T. (2003). Is emotional intelligence a viable concept? *Academy of Management Review, 28,* 192–195.
Birdwhistell, R. L. (1970). *Kinesics and context.* Philadelphia: University of Pennsylvania Press.
Blesius, R. (1989). The concept of empathy. *Psychology: A Journal of Human Behavior, 26*(4), 10–15.
Bostrom, R. N. (1990). *Listening behavior: Measurement & application.* New York: The Guilford Press.
Boyatzis, R., Goleman, D., & Rhee, K. (1999). Clustering competence in emotional intelligence: Insights from the emotional competence inventory. In R. Baron and J. D. Parker (Eds.), *Handbook of Emotional Intelligence.* San Francisco, CA: Jossey-Bass.
Boyatzis, R., & Van Oosten, E. (2003). A leadership imperative: Building the emotionally intelligent organization. *Ivey Business Journal, 67*(2), 43–61.
Brownell, J. (1994). Relational listening: Fostering effective communication practices in diverse organizational environments. *CHRIE Hospitality and Tourism Educator, 6*(4), 11–16.
Bruneau, T. (1989). Empathy and listening: A conceptual review and theoretical directions. *Journal of the International Listening Association, 3,* 1–20.
Bruneau, T. (1993). Empathy and listening. In A. D. Wolvin and C. G. Coakley (Eds.), *Perspectives on Listening,* pp. 185–200. Norwood, NJ: Ablex Publishing.
Buber, M. (1965). Elements of the interhuman. In M. Friedman (Ed.), *The Knowledge of Man: Selected Essays,* pp. 72–88. New York: Harper and Row.
Buie, D. H. (1981). Empathy: Its nature and limitations. *American Psychoanalytic Association Journal, 29,* 281–307.
Clore, G. L., Wiggins, N. H., & Itkin, S. (1975). Gain and loss in attraction: Attributions from nonverbal behavior. *Journal of Personality and Social Psychology, 31,* 706–712.

Cortes, J. B., & Gatti, F. M. (1965). Physique and self-description of temperament. *Journal of Consulting Psychology, 29,* 434.

Davitz, J. R. (1964). A review of research concerned with facial and vocal expressions of emotion. In J. R. Davitz (Ed.), *The Communication of Emotional Meaning,* pp. 13–23. New York: McGraw-Hill.

Dawda, R., & Hart, S. D. (2000). Assessing emotional intelligence: Reliability and validity of the Bar-On emotional quotient inventory (EQ-i) in university students. *Journal of Personal and Individual Differences, 28,* 797–812.

Day, M. E. (1964). Eye movement phenomena relating to attention, thought and anxiety. *Perceptual and Motor Skills, 19,* 443–446.

Druskat, V. U., & Wolff, S. B. (2001). Building the emotional intelligence of groups. *Harvard Business Review,* 81–90.

Egan, G. (1977). *You and me: The skills of communicating and relating to others.* Belmont, CA: Wadsworth Publishing Company.

Ekman, P., & Friesen, W. V. (1969). The repertoire of nonverbal behavior: Categories, origins, usage and coding. *Semiotica, 1,* 49–98.

Ekman, P., Friesen, W. V., & Tomkins, S. S. (1971). Facial affect scoring technique: A first validity study. *Semiotica, 3,* 37–58.

Fineman, S. (2003). *Understanding emotions at work.* London: Sage Publishers.

Goffman, I. (1974). *Behavior in public places: Notes on the social organization of gatherings.* New York: The Free Press.

Goleman, D. (1995). *Emotional intelligence.* New York: Bantam Books.

Goleman, D. (1998). *Working with emotional intelligence.* New York: Bantam Books.

Goleman, D. (2004). What makes a leader? *Harvard Business Review, 82*(1), 82–97.

Harman, J. J. (1986). Relations among components of the empathetic process. *Journal of Counseling Psychology, 33*(4), 371–376.

Henley, N. (1977). *Body politics: Power, sex and nonverbal communication.* Englewood Cliffs, NJ: Prentice Hall.

Howell, W. S. (1982). *The empathic communicator.* Belmont, CA: Wadsworth Publishers.

Jenkins, S. J., Stephens, J. C., & Chew, A. L. (1992). Examination of the relationship between the Myers-Briggs Type Indicator and empathetic response. *Perceptual and Motor Skills, 74*(3), 1003–1009.

Kalbfleisch, P. J. (1990). Listening for deception: The effects of medium on accuracy of detection. In R. N. Bostrom (Ed.), *Listening Behavior: Measurement & Application,* pp. 155–176. New York: The Guilford Press.

Katz, R. L. (1963). *Empathy: Its nature and uses.* New York: Free Press.

Kendon, A., & Ferber, A. (1973). A description of some human greetings. In R. P. Michael and J. H. Crook (Eds.), *Comparative Ecology and Behavior of Primates,* pp. 74–86. London: Academic Press.

Knapp, M. L. (1978). *Nonverbal communication in human interaction.* New York: Holt, Rinehart, & Winston.

LaFrance, M., & Mayo, C. (1976). Racial differences in gaze behavior during conversations: Two systematic observational studies. *Journal of Personality and Social Psychology, 33,* 547–552.

Leathers, D., & Emigh, T. (1980). Decoding facial expression: A new test with decoding norms. *Quarterly Journal of Speech, 66,* 418–436.

Macarov, D. (1978). Empathy: The charismatic charmers. *Journal of Education for Social Work, 14*(3), 86–92.

Mehrabian, A. (1971). *Silent messages.* Belmont, CA: Wadsworth Publishing.

Mills, J., & Aronson, E. (1965). Opinion change as a function of the communicator's attractiveness and desire to influence. *Journal of Personality and Social Psychology, 1,* 73–77.

Nguyen, M. L., Heslin, R., & Nguyen, T. (1976). The meaning of touch: Sex and marital status differences. *Representative Research in Social Psychology, 7,* 13–18.

Redmond, M. V. (1983). Towards resolution of the confusion among the concepts empathy, role-taking, perspective-taking, and decentering. Paper presented at the meeting of the Speech Communication Association, Washington, D.C. ERIC document 236748.

Reece, M., & Whitman, R. (1962). Expressive movements, warmth, and verbal reinforcement. *Journal of Abnormal and Social Psychology, 64,* 234–236.

Rosenfeld, L. B., & Civikly, J. M. (1976). *With words unspoken: The nonverbal experience.* New York: Holt, Rinehart, & Winston.

Rosenthal, R., Archer, D., DiMatteo, M. R., Koivumaki, J. H., & Rogers, P. L. (1979). Measuring sensitivity to nonverbal communication: The PONS test. Unpublished manuscript, Harvard University, 1975.

Salovey, P., & Mayer, J. D. (1990). Emotional intelligence. *Imagination, Cognition, and Personality, 9,* 185–211.

Scheflen, A. E. (1966). Natural history method in psychotherapy: Communication research. In L. A. Gottschalk and A. Auerback (Eds.), *Methods of Research in Psychotherapy,* pp. 280–287. New York: Appleton-Century-Crofts.

Singer, J. E. (1964). The use of manipulative strategies: Machiavellianism and attractiveness. *Sociometry, 27,* 128–151.

Stewart, J. (1983). Interpretive listening: An alternative to empathy. *Communication Education, 32,* 379–391.

Stewart, J., & Thomas, M. (1986). Dialogic listening: Sculpting mutual meanings. In J. Stewart (Ed.), *Bridges Not Walls: A Book About Interpersonal Communication,* pp. 192–210. New York: McGraw-Hill.

Thomlison, D. (1991). Intercultural listening. In D. Borisoff and M. Purdy (Eds.), *Listening in Everyday Life: A Personal and Professional Approach,* pp. 87–138. New York: University Press of America.

Verderber, R. F., & Verderber, K. S. (1989). *Inter-act: Using interpersonal communication skills.* Belmont, CA: Wadsworth Publishers.

Walp, B. (2001). *Project management and emotional intelligence.* Monograph completed in fulfillment of the requirements of the MMH degree, School of Hotel Administration, Cornell University.

Weaver, R. L., II. (1990). *Understanding interpersonal communication.* Glenview, IL: Scott, Foresman Company.

Widgery, R. N. (1974). Sex of receiver and physical attractiveness of source as determinants of initial credibility perception. *Western Speech, 38,* 13–17.

CHAPTER 7

THE PROCESS
OF EVALUATING

Folks who think they must always speak the truth overlook
another good choice—silence.

—C. L. NULL

OUTLINE

CHAPTER OBJECTIVES

After completing this chapter, you will

Become more aware of:

- the importance of critical listening in decision-making and problem-solving
- the influence of speaker credibility on perceptions of the message
- the ways in which communicators use logic and emotion to influence

Better understand:

- listening problems created by inappropriate habits of thought
- the impact of speaker credibility on influence attempts
- the principles of logic and reasoning
- types of evidence
- the differences between facts, opinions, and inferences
- propaganda and emotional appeals
- the use of language in persuasion

Develop skills in:

- analyzing source credibility
- analyzing a communicator's reasoning
- analyzing a communicator's evidence
- analyzing a communicator's emotional appeals

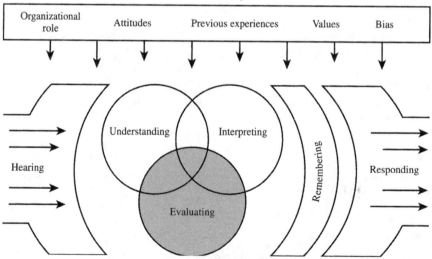

A Model of the Six-Component HURIER Listening Process

■ ■ ■ ■ ■

EVALUATING: SITUATION AND PURPOSE

Sound evaluation is essential, particularly in persuasive contexts where you are asked to make choices among competing ideas. On other occasions, such as when you listen for enjoyment, the need for critical analysis decreases. Be aware, however, that purposes may change from one moment to the next; you may begin listening to music or the radio for enjoyment but find yourself suddenly drawn to evaluate the effectiveness of a commercial.

As you communicate more frequently with those whose ideas and experiences are different from your own, the ability to recognize bias and stereotyping, and to withhold immediate judgment, becomes even more vital. Valuing diversity implies openness and the ability to withhold evaluation so that alternative viewpoints can be fully explored. You must first hear and understand what your partner says before you evaluate its worth.

Critical listeners apply the principles of sound thinking, logic, and reasoning to the messages they hear. They also recognize propaganda devices and can remain objective in the face of strong emotional appeals.

CASE: TOUGH SELL

Kurt put down the consumer guide and yawned. Enough reading. He felt he now knew almost everything there was to know about compact cars and was ready to have some live encounters at a showroom. He closed his eyes and thought about how many years he had been saving up for his first car. His mom and dad had agreed to pay for the insurance, and he was now ready to visit some dealers.

"I'm going to pick up Sara and then we're going on our mission," Kurt yelled to his mother as he zipped up his jacket. "Should be home for dinner."

"Wait just a minute," his mother answered as she followed him to the door. "Don't you want your father to go with you? I really wish you would let him. You can make your own decisions, but it might be good to have him there just in case."

"In case of what?" Kurt asked, beginning to get annoyed. This was not a new request.

"I don't know," his mother replied. "I don't know. I just think he should go with you."

"I don't," said Kurt with a smile. He left the house and got into the family's second car, which he had been driving since he had gotten his license last year. Sara lived only a few blocks away. Her opinion mattered; after all, they spent most of their time together now that she had transferred to the local college Kurt was attending. Although it wasn't his first choice, living at home had its advantages.

He picked up Sara and headed to the Chevy dealer. After listening to a salesperson talk about the advantages of buying American-made cars, they headed on to test-drive a Plymouth and then a Honda. It was exhausting. Their final stop was at a Toyota dealer, where they took a Tercel for a spin. New model cars were coming in to the showroom, and the salesperson was anxious to sell last year's floor models. The dealer was running an employee contest, and whoever made the greatest number of sales would win a round trip to Bermuda. Sandy Snider was determined not to be outsold.

"It's perfect for you," Sandy stated emphatically as she greeted them upon their return to the parking lot. "Come on in to my office where we can talk."

"Well," Kurt began, "I'm really not ready to take the next step just yet. . . ."

"Nonsense," Sandy replied as she guided the couple into her office. "You don't want to wait. Prices are going up every day; when you see a good deal, you have to grab it. You know, I've sold more cars in the last week than in the entire time I've worked here. Do you know why?" She paused, smiling, "Because smart people know when they see a good deal, and we have one for you."

Kurt fumbled for the list he had made of the features he was looking for and the questions he had planned to ask. As they sat down, he located the crumpled paper.

"I had been looking for a smaller engine," Kurt tentatively began. "I understand there's a difference in mileage and my dad said. . . ."

"No, you don't want a smaller engine!" Sandy leaned back in disbelief. "My goodness, with all the hills around here? If you're only running on 4-cylinders, every time you go up an incline you're going to slow down. Even on a straightaway, there's nothing like the feeling of real power when you go to pass and you only have a few seconds before that turn comes up." Sandy turned to Sara and said with a laugh, "You like a man with power, don't you?"

"Ah, sure," Sara said as she shifted in her chair.

"Actually," Sandy continued, "I've always said a 4-cylinder engine is dangerous, just for that reason. You think you can pass and, suddenly, you find yourself heading right toward an oncoming car. Has that ever happened to you before? You've been following some jerk for miles, waiting for an opportunity to pass. You get to a short stretch in the road where you think you can get by. You pull out, step on the gas—and nothing happens! The curve gets closer and closer, you're just about even with the guy and you see a car headed toward you in the other lane. No thanks. I'll pay for the power and the peace of mind."

After a pause Sandy continued, "And what else were you looking for?"

"I guess it's more a matter of what I wasn't looking for," Kurt replied. "This car has a lot of features I really don't need. I mean, the satellite radio, the heated seats, the expensive upholstery—I had been thinking in terms of basic necessities rather than luxury items."

"You think it's not essential now," Sandy said as she leaned forward and looked intently at Kurt, "but let me tell you, every feature has a purpose. You deserve to have a car that makes you feel good. It's not luxury—it's necessity. It makes a statement."

Kurt cleared his throat, ready to end the conversation, when Sandy interjected, "You know Ted Banks, our famous attorney? He said himself that Toyotas are the only car he'd ever own. Besides," Sandy concluded, "everyone knows Toyota makes the best cars. The cars we have are the best because they're Toyotas. You can't do better than that."

"Well, I'll have to think about it some more," Kurt said politely as he stood up. He glanced at Sara to make sure that she, too, was ready to exit quickly.

"Remember, this car won't be here long," Sandy warned as she placed one of her cards firmly in Kurt's hand. "The people who really know a good deal when they see one aren't passing up this opportunity."

As Kurt pulled out of the lot, he sighed in relief. "What do you think?" he said to Sara as he headed for Jenny's, their favorite coffee spot.

"I don't know," Sara shook her head. "I think you should buy an American car regardless."

"Why should I buy American, when the Japanese build cars just as sound and sell them at competitive prices? Don't be silly. What did you think about the Tercel?"

"I wasn't really paying too much attention—I thought Sandy was obnoxious. Do you realize she only looked at me once the entire time we were in her office? Did you see those long nails?" There was a short pause. "And I'm not silly." Sara suddenly took offense at Kurt's comment. "I just think we need to support American products, that's all. Besides, I heard that several auto plants will close if sales don't go up this year. Do you want to be responsible for putting Americans out of work?"

"Where did you hear that?" Kurt asked sharply.

"Kim told me," Sara replied.

"Kim! What does Kim know about cars?" Kurt shook his head as he spoke.

"Her sister dates a mechanic, that's what," Sara said, sliding down in the seat.

"Well, I can't talk with you about it if you don't have better reasons than that," Kurt replied. "It was probably a waste of time for you to even come with me." They rode the rest of the way in silence.

When they got to Jenny's it was crowded and smoky, but since neither Kurt nor Sara wanted to be the one to break the silence, they went ahead and found a table.

"Sara!" A man waved from across the room and began to make his way toward them.

Sara turned and immediately recognized Cody Morgan. Cody had been her supervisor the previous summer when she worked at BurgerWorld, a local fast-food restaurant.

"Cody!" The well-dressed man held out his arms and gave her a big hug. "It's so good to see you! I've stopped by BurgerWorld several times but I haven't seen you there."

"We've missed you," Cody said, staring intently at Sara. "I've had a couple of big promotions since you left. I'm a district manager now."

"Congratulations!" Sara replied. "Oh, I'm sorry—this is Kurt Freeland." Sara turned to Kurt. *"Kurt, you remember Cody. He managed BurgerWorld the summer I worked there."*

The two men nodded toward each other, and Cody immediately turned his attention back to Sara.

"You know, there's a lot of opportunity with BurgerWorld for a smart, responsible person like you. I mean it." Cody pulled up a chair and sat down at the table.

"Management positions are opening up all the time. I could get you in right away if you were interested. The salary is good, the benefits are excellent, and you could still work on your degree part time. What's the point in going to college for four years, getting yourself deeply in debt, and taking the risk that you won't even be able to find a job when you graduate?"

"Sometimes I do wonder if I'm doing the right thing, especially with all of my student loans, but. . . ." Sara paused and Cody immediately interrupted.

"Look, you want security, right? And a job where you can really go somewhere—where you'll be recognized for your hard work and talents? Trust me. BurgerWorld is perfect for you."

"I'll think about it," Sara offered. *"I really will. I just can't give you an answer right now."*

"Tell you what. I'll be in town this Thursday evening. Why don't I meet you at the restaurant and we'll talk. I can give you some more information and tell you exactly how to go about getting involved. With my recommendation," Cody assured her, *"you should have no trouble coming in as an assistant manager. What do you say. Thursday at 6:30 p.m.?"*

"Okay, I guess" Sara was still somewhat uncertain but figured she had nothing to lose.

"Great," Cody hit the table with his hand, as if to close the deal, and then stood up. *"I'll see you on Thursday. Nice meeting you, Kurt."*

As Cody made his way back across the dining room, Kurt shook his head. *"What a jerk!"*

"What do you mean, jerk?" Sara countered somewhat defensively. *"He's just trying to help me out. Look at how successful he's been in just a short time."*

"It's probably because everyone else is quitting," Kurt replied with a snicker. *"I heard BurgerWorld was in deep financial trouble and that they take advantage of their employees. Not even the high school kids want to work for that company. They're probably desperate for some help. Did you ask him what kind of hours he puts in?"*

"Just what makes you such an expert on this subject, anyway?" Sara responded. *"I assume you don't think I should take him up on his offer for Thursday?"*

"What offer?" Kurt was annoyed that they were spending so much time talking about this subject. *"I could tell he didn't have anything worthwhile to say, so I was thinking about something of consequence—like the decision I have to make about a car, for instance."*

"Let's go home," Sara suggested.

THE PROCESS OF EVALUATING: PRINCIPLES

You make a judgment, in one way or another, about almost everything you hear. Look at how often Kurt had to evaluate the validity of Sandy's arguments in the course of one short conversation. As you move into positions of responsibility and decision-making in the workplace, the quality of your decisions will affect others in important ways. Who gets to attend the leadership conference? Which candidate do you choose for your new administrative assistant? What benefits do you provide to your employees? What department is targeted for downsizing? It is therefore essential for both personal and professional effectiveness that you become a critical listener, that you learn the principles that contribute to sound judgment and wise decisions.

Keep in mind that *critical* does not mean *negative,* and the deliberate process of *evaluation* that you learn about in this chapter is not the same as being *judgmental.* When you become a critical listener, you know *how* and *when* to evaluate what you hear. Unlike hearing, which is prerequisite to all listening contexts, critical listening is situational. The appropriateness of critical listening is determined by your listening purpose and goals.

Critical listening is particularly relevant to persuasive communication situations. When someone wants to change your opinion or behavior, as Sandy tried to do to Kurt, you must determine whether to accept or to reject what you hear. Persuasion implies *free choice among alternatives.* Your decision is best made rationally, on the basis of clear thinking, sound logic, and valid reasoning.

In almost all instances, critical listening *follows* the related processes of hearing, understanding, remembering, and interpreting. Until you are confident that you share the speaker's meanings and have taken nonverbal and situational aspects into account, you cannot make a wise decision or come to a valid conclusion. As you learn more about this process, you will see its relevance to your daily activities.

Sara Lundsteen (1979) is among the many educators who emphasize the importance of critical listening skills. She provides a list of common listening tasks which include:

1. judging the validity and adequacy of both main ideas and supporting arguments;
2. distinguishing statements of fact from opinions and judgments;
3. inspecting, comparing, and contrasting ideas and arriving at a conclusion;
4. identifying the use of logical fallacies;
5. detecting speaker bias;
6. evaluating the speaker's qualifications. (pp. 65–67)

All persuasion is not intentional and deliberate. You are constantly exposed to subtle influence attempts, from that guy or girl who always smiles and says "hi" to you, to your mother's parting "we know you're busy but we really miss you and hope you'll find some time to come see us over your break. . . ." Just as you might view all human communication as relational, so, too, you might adopt a framework that suggests that most of your daily interactions have some persuasive component; your encounters provide opportunities for you and others to exert influence.

In this discussion, persuasion refers to all communication that either intentionally or unintentionally influences your choices. Yet, in keeping with our emphasis on the co-creation of meanings, you know that regardless of what your partner says or does, you persuade yourself. All persuasion is self-persuasion; meanings are elicited, not forced. In order for cognitive change to occur, you must participate in the process (Larson, 1989).

> Do you have an ethical responsibility to objectively evaluate what you hear? Will your answer be affected by your cultural orientation?

Given the wide range of persuasive efforts that occur continuously, it is wise to listen objectively as a matter of habit. Although there are situations where critical listening is of extreme importance, and occasions where you listen to relax and enjoy the message, effective communicators are aware of their evaluative process as it occurs in all encounters. For better or for worse, it is almost impossible for you *not* to evaluate unless you deliberately postpone this process. Consequently, it is essential for you to learn the principles that guide sound judgment.

Kelly (1982) convincingly argues that a competent critical listener *first* suspends judgment to consider his partner's ideas objectively. If evaluation occurs immediately—if you let your personal bias or preconceived notions influence your listening—it is almost impossible to clearly hear another's viewpoint. You know from earlier chapters that selective attention and other aspects of your mental framework influence how you view and process information. In their listening taxonomy, Wolvin and Coakley (1992) also argue that, ideally, understanding precedes evaluation. You can reduce your tendency to immediately judge what you hear only if you deliberately work to control your mental processing. Self-reflection is key to critical listening. Larson's point is well taken:

> *We need to watch ourselves being persuaded, and try to see why and how it happens so that we can be more conscious of our changes. Our knowledge will allow us to be more critical and therefore more effective in rejecting persuasive messages when appropriate—and in accepting others when it seems wise to do so.* (1989, p. 10)

> How is self-reflection key to critical listening?

This chapter is your guide to becoming a more effective critical listener. You will learn how persuasion works and be introduced to several important mental principles that will help you approach persuasive situations more objectively. The three traditional dimensions of persuasion—speaker credibility, logic and reasoning, and emotional appeals—are then examined in turn.

THEORIES OF PERSUASION

Numerous theories have been proposed to explain how and why persuasion affects listeners. In some cases, you might be motivated by the need for recognition or approval; on other occasions, you seek peace of mind, or what is called internal consistency. In helping you understand this complex process, three well-known theories are examined briefly: attitude change theory, consistency theory, and social judgment theory.

Attitude Change Theory

Existing attitudes and beliefs influence your behavior. Consequently, you are persuaded to act only to the extent that communicators influence the underlying attitudes that affect the targeted behavior. For instance, if Kurt believed that he had an obligation to buy American cars, nothing Sandy could have said in the showroom about the selling points of a Toyota would have changed his mind; the persuasive messages were not targeted to Kurt's key attitudes.

Researchers (Hovland, Janis, & Kelly, 1953) maintain that a communicator's ability to influence attitude change is dependent upon her ability to accomplish five interrelated steps: (1) getting your attention, (2) ensuring your understanding of the message, (3) convincing you to accept the message, (4) ensuring that you remember the message, and (5) describing the action you should take as a result of the encounter.

You can see how Sandy followed this basic pattern as she attempted to convince Kurt that buying a Toyota was a smart decision. She immediately escorted Kurt and Sara into her office, where she would have their undivided attention. Sandy then engaged in a dialogue with the couple, restating the points she wanted to make sure were clear. She made a vivid argument, for instance, regarding the value of a large engine by describing dangerous driving situations where power was critical. Her ability to connect directly to Kurt's reservations ensured that her message would be more meaningful and memorable than if she had simply read the selling points from a brochure. Repeatedly, Sandy made clear the action she advocated: buy a Toyota.

Consistency Theories

Consistency theories are based on the assumption that you feel psychologically uncomfortable when two pieces of information are logically inconsistent. To overcome this imbalance, you are often willing to change one of your beliefs so that it is compatible with the other information—with your existing schema. Persuaders use this desire for psychological balance to influence your choices.

In their persuasive efforts, then, speakers intentionally create imbalance to persuade you to change your mind about an existing opinion or belief. The simplest model of this process (Heider, 1958) is illustrated through the dynamics of your relationship with two communication variables: (1) the speaker, and (2) the speaker's proposition or idea. You experience inconsistency under the following conditions:

1. When you like the speaker but disagree with the speaker's ideas.
2. When you dislike the speaker but agree with the speaker's ideas.

You may recall examples of this principle from your experiences listening to politicians (Figure 7.1). If you think a particular mayor is a jerk, it can be uncomfortable to agree with her major policies. You experience much more comfort when you can identify evidence that confirms your belief in her incompetence.

A more complicated explanation of consistency is proposed by Festinger (1962), whose theory accounts for the strength of the relationship's imbalance as well as for its presence. He hypothesizes that any imbalance you experience produces psychological tension, and that you will seek to relieve this tension in one of

> Does our need for psychological balance—and our tendency to seek consistency as explained by Festinger—have a positive or negative impact on communication?

several ways. You might change one of your beliefs so that the two conflicting ideas are more similar, or you might rationalize to explain away the competing idea. In other cases, you might choose to discredit the source, assuming that the person expressing the idea doesn't know what he is talking about. You might also escape from discomfort through selective perception or retention—you ignore or choose not to be exposed to information that doesn't fit into your existing framework.

Review the meeting between Sara and Cody in "Tough Sell," and see if you can identify instances where dissonance was created. Then determine how the listener went about reducing it.

Given that individuals from different cultures are likely to have different attitudes and belief systems, how do you think foreigners keep their psychological

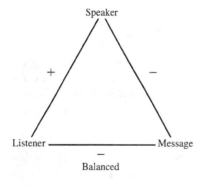
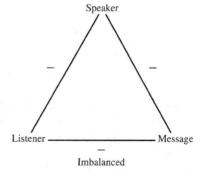

FIGURE 7.1   Heider's Balance Theory

stress at a reasonable level? Do you think that visitors abroad experience more dissonance than the average citizen?

Social Judgment Theories

Social judgment theory builds on the notion that you develop attitudes and learn how to behave as a result of your interactions with others (Bandura, 1977). Social judgment is often expressed through rewards and punishments; you get a certificate for volunteering at a local hospital, a trophy for excelling in a sport, an A for doing well in class, a hug for being considerate, attention from your friends for wearing the right clothes.

Each person has an internal anchor, a reference point that he uses to make judgments about the people and events he encounters. This anchor is a personal and unique position, developed over time, that determines the degree to which you find a particular idea acceptable. For instance, while I might be willing to spend a lot of money on "frills" for a car—satellite radio, heated seats, and so forth—you might be convinced that these luxury items serve no useful purpose. Clearly, Sandy's proposition that "luxuries are really necessities," falls within my latitude of acceptance but not within yours. Furthermore, if you make your views public, your commitment to a position is even stronger.

In addition to latitudes of acceptance and rejection, you also have a latitude of noncommitment, an area where you are particularly vulnerable to persuasive efforts since you have no opinion on the topic. It is within the boundaries of noncommitment that persuasive efforts can affect the greatest degree of attitude and behavior change.

These three theories make it obvious how you, as a listener, play a central role in determining the extent to which persuasive techniques will be effective. Building on your understanding of these strategies, you can better prepare yourself to handle the wide range of persuasive messages that reach you every day.

PREPARE YOURSELF FOR CRITICAL LISTENING

Ask anyone and she'll tell you, "Sure, I'm open-minded!" It is unlikely, however, that any of us are as open-minded as we think we are—or would like to be. As you encounter increasing diversity in your classrooms, communities, and organizations, it is particularly important to objectively consider a wide variety of options and to accommodate a range of values and opinions. Cross-cultural communication has profound implications for critical listening, since individuals from different cultures may apply a different set of criteria in making decisions and may even have a different ethical framework.

As you work toward more effective critical listening skills, keep the rules of objective thinking in mind. Objectivity—and effective listening—are impossible to achieve when you are emotionally involved or defending your personal viewpoint.

The following principles may be helpful as you work to maintain an objective response to what you hear.

There's Always More to Know

Regardless of how strong your convictions, they are based on limited information—what you already know. It's tempting to behave as if you know everything about a topic and to use familiar scripts rather than continuing to evaluate new, incoming information. Personal schema are used to make inferences and predictions which, in some cases, are helpful. In other situations, however, they prevent you from searching for more current or complete information.

Be Ready to Modify Your Position

Rather than listening well to those who disagree with your ideas, it's tempting to simply wait for your turn to present the opposing point of view. Watch two individuals who are arguing and determine how much real listening is taking place!

What are the risks associated with open-mindedness?

A position of certainty can be dangerous since it implies that new information will not change your mind. Part of *open-mindedness* is realizing that new facts and new ideas may change or modify currently held beliefs. The most effective listeners recognize the limitations of their own knowledge and listen to others with the understanding that their opinions may be altered as a result.

Consider Differences As Well As Similarities

There are stereotypes for almost every imaginable category. The practice of drawing upon the similarities within a group and attributing those characteristics to all members is something many people do automatically. You expect a teacher to treat you fairly, a two-year-old to get into mischief, and a man to be physically stronger than a woman. Stereotypes affect the way you process information, since they influence your expectations and, subsequently, your perceptions. Ethnocentrism also leads to stereotyping, since people have a greater need to categorize when dealing with those who are unlike them (Thomlison, 1991).

Recognize Self-fulfilling Prophecies

What expectations do you hold that easily could turn into self-fulfilling prophecies?

A major danger of stereotyping is that it can create a self-fulfilling prophecy, a situation in which a judgment—good or bad—is made about an individual that encourages you to perceive information in such a way as to reaffirm that expectation. One study described an elementary school teacher who was told that one group of children were poor performers and the other group exceptionally bright. Such, in fact, was not the case; the two groups had identical abilities. When the teacher tested the groups and reported her findings, the results were significant. The group of "poor performers" were rated much lower than the children who were identified as above average.

Use Indexing to Focus on Individuals Rather Than Categories

While useful and efficient, stereotyping has its costs. The most significant potential problem is that listeners will overlook the unique, idiosyncratic characteristics of each individual and focus instead on more convenient generalizations. You may not like country music singers, but . . . what about that woman you heard performing at the State Fair?

One way you can reduce stereotyping is to pay attention to the differences between individual members of a group as well as to the similarities. Notice how female manager 1 is different from female manager 2 and female manager 3. Such *indexing* encourages you to view each person or situation independently rather than relying on past information or generalizations. Your challenge is to withhold judgment until you've observed a particular case long enough to draw some concrete conclusions. This consciousness helps prevent the acceptance of unwarranted generalizations that may not apply to the person or situation in question.

Date Your Information and Constantly Reassess the Situation

> With the constant pace of change, is dating the best or only way to acknowledge changes?

Another principle that helps increase objectivity is called *dating*. Dating focuses your attention on the changes that take place over time. Just because Sam Smith was irresponsible on his first job in 1990 does not *necessarily* mean that he still behaves that way. Although information may be useful, it is important not to build a communication framework that prevents someone from overcoming a past circumstance.

There's a Lot of Gray between Black and White

The English language makes it easy for you to think in extremes. If something isn't good or bad, what is it? What is in-between fair and unfair? Mean and kind? Although our language may encourage you to think in either–or terms, most situations you encounter are not clear-cut. Ideas aren't completely bad or completely good, completely useful or useless.

In addition, because there are so many competing messages, it is easy to get into the habit of exaggerating to get a point across. If you had a good time it was "terrific"; if you didn't do quite as well on an exam as you thought you would, it was "a total bomb." As a listener, it's useful to be aware of this tendency and to ask clarifying questions whenever necessary so that your understanding of the actual situation is as accurate as possible.

ELEMENTS OF PERSUASION

So far you have been introduced to three theories that explain how persuasion works, and have reviewed several principles of critical thinking that may help you maintain objectivity in persuasive situations. Now we examine three elements that are associated with effective persuasive appeals: speaker credibility, logic and reasoning, and emotional appeal.

First, the effective critical listener considers the source of the message in making judgments about its content. Then she evaluates the message on the basis of sound logic and reasoning. Finally, the critical listener recognizes propaganda devices and emotional appeals and responds accordingly. She realizes that effective decision-making depends upon sound judgment and analysis, upon weighing the right facts and asking the right questions.

Evaluate Speaker Credibility

Speaker credibility is judged on both the communicator's character and competence. Credible communicators are perceived as trustworthy, dynamic, and as having expertise in their subject (Brembeck & Howell, 1976).

How do you establish your trustworthiness through communication?

Trust is established in many ways. A person's nonverbal communication and appearance affect your perceptions of his trustworthiness, as do any previous experiences you may have had with him. Managers who work effectively with their employees have gained these individuals' trust and respect. Dentists, doctors, counselors, and educators are among other groups where trust is critical to credibility.

The second feature of credibility, dynamism, is related to a trait referred to as charisma. Individuals who have a presence, an intangible manner about them that others find attractive, are more persuasive than their peers. Although dynamism is sometimes related to physical attractiveness, such is not necessarily the case. Delivery factors, as you know, contribute to perceptions of expertise even though such indicators may be misleading. A dynamic image can be created through vocal variety, powerful language, facial cues, and strong eye contact.

Finally, expertise is a more straightforward and somewhat easier dimension to judge objectively than either trustworthiness or dynamism. Speakers are often coached to provide listeners with information that establishes their knowledge of the topic. On other occasions, your responsibility as a listener may include researching the speaker's background.

In their text on persuasion, Brembeck and Howell (1976) provide additional insight into what makes someone credible and what impact that variable has on your listening. Among their findings are the following:

- The greater the source's credibility, the more impact his message has on you.
- An effective introduction can substantially increase a speaker's initial credibility.
- You are most easily influenced by someone whom you perceive to be similar to you in important ways.
- It is more difficult for females to establish credibility than males.
- A speaker with high initial credibility who does not present his information well will lose much of his credibility.

Credibility, as you might suspect, is also culture-bound. Persuasive factors that appear to enhance a U.S. speaker's credibility include orderliness, clarity, and directness, concreteness, and accuracy (Brembeck & Howell, 1976). In the United States, listeners feel comfortable with messages demonstrating these characteristics and, hence, are likely to accept them. In other cultures, however, the effectiveness of various persuasive strategies may be surprising. When you

> How would either high or low cultural contexting affect persuasive efforts?

encounter classmates or group members who hold values and beliefs different from yours, or who make judgments you do not agree with, it is difficult to perceive them as trustworthy. New definitions of trust must be developed as we move into increasingly international communication contexts.

Initial, Derived, and Terminal Credibility

A speaker's credibility can be assessed at three points in the communication process: before speaking, during the presentation or interaction, and following the encounter. Initial credibility refers to the way a speaker is perceived before the communication begins. Have you ever heard of this person before? Are there rumors about her competence, personality, or knowledge of the subject? If not, then initial credibility has little impact. If, however, you do have prior information about the speaker, this information can be a very powerful factor in shaping your perceptions.

Imagine that you go to a class prepared for a well-known researcher to make a presentation. At the last minute, however, she gives her notes to her new teaching assistant because she is called out of town. The assistant, who just began his job that semester, would have low initial credibility. It would be up to him to use this speaking opportunity to establish his trustworthiness, expertise, and to win your good will.

Derived credibility is determined by the degree of perceived trustworthiness and expertise the speaker generates *during the communication event*. The new assistant director of personnel has no control over the fact that he is inexperienced. He does, however, have a good deal of control over how he presents himself in the immediate speech situation, how he organizes his information, how professionally he prepares his visuals, and how carefully he checks his facts.

A speaker derives credibility in various ways, and the perceptive listener recognizes these efforts. Among the most common methods are:

1. references to personal experiences with the subject, general credentials
2. citing reliable sources from which information was obtained
3. effective delivery: appropriate pitch, gestures, appearance, fluency
4. knowledge of the audience or listener: ability to create rapport, demonstrate sincere interest in the listener's needs, and relate material to the specific group

After an individual has finished speaking, you make your final judgment concerning his character. While most speakers hope to have gained credibility, this does not always happen. Terminal credibility may be either higher or lower than initial credibility. You judge the speaker's character, documentation, credentials, and manner and determine whether or not his reputation has been enhanced.

EVALUATE RATIONAL APPEALS

Communicators design the content of a persuasive message on the basis of its power to elicit the desired response from you, the listener. What may be sufficient and convincing content for you may not be sufficient for someone else. Often, a communicator hopes to persuade you on the basis of evidence and reasoning, or what is called the rational approach. As you consider this dimension of persuasion, first determine the type of information that is being presented.

Distinguish among Facts, Opinions, and Inferences

One of the first tests a critical listener applies is to ask whether the information presented is a fact, or whether it is an opinion (Box 7.1).

Fact.   A fact can be verified; potentially, everyone can agree on a matter of fact. Take the following case:

> *Your classmate sees you in the hall and says anxiously, "We've just got to get underway on this project! It's due Tuesday morning, and almost nothing has been done." Recalling the initial assignment, you respond, "No hurry. The deadline is a week from Tuesday, the 15th. We've still got plenty of time." "No," your friend insists, "it's due this coming Tuesday and we've got a. . . ."*

Stop arguing. The matter is one of fact. Somewhere you will be able to find an answer, and the answer will solve your conflict. It's all too common for people to spend valuable time disagreeing about something that is a matter of fact. Remember, too, that facts in themselves are not always useful. It takes a skilled com-

■ ■ ■ ■ ■

BOX 7.1

DISTINGUISH AMONG FACTS, INFERENCES, AND OPINIONS

Statements of Fact	Inference	Opinion
Can be made only after direct observation.	Can be made at any time.	Can be made at any time.
Sticks with what was actually observed.	Goes beyond what was observed.	Goes beyond what was observed.
Objective presentation.	Interpretation.	Interpreted in light of individual values.
In terms of truth.	In terms of probability.	In terms of agreement.

---

municator to interpret them accurately and use them wisely. Overemphasis on the acquisition of unrelated facts as an end in itself is unproductive. Facts do not take the place of true understanding; it's one thing to know the principles, but quite another to use them appropriately in problem-solving. Fragmentation of thinking results in inadequate analysis and poor judgment (Reese & Floyd, 1987).

Opinions.   Opinions, in contrast to facts, are subject to continuing modification. Sound opinions are based on careful examination and evaluation of the facts at hand. Since they depend to some degree upon the individual's particular goals, values, and expectations, they remain personal rather than universal. The "best" course of action, candidate for office, or computer on the market remains largely an individual choice based on the available information and the individual's frame of reference. It is in this arena that persuasive efforts are most effective.

> How often do you change your opinions about really important issues?

Inference.   Inferences, unlike facts, are not obtained by direct observation or description. Think of an inference as a "good guess." It takes you from the facts to *probable* outcomes or conclusions. A story that illustrates this point concerns two men who were riding on a bus. As one of them gazed out his window, he said to his friend, "Look at that sheep! He just got his coat sheared." "Yes," replied the other man, "at least on the one side." Knapp (1978) provides another view of how inferences may lead us astray.

> *Failure at the 'inference' stage is aptly illustrated by the scientist who told his frog to jump and, after a few minutes, the frog jumped. The scientist recorded this behavior and then amputated one of the frog's hind legs. Again he told the frog to jump. 'Jump!'*

▬ ▬ ▬ ▬ ▬▬▬▬▬▬▬▬

Describe someone who was harmed by inferences that others made based on the person's cultural orientation.

▬▬▬▬▬▬▬▬▬▬▬

he shouted. 'Jump!' In time, the frog made a feeble attempt to jump with the one hind leg. The scientist then cut off the frog's other hind leg, and repeatedly ordered the frog to jump. When, after quite some time, no jumping behavior occurred, the scientist recorded in his log:

> *Upon amputation of one hind leg, the frog begins to lose its hearing.*

> *Upon amputation of both legs, the frog becomes totally deaf. (p. 176)*

Inferences are created in any number of ways. Often, information is added to complete a missing piece and to make the situation consistent with the listener's expectations. Inferences are most likely to occur, then, when messages are incomplete and you are required to "make sense" of the situation (Fitch-Hauser, 1990).

Those who have decision-making responsibilities realize that seldom are all the facts available. Good guesses—inferences—become a necessary means of getting things done. Yet, as you move from the certain to the probable, it's important to hesitate long enough to recognize that you are also moving into a riskier domain.

Types of Evidence and Support

You are probably familiar with the concept of proof. While you may think of proof as something "out there" that a communicator brings to bear on his argument, proof is actually a relative concept and varies from one situation to the next. It may not take much evidence, for instance, to convince you that diet affects your memory. If you have a friend who is a nutritionist, however, proving this proposition to her might be very difficult, especially if she has already formed an opinion on the subject. Proof, then, is "enough evidence" connected through reasoning; it is whatever it takes *in a particular situation* for you to accept the speaker's advice (Larson, 1989). Types of evidence include statistics, testimony and quotations, literal comparisons, and stories. Each has a slightly different purpose and impact.

▬ ▬ ▬ ▬ ▬▬▬▬▬▬▬

Compared to your peers, do you think it takes more or less evidence to convince you?

▬▬▬▬▬▬▬▬▬▬▬

Statistics make points specific and concrete. Since you often attribute increased credibility to someone who uses numbers to back up his point, there is a tendency to take the figures at face value. Critical listeners must not only apply the standard tests for sound evidence, but ask the following questions as well:

1. How were the statistics gathered?
2. Do the statistics cover a sufficient period of time?
3. Is it clear exactly what they represent?
4. Can the results be verified in other ways?

Numbers, no matter how striking, do not give a speaker credibility. They must meet the tests for sound evidence.

Both testimony and quotations can add interest and make an idea more vivid. Valid testimony comes from individuals who are knowledgeable or have relevant expertise. There are no conflicts of interest, bias, or hidden agendas. When evaluating this type of evidence, ask the following questions:

1. Is the information consistent with what I already know about the subject?
2. Is the information clear—do I understand it?
3. Is the support directly related to the main point?
4. Is the source of the information reliable?
5. Is the information recent enough to be valid?

A comparison can be used to clarify an idea or point, or can be used in persuasion as logical proof. If the comparison is figurative, it compares two things from different types or classes of information. Figurative comparisons can be used only for clarification. If the comparison is literal, however, two things within the same class are compared. This type of analogy is often used in reasoning if the communicator can demonstrate how there are enough similarities between two schools, two cars, or two other items for you to be convinced that the principles that apply to one will also apply to the other.

Finally, narratives and stories are effective in making points vivid and in eliciting a memorable, and often emotional, response. Think about the stories you have heard that left a lasting impression on you. Perhaps they were descriptions of squalid living conditions, or acts of kindness, or exciting experiences.

Box 7.2 provides examples that illustrate some of the more common types of support used to clarify or substantiate a communicator's ideas.

Types of Reasoning

Communicators seldom expect to influence you by presenting isolated pieces of evidence. Recall that in order to convince, "enough evidence" must be connected by sound reasoning. Persuasive strategies involve linking information together in some systematic manner so that key ideas have meaning and impact. When a speaker's logic is clear, not only are her ideas easier to follow, but they also are more convincing. You will make more valid and objective judgments if you know some basic patterns of reasoning.

Inductive Reasoning.   Inductive reasoning moves from specifics to a conclusion. It is a scientific method whereby, if it were possible, all individual cases would be observed and the results recorded. Rarely, however, is this feasible. Inductive reasoning, therefore, most often establishes the *probability* of a statement rather than its certainty. Available evidence is examined and a conclusion drawn.

If, for instance, you were interested in determining student attitudes toward a new parking regulation, you might survey members of your class to find out how they feel about the rule. By asking each person her opinion and then drawing a

---

BOX 7.2

TYPES OF EVIDENCE AND SUPPORT

Statistics

Main Point: The SR program is a proven training program.

Statistics: Over 400 firms in New York State alone have used the SR method.

Main Point: Sales have grown drastically over the last three years.

Statistics: Our company did $6 thousand worth of sales in 1980. In 1983 the figure more than doubled to $14 thousand. 1984 was the best year yet with total sales reaching $20 thousand.

Testimony and Quotations

Main Point: The SR training program has had excellent results.

Testimony: Mr. Roger Bell, Vice President of Personnel at Mentel Corporation, wrote that "the SR program has made a world of difference in the competence and morale of our employees."

Main Point: There are times when it is necessary to take a risk.

Quotation: Lawrence Graham, in his best-selling novel, summed it up like this, "Nothing ventured, nothing gained."

Literal Comparisons

Main Point: The new MEG-11 will save your office staff valuable time.

Literal: Wemel corporation just replaced their REC-41s with new MEG-11s. Their staff has saved over 200 hours a week in typing time over the past three months. The Wemel corporation is like ours in several important ways. First . . .

Stories

A lot of students have been afraid to walk through the east hill parking lot at night. Patty was no exception. Last weekend she worked late on the school newspaper and found herself alone around 11:30 p.m. She . . .

---

conclusion, you would be using an inductive approach. In determining the validity of your results, you would need to keep the following questions in mind:

1. Was your sample representative?
2. Did you include enough cases in your sample?
3. Can the results be verified?
4. Are those in your sample reliable? Is there any reason to assume they would be biased?
5. Are there any exceptions that should be considered?

Careful listeners analyze a speaker's inductive method whenever they hear a generalization. By asking some of the questions listed above, you can determine for yourself whether the reasoning presented is sound.

Deductive Reasoning.   Deduction is the process of applying a conclusion or generalization to an individual case. You might know that glass shatters when it strikes a hard surface (your conclusion), so you know that if you drop the cup you're holding, it is likely to break. Deductive reasoning is best illustrated through the use of syllogism. If you understand the syllogistic method you can determine whether or not the deductive reasoning is valid. Since syllogisms always begin with a major premise or generalization, however, you must go back to the facts from which the generalization was derived in order to make any judgments concerning its truth. Generalizations derived from faulty inductive methods may make a valid syllogism, but will never yield accurate information.

Take, for example, the statement "All faculty at State University drink wine." This generalization is our major premise. From it we may continue deductively:

Major premise: All faculty at SU drink wine.
Minor premise: Jack is a faculty member at SU.
Conclusion: Jack drinks wine.

Valid deduction, yes. But is it *true*? You don't know. If you discover that the speaker went to a faculty party at which all guests were drinking wine and consequently arrived at this generalization, you would then know that his major premise is shaky. Did all faculty members attend the party, or only those who like to drink wine? What percentage of the total number of faculty attended? We might find that the sample is neither representative nor large enough. Regardless, the speaker may still use it to construct a syllogism that is logically *valid*—but, in this case, would not be *true*.

There are several types of syllogisms. The most common are presented in Box 7.3. Regardless of the particular form of a syllogism, all share some common features:

1. There are three statements: a major premise, a minor premise, and a conclusion.

BOX 7.3

TYPES OF SYLLOGISMS

Categorical Syllogism: Application of a Category to a Specific Case

Major Premise: All secretaries can type.	Term 1: secretaries (*middle term*)
Minor Premise: Jane is a secretary.	Term 2: type
Conclusion: Jane can type.	Term 3: Jane

Hypothetical Syllogism: If–Then Format
Major Premise: If selling candy works for the RFT firm, it will work for us.
Minor Premise: Selling candy works for the RFT firm.
Conclusion: Then selling candy will work for us.

Disjunctive Syllogism: An Either–Or Approach
Major Premise: Either Joe will be transferred or he will stay at our plant.
Minor Premise: Joe will be transferred.
Conclusion: Therefore, Joe will not stay at our plant.

2. There are three main terms.

3. The middle term is found in the major and the minor premises but not in the conclusion.

4. If the major premise is qualified by a word like *some* or *many*, the conclusion must also be qualified.

Understanding and analyzing deductive reasoning is important for the critical listener who must determine both the truth and the validity of the information presented.

Cause to Effect.   In this form of reasoning, your partner tells you that if certain conditions exist, a particular result is likely to follow. Think of the statements parents frequently make to their children, or advertisers make to their markets. "If this happens, then this is what you can expect." If you don't wear your mittens, your hands will get cold. If you use Brand R toothpaste, you will have fewer cavities. If you drink lemonade, you will feel refreshed.

> What are some of the cause–effect statements that you heard as a child that were not based in fact?

Reasoning from a Comparison.   Communicators often reason from comparisons, or literal analogies, which apply a known situation to illustrate what is likely to happen in an unknown case. If, for instance, an administrator wants to convince her colleagues that meal coupons would work at a particular university, she might first discuss a college where meal coupons have been successful. Her next step would be to compare the institutions described with her own, emphasizing important similarities and reasons why conclusions from her example would hold true in the unknown case.

Compelling Reasons.   In some instances, your partner's strategy may be to provide you with so many different reasons that you become convinced that the advantages of his or her proposal outweigh the disadvantages. The sequencing of reasons is often an important factor in the effectiveness of the appeal. In most cases, influence is greatest when stronger arguments or reasons appear at the end and in the beginning. This strategy takes into account the primacy and recency effect that you read about in Chapter 5; you are likely to remember best what you hear first and last.

> Do reasons affect all listeners in the same way? How do you define a "good" reason?

Unfortunately, your job as a critical listener is not a simple matter of assessing the validity of a persuader's logic and reasoning. You must also recognize logical fallacies, arguments that at first appear valid but, upon further examination, prove faulty.

Identify Logical Fallacies

A communicator who uses logical fallacies may not deliberately intend to deceive you; often, he has simply not given enough thought to the development of his arguments and communication strategy. Remember, any piece of evidence can be misused; it is up to you to detect fallacies such as the ones listed below, and to request further information or clarification.

Begging the Question.   When a question is begged, the speaker never really proves the point she is trying to make. The individual argues in a circle, using one unsupported proposition to "prove" another. In "Tough Sell," Sandy states, "Everyone knows Toyota makes the best cars." How do we know that? They're the best "because they're Toyotas." It doesn't take much analysis to recognize that neither assertion has been substantiated.

Hasty Generalization.   You'll recall our discussion of hasty generalizations as a problem of faulty induction. They occur when the communicator does not have enough support for the conclusion she draws. Perhaps, during a recent visit to a Denver company, your sister dined at three restaurants. When she describes her trip, she tells you she'd never eat out in Denver again because "the restaurants there are terrible." Obviously, all restaurants in Denver are not poor just because she didn't like the three she sampled. A hasty generalization was made on too few instances.

> Does cultural orientation affect the impact of various logical fallacies?

Either-Or.   At times a person feels so strongly about an issue that he begins to look at the situation as black and white. Either a particular proposal is adopted entirely, or it's dropped. Either funds are allocated to create a scholarship, or they're not. Either someone is your friend, or he isn't.

Although there are some things that are truly either one way or the other (an elephant is either pregnant or it isn't), many problems have more than two possible solutions and many questions have more than two answers. Portions of a proposal may be adopted, other aspects modified or replaced. Funding for a scholarship may not be as extensive as its organizers envisioned, but perhaps some money can be allocated.

> Is looking for a middle ground always the best approach? When might an either–or approach be the wisest strategy?

Post Hoc, Ergo Propter Hoc.   In this fallacy, the speaker reasons that because one event followed another, there must be a cause–effect relationship. Superstitions belong here. A black cat crosses your path and the next day someone backs into your car in the parking lot; the cat brought you bad luck.

Post hoc, ergo propter hoc is an example of non sequitur or "false cause." Although this type of fallacy is easy to spot when exaggerated, in daily interaction it may easily go undetected. People often look for easy answers to explain unpleasant circumstances. Perhaps you heard that a classmate had just broken up with her long-time steady and quickly concluded, "Now I know why she acted that way. . . ."

Ignoring the Issue.   One of the most common ways in which speakers ignore an issue is through the use of a fallacy called *ad hominem*. Rather than presenting evidence in support of a position, the speaker attacks his or her partner's personal characteristics. The conflict becomes one of personalities rather than ideas. Listen to political presentations for good examples of this fallacy. Politicians frequently argue, "I'm right because, obviously, you can't trust my opponent."

> What is the balance between listener and speaker responsibilities with regard to the use of logical fallacies?

While you may sometimes be convinced on the basis of logic and reasoning alone, emotional appeals play an important role in motivating action. In addition to judging the elements of credibility and the principles of sound reasoning, you also need to identify the emotional appeals applied by persuasive communicators to influence your opinions and actions.

EVALUATE EMOTIONAL APPEALS

Consider the variety of things that you "know" to be true—staying in bed after the alarm rings will cause you to be late to your morning class, a green salad is better for you than chocolate cake—the list is endless. Yet, how often do you go right ahead and behave in ways that are inconsistent with what you acknowledge to be reasonable? Unless what you know is also limited to something you can vividly *feel,* behavior is unlikely to change. As a salesperson, Sandy recognized this principle. In her conversations with Kurt and Sara, she repeatedly framed her propositions in emotional terms by associating Toyotas with "power," "safety," and "smart buyers."

Emotion has been defined simply as a "stirred-up" state, often caused by the perception of a situation as either very threatening or very rewarding. What is emotionally arousing for one person may not be so for the next. It is your individual perceptions and the way you internalize or assign meanings that determine the type of reaction you have. Emotional responses can be triggered by your partner's personality, language, or the substance of the message itself. In fact, there is an emotional component to almost all decision making. Studies have shown that brain-damaged individuals, no longer able to access intuitive signals or "somatic markers," struggle with even the simplest everyday decisions (Damasio, 1994; Brown, 2003). The important point to keep in mind is that while emotion-based intuition plays an important role in forming judgments, effective listeners do not allow their emotions to compromise their ability to identify logical fallacies or propaganda devices.

Emotions vary in intensity. They run high when your need is great and when you perceive the situation as capable of completely satisfying or frustrating this need. Moderate to strong emotional states facilitate appropriate behavior while extreme emotions often lead to disorganized, less effective responses. Intense fear, for instance, may produce aggressiveness toward the communicator, while intense anxiety is likely to cause a defensive–avoidance reaction. When emotional involvement is too intense, you are likely to turn your focus inward and your ability to concentrate decreases. If your instructor begins by announcing that forty percent of the class failed an exam that you desperately needed to pass, it's likely that your listening during the remainder of the session will be affected.

Although any emotional response affects your listening behavior, moderate emotional involvement appears to help you focus attention on the message and prevents your mind from wandering. Recall that your attention is often directly related to your degree of interest in the subject. Speakers incorporate ideas or items that you value in order to influence your thinking and behavior. An internal push increases your chances of understanding and retaining the information you hear.

> Is it possible to design emotional appeals that are equally effective across cultures?

Communicators use a number of techniques to elicit an emotional response. The more they know about you, the better able they are to connect their messages in ways that stimulate your interest and involve your emotions. Listen for the following:

1. Appeals to your values create an emotional response as speakers relate their ideas to your needs and concerns (Box 7.4). It's important to recognize that your personal values are culture-bound and that they have a profound influence on your listening. Attitudes toward such things as change, self-help, competition, openness, efficiency, privacy, and time all have an effect not only on how you interpret a message, but also on how you evaluate the communication. Again, this list varies not only across cultures, but even locally. In general, people in the United States share a set of values—about looking good, eating healthy, keeping current—that the skillful communicator links to his or her message.

BOX 7.4

VALUES USED IN PERSUASIVE APPEALS

health	sex	curiosity	status
cooperation	power	independence	attractiveness
pleasure	belonging	protection	property

2. Visual descriptions of an emotion-producing situation are used to involve you. Sympathy, fear, and curiosity all can be evoked quite readily through short stories or illustrations with vivid imagery.

3. Displays of emotion are used to arouse an identical response in listeners. If the speaker shows sincere enthusiasm for a topic or proposal, listeners are likely to share this wholehearted interest and, subsequently, accept the speaker's position more easily than if they had remained passive.

Wolvin and Coakley (1992) provide suggestions to help determine whether the emotional appeal is leading you astray or whether the speaker's purpose is sound. They recommend that you ask yourself such questions as:

- What is the communicator's intent? Are his or her motives honest and straightforward?
- Who will benefit if the speaker's purpose is accomplished?
- Does the communicator demonstrate sound logic and reasoning in addition to the emotional appeals?
- Is my response completely emotional, or am I also analyzing the message objectively?

Some of these questions may be difficult to answer; however, they serve as a guide in making objective choices in the face of strong emotional appeals (Box 7.5).

4. Language is often used to arouse emotions. The creation of symbols is a uniquely human process, and these symbols have a profound influence on the impact of any message. As you well know, however, the meaning of a word is never the same for any two people; consequently, words can be manipulated to serve a variety of purposes. Recall Eisenberg's (1984) discussion of intentional ambiguity, or the deliberate selection of words that allows listeners to create their own interpretations.

Emotion-laden words are particularly effective in persuasion. Recall the discussion of semantic reactions in Chapter 4, the habit of responding to a word as if

■ ■ ■ ■ ■ ▬▬▬▬▬▬▬▬▬▬▬▬▬▬▬▬▬▬▬▬▬▬▬▬▬▬▬▬▬▬

BOX 7.5

GUIDELINES FOR MODERATING AN EMOTIONAL RESPONSE

- Everyone has "hot buttons"; acknowledging and identifying them is essential to effective listening.
- Anticipate situations in which you may become highly emotional so that you can plan a strategy in advance.

- Use self-talk to calm yourself and maintain your objectivity.
- If you become increasingly emotional during the encounter, you may want to delay your final evaluation until you have an opportunity to distance yourself from the situation.

it was the idea or object it represents. A speaker who uses *mother, freedom,* or *lazy* is depending on your semantic reactions and strong emotional associations to help accomplish her persuasive purpose. Organizational leaders, interested in increasing employee morale, are becoming more careful about the words they choose to motivate workers and create shared visions.

Language is an essential leadership tool as stories, myths, and metaphors help to shape organizational images and cultures. Slogans used during past presidential campaigns in the United States illustrate how language shapes culture: John Kennedy's "New Frontier," Jimmy Carter's "Leadership—For a Change," Ronald Reagan's "New Beginning," Bill Clinton's "Growing of the Economy," or the Army's "Be All You Can Be." Analysts have described George W. Bush as a master of negatively-charged emotional language. In his 2002 policy speech on Iraq, for instance, Brooks (2003) found that he included 44 statements referring to the crisis and its catastrophic repercussions. Regardless of the speaker's specific purpose, vivid language and strong images characterize messages that stimulate an emotional response and inspire listeners to action.

> Think of a current political or organizational leader. How has this person used language to elicit an emotional response? Was it effective?

Propaganda Devices

Effective critical listeners also recognize propaganda techniques. A clever propagandist appears to be presenting facts when he is really using deceptive verbal devices to elicit an emotional response. The skilled critical listener identifies, and discounts, these techniques.

1. *Name-calling:*   In name-calling, the speaker gives a person or an idea a negative label without providing any evidence to prove the assertion. When you hear a speaker call someone a "liar," "crook," or "jerk," don't be misled. Make sure the speaker presents good reasons for using these emotion-laden labels.

> Could you readily identify propaganda techniques when you encounter them in another culture?

2. *Card-stacking:*   Card-stacking is a method where the speaker, instead of presenting all of the important evidence, tells you only those facts that support the point he is trying to make. The communicator leaves out the negative aspect of the idea and neglects to point out any benefits of other positions. This device is particularly difficult to detect when you are unfamiliar with the topic. Those who are knowledgeable about the issues, however, quickly become alienated by one-sided presentations.

3. *The Bandwagon:*   In this appeal, the speaker tries to convince you to "jump on the bandwagon" by telling you that everyone else is doing something—whether it is purchasing a particular computer or drinking a certain beverage. The strong implication is that you should do it, too, or you will be left out. Television commercials regularly use this approach. Teenagers test this technique when they argue, "All my friends' parents are letting them go to the party."

4. *Glittering generality:*   A glittering generality is a word so vague that everyone agrees on its appropriateness and value—but no one is really sure just what it means. When your instructor says she is in favor of "fair grading policies" or "flexibility in the submission of assignments," you may think, "Hey, she's not so bad after all." Later, however, you may discover that your interpretation of these terms is quite different from what she intended.

5. *Testimonial:*   When a communicator presents the opinion of some well-known person to support his view, the strategy is called a testimonial. Often, the particular individual, although famous, is not qualified to judge or speak on the idea he advocates. Do football players really know about breakfast cereal? Is a movie star more knowledgeable about detergents than your neighbor? Whenever you hear a testimonial, ask yourself, who is this person and what is his area of expertise? Is this person a credible source?

> Under what circumstances does the use of propaganda devices become unethical?

6. *Doublespeak:*   When you hear that a communicator is using doublespeak, it means that he is trying *not* to communicate clearly and accurately. It is likely that he is concealing the truth and deliberately misleading or distracting you. Many examples of doublespeak occur in the political arena: "income enhancement" has been used to refer to taxes; an important issue is said to be at the "vortex of cruciality."

In many respects, critical listening is an orientation, an approach to persuasive listening situations that recognizes the many ways in which you are potentially influenced every day. The critical listener takes responsibility for the decisions she makes. As Larson (1989, p. 428) reminds us, all persuaders ask to borrow just a bit of your mind, just for a little while. Understanding the principles of persuasion will ensure that your mind is safely returned.

SUMMARY

Critical listeners are first concerned with accurately and completely understanding what they hear. The nature of the listening situation, however, requires that you take an additional step to evaluate messages in order to make wise choices and solve problems effectively. The most frequent critical listening context is persuasion.

In responding appropriately to persuasive efforts, you must first understand the principles of key persuasive theories. Further, as a critical listener, you strive to remain open-minded and objective by adhering to principles such as indexing, dating, and acknowledging differences as well as similarities.

There are three dimensions to persuasive appeals, and critical listeners evaluate each as it influences their perceptions of the message. The first is the impact of the speaker, or her credibility. You are affected by judgments of the individual's character—her trustworthiness, dynamism, and expertise. Perceptions of credibility can change during the communication encounter itself, so that an individual's initial credibility may be higher or lower than her terminal credibility.

To evaluate the next element, rational appeals, you must understand logic and reasoning and be familiar with the types of information and evidence you are likely to hear. Your partner must prove his or her position; the amount of evidence it will take to be effective depends on your background, previous knowledge, current beliefs, and other individual factors. There are a variety of patterns communicators can use to link their evidence into logical arguments such as induction, deduction, cause–effect, and literal comparisons.

Finally, persuaders often rely on the use of emotional appeal as well as evidence and reasoning. Critical listeners understand the influence language has on their reactions, and how effective persuasive appeals involve strong references to their values and needs. They also recognize propaganda devices and are careful not to be overly influenced by manipulative techniques.

APPLICATIONS

Application 1: Mentally Prepare Yourself to Listen Objectively
Application 2: Analyze Source Credibility
Application 3: Analyze the Speaker's Evidence
Application 4: Analyze the Speaker's Reasoning
Application 5: Analyze the Speaker's Emotional Appeals

_____ I readily consider new evidence and circumstances that might prompt me to reevaluate my previous position.
_____ I am constantly aware that people and circumstances change over time.
Application 1: Mentally Prepare Yourself to Listen Objectively

_____ I consider my partner's personal expertise on the subject when *he or she* tries to convince me to do something.
Application 2: Analyze the Speaker's Credibility

_____ I weigh all evidence before making a decision.
Application 3: Analyze the Speaker's Evidence

_____ I take time to analyze the validity of my partner's reasoning before arriving at my own conclusions.
Application 4: Analyze the Speaker's Reasoning

_____ I listen carefully to determine whether the speaker has solid facts and evidence or whether she is relying on emotional appeals.
Application 5: Analyze the Speaker's Emotional Appeals

Application 1: Mentally Prepare Yourself to Listen Objectively

By following the principles of objective thinking, you can prepare yourself to listen effectively in almost any persuasive encounter. The most difficult critical listening situations involve daily interactions in which you may be subtly influenced by the unplanned, informal messages around you. In these and similar situations, the habits of clear thinking will enable you to make wise decisions.

Although you strive to withhold judgment until you have completely understood your partner, it is virtually impossible not to view the situation from your own perspective, coloring what you have heard as you put your partner's ideas into the context of your own past experiences, values, and attitudes.

Activities

1. What are some of your strongest opinions or biases? How did you come to take these positions?

    List some situations in which your bias could interfere with effective listening. Is being aware of your predispositions enough to prevent them from distorting incoming messages? What else might you do?

2. Choose one stereotype you know you have. Using it as an example, complete the following:

    a. How would the rule "There's always more to know" help you become more open-minded on this subject?
    b. How would indexing influence your thinking on this issue?
    c. Would dating help overcome this bias? If so, how?

3. List several groups to which you belong—brother, daughter, student, server. Make a list of the things all members in each group have in common. Then list the ways in which you differ from other members of each group.

4. It is essential that you first listen to understand before you evaluate what you hear.

    Under what circumstances is this particularly difficult?

    In the past, what situations have you encountered where someone's message was immediately accepted or rejected before it was completely understood?

    How can you guard against this tendency?

5. How have you changed over the past three years? Have others recognized the changes? Why or why not?

Group Activities

Form a small group of four to six people. You may want to keep the same group for all activities, or you may find it more interesting to change groups so that you get to hear the opinions and ideas of a greater number of your classmates.

1. Generate two examples of a stereotype that is common to everyone in your group. Focus on each example in turn, identifying how the following principles might help you to overcome these blocks to effective evaluation.

    a. There's Always More to Know (open-mindedness)
    b. Every Person Is Unique (indexing)
    c. Allow for Change over Time (dating)

2. Find examples from the print media where the bias of the source has influenced the content of the story (perhaps you can find articles in two different publications on the same incident or event). As a group, rewrite the story eliminating any bias. Read both articles aloud.

3. If we agree that every person is biased to some degree, is there such a thing as pure objectivity? Is it desirable? What can we do to recognize bias in the messages we hear? Make a list of some questions we should ask ourselves, building on the ideas provided in the text.

4. How do you determine when dating is appropriate, and when knowledge of past behaviors and attitudes should influence present actions?

    Consider the following examples and discuss what appropriate behavior might be in each case. Note differences of opinion among group members:

    - a child is known to be anxious and shy
    - a parent is known to be abusive
    - a student is known to always volunteer
    - a child care provider has a criminal record
    - a friend is repeatedly unreliable
    - a teacher has a reputation for giving low grades

5. Our language tempts us to exaggerate and see the world in black and white terms. Work in competitive teams to generate answers to the "middle" value in each of the situations below.

black	white
success	failure
polite	rude
honest	dishonest
stingy	generous

6. Events are often colored by the words you choose to describe them. Increase your sensitivity to language by completing the exercise below. The "I" column is the most positive interpretation of an event. "He" or "She" is used for the most negative interpretation of the same behavior or situation.

    As a group, your task is to come up with "You" sentences that are somewhere in-between the two extremes of the "I" and "He/She" categories. Then, see if you can generate sentences for both "he/she" and "you" columns for the final six items.

I	*You*	*He/She*
a. I am a casual housekeeper.	?	She is a slob.
b. I am healthy-looking.		She is a fat pig.
c. I am fun-loving.		He is out of control.
d. I am tactful.		He is deceitful.
e. I use discretion.		She is a liar.
f. I am sensitive.		
g. I need plenty of rest.		
h. I daydream.		
i. I am firm.		
j. I am high-spirited.		
k. I like to have a good time.		

7. It's difficult to identify all of the assumptions in our heads that affect how we think about the world around us. Individually, fill in the blanks below. Then as a group, compare your answers. Discuss the explanations for any significant differences that arise.

   a. Mrs. Smith is a tall woman. She must be at least_____tall.
   b. Mr. Jones is middle-aged. He has got to be_____old.
   c. Mrs. Randall wears nice clothes. That dress must have cost her_____.
   d. Mr. Arnold is a short man. He must be_____tall.
   e. Mrs. Perry has a lot of children to worry about—she's the mother of_____.
   f. Mrs. Bentley lets her 16-year-old daughter go out way too much. She has a date_____times a week.

8. Take turns responding out loud to each of the following statements. Be candid. At the end of each round, discuss your responses and how they might influence your judgments and evaluations.

   a. When I see a student come out of class crying, I assume . . .
   b. When I see a very orderly desk, I assume . . .
   c. When I hear that someone meditates, I assume . . .
   d. When I discover that a friend is taking a time and stress management seminar, I assume . . .
   e. When a student says to a secretary, "How long will it be before Professor Smith can see me?" I assume . . .
   f. When my roommate says she cannot be interrupted during a particular period, I assume . . .
   g. When a classmate has a headache almost every day, I assume . . .
   h. When someone says that he or she never knows what to do next, I assume . . .
   i. When a friend takes a long time to make a relatively minor decision, I assume . . .
   j. When someone has no long-range goals, I assume . . .

Application 2: Analyze Source Credibility

Questions about your partner's credibility will soon arise almost automatically. "Who is this person, anyway?" you'll think to yourself. The dimensions of trust, expertise, and dynamism are always present; in every encounter you make judgments about how much credibility your partner has on the topic at hand.

You can also analyze the on-going communication situation to determine how credibility is either enhanced or lost during the encounter. Remember that while a speaker may have high credibility on one subject, he or she may know very little about other topics. Make sure that you don't attribute unwarranted credibility to a speaker who has demonstrated expertise or trustworthiness in the past, but who may not know much about the current topic.

Activities

1. On what topics do you have credibility?
   On what topics is your credibility low?
   On what topics would you like to improve your credibility?

2. Watch a TV news broadcast. Why do newscasters have so much credibility? What do they do to establish their credibility?

3. Rank order the following according to the importance of credibility to each profession (1 = most need for credibility, 10 = least need).

    Repeat this exercise in your group. How similar were your rankings? Justify your choices.

    _____ college teacher
    _____ surgeon
    _____ pilot
    _____ truck driver
    _____ computer programmer
    _____ school bus driver
    _____ elementary school teacher
    _____ car salesman
    _____ home contractor
    _____ quality control inspector

Group Activities

Form a small group of four to six people. You may want to keep the same group for all activities, or you may find it more interesting to change groups so that you get to hear the opinions and ideas of a greater number of your classmates.

1. Together, generate a list of public personalities—television, movie, political—whom you respect. Create a second list of those individuals you distrust.

    a. How do your feelings about each person affect the way you listen to his or her message?
    b. Do you agree more frequently with people whom you perceive as credible?
    c. If there are differences among the members of your group, try to determine the cause of the disagreement. It is likely that different members of your group listen differently to each of the individuals listed because of their own personal attitudes and opinions.

2. Think of an example where someone had relatively low initial credibility but was effective in deriving more credibility during his presentation.

    What was the occasion?
    What did this person *do* to increase your confidence?

3. As a group, list four people you find exceptionally credible. Consider their listening skills. Individually, rate each person's overall listening competence.

Name	Poor Listener						Effective Listener			
1._____	1	2	3	4	5	6	7	8	9	10
2._____	1	2	3	4	5	6	7	8	9	10
3._____	1	2	3	4	5	6	7	8	9	10
4._____	1	2	3	4	5	6	7	8	9	10

Compare the ratings on your list with those of other group members. Is there any consistency among group members' ratings?

Do individuals with high credibility tend to be perceived as effective listeners? Explain.

Application 3: Analyze the Speaker's Evidence

There's a well-known cartoon that shows college students diligently writing in their notebooks as their science teacher lectures. He's talking about astronomy, and the students are writing, "The moon is really made of a synthetic material called Luberfill that was first produced in 1430. . . ."

The point, of course, is that no one is questioning what the professor is saying. They are dutifully repeating without asking questions—without asking for proof of statements that seem outrageous. You know that some people are more difficult to convince than others, but a healthy attitude requires that you constantly assess the validity of what you hear.

Activities

1. Consider your most frequent listening situations. Which components of the HURIER model are most essential for each?

    In what types of listening situations do you feel most comfortable?

    What do you know about your personal style that helps to explain your preferences?

2. What inferences have others made about you? Were they true?

    How and why did they begin? What did you do about it?

    What can you do when false information is circulated?

3. do you believe that all communication is persuasion? Why or why not? Share your opinions with other group members and discuss your reasons for taking the position you did. Can your group come to a consensus?

Group Activities

Form a small group of four to six people. You may want to keep the same group for all activities, or you may find it more interesting to change groups so that you get to hear the opinions and ideas of a greater number of your classmates.

1. Read the passage below and respond to the six questions that follow. Mark the statements "T" that you believe to be true. Mark statements "F" that you believe to be false. Mark statements with a question mark when you are not sure if they are true or false from the information provided.

    Incident: A businessman had just turned off all the lights in his store when a man appeared and demanded money. The owner opened one of the cash registers. The contents of the cash register were scooped up, and the man hurried away. A member of the police force was called immediately.

    _____ a. A man appeared after the owner had turned off all the store lights.

    _____ b. The robber was a man.

    _____ c. The man who opened the cash register was the owner.

    _____ d. The store owner scooped up the contents of the cash register and ran away.

    _____ e. After the man who demanded the money scooped up the contents of the cash register, he ran away.

    _____ f. While the cash register contained money, the story does not state how much.

    How did you score?

    Review your responses to determine how you came to each conclusion.

    Discuss your answers with other group members. What does this exercise illustrate about our tendency to make inferences?

What *evidence* did you have on which to base your conclusions?
(Answers to these questions appear at the end of this section.)

2. Take five minutes and prepare to explain a process or describe an item to other members of your group. You must use at least three different types of development. (You can make up this information.) Other members of your group must identify each type correctly.

3. Construct a sound case for the adoption of a specific plan or idea. Present your case to the entire group. Limit your presentation to five minutes. Other group members will challenge your:

   a. use of reasoning
   b. support for your main points
   c. application of fact, opinion, and inference

4. Cut out a picture from a magazine—the more complex it is, the better. Don't let other members of your group look at the picture. Describe it to them verbally as they try to draw from your verbal description. Stop after four minutes. Compare all pictures with the original. Notice what the speaker *selected* to describe and note any *inferences* that were made by the listeners. Did they "read in" information in order to make sense of the directions? What accounts for the differences between the pictures?

5. As a group, prepare in writing a set of instructions for someone to put on a coat. Assume this person knows nothing about coats—collar, lapel, lining, belt, pockets, buttons. Each group takes a turn reading its directions to an individual who will follow them *exactly* as they are presented. The individual who is reading should have his back to the person performing. The speaker cannot add information to what was written down, and the listener can do only what she is instructed to do. After the exercise is complete, discuss the following:

   Were the directions complete?
   What assumptions were made about what the listener "knew"?

6. Review the list of statements below and determine what it would take to convince you to accept that particular position; in other words, how much (and what type) evidence would it take to persuade you?

   When everyone has finished, take turns within the group sharing your responses.
   Were there differences among group members?
   What accounts for these differences?

Statements:
a. Flying saucers from outer space have landed on the earth.
b. Ghosts exist.
c. It is best to have just two children.
d. College grades do not affect job success.
e. Praying works.
f. Events in your life are largely predetermined.
g. You should buy a new computer.
h. College is a waste of time.
i. Listening is the most important communication skill.
j. Be an organ donor.

7. Select one of the topics below. As a group, discuss how you would adapt your message for each audience by selecting different evidence in support of your point. Note other changes you would make in language, amount of information presented, and so forth.

Topics	Audiences
Don't drive—car pool	vice presidents of major companies
Join our aerobics class	secretaries
Retirement planning—don't wait	sales and marketing personnel
You need a kitten	working mothers

       Answers to Group Activity 1 were all "?" Can you explain why? When you give up, look below.

a. The owner and the businessman may or may not be the same person.
b. We do not know that a "robbery" occurred.
c. The owner may be a woman.
d. The contents were scooped up, we don't know by whom.
e. We do not know if the same person did these three things.
f. The contents of the cash register may not have been money.

Application 4: Analyze the Speaker's Reasoning

Listening for a speaker's use of logic and reasoning is a valuable exercise. Not only does it help you concentrate on the message, but it reinforces critical thinking habits. Keep in mind, however, that we are talking primarily about those formal and informal situations in which someone is trying to influence behavior. There are other times when an analysis of this sort would be inappropriate, where the communicator's purpose is to lend support, to entertain, or to accomplish some other objective.

Activities

1. Identify several critical listening situations that you have been in recently.
   How satisfied are you with the way you managed these encounters?
   Do you habitually ask probing questions about the information you hear?

2. Keep a journal and record disagreements or arguments that you have with friends or family.
         What kind of logic was used?
         How rational were the participants?
         What was the outcome of the argument?

3. List five things you know to be true. Determine whether these conclusions are based on inductive or deductive reasoning.

Group Activities

Form a small group of four to six people. You may want to keep the same group for all activities, or you may find it more interesting to change groups so that you get to hear the opinions and ideas of a greater number of your classmates.

1. Bring in the text of a persuasive speech or essay.

What is the writer's main objective?

What types of logic and reasoning are used?

Determine the major premises and identify how these were supported.

2. Bring an example of induction (from any written source) to class. Share your samples with other group members. Put each sample to the tests suggested in your reading:

   a. Was the sample representative?

   b. Did it include enough cases?

   c. Can the results be verified?

   d. Are those in your sample reliable? Is there any reason to assume they would be biased?

   e. Are there any exceptions that should be considered?

3. Find examples of logical fallacies from any communications media. Share your samples with other group members.

   Identify the type of fallacy and discuss its effectiveness.

   Who would be taken in by the argument? Why?

4. Make a small slip of paper for each group member. Put an X on one slip and then fold all pieces. Give out slips randomly. Each person creates and then shares a valid (but possibly untrue) syllogism. The individual who drew the X presents an *invalid* syllogism. Members listen carefully to determine who drew the X.

Application 5: Analyze the Speaker's Emotional Appeals

In many circumstances, emotional appeals are highly effective. It is your job as a critical listener to recognize how they also serve as filters, preventing you from hearing the entire message or from logically assessing the value of your partner's ideas.

Recognizing emotional appeals, and the way they affect you, is the first step to reducing the impact they have on your ability to listen objectively. Emotions can be aroused by the communicator, by the subject, or by the language used to express ideas. Although some emotional involvement is necessary and desirable, realize that whenever you respond emotionally, your listening is affected and the likelihood of making an objective, logical decision is decreased.

Activities

1. Explore some of the propaganda devices as they have been used in political campaigns or by various cults. Bring specific examples to class.

   Why are they so effective?

   What can you do to protect yourself from this type of persuasion?

2. Do you believe the visual or verbal medium is best for eliciting a strong emotional response? What types of emotional appeal affect you the most? Does the effectiveness of emotional appeal depend on the individual? The circumstances? Both?

3. List five values that could be used to persuade you.

   a. Which of the above do you share with your family? Which have you held for more than ten years? Do your values change over time? Why?

b. Should you attempt to reduce the emotional impact of value appeals? Why?

c. How would you go about controlling your emotional response?

4. How might you use self-talk to reduce the impact of strong emotional appeals? Keep track of situations in which you become emotionally involved, and deliberately apply this suggestion. How effective was self-talk in helping you maintain objectivity?

Group Activities

Form a small group of four to six people. You may want to keep the same group for all activities, or you may find it more interesting to change groups so that you get to hear the opinions and ideas of a greater number of your classmates.

1. Do public relations offices use propaganda to increase morale or influence the company's image? Is this ethical? Does your college or university engage in any activities (recruitment and admissions, placement, public relations) that could be classified as propaganda?

2. Bring in print advertisements that have a strong emotional appeal. Determine what particular group the ad was designed to persuade. Do you think it is successful? What values are targeted?

3. Select a product and a market. Create your own advertisement using appeals from the list of propaganda techniques. Would different techniques work better on some listeners than others? Why?

   a. bandwagon
   b. card stacking
   c. testimonial
   d. doublespeak
   e. glittering generality

4. Bring in a short passage that you believe will elicit a strong emotional response from members of your group. Read it to them.
   Discuss the following:

   a. What type of audience is this message designed to persuade?
   b. What are the needs and values of this group?
   c. What response does the author want?
   d. How effective was the message in accomplishing its purpose?
   e. How else might the author have accomplished his goal?

   Now rewrite the passage using a logical approach so that the emotional impact is reduced (you can make up your own evidence). Read it to the group once again. Analyze the changes that resulted from the increased objectivity.

5. **Value Action**

   Each person in a large group (from fifteen to twenty participants) is given ten $10 tokens. Each of the following values will be auctioned off to the highest bidder. Choose an auctioneer and a recorder. Before bidding, fill out a personal budget of the way you think tokens will be distributed. You are not obligated to stick to your original plan. A designated class member will conduct the auction until all values have been sold.

	My budget	Amount I bid	Top bid
a. A satisfying marriage	_____	_____	_____
b. No responsibilities	_____	_____	_____
c. The respect of friends	_____	_____	_____
d. Travel to different cultures	_____	_____	_____
e. Complete self-confidence	_____	_____	_____
f. Recognition by professional colleagues	_____	_____	_____
g. A life free of illness	_____	_____	_____
h. A year's vacation with salary	_____	_____	_____
i. A lovely home	_____	_____	_____
j. Success in your chosen profession	_____	_____	_____
k. Lifetime health for your pets	_____	_____	_____
l. Constant excitement and fun	_____	_____	_____

After the auction, discuss why you bid on each item. Why did some items receive high bids from many people while others went for much less?

How would the auction have been different if the following groups had participated:

- elderly
- parents
- children
- terminally ill patients
- all women or all men
- individuals from a third world country

6. Is logic valued more than emotion in a business environment? When is an emotional response appropriate in making business decisions? Do you believe there are gender differences in the degree to which decisions are made on an emotional basis? Cultural differences? Discuss your opinions.

EVALUATING MESSAGES: SHORT CASE

Natural Resources

A successful sales representative, Ted Banks, just retired. When his co-workers, Paul and Bev, realized that his secretary would be available, each wanted to work with her. They appealed to Ed Franklin in their separate efforts to convince him. Ted's secretary, Barb, had been in her position for eleven years. She knew the accounts inside and out and was dependable, easy to work with, and extremely knowledgeable.

Paul argued that he could best use her services because he was relatively new and her expertise could make a substantial difference in his performance. He had new facilities, a plush office available to her, and his region was much larger than Bev's.

Bev was angry when she realized that Paul was trying to get Ed to assign Barb to him. She had had her request in two days before his. She felt that as a woman, Barb would prefer to work with her. She also had seniority, having worked for the company for seven years; Paul was only in his second year on the staff. Besides, everyone had heard that Paul might be leaving the company soon, and it seemed foolish to assign such a good secretary to someone who might not be around much longer.

1. Evaluate the reasons presented by Paul and Bev. Which are valid? Why? Which are invalid? Why? What emotional appeals are involved?

2. What other questions does Ed need to make a decision? What questions should he ask of Paul and Bev?

3. How should Ed make the decision?

4. Who do you think will get Barb for his or her secretary?

TOUGH SELL: CASE QUESTIONS

1. How much credibility did Sandy have in her discussions with Kurt and Sara? Explain.

2. What inferences are made in the case that cause problems for the individuals involved? In terms of criteria for buying a car, how did the opinions of Kurt, Sara, and Sandy differ?

3. What emotional appeals did Sandy use on Kurt and Sara in trying to sell them a Toyota? How effective were they? What values were involved?

4. What persuasive techniques did Cody use in trying to persuade Sara to consider working at BurgerWorld?

5. Can you identify any ethical dilemmas in any of the situations described in "Tough Sell"? Explain your position.

6. Identify examples of consistency theory at work in "Tough Sell."

7. What rules of critical listening (there's always more to know, things change, and so forth) would have been most helpful to Sara in her discussions with Cody?

8. Role-play interactions between Sandy and Kurt, illustrating the following:
   a. Sandy uses only logical appeals.
   b. Sandy knows that Kurt is heavily influenced by emotional appeals.
   c. Sandy knows that Kurt will be persuaded only if Sara is convinced.

9. To what extent did Kurt apply the rule of "understand before you evaluate." What about Sara?

10. What examples of effective or ineffective hearing, understanding, remembering, or interpreting did you notice with regard to the characters in "Tough Sell"?

BIBLIOGRAPHY

Bandura, A. (1977). *Social learning theory.* Englewood Cliffs, NJ: Prentice Hall.
Brembeck, W. L., & Howell, W. S. (1976). *Persuasion: A means of social influence.* Englewood Cliffs, NJ: Prentice Hall.
Brooks, R. (2003, June 22). Bush dominates a nation of victims. *The Nation,* 4.
Brown, R. (2003). Emotions and behavior: Exercises in emotional intelligence. *Journal of Management Education, 27*(1), 122–135.

Damasio, A. R. (1994). *Descartes' error: Emotion, reason, and the human brain.* New York: Avon Books.

Eisenberg, E. (1984). Ambiguity as strategy in organizational communication. *Communication Monographs, 51*(3), 227–242.

Festinger, L. (1962). *A theory of cognitive dissonance.* Stanford, CA: Stanford University Press.

Fitch-Hauser, M. (1990). Making sense of data: Constructs, schemas, and concepts. In R. N. Bostrom (Ed.), *Listening Behavior: Measurement & Application,* pp. 76–90. New York: The Guilford Press.

Heider, F. (1958). *The psychology of interpersonal relations.* New York: Wiley & Sons.

Hovland, C. I., Janis, I. L., & Kelly, H. H. (1953). *Communication and persuasion.* New Haven, CT: Yale University Press.

Kelly, C. M. (1982). Empathic listening. In J. Stewart (Ed.), *Bridges not walls,* 3rd Ed., pp. 214–223. Reading, MA: Addison-Wesley.

Knapp, M. L. (1978). *Nonverbal communication in human interaction.* New York: Holt, Rinehart, and Winston.

Larson, C. U. (1989). *Persuasion: Reception and responsibility.* Belmont, CA: Wadsworth.

Lundsteen, S. (1979). *Listening: Its impact on reading and other language arts.* Urbana, IL: ERIC Clearinghouse on Reading and Communication Skills.

Reese, R. G., & Floyd, J. J. (1987). Listening theory in modern rhetorical thought. *Journal of the International Listening Association, 1*(1), 87–102.

Thomlison, D. (1991). Intercultural listening. In D. Borisoff and M. Purdy (Eds.), *Listening in Everyday Life: A Personal and Professional Approach,* pp. 87–138. New York: University Press of America.

Wolvin, A., & Coakley, C. W. (1996). *Listening.* Dubuque, IA: Wm. C. Brown.

CHAPTER 8

THE PROCESS OF
RESPONDING

If people listened to themselves more often,
they would talk less.
—ANONYMOUS

OUTLINE

CHAPTER OBJECTIVES

After completing this chapter, you will

Become more aware of:

- the importance of your response in facilitating effective interactions

- the variety of response choices available to listeners

- the range of nonverbal elements that affect listening environments

Better understand:

- transactional analysis and ego state responses

- common response styles

- the assertive response

- supportive responses

- the ways in which distance, time, and other nonverbal elements affect the listening environment

Develop skills in:

- analyzing behavior in transactional analysis terms

- identifying a variety of response styles
- demonstrating assertive skills
- recognizing and applying supportive communication behaviors
- using distance and timing to facilitate supportive listening environments

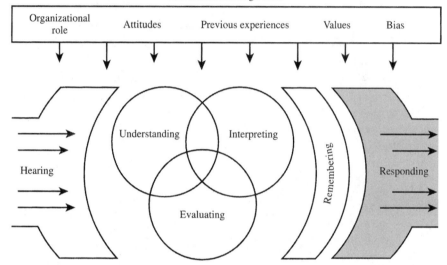

A Model of the Six-Component HURIER Listening Process

RESPONDING: SITUATION AND PURPOSE

Others judge the effectiveness of your listening by the nature of the response you make to what you hear. Your response can be overt or covert, verbal or nonverbal. Whenever there is a strong stimulus, it is likely that you will have some reaction to it. When you are comfortable with a wide range of responses, you can adapt to almost any listening situation.

The consequence of your response is perhaps nowhere more powerful than in relational listening settings. Whether your purpose is to provide support, confirm understanding, or offer advice, the face-to-face setting provides the richest opportunities to connect with another person. Keep in mind, too, that your response reflects your value and character as well as your listening ability.

Through your response, you have an opportunity to influence your partner. You can improve relationships and ensure more accurate understanding. Recognizing and identifying your own response, and the manner in which it is perceived by others, is the first step to improving your overall listening competence.

CASE: THE INTERVIEW

Martina was on the job market. She had come back to her dorm room early to prepare for an important interview with one of the major sales and marketing firms, HBH. She had made it through the on-campus screening process, and this would be her second interview. She knew she was one of only three final candidates, and she wanted to be fully prepared. Martina took a deep breath. For the moment, at least, she had to put all other problems aside. Martina looked at herself in the mirror one last time, and left her room feeling reasonably confident.

As she got off the subway and approached the towering HBH building, she could feel her heart beating faster. "You've got to stay calm," Martina told herself. "You can't blow this opportunity." She entered the building and took the elevator to the fifth floor. There, she entered a waiting room filled with briefcases and young people in business suits. She checked in with the receptionist and was escorted to an exceptionally large office and asked to wait for Ms. Toni Rogers, Director of Sales.

It was almost twenty minutes before Ms. Rogers appeared. Her arms were full of file folders and she began talking as soon as she entered the room. Without formally acknowledging that Martina was sitting there in front of her, Ms. Rogers set down the folders on the table and sighed loudly, "It's been one of those days. There's never enough time. Never."

Martina sat in silence as Ms. Rogers moved past her to a dark oak desk. Ms. Rogers sighed as she opened her briefcase and sorted through more files. "Well, it's here somewhere," she said, sounding slightly irritated. "John gave it to me yesterday to review. Not that I've had any time to look at anything except papers related to my sales plan." Ms. Rogers continued to sort through the papers, then gave up, closed her briefcase, and looked up at Martina. "So," she said, leaning back in her chair. "It seems you'll have to tell me who you are and why you're here."

"This is a nightmare," Martina thought to herself. "This woman has no business interviewing me—she hasn't even read my resume. She probably hasn't even read the job description."

"Well," Martina began, but she was abruptly interrupted.

"Please, don't begin your sentences with 'Well,'" Ms. Rogers said firmly. "It sounds tentative, weak. When you have something to say, just say it directly. I hate it when my people begin their sentences with 'well,' or 'um,' or some other weak word." Ms. Rogers leaned forward and removed a piece of hard candy from a dish on her desk. She stared intently at Martina as she methodically took off the wrapper.

Martina was ready to leave, but she knew she had to say something. "My name is Martina Tantonic. I'm a first semester senior over at Delrose College, majoring in business administration."

"So?" Ms. Rogers responded impatiently.

"So," Martina felt herself on the verge of tears. She couldn't believe how rude this woman was to her. "So, I've been doing a lot of work in sales and marketing and I was interested in your company."

"A lot of people are interested in our company," Ms. Rogers replied, looking intently at Martina over her huge desk. "This is a growing, profitable company. You should be interested. The question is, why should I be interested in you?"

"You should be interested in me," Martina paused momentarily. Ms. Rogers took the opportunity to once again interrupt. "Please speak up," she said.

Martina continued, noticeably louder this time, "because I'm very good at sales. My junior project won first place out of all two hundred students in our class, and I've had two summer's work experience selling door-to-door. Right now I work at the student headquarters where I designed and help manage a major fund-raising campaign."

"I see." Ms. Rogers continued to look directly at Martina. After this last response, Martina began to feel a little more confident. Martina decided that she would stare right back at Ms. Rogers and try not to let her know how intimidated she really felt. Martina caught herself fidgeting with her hair and quickly stopped.

"I am interested in HBH," Martina continued, "because I understand that you give your sales staff a lot of autonomy. I am looking for a company where I can be creative and where I can develop my sales skills. I don't need a lot of supervision."

"So, you think you're creative," Ms. Rogers sat back in her chair, still keeping her eyes on Martina. "What do other people think?"

Martina felt herself getting flushed and upset once again by Ms. Rogers' manner, but she forced herself to stay calm. "Here are some samples of the ads I created as part of my junior project," Martina said as she reached into her briefcase for her portfolio and handed it across the wide desk to Ms. Rogers.

Ms. Rogers was silent for what seemed to Martina like hours. Then she laid the portfolio down, stood up, and walked to the door. Martina thought she heard her say something like "One moment," as she disappeared into the hall.

When Ms. Rogers returned several minutes later, she was followed by three men who all looked to be in their late twenties or early thirties. Each of the men shook hands warmly with Martina and introduced himself before taking a seat at the conference table.

"Come join us," Ms. Rogers said to Martina with a smile as she motioned to a seat at the head of the table.

Once again, Martina felt the awkwardness of her position. Sitting there facing four older business people made her want to slide underneath the table. She sat straight, however, and looked out at them.

"Well, Martina," the man to her left, John Carlsen, was the first to speak. "Toni tells me that she's talked with you for a few minutes and is very impressed with what she's seen."

"Thank you," Martina replied, trying not to show her surprise at his compliment. She felt weak and hoped she wasn't shaking visibly.

"Yes, Martina," Ms. Rogers added. "I know the interview was stressful, but you did a marvelous job of answering my questions clearly and directly and of supporting your claims with solid evidence. You also stayed calm and professional. I

know that wasn't easy. Some candidates have simply walked out of the room, as you can probably imagine!" She took a drink of coffee and continued, "You probably wonder why we put you through all of this. It's because you're thinking about taking on some very stressful work. Sales isn't easy and your clients aren't always polite. You need self-discipline, confidence, and interpersonal skills as well as sales expertise. It's our job to make sure that we only make an offer to a candidate who has the potential to be successful at this business. From what I've seen so far, you certainly qualify."

"Thank you, Ms. Rogers. There were times when I was really upset, but I tried to remain as calm and professional as I could." Martina felt herself relaxing for the first time since she'd entered the office.

"You did a good job," Ms. Rogers replied. "And please, call me Toni."

The rest of the afternoon passed quickly. Martina met with several other sales representatives and talked with the vice-president of marketing. When she finally left HBH and entered the subway bound for campus, it was after 5:30 p.m. and she was exhausted. Toni has promised to get back to her within a week. As she reflected on the day's events, Martina felt confident that she had done her best.

RESPONDING TO MESSAGES: PRINCIPLES

Effective listening is prerequisite to demonstrating an appropriate response. As emphasized in Chapter 2, unless you listen well, it is impossible to construct an effective message—a response that has meaning for your partner relative to what was said. Key factors that influence the development of your response have to do with the listening situation and your listening purpose. Each of Chapters 3 through 8 has opened with thoughts on how situation and purpose affect the degree to which each component of the listening process is relevant. You'll recall that *situations* include intrapersonal, interpersonal, small group, public, and mediated. From our perspective, speaking and listening are inseparable dimensions of a relational communication process that can take place, to some extent, on each of these levels.

Distance communication, most notably in mediated settings, creates one of the greatest distinctions between the communication functions of speaking and listening. Your response may be constrained further by the nature of the technologies involved. Chat rooms, videoconferencing, and other forms of distance communication each has its own unique impact on the communication process and, subsequently, on your choice set when it comes to creating an appropriate response.

Even the most formal communication occasions, however, are profitably viewed as extensions of the relational model. In these settings, you engage in inner speech as you silently respond to what you hear. Skilled presenters attend to nonverbal cues and use them as guides to better understanding the

> How do you respond when you listen to a presentation? Which elements of this response are private and which are public?

response that their messages have elicited. In this way, adaptations to listeners continue.

The box at the beginning of this chapter noted that the nature of your verbal and nonverbal response is perhaps most powerful in interpersonal and small group situations where feedback is immediate and all participants are within close proximity. When you take the co-creation of meaning seriously, you recognize that individuals engaged in the relational listening process must constantly respond in order to provide feedback to their partners. Keep in mind that your partner can only judge the quality of your listening through the response that you make to his overtures. He cannot read your mind; his conclusions about your listening effectiveness are based on your behavior in this multidimensional encounter.

> Is the nature of your response the *only* way for a speaker to know what his impact has been?

While the nature of the situation affects your response and its impact on your partner, it is only one of two important variables. Your *purpose* for listening has an equally significant influence on the decisions that you make as a listener and on the consequences of your choices. You may recall that five listening purposes were presented in Chapter 2: discriminative, comprehensive, critical, therapeutic, and appreciative. These purposes affect the degree to which each component of the HURIER model affects your listening. If you are listening to music, for instance, hearing is critical, while understanding may be less important. When we focus on response as the key listening variable, identifying your purpose provides particularly valuable direction. As you develop behavioral flexibility, that is, as you increase the number and nature of responses available to you, your chance of being effective increases.

Imagine that you are a participant in a videoconference as part of a required course. The fact that you must clearly *comprehend* what you hear will influence your response, which may be to ask questions, rather than simply to ignore ideas that are unclear. If a friend has come to you after a traumatic experience and your purpose is to provide support through *therapeutic* listening, you will create your responses accordingly. Listening to make a wise purchase, on the other hand, necessarily involves *critical* listening skills and a more objective, fact-centered approach.

An important part of effective listening, then, is to respond in a manner that will facilitate shared meanings, contribute to accomplishing tasks, and develop satisfying relationships. The term listening response is used to describe the mindful behavior that occurs as a result of effective listening. In this chapter you will be introduced to response styles that will enable you to make better informed, wiser choices. Emphasis will be on transactional analysis as a framework for understanding your behavior, followed by descriptions of the assertive and supportive styles. These lis-

> Do you believe that the listener's response should be considered a component of the listening process?

tening responses can best be understood in relation to your habitual responses and your personal style.

Developing Your Listening Response

We all develop habitual patterns of response to common situations. Instead of ana-lyzing each occasion and determining the most effective course of action, you tend to rely on already established schema, communication frameworks developed early in relationships. The way your mother responds when you enter the house after a long absence is predictable. In fact, she may say or do exactly the same things she did when you were in high school. The way your sister behaves when you've been too long in the bathroom, or the way your friends react when you come by to pick them up, all are likely to be examples of behaviors you have learned to expect.

These habitual responses may, in fact, serve you well most of the time since they make conversations and verbal exchanges effortless. Problems arise when you are confronted with a new or particularly difficult situation, or when you are dissat-isfied with the way a relationship is progressing. It is in these instances that you re-alize most vividly how little listening was taking place and how important it is for you to expand your comfort with alternative response styles. Remember that the outcome of any encounter is largely dependent on *your* listening behavior.

A significant obstacle to change is the lack of comfort people experience when experimenting with new and unfamiliar responses. If you have always smoothed over conflicts and avoided confrontation, you might find it uncomfortable to begin challenging others' opinions. If you are accustomed to speaking your mind, you may find it difficult to remain silent. Expanding your comfort zone, however, is critical if you are to become a more effective listener and improve the quality of your relationships.

The greater the variety of response styles at your command, the more likely you will be to select one that communicates your understanding effectively and ac-complishes your purpose. Remember that regardless of your specific communication goal—to persuade your uncle to give you a job or to teach your friend how to play golf—there are always two functions your communication must serve. You need to accomplish your task and at the same time maintain or develop your relationship. Each communication encounter moves you in one direction or the other along these two dimensions. If you respond appropriately—which is only possible if you have listened carefully—your chances of accomplishing both goals will increase.

Your Listening Response and Your Personal Style

We have emphasized repeatedly that personal style has a strong influence on listen-ing behavior. Recall that high self-monitors, for instance, more readily adapt their communication behaviors in light of their perceptions of their partner's response. Imagine that your recent participation in a computer dating service was successful, and you find yourself sitting across from a really cool date who says casually, "*Beginnings* was a great movie. I just loved the way Parker played the part of the clown." You could envision a response of general agreement from the high self-monitors in the group.

As a low self-monitor, however, you would be more likely to speak your mind, particularly if you were asked directly what you thought. Instead of going along and saying, "Yes, I really enjoyed it," you would be more likely to reflect, "It really didn't do much for me. I thought Parker should have been much more subtle in his interpretation." Look back at "The Interview" and determine whether Martina is a high or low self-monitor as she interacts in her stressful interview situation.

Although you can change and develop new responses, there will always be some ways of responding that are easier or more comfortable, that require less energy. Ms. Rogers, for example, was deliberately creating a stressful situation for Martina. Her behaviors in the early part of the interview were quite different from what her normal responses would have been. Yet, apparently, her performance was convincing. How can you explain her ability to communicate so convincingly in a range outside of her personal style?

How are judgments of personality made? If you change your response to what you hear, might it be perceived by others as a change in *personality*?

Suggesting that you learn new ways of responding does not imply that you should, or even could, change your personality. If you listen carefully and analyze the listening situation, however, you are certain to conclude that each encounter requires a slightly different response. Since your listening effectiveness will be judged by others on the basis of this response, it is only reasonable to suggest that increasing your behavioral flexibility will have a positive effect on your communication outcomes.

THE TRANSACTIONAL ANALYSIS FRAMEWORK

Transactional analysis is a framework for analyzing your listening response. It explains and directs your behavior by examining the development and functioning of three *ego states,* or behavioral modes: Child, Parent, and Adult. Ego states are manifested through both your verbal and nonverbal behaviors (Box 8.1).

Recognizing and identifying behavior in terms of ego states helps you choose the most appropriate listening response for each situation. Analyzing interactions in transactional analysis (TA) terms not only provides a powerful means of influencing communication outcomes, but each ego state also has implications for the nature and quality of your listening.

Child Ego State

Regardless of where in the world they are born, infants display one ego state, the Child. This mode is characterized by spontaneity and the expression of emotions.

■ ■ ■ ■ ■ ▬▬▬▬▬▬▬▬▬▬▬▬▬▬▬▬▬▬▬▬▬▬▬▬▬▬▬▬▬

BOX 8.1

NONVERBAL CHARACTERISTICS OF EACH EGO STATE

Parent
Hugging
Pointing a finger
Hands on hips
Crossed arms
Tense lips and facial muscles

Adult
Confident, good posture
Comfortable, calm

Appropriate eye contact
Forward lean
Head nods

Child
Kicking or hitting
Jumping up and down
Slamming things around
Pouting
Smiling spontaneously

The Child feels angry and screams, throws things, jumps up and down, laughs hysterically. A little person smiles, hugs, says "Oh, boy!" and pouts. Whatever the emotion, it is expressed both verbally and nonverbally in a manner that can be observed and identified.

In this ego state, you also demonstrate such tendencies as self-centeredness and creativity. One part of the Child is called the Little Professor because in this state you are free to be spontaneous and use your imagination for creative, uninhibited exploration and discovery. Child behaviors are not constrained by social convention or norms; the Child is your free spirit.

When you feel yourself respond emotionally, you can be sure you are in your Child ego state. Defensiveness, anger, jealousy—all are Child responses. Because of this emotional involvement and egocentricity, you seldom listen effectively when you are in your Child ego state. As you become more emotionally involved, you are likely to take things personally, interrupt, and distort much of what you hear.

Parent Ego State

Even before a little person begins to walk and talk, she becomes aware of the rules that govern her behavior. Mother says "No!" whenever she touches the television; she learns that food should not be thrown on the floor or eaten with fingers. As the young person internalizes these rules and values, she develops a Parent ego state. Analogous to a self-monitoring system, she begins to impose internal constraints on her behavior, which are highly culture specific.

There are two different forms of Parent behavior. One is the Nurturing Parent, the other the Critical Parent. The Nurturing Parent, as you might suspect, is supportive, sympathetic, and helpful. Children can be seen modeling this behavior in their play as they pretend to be doctors, nurses, parents, and other care-givers. This sympathetic response is not to be confused with empathy.

The Critical Parent, on the other hand, sets up guidelines about what is proper, what you "should" or "shouldn't" do, what is "good" and "bad." In fact, the rules authority figures establish for the young person, and which are subsequently internalized in the Parent ego state, are almost never completely forgotten. Called Parent Tapes, they remain active long after the message was received, and serve as the foundation on which future decisions are based.

The Parent ego state inhibits effective listening by filtering ideas and information through a set of rigid guidelines. Individuals with a strong Parent ego state are likely to adhere strictly to values and rules acquired in childhood, even after circumstances change and they no longer are appropriate (Box 8.2). When in the Parent ego state, it is almost impossible to reason with a person because he is not basing decisions on the information at hand, but rather on the Tapes already in his memory. Following your Parent Tapes without reevaluating their relevance or accounting for new information can lead to unproductive habits and resistance to change, as the story below illustrates.

A newly married woman was preparing the first big meal for her husband when he happened to pass through the kitchen. Noticing that she had sliced both ends off the roast, he questioned the reason for this unusual procedure. The woman shrugged and responded, "I don't know—I guess because my mother always did it that way."

Fortunately, the mother lived next door. That afternoon her daughter asked, "Mom, why do you always cut the ends off a roast before putting it into the oven?" "Well," replied her mom, "I never gave it much thought. That's the way my mother used to cook them. Let's see if she has the answer."

The two women then went across the street to the grandmother and posed the same question. "Grandma," the woman asked, "Mom tells me you always cut both ends off a roast before putting it in the oven. Why?"

"Well," replied the grandmother, "I had to. The butcher always had eleven-pound roasts that were just a bit too big for my pan, so I always cut off the ends to make the meat fit."

Think about your own Parent Tapes—your old habits and ideas about the "right way" to behave. You may be surprised at the number of things you do just because it's what you've always done. You may also be surprised to find how difficult it is to accept change and consider new ideas when in your Parent ego state. Critical listeners,

■ ■ ■ ■ ■ ▬▬▬▬▬▬▬▬▬▬▬▬▬▬▬▬▬▬▬▬▬▬

BOX 8.2

If you always do what you always did, you always get what you always got.

in particular, need to watch for signs of their Parent: indicators include stereotyping, attitudes of certainty, and premature judgments.

The Parent ego state may interfere with cross-cultural communication and work against open-mindedness and flexibility. Parent norms vary from one culture to the next. Imagine visitors from Asia, or from an Arab country, at their first fraternity party and consider how their behavior might differ from yours.

> Why do you think the elderly have a particularly difficult time moving out of the Parent ego state?

Adult Ego State

When internal conflicts arise between the Child (what you want to do) and Parent (what you think you should do) ego states, it may be useful to put yourself into the Adult position. Consider Stacy's behavior in the following example.

Stacy is at a lecture on auto mechanics. She doesn't drive and sees no point in the material. Long before the lecture is over, she begins doodling and talking periodically to her friends in the next row. When the lecture ends, she realizes that she heard almost nothing of what the speaker had to say. Since she's worked hard to put herself through school, she feels guilty for wasting a class period even though she questioned the value of the information.

Your best decisions in such instances aren't made on the basis of impulse (Child) or habit (Parent), but rather on critical thinking. You may decide you can afford to be inattentive, or you may summon your will power and practice the vocalized listening technique. The point is that *you* decide and *you* take responsibility for the decision.

The Adult ego state, then, is characterized by mental objectivity and rationality. It is reality oriented, calm, and most appropriate for problem solving. The Adult ego state also helps you align your response with your ethical framework by guiding you to a thoughtful and reasoned response to moral dilemmas. When in your Adult ego state, you look at the facts at hand and assess your position in light of current circumstances and goals. Each ego state has implications for the effectiveness of your listening behavior (Box 8.3). *The Adult ego state is the most effective mode for almost all professional or formal*

> Under what circumstances would the Adult ego state be an *inappropriate* response?

listening situations. In fact, as soon as you feel yourself moving into the Child or Parent ego states, you know that empathic, rational, objective listening has decreased.

True empathic listening only takes place in the Adult ego state. When in this mode, you are caring and concerned, patient and interested, but not overly emotional. Your focus is on your partner, not your own agendas (Child behavior); you don't impose your values on the other person (Parent behavior). Objective does not imply uncaring or cold; it describes a state where you are able to put things into perspective and listen nonjudgmentally.

■ ■ ■ ■ ■ ▬▬▬▬▬▬▬▬▬▬▬▬

BOX 8.3

EGO STATES AND LISTENING

	Ego States	*Typical Response Style*	*Typical Listening Behaviors*
PARENT	Critical Nurturing	Advice Evaluative Sympathetic Opinions	Selective in choosing information Influenced by personal bias Resists change and new ideas Judgmental—creates defensive climate
ADULT	Logical	Questions Paraphrase Empathy Assertive	Open-minded Thoughtful Fact centered Projects empathy Tries to create win–win situation
CHILD	Egocentric Creative	Emotional Spontaneous Manipulative	Easily defensive Emotions block listening Jumps to conclusions without support Focus on self Tendency to create win–lose situation

RESPONSE STYLES

You can use the Transactional Analysis model as a framework for determining the most appropriate listening response or for assessing the effectiveness of the behaviors you choose. Since communication is situational, your best preparation is to practice a variety of effective listening responses so that you have alternatives from which to choose when confronted with challenging listening situations.

Assertive and supportive responses may appear at first to be quite different; both, however, are Adult ego state behaviors. Can you see why this is the case? They are each reviewed here in turn, both because they are effective listening responses and because they seldom occur automatically—each behavior must be learned and practiced.

What would happen if everyone you know suddenly developed strong assertive skills?

The Assertive Response

Do you have difficulty listening to negative feedback? Do you listen to a friend's request and then say "yes" when you would like to have said no? Do you ask for clarification when you're not sure you've understood what you've heard? Each of these situations requires an assertive response characteristic of the Adult ego state.

Assertive skills are learned; they seldom come naturally. Keep in mind, too, that this response is not always appropriate. When you choose to be assertive, you

1. demonstrate that you have listened to and considered the other person's viewpoint;
2. have the satisfaction of knowing that you expressed yourself clearly and honestly;
3. allow the other person to maintain his self-respect.

A definition of assertive communication is presented, and then several specific assertive responses are examined.

Definition of Assertiveness. The assertive response is best understood in contrast to aggressive and nonassertive behaviors. Remember that aggression, like any other emotion, comes from the Child ego state. As soon as you feel yourself becoming angry, be on guard for cues that indicate aggressiveness. Tone of voice, facial expressions, and body posture are among the most obvious indicators of Child behavior. It is common for aggressive individuals to believe they are being assertive because they are speaking up. There is, however, a significant difference. When you are aggressive, you can be sure that you are *not listening effectively.*

Recall the last time you complained to a friend about a person or situation. This behavior is nonassertive. Rather than confronting the problem directly, a person who complains is choosing a less threatening and indirect course of action. Nonassertion is seldom productive, since the person who is able to do something to solve the problem is never approached. Complaining to a friend about a grade on your exam, for instance, does little to remedy the situation. Although others may provide support and advice, they cannot make your decisions or solve your problems.

Avoidance is also characteristic of the nonassertive response. If, for example, you don't like the way you are treated by the customer service people at a particular store, taking your business elsewhere is not assertive. The assertive individual would first confront the customer service person with the facts of the situation and her feelings about the way she was treated, and then pursue further action if necessary, perhaps by speaking with the manager. Although there is no guarantee that the problem will be remedied, she took constructive action.

The assertive person, then, is straightforward, honest, and objective. He or she manifests characteristics of the Adult ego state. Ideas, opinions, and feelings are expressed clearly and directly. In fact, the *way* you communicate your ideas is often as important as *what* you say (Box 8.4).

Most important of all, the assertive communicator *listens.* The actions he or she takes are timely and directed to the appropriate source. The assertive person focuses on solving the problem, not "winning" the conflict at the expense of his

▪ ▪ ▪ ▪ ▪

BOX 8.4

NONVERBAL COMPONENTS OF ASSERTIVE BEHAVIOR

1. Eye Contact	Look directly at the other person to communicate sincerity.
2. Body Posture	Face the person and lean toward them. Be as direct as possible.
3. Gestures	Accent ideas with gestures for added emphasis.
4. Facial expression	Effective assertions require expressions consistent with the message.
5. Voice	Strive to be convincing but not intimidating.
6. Timing	Be spontaneous when possible; hesitation may diminish the effect of an assertion—or you may change your mind!

partner. As one employee explains, "I know my manager listens because she pays attention to what I have to say, tells me exactly what she's going to do, and then she does it."

Whenever you assert yourself you are taking a risk, and you must be willing to accept the possible consequences of your behavior. If, after two days, you get up the courage to tell your instructor you don't think the grade on your paper was fair, you have to be prepared for disagreement and the possibility that nothing will be changed. Then what have you gained? Your self-respect, for one thing. You know that you spoke up about something you felt was unfair and that you took action and behaved in a professional, self-confident manner.

Types of Assertive Response.   There are numerous occasions where assertive skills are appropriate, and each situation requires a slightly different approach. You may discover that while you are confident and assertive with some people, other individuals make you anxious. While you may find you handle some assertive situations easily, others may be stressful or troublesome. Box 8.5 lists some of the skills that may be required in the situations you encounter. Note which ones you would like to develop.

What are the personal risks associated with becoming more assertive?

Your verbal assertive response may be situation-specific, or it may conform closely to one of several assertive techniques. Since these techniques may prove useful as you begin to practice your Adult ego state behaviors, five of them are described next.

1. Broken record.   Your supervisor wants you to stay after work and finish up a report that's due the next day. He doesn't mind getting home late because on Wednesdays his wife has an aerobics class and dinner is delayed anyway.

BOX 8.5

ASSERTIVE SKILLS

- Saying no when you want to
- Receiving criticism
- Giving criticism
- Expressing feelings
- Terminating conversations
- Not allowing others to give you their problems

- Expressing ideas concisely
- Giving others compliments
- Standing up for unpopular opinions
- Stating personal needs
- Initiating conversations
- Demonstrating appropriate nonverbal behaviors

Boss: Hey, how about staying after work for a few minutes and getting this report out of the way? I've got a few things I'd like to talk to you about before Marge does the final copy tomorrow.

You: I'd like to help you out, but I can't stay late tonight. Promised my friend I'd be home before 6:00 o'clock.

Boss: So give her a call, tell her you'll be a little late—all for a good cause!

You: Well, we've made some plans with Fred and Jane tonight and I don't want to cancel. The weather's terrific, and we've been planning a picnic for months.

Boss: Look, have your wife show up and tell them you'll meet them there a little later. How about it? Takes an hour or so to get the food ready anyway. If you're just going over to the State Park, I can drop you off on my way home.

Trapped. Your excuses have allowed your supervisor to back you into a corner as he finds solutions to each objection. No matter how well you present your case, as long as you keep offering details your boss has the upper hand. Broken record, a basic assertive technique in which you repeat your initial response, prevents this kind of exchange by limiting the information provided. Notice the difference this technique makes in the same situation.

Boss: Hey, how about staying after work for a few minutes and getting this report out of the way? I've got a few things I'd like to talk to you about before Marge does the final copy tomorrow.

You: I'd like to help you out, but I can't stay late tonight.

Boss: So what's up?

You: I realize this is a good night for you to work late, but it's not for me. I'd like to help you out, but I can't stay late tonight.

Boss: Well, how are we going to get this thing done?

You: How about coming in earlier tomorrow morning? I could meet you for coffee at Dino's and we could talk over the details then.

Notice here the focus of the encounter is on the topic at hand—on solving the problem rather than on avoiding a confrontation. The boss was not given ammunition to force his subordinate into doing something he obviously did not want to do. Yet, the subordinate still listened—*he showed his concern with his employer's need to get the job done*—and the problem appeared to be resolved to the satisfaction of both parties. The decision whether to use Broken Record is yours, and should be made after listening carefully to the people involved and analyzing your objectives.

2. Negative inquiry. Your professor says she doesn't like your work. She has told you that it was submitted late, that it doesn't conform to the specifications she required, and that it's difficult to read. You disagree. As she speaks, you can feel yourself becoming increasingly angry and defensive. You know your Child has been hooked; you feel threatened, and you stop listening. You need to maintain a working relationship with your professor; in fact, you like the class.

You have several choices. First, you can be nonassertive, swearing under your breath. You might even act indifferent or disinterested in order to avoid a confrontation. Only when you get home—or meet a friend a little later that day—do you complain and vent your frustration. On the other hand, you may become aggressive when criticized. You could immediately defend your actions, raise your voice, and throw your paper on the desk. In either case, you gain nothing from such behaviors.

Negative inquiry may be a wise choice in this type of situation but, to be effective, you need to listen carefully. Negative inquiry requires practice and self-control. Here are the basic steps.

a. Make sure you are in your Adult ego state. Your Child would, most likely, derive great pleasure from name-calling, shouting, or arguing, behaviors that would cause your professor to become defensive.

b. Acknowledge the fact that you understand how your professor could see things the way he or she does. You do not indicate that you agree—you simply acknowledge your understanding of his opinions.

c. Instead of refuting or disagreeing, draw him out. Request more information. Politely ask for clarification and examples. Make sure you understand exactly what he believes to be the problem and how your performance differs from his expectations. Do not apologize or defend your behavior; simply listen.

d. Wait to present your point of view. Schedule a specific appointment, and be ready with examples and details to demonstrate your case—whether you still disagree with your professor's position or whether you have come with an action plan for change. This interval will allow you both time to gain perspective.

3. Fogging.   Fogging is also appropriate when you are listening to criticism. Since this is one of the most difficult situations to handle effectively, it is wise to practice skills that defuse anger or hurt feelings. Fogging requires that you listen to the person's opinions or judgments without reacting defensively. It is used in situations when you realize immediately that what the other person is telling you is true. Simply agree with your partner's criticism, letting her know that the message has been understood. Then, work toward problemsolving. Here is an example of fogging.

On Wednesday morning you're at your apartment working on a term paper that has been on your mind for several weeks. Paula knocks on your door, and when you see her you suddenly remember that you had promised to have some visuals ready for her presentation later that morning.

Paula: Won't keep you. Just dropped by to pick up those visuals you prepared for my talk this morning.

You: Paula, I'm afraid I just plain forgot all about it! They're not ready. In fact, I haven't even started them.

Paula: I can't believe you could forget! We talked about it several times. These figures are essential support for my final project. I should have known . . .

You: You're right. I let you down. You gave me plenty of time and reminded me about them just last week. (*Negative assertion*)

Let's see, though. I still may be able to help you out. How much time do we have before class? (*Problem solving*)

> The various types of assertive responses are quite different. Which fall outside your current comfort zone?

Whenever you listen openly to a person's criticism, conflicts can be managed by admitting the negative aspect of your behavior, reducing the other person's anger, and allowing problem solving to begin.

4. Workable compromise.   When there is disagreement, it may be possible to negotiate a compromise. Having expressed your ideas and feelings, you may decide to work toward a resolution that maintains the essential elements of each position. In such cases, effective listening contributes to your accurate understanding of the other person's point of view and increases the probability that the conflict will be managed fairly and successfully.

5. Express feelings verbally.   Emotions are communicated largely through nonverbal behavior. You know from your earlier reading on voice that the *way* you speak conveys as strong a message as your words. Gestures, facial expressions, and posture, however, are *indirect* cues and easily misinterpreted. Statements such as

"It's about time," "Please, won't you let me stay?" or "I've had enough of your wise remarks!" all potentially convey feelings, but in a way that makes identifying them something of a guessing game. In addition, when these remarks come from the Child ego state, they are likely to create defensiveness, anger, and damaged relationships as well.

Assertive communicators name their feelings clearly and make the feeling part of the *content* of their messages. This allows for more straightforward, constructive, and clear communication. Let's use the examples in the preceding paragraph. A description of feelings is provided for each of the three responses.

a. "It's about time." *The person means*: I feel very frustrated that you made me wait.

b. "Please, won't you let me stay?" *The person means*: I'm afraid to be alone. Can I stay with you for a while?

c. "I've had enough of your wise remarks!" *The person means*: I feel hurt and upset by what you said to me.

Descriptions of feelings almost always include the pronoun *I*. Don't confuse this, however, with judgments that also begin with a personal pronoun. "I feel inadequate" is a description and expresses something very different from "I am inadequate," which is a judgment. Feelings are most clearly expressed by "owning" them.

How might cultural orientation affect the listener's comfort with expressing feelings verbally?

Describing your feelings may be difficult. You must first be convinced that your response is appropriate, and then practice as much as possible (Box 8.6). Begin by sharing your feelings with people you know well and who are likely to respond in positive and supportive ways.

BOX 8.6

STEPS TO MORE ASSERTIVE BEHAVIOR

Step 1: Identify your current behavior; what is your typical listening response?

Step 2: Select one type of situation to work on, or one person with whom you would like to communicate more effectively.

Step 3: Use positive self-talk; see yourself handling the situation assertively.

Step 4: Just do it! When you have the opportunity, use an assertive response.

Step 5: Get feedback if you can on the effectiveness of your efforts.

Step 6: Reflect on your behavior. How can you improve?

Supportive Responses

Listening stops when you feel threatened. No one likes to be proven wrong in front of others, criticized, or ignored. Defensive individuals are generally in their Child ego state; they are more concerned with protecting their self-concept and saving face than with promoting relational communication (Egan, 1977). The more defensive a person becomes, the less able he is to perceive his partner's motives, values, and emotions accurately. Box 8.7 describes some of the most common defensive reactions that you readily can learn to identify—and reduce.

Your goal is to create and maintain environments which contribute to open, nonevaluative interaction. Gibb (1977) has called this type of atmosphere a supportive communication climate. Although it is not always easy, a listener who practices supportive behavior will undoubtedly minimize defensiveness and encourage objective analysis, problem solving, and healthy relationships. Gibb provides the following guidelines for open interactions.

"I" Language versus "You" Language.   When you're judgmental, your partner's first response is to become defensive. To avoid evaluative language, become aware of the *way* in which you present ideas.

BOX 8.7

COMMON DEFENSIVE "NOT LISTENING" RESPONSES

Rationalization
Do you ever create untrue but logical explanations for your unacceptable behavior? When you're late for work, was it because you spent too much time drinking coffee with a friend or because the bus was late? It's easy to save face by presenting a slightly distorted version of the truth.

Projection
In this case, blame is put on a specific person or an "active force." The assistant who makes a mistake because of new glasses or an old typewriter has found an effective way to avoid admitting to poor typing skills.

Displacement
Nonassertive individuals are likely to go home and yell at the dog, the kids, the letter carrier, in order to vent hostile feelings held toward a much more threatening source. When you're angry at your supervisor, think about who is on the receiving end of your wrath.

Verbal Aggression
When we can get away with it, the easiest (and momentarily the most satisfying) way to deal with a troublesome situation is to yell and scream about it.

Apathy
Hurt feelings can be avoided by pretending indifference. When your friend was passed over for a promotion or not invited to a housewarming party, how did she behave? "It doesn't matter" helps smooth the situation and save the individual's self-image.

DEFENSIVE: You're never around when I need you. You really let me down yesterday when I wanted some help studying. It's a good thing Ted was there .

SUPPORTIVE: I feel frustrated because yesterday, when I needed your help, I couldn't find you. I had a big exam in political science and I was under a lot of pressure. I called in Ted to help . . . .

Problem Solving versus Placing Blame.   What reaction do you have to someone who always sounds as if she knows what's best for you? Most likely, you become angry and annoyed. People object to being controlled or to having their decisions made for them. Much more support can be obtained if problems are approached from a problem-solving orientation, where everyone involved is asked for his or her input.

Is it possible, or desirable, to completely eliminate defensiveness?

DEFENSIVE: Everyone around here is slowing down. Don't you care whether we get this project finished on time? There have to be some changes around here soon. I'll let you know next week what they will be.

SUPPORTIVE: I don't feel we're as productive as we could be. What do you think? Let's have a brainstorming session tomorrow and see if we can't find some better ways of doing things.

Empathy versus Indifference.   The empathic listener, as you know, encourages honest, two-way interaction by asking for clarification, reflecting the speaker's feelings, and demonstrating supportive, open, nonverbal behavior. This is in contrast to indifference or apathy, an attitude of "I don't care" or "it's not my problem," which encourages defensiveness.

The paraphrase is an appropriate response style in communicating empathy because it does not "lead" the speaker in any particular direction; rather, it allows your partner to take responsibility for her own problems and decisions. When someone is under stress, uncertain, or emotionally involved, the paraphrase can be an effective listening tool.

You can paraphrase both the content of the message or your partner's feelings about what he or she has said. In either case, it is important to reflect content and feelings in your own words so your partner can determine the degree of your understanding. This response also helps your partner to clarify his or her self-understanding. An effective paraphrase is simple, clear, and in the Adult ego state (Johnson, 1982). While the paraphrase is used primarily in empathic listening situations, you may recall that a closely related response, the perception-check, ensures the accuracy of your listening comprehension. An example of the use of paraphrase illustrates how it reflects empathy.

Under what circumstances would indifference be a more effective response than empathy?

STUDENT:	My car broke down on the highway.
INDIFFERENT:	Well, now that you're finally here we can get started.
STUDENT:	My car broke down on the highway.
SUPPORTIVE:	It must have been frustrating to have your car break down like that; I hope you were able to take care of the problem. I'm glad you're here so now we can get started.

Provisionalism versus Certainty.   Good listeners are open to new information and viewpoints. They present their ideas assertively, but they realize that no one can know all there is to know. As you learned in Chapter 7, things change. With the introduction of new information, you expect to modify your position. Therefore, it's appropriate to qualify your statements with such phrases as "it seems to me" or "as far as I know." When you see your way of doing things as the only "right way," barriers to communication and a defensive climate result.

DEFENSIVE:	Hey, what are you trying to do? You don't download those programs like that. Where have you been?
SUPPORTIVE:	Loading that software is a tricky job. I've tried a lot of ways to get it on the server, and I'd like to share one with you that seems to work well. You might want to give it a try. . . .

These distinctions make a significant difference in the way your relationships develop and in your partner's perceptions of your listening effectiveness. Equally important to facilitating effective relational communication are the often taken-for-granted nonverbal aspects of the listening situation.

NONVERBAL DIMENSIONS: CREATING LISTENING ENVIRONMENTS

You have already read about the importance of interpreting nonverbal cues as you listen supportively, and of demonstrating appropriate nonverbal behavior in communicating empathy to your partner. In addition to your nonverbal response, there are other dimensions of nonverbal communication over which you have control and that significantly affect the quality of your interactions. Through the choices you make about aspects of the physical setting, distance, and the use of time, you can create a supportive listening environment.

> To what extent is it appropriate to control or manage the environment to accomplish your purpose?

Communication Settings

The environment in which communication occurs has a major impact on how you attend to, understand, remember, interpret, and evaluate what you hear. In addition to the skills each communicator brings to the situation, the degree to which effective listening is possible depends upon a number of environmental variables.

Listening situations vary in (1) the degree to which they stimulate participants, (2) the degree to which participants feel comfortable, and (3) the degree to which you feel dominant or in control (Sommer, 1969; Mehrabian, 1976; Rosenfeld & Civikly, 1976). The difference between a discussion in the student cafeteria and one in an instructor's office can be dramatic. Similarly, a poolside meeting is qualitatively different than one carried out in a formal conference room.

One researcher (Knapp, 1978) distinguishes six significant characteristics of listening environments: formality, warmth, privacy, familiarity, constraint, and distance. These may be present in any combination to produce dramatically different results. You may want an environment of warmth and privacy for one type of interaction, but find a formal setting more appropriate for another.

> Are there gender or cultural differences that might explain an individual's sensitivity to environmental variables?

The type and style of furniture, the seating arrangement, the colors, music, and the time of day together create a unique atmosphere that can either encourage or discourage interactions (Ketcham, 1958). An oversized chair, a forbidding desk, and wicker furniture all communicate different messages. Think back to Martina's perceptions of her interview environment and the impact her surroundings had on her listening. There's a story about a woman entertaining her date that also illustrates how the environment can become a significant aspect of communication. After repeated attempts to demonstrate her disinterest, she finally resorts to putting on some "not-in-the-mood" music to get her message across.

In another case, Knute Rockne is said to have kept his players stimulated throughout their halftime break with a red-walled dressing room, while he sought to lull visiting teams with restful blue in their quarters. Color has been similarly used by doctors to relax patients and by restaurants to stimulate the appetite. Red is hot, exciting, passionate, dangerous. Blue is lonely, cool, passive. White connotes delicacy, purity, and simplicity; purple is perceived as symbolizing courage and virility (Box 8.8). Whether you agree with these descriptions or not, it's clear that color does have the potential to influence participants' behavior.

Space and Communication

Small group ecology, or the spatial arrangements individuals make when they are in small group settings, also influences your listening. Once again, there are many variables involved: your personality, your relationships with the other people, the topic of discussion or task, and the available space. Your position relative to others in your group can have a major impact on your listening as well as on your participation.

Positioning affects communication flow, perceptions of status, and degree of formality. At conference tables, the person with greatest authority generally sits at the head of the table. If this individual is also sitting in a larger, padded chair, relin-

---

BOX 8.8

DO YOU AGREE WITH THIS CHART?

Mood	*Color*
Stimulating	Red
Comfortable	Blue
Upsetting	Orange
Melancholy	Brown
Calm	Green and blue
Dignified	Purple
Cheerful	Yellow

---

quishing the position may mean giving up some control as well. Recall the change Martina experienced when she moved from the chair across from Toni's large desk to a seat around a conference table.

The distance between communicators also affects your listening (Box 8.9). Hall's (1959) pioneering work on cross-cultural differences in the use of space is not only fascinating, but offers important insights to improve your listening effectiveness. Hall identifies four distance categories that have implications for how participants interact.

1. *Intimate distance:* At intimate distances—from physical contact to about 18 inches—you are so close that communication behaviors need to be modified.

BOX 8.9

EXAMPLES OF DISTANCE CATEGORIES

Intimate Distance
looking at a paper with a classmate
reading a memo over someone's shoulder
standing in line
sharing a message in confidence (standing)

Social Distance
the employment interview
discussion across a conference table or desk
meeting with your instructor

Personal Distance
the coaching interview
talking with a friend before going into class

Public Distance
shouting across a parking lot
making a presentation

You are conscious of odors, and touching is almost unavoidable. A large percentage of your communication is likely to be nonverbal. Unless you know your partner well, intimate distance may create anxiety which reduces listening effectiveness.

2.   *Personal distance:*   Most conversations take place at the edges of your personal bubble, or what Hall terms personal distance. Here, rapport can be established and personal information disclosed. A variety of nonverbal and vocal cues are readily accessible. Personal bubbles, or the distance at which you feel comfortable communicating, vary. Culture, in particular, has a major impact on perceptions of space. Although people in the United States generally feel invaded if their partners stand closer than eighteen inches, the distance at which individuals from other cultures begin to feel threatened may be as close as 12 inches or as much as 2 feet. These differences have obvious implications for your listening behavior.

3.   *Social distance:*   Social distances are appropriate for less personal, more formal conversations. At four to twelve feet, it may be difficult for you to feel comfortable sharing personal information. Although you still have easy access to all of a speaker's nonverbal cues, there is likely to be much less emotional content and more information in the messages. Small groups of eight or fewer participants generally communicate at social distances. If you want to encourage more personal disclosure, your partner will have to move closer to you.

4.   *Public distance:*   Not only do the topics of conversation tend to be more general at public distances, but the listening situation itself becomes more complex. To get a message across to a number of listeners simultaneously, communicators must use broader gestures, speak more loudly, and work harder to maintain a direct rapport with the group. Message design is also more complicated, since listeners are likely to have different backgrounds and different levels of understanding. At public distances—12 feet or more—you have to work a lot harder to interpret meanings.

Most relational encounters take place at personal distances, so we are particularly interested in how this dimension affects your listening. You may have had the experience, for instance, of backing away from your communication partner because of a perceived discomfort. In some cases, you may not even have been conscious of the fact that your partner invaded your personal space. When communicators begin to feel anxious, they may back up, shift their weight, turn their shoulder toward you, look away, cross their arms—anything to maintain more physical and psychological distance.

There are a variety of other reasons why communicators either move toward or away from their partners. Researchers have found that participants stand closer together if they are communicating good news, if they feel positively about each other, and if

> If someone knew you only as a public speaker, what impression would they have of you? What aspects of your personality would they be missing?

they perceive the other person as friendly. Yet, moving too close to your partner may be perceived as threatening or uncomfortable, therefore interfering with effective listening.

The distance at which you listen is often a product of negotiations with your partner. Although culture is a significant factor, distance is also affected by age, gender, subject matter, the physical characteristics of the communicators, individual personality traits and attitudes, and the emotional relationship between the individuals (Burgoon & Jones, 1976). See if the following patterns hold true from your observations:

- Pairs of women stand closer when speaking than male-female pairs.
- Male-female pairs stand closer to the very old or the very young.
- Individuals stand closer to the very old or the very young.
- Listeners stand closer to those perceived as pleasant and friendly.
- Speakers seeking approval tend to stand closer to the listener.
- Individuals with high self-confidence stand closer.
- Those with high affiliative needs stand closer than introverts.
- The setting affects the distance at which individuals stand.

In addition to distance, time also influences your listening environment.

Time as a Communication Variable

Consider how Martina felt when she was left to wait in Ms. Roger's office for so long before the interview. Was this use of time intentional? What was communicated? We talk about saving time, spending time, wasting time, making time, and taking time. Increasing your consciousness of how time affects communication can help you become a better listener.

Time of day affects your ability to listen. Everyone has personal ups and downs that occur on a fairly regular basis. These high and low points influence both your ability to listen and the quality of your response. In addition, if you know the participants involved, you can make some safe assumptions about how time of day affects moods and perceptions. The atmosphere of a group meeting held at 8:00 a.m. may be very different from one held at 5:00 p.m., or 9:30 p.m.

> How often do you "make time" to listen? What does "making time" mean to you?

The amount of time spent on a given task is often a clue to its importance. If you schedule a 20-minute interview with one person and a 2-hour session with another, it may be an indirect indicator of the relative importance you assign to each. Lead time may also influence how actions are perceived. If advance preparation is required for a particular occasion, chances are communicators will view it as more important and listening may be improved. Making an appointment to see someone encourages better listening than dropping by unexpectedly.

Appropriate timing of communication, too, is essential. You know that if your mind is elsewhere, you're not going to be receptive to what you hear, regardless of how well your partner presents her ideas. If you are rushed, upset, or preoccupied, listening effectiveness is reduced—and misunderstandings are likely to result. If you sense that it's a bad time for communication, reschedule or check back when things have calmed down.

It is clear that your listening, in addition to being influenced by elements of the situation and your overall purpose, is affected by a range of both verbal and non-verbal dimensions. Understanding these dimensions will enable you to make informed choices regarding your listening response and the environment in which it occurs.

SUMMARY

Your partner makes judgments regarding the quality of your listening based largely on the nature of your response. As you recall from earlier chapters, both the listening context (intrapersonal, interpersonal, small group, public, and mediated) and your listening purpose (discriminative, comprehensive, critical, therapeutic, appreciative) help you better to define the range of response possibilities and the relative emphasis that appropriately is placed on each component of the HURIER model.

Understanding response styles and learning how nonverbal elements contribute to creating supportive environments are essential to making wise response choices and identifying behaviors that will contribute to effective communication. As always, understanding yourself and acknowledging your own comfort level with various behaviors is the first step.

Transactional Analysis provides a useful framework for identifying your behavior and making appropriate adjustments based on the situation. Most common responses can be placed into one of three ego state categories; Parent, Adult, or Child. Although each ego state has advantages, the most effective listening takes place in the Adult mode.

Two Adult ego state responses are particularly useful to effective listeners, the assertive, and the supportive responses. There are a wide range of situations in which assertive behavior is appropriate, and learning specific assertive behaviors provides a starting point in encouraging honest and direct interactions.

As you know, listening is also facilitated by supportive communication. Using *I*-language, adopting a problem-solving approach, demonstrating empathy, and expressing opinions provisionally, all contribute to open, two-way exchanges.

The nonverbal dimension is also important to consider when your goal is to create a supportive listening environment. Color, spatial relations, distance, furniture, and time all influence relational communication. Understanding the effect these nonverbal dimensions have on both you and your partner will enable you to become more effective in achieving mutually satisfying relationships and shared meanings.

APPLICATIONS

Application 1: Expand Your Comfort Zone
Application 2: Identify the Transactional Analysis Ego States
Application 3: Develop Your Assertive Skills
Application 4: Practice Supportive Responses
Application 5: Create Supportive Listening Environments

_____ I adapt my response according to the needs of the particular situation.
Application 1: Expand Your Comfort Zone

_____ I do not let my emotions interfere with my listening or decision making.
Application 2: Identify the Transactional Analysis Ego States

_____ I provide clear and direct feedback to others.
Application 3: Develop Your Assertive Skills

_____ I encourage information-sharing by creating a climate of trust and support.
Application 4: Practice Supportive Responses

_____ I recognize and take into account personal and cultural differences in the use of time and space that may influence listening effectiveness.
_____ I make sure that the physical environment encourages effective listening.
Application 5: Create Supportive Listening Environments

Application 1: Expand Your Comfort Zone

You may be surprised by how much you rely on one or two types of response in your daily encounters. The greater your awareness of response styles, the better able you will be to analyze interactions and make informed decisions about how to facilitate shared meanings and healthy relationships.

The following exercises encourage you to think more specifically about your habitual behaviors and to experiment with a variety of response styles.

Activities

1. Use a journal to keep track of your response styles for at least a week. Analyze your behavior in Transactional Analysis terms.

   a. In what situations do you feel uncomfortable with your response?
   b. In what situations, and with whom, do you tend to use unproductive responses— blaming, advice, ignoring, clichés?
   c. Do you currently use paraphrase? Are there occasions when it might be helpful?
   d. What responses would you like to develop? Which do you feel you already use effectively?

2. Do your different roles—student, son or daughter, employee, and so forth—require different types of response styles? Which ones are most comfortable for you? Which ones do you need to develop?

3. Think of two relationships that you would like to improve.

    a. What behavior does your partner display in each case that elicits an ineffective or inappropriate response from you?

    b. What can you do to break this cycle?

Group Activities

Form a small group of four to six people. You may want to keep the same group for all activities, or you may find it more interesting to change groups so that you get to hear the opinions and ideas of a greater number of your classmates.

1. Any volunteer from the group makes a statement such as, "I'm going to the zoo tomorrow" or, "The movie about cats was excellent." Group members then respond in turn, with:

    a. a paraphrase,

    b. advice,

    c. a question,

    d. evaluation, or

    e. other specific responses that may occur spontaneously.

       Each participant takes a turn making statements and then identifying the various types of feedback they receive. The person making the statement also shares his reactions and feelings about the different types of response.

2. As a group, generate a list of responses that might be expected of someone in each of the following roles. Then, make a list of responses that would be unexpected and/or inappropriate.

Example: Student to instructor:	"Could you explain why I got a C on my term paper?"
Anticipated response:	"You were assigned a C because your paper was incomplete."
	"Why do you think you received a C?"
Unanticipated response:	"No. Go away."
	"You aren't very smart."

    a. Parent to child: Please pick up the clothes in your room.

    b. Child to parent: I'm really hungry.

    c. Employee to supervisor: Could you show me how to work the PCF?

    d. Supervisor to employee: You've been doing a really good job lately.

    e. Guest to hotel front desk employee: My television doesn't work.

    f. Male colleague to female colleague: That's a beautiful suit you're wearing.

Application 2: Identify the Transactional Analysis Ego States

The transactional model, although simplified for our purposes, provides a useful framework for analyzing relational communication. If your goal is effective listening, you can develop a productive action plan to improve your performance simply by recognizing how your ego state is affecting your listening. Remember that Child ego state emotions may well interfere with listening, and that when in the Parent ego state you are likely to be filtering information, thereby reducing your ability to interpret and evaluate what you hear.

Activities

1. Everyone has some conclusions that they have come to about themselves. Identify at least one statement that you began to believe at an early age concerning your capabilities, personality, or appearance.

I'm inefficient	I try hard	I can't do anything right
I'm silly	I'm athletic	
I'm generous	I'm uncoordinated	I'm as good as anybody else
I'm clumsy	I'm stupid	
I'm good-looking	No one likes me	Everything bad happens to me
I'm nice	I can't sing	

When did you first form these perceptions? What "older people" influenced you?

2. Keep track of your ego state reactions. Do you have a favorite state? Does it change depending upon the situation, your role, and the other person? When do you feel most comfortable as a listener?

3. Share some of your perceptions about your response styles and ego states with a close friend or family member. Ask if he or she agrees with your conclusions.

4. Consider your ideal relationships. What ego state would each of you display in the following situations?

    SITUATION
    a. Leading a task-oriented group
    b. Going to a movie
    c. Going to exercise class
    d. Discussing a personal problem
    e. Working on a project
    f. Eating lunch

Group Activities

Form a small group of four to six people. You may want to keep the same group for all activities, or you may find it more interesting to change groups so that you get to hear the opinions and ideas of a greater number of your classmates.

1. The more familiar you become with each ego state, the more useful this model will be in developing appropriate listening responses.

    As a group, identify the most likely ego state for each of the responses provided below.

Ego-state Quiz

A. A secretary can't find an important memo:
    a. You're always losing things! Try taping it to your nose!
    b. Don't tell me you lost another memo. Can't you keep track of anything?
    c. Let's think for a moment. When was it typed?

B.   The copy machine breaks down:
   a.   Jane, please call a repairperson and find out how soon it can be fixed.
   b.   What a stupid machine! Let's just get rid of the monster.
   c.   Some careless secretary probably misused it. No one takes care of anything around here.

C.   A supervisor is unhappy with a letter his secretary wrote:
   a.   I'd like to discuss this letter with you. Do you have a minute?
   b.   You really passed the third grade? This letter is terrible!
   c.   First of all, you should never put the date at the bottom of the page.

D.   A supervisor just received a poor evaluation:
   a.   Whoever created these evaluations clearly didn't know what he was doing.
   b.   What a jerk! Thinks he knows everything.
   c.   I'm feeling very upset. My evaluation didn't go as well as I had hoped.

E.   Some children run through the hall:
   a.   There they go! After them!
   b.   I wonder what children are doing here this time of day?
   c.   Children should not be allowed in the building.

2.   Personalize each ego state by discussing the following with members of your group:

Child

   a.   Think of something you did for fun as a child that you still do now.
   b.   Describe a recent situation in which you used Child words or behaviors. Were they appropriate?
   c.   What do you do in your Child ego state to express your creativity?
   d.   Is it easy for you to be spontaneous in most situations? Do you feel, generally, that your Child ego state is active and healthy?

Parent

   a.   Do you repeat a message to your spouse, friends, children, and others that came from one of your parents? What?
   b.   Identify a Parent Tape that you still hear and either obey, rebel against, or have a conflict about. Discuss.
   c.   Give an example of a recent situation in which you were nurturing, and one in which you were critical.
   d.   Would you say that you have a strong, moderate, or weak Parent ego state? Why?

Adult

   a.   Think of a recent situation where you collected information and, on the basis of your facts, made a decision.
   b.   Describe a recent situation in which you calmed your emotions through deliberately putting yourself into your Adult ego state.
   c.   How are most of your decisions made?

3. Form groups of three. As a group, identify a typical decision that you can all relate to where the Child ego state wants to do one thing and the Parent ego state pulls in the opposite direction. Examples might be:

Child	*Parent*
Go to a party	Stay home and clean the apartment
Stay in bed	Get up and go to class
Buy that record you've wanted	Save your money
Throw broken item away	Take item to be fixed

After you have determined the situation, assign an ego state role to each participant in your group (if there are four individuals, use two Adult roles). As a group, you represent the ego states of *one individual*. Your objective as either Child or Parent is to convince the Adult to take action on your behalf. Allow 3 minutes for the Child and the Parent to try to persuade the Adult to take their side. *Remember*: Use appropriate nonverbal as well as verbal behaviors.

After your time is up, the Adult makes a decision. (Compromises are acceptable.) Change roles, choose another situation, and role-play again. What did you notice about your listening behavior while playing the different roles?

Application 3: Develop Your Assertive Skills

It takes effort and practice to fine-tune your assertive skills. Keep in mind that becoming more assertive requires a change in attitude as much as the acquisition of new skills. Even if you demonstrate assertive behavior effectively in the classroom, this doesn't mean that you will feel comfortable asserting yourself when you participate in everyday encounters. You need to believe that assertive communication is the best choice in responding to a particular situation. Only then will you be able to assert yourself effectively.

Activities

1. You may find that you are assertive with some people and not with others. It is helpful to review these relationships. Consider how you respond to the following:

spouse/significant other	strangers
children	neighbors
co-workers	classmates
professors	salespeople

Are you too assertive in some instances? With whom? When are you nonassertive? Why do you think this is the case? Analyzing your habitual patterns of assertion might provide useful insights into your motives, fears, priorities, and personal goals.

2. What emotions would you like to communicate more easily? Do you find it easier to express some than others? Think about how you express each of the following:

anger	hurt
tiredness	fear
rushed, busy	affection
sad	happiness

3. Most people find it easy to demonstrate some types of assertive skills but very difficult to express others. Review the list in Box 8.5. In each of these situations, do you tend to act assertively, nonassertively, or aggressively? Do you avoid some situations? Select one or two of the skill areas and begin to consciously work on improving your assertiveness in that area. Remember, progress is gradual.

4. One of the best ways to begin developing assertive skills is to find a role model, someone you know who practices effective assertive communication. Take a few days and then describe the person you've chosen. Be sure to include information about your role model's listening behavior. Observe this person in a variety of situations, and then reflect on what you've learned that you can incorporate into your own style to become more assertive.

Group Activities

Form a small group of four to six people. You may want to keep the same group for all activities, or you may find it more interesting to change groups so that you get to hear the opinions and ideas of a greater number of your classmates.

1. One group member will be the "borrower" and will speak to each of the other members in turn, asking (pleading, begging, threatening) to borrow something. The other members of the group practice their assertive skills and, in turn, refuse to lend the item. Discuss the effectiveness of the assertive response in each case.

2. Identify several situations in which the assertive skill of giving or taking criticism would be required. Decide on a specific case, and choose participants to role-play the situation for the rest of the group. Discuss alternative approaches, and the benefits and risks of assertive behavior in this situation.

3. Identify several situations in which the assertive skills of asking for help or starting conversations would be required. Generate a specific case, and choose participants to role-play the situation for the larger group. Discuss.

4. Identify several situations in which the assertive skills of standing up for personal beliefs expressing an unpopular opinion would be required. Generate a specific case, and choose participants to role-play the situation for the larger group. Discuss.

5. Discuss the following questions:
   a. What are the implications for listening effectiveness if suddenly everyone decided to become more assertive?
   b. Is the assertive response always appropriate?
   c. On what basis do you decide when to be assertive?

Application 4: Practice Supportive Responses

Your ability to establish a supportive communication climate will pay off in many ways. Your partner will feel comfortable expressing his ideas in an open and nonevaluative atmosphere. By reducing defensiveness, both of you are encouraged to focus on the situation at hand rather than protecting your self-concept. If effective listening is important to you, it will be well worth your time to learn and practice the skills that promote supportive climates.

Activities

1. Under what circumstances do you become defensive? Is there someone who provokes a defensive response without even trying? Why do you suppose that's the case? List at least four actions that you can take to minimize defensiveness in yourself and others.

2. Keep a journal of your defensive reactions. What types of response are most typical? Do you rationalize? Display apathy? Refuse to accept responsibility for problems?

3. What do you do that might cause others to become defensive? Do you know of someone who becomes defensive when you talk with them?

4. Identify a person with whom you would like to build a more supportive relationship. Set a concrete action plan regarding how you will use more supportive responses in your encounters.

Group Activities

Form a small group of four to six people. You may want to keep the same group for all activities, or you may find it more interesting to change groups so that you get to hear the opinions and ideas of a greater number of your classmates.

1. Form five groups. Each group chooses or is assigned one of the following defensive behaviors (see Box 8.7 in your reading). Generate two or three good examples of the behavior to share with the other groups.

   a. Rationalization
   b. Projection
   c. Displacement
   d. Verbal aggression

   What are your choices as a listener when someone becomes defensive?

   Alternative activity: Role-play the examples generated above. Discuss how defensiveness might have been reduced. Role-play the situation a second time, illustrating the new listening behaviors.

2. Choose one of the defensive–supportive climates listed below.

   Spend 10 to 15 minutes sharing situations in which a defensive climate resulted in unproductive interactions. Select one situation to role-play. Role-play the situation as it occurred, with the defensive climate. What happened? Role-play the same situation a second time, using behaviors that encourage a supportive climate. Discuss the differences you noted, particularly with regard to listening behavior.

   a. *I* versus *You* language
   b. Problem versus Blame orientation
   c. Empathy versus Indifference
   d. Provisionalism versus Dogmatism

3. Form groups of three. Person A chooses one of the topics listed below and will talk about the topic for 8 minutes. While he speaks, Person B, the listener, practices paraphrasing, perception-checking, and questioning. Person B should *avoid giving opinions or advice, relating his own experiences, or any other types of response.*

Person C serves as an observer and records the type of responses Person B makes on Part I of the *Listening Response Feedback Sheet*. Immediately following the interaction, Person B fills out Part II of the *Listening Response Feedback Sheet*.

Take approximately 5 minutes to share feedback (from both Person A and Person C) with the listener, Person B. Reverse roles, as time permits, until all three members have played each role.

Topics

   a. When I relate to people I . . .
   b. I'm at my best when . . .
   c. Those who don't know me well . . .
   d. An important value for me is . . .
   e. My family . . .
   f. I enjoy people who . . .
   g. One important thing I've learned this year is . . .
   h. One of my biggest regrets is . . .
   i. Too many people . . .
   j. I'm really proud of the fact that . . .

Listening Response Feedback Sheet: Part I

(To be completed by Person C, the Observer)
Be as *specific* and as *complete* as possible in filling out this sheet.

Verbal Behavior

OTHER-CENTERED RESPONSES	YOU-CENTERED RESPONSES
Questions _____	Advice _____
Paraphrase _____	Opinions _____
Descriptions _____	Judgments _____
Empathy _____	Joking _____
Perception checks _____	Emotional _____

Other verbal responses:

Nonverbal Behavior

Eye contact _____
Mannerisms _____
Vocal cues _____
Posture _____
Gestures _____
Facial expressions _____

General Comments

Listening Response Feedback Sheet: Part II

(To be completed by Person B, the listener)

1. I felt _____ talking with you because _____

_____

uncomfortable   *slightly uncomfortable*   *fairly comfortable*   *comfortable*

2. You encouraged me to speak _____ by _____

_____

3. You seemed _____ in what I had to say because you _____

_____

disinterested   *slightly interested*   *fairly interested*   *interested*

4. You seemed to understand _____ of what I said because you _____

_____

very little   *some*   *almost all*   *all*

Application 5: Create Supportive Listening Environments

Effective listeners take into account as many variables as possible in order to maximize the comfort levels of all participants. Factors that affect your listening environment, and over which you exercise control, include:

- Furniture and movable objects: these factors determine interaction patterns and influence perceptions of status, formality, and degree of comfort;
- Distance between communicators;
- Communication aspects related to time: the time of day, amount of time scheduled for the activity, the lead time given participants, and so forth.

Activities

1. Design your ideal environment for the following situations. Use your imagination, and be thorough in your description. Select the colors, the style and placement of furniture, and describe use of decorative objects.

   a. An interview (you are the interviewer)
   b. A meeting of ten
   c. An office
   d. A birthday party for fifteen 10-year-olds
   e. A classroom for thirty-five college sophomores
   f. Your living room or recreation room

2. How do you react in the following situations (both verbally and nonverbally)?

   a. You're in a hurry to leave for class and someone stops by to talk to you.
   b. You've just had an argument and the other person begins to be verbally aggressive.

c. You need to leave a party and the person you're with keeps on socializing.

d. You have a lot on your mind and someone asks you to help her make a big decision.

e. You're studying in the library and your friend keeps talking to you loudly.

3. What is your best time of the day? Keep track of your physical and mental states each day for a week. Note when you feel most alert, when you begin to feel tired, when you concentrate easily, and so forth. Graph your highs and lows.

a. Does the graph coincide with your normal routines?

b. Do you save your planning and large projects for your peak hours, or do you try to fit in these activities randomly?

c. When are your classes?

d. How can you modify your schedule to fit more closely with your personal rhythms?

4. What are some of the changes you notice when speaking at public distance? How is your delivery influenced? How is the content of your message affected by distance? What kind of listening do you do in this setting?

Group Activities

Form a small group of four to six people. You may want to keep the same group for all activities, or you may find it more interesting to change groups so that you get to hear the opinions and ideas of a greater number of your classmates.

1. Choose one of the following environments:

- student lounge
- classroom
- cafeteria
- bus station or airport
- restaurant
- faculty office

Discuss how the physical space affects communication in that situation. Under what circumstances is it easy to listen? What factors in the environment encourage or discourage effective listening? Can anything be done to make some situations more conducive to effective communication?

2. Sketch a rough floor plan of your living room. Trade papers with another member of your group. Look at the diagram in front of you, and comment on how you believe it would affect communication. Return the paper to its owner and discuss your response. Repeat using other floor plans.

3. Identify an environment that makes a strong statement—positive or negative. Perhaps a doctor's office has diplomas hanging on the walls, soft music playing, uncluttered spaces with objects all arranged in rows. How do you feel in this particular environment? Do you feel the way the owner/designer wants you to? Share your example and your impressions with group members.

4. Discuss the nonverbal cues that let you know someone is not in the right frame of mind to talk. Think of a specific individual and identify some of the cues this per-

son sends that let you know he or she would not be receptive to your message. Share as many details as possible with members of your group. Then, choose participants to role-play this situation. What variables influence your decision about how to react?

5. You have something very important to discuss with a friend. What must you take into consideration in determining the best possible circumstances under which to approach this person? Brainstorm a list of all the factors that need to be considered. Then, indicate what you would consider the *ideal* situation for each.

> *Example:*   *Factor*   *Ideal*
>   time of day   between 8:00 a.m and 11:00 a.m.
>   color scheme   blue

6. Stand up and face a partner at a distance of approximately 3 feet. Begin speaking with this person, facing him or her squarely. Take a small step forward every few seconds until you reach a point where one of you feels uncomfortable. Measure the distance. Compare your results with the results of others in your group.

   a. Is your distance about average, or do you feel uncomfortable more or less quickly than others?
   b. What might account for differences?
   c. How did the discomfort you began to experience affect your listening?

THE INTERVIEW: CASE QUESTIONS

1. How would you have responded if you were Martina and Ms. Rogers had kept interrupting you? Do you think Martina handled the situation well? What were her choices?

2. Role-play the scene between Martina and Ms. Rogers before the three men entered the room. Would you say that Ms. Rogers was aggressive or assertive? Explain. Role-play the situation again, keeping Ms. Rogers' role the same but experimenting with different responses for Martina. Role-play her in the Parent ego state and then in the Child.

3. Do you feel it is ethical to put an interviewee through the type of stress interview in which Martina participated?

4. Do you think Martina had to work hard at being assertive? Was she listening well? What indicators do you have of her listening behavior?

5. Was Ms. Rogers listening to Martina? Was her listening effective?

6. What do you know about the physical environments Martina was in from the case? How did the physical environment of Toni's office influence listening? Draw a floor plan of a room that you believe would have been ideal for this type of interview. Indicate the time of day, colors, and other nonverbal aspects.

7. How did Martina's comfort level in the situation influence her listening? How do you imagine she behaved nonverbally in response to stress? How might her nonverbal behavior change when the men entered the room and Ms. Rogers told her she had done well?

8. What are some of the listening challenges Martina might encounter when there are several interviewers talking with her at one time?

BIBLIOGRAPHY

Burgoon, J. K., & Jones, D. B. (1976). Toward a theory of personal space expectations and their violations. *Human Communication Research, 2,* 131–146.

Egan, G. (1977). *You and me: The skills of communicating and relating to others.* Belmont, CA: Wadsworth Publishing.

Gibb, J. R. (1977). Defensive communication. *Bridges not walls: A book about interpersonal communication.* Reading, MA: Addison-Wesley.

Hall, E. (1959). *The silent language.* Garden City, NY: Doubleday.

Johnson, D. (1982). *Reaching out: Interpersonal effectiveness and self-actualization.* Englewood Cliffs, NJ: Prentice Hall.

Ketcham, H. (1958). *Color planning for business and industry.* New York, NY: Harper and Brothers.

Knapp, M. L. (1978). *Social intercourse: From greeting to goodbye.* Boston: Allyn and Bacon.

Mehrabian, A. (1976). *Public places and private spaces.* New York: Basic Books.

Rosenfeld, L., & Civikly, J. M. (1976). *With words unspoken: The nonverbal experience.* New York: Holt, Rinehart and Winston.

Sommer, R. (1969). *Personal space.* Englewood Cliffs, NJ: Prentice Hall.

PART III

LISTENING: RELATIONSHIPS AND CHALLENGES

PEANUTS Reprinted by permission of United Features Syndicate, Inc.

CHAPTER 9

LISTENING RELATIONSHIPS

We listen a book a day, we speak a book a week, we read a book a month, we write a book a year.

OUTLINE

CHAPTER OBJECTIVES

After completing this chapter, you will

Become more aware of:

- the importance of listening to family members
- the variety of ways in which you listen to learn
- your responsibility as a listener in presentational speaking situations
- the ways in which you can derive the most benefit from a coaching relationship
- the role you play as a listener in providing help
- the differences in listening to employees and listening to your supervisor
- the ways in which you can facilitate effective group process through listening
- the ways in which rumor affects employees' perceptions

Better understand:

- the special requirements of listening to family members, including children and the elderly
- the principles of listening in classroom and lecture situations
- the nature of listening in coaching relationships
- the listening principles involved in formal and informal counseling situations
- the ways in which you can gain more information in the patient-doctor encounter
- your responsibilities when listening to employees
- techniques of listening more effectively to supervisors
- the principles of listening in small group discussions
- the characteristics of rumors

Develop skills in:

- listening to members of your family, including children and the elderly
- taking advantage of listening opportunities in the classroom
- listening to presentations
- listening in a coaching relationship
- providing support as a listener to friends in trouble
- listening in the patient–doctor relationship
- listening to employees and supervisors
- leading small groups
- using rumors productively to facilitate information sharing

CASE: HOME FOR THE HOLIDAYS

"It's going to be wonderful to be home for the holidays," Meg thought as she pulled into her parents' driveway. She was looking forward to seeing her brothers and parents during the three-week winter break. Although she could get home from college in less than six hours, she was just far enough away that her visits home were infrequent.

Meg knew her mother had been waiting by the window all afternoon, looking for her red Volvo. As she entered the living room dragging her suitcases, she was suddenly glad she had chosen to spend the holidays with her family rather than head to Bermuda with her housemates. Everyone looked so happy to see her. Larry and Ken, fourteen-year-old twins, were too cool to greet her at the door, but they looked up and yelled a greeting, and she knew they had missed her. Her little brother Tim was most demonstrative, jumping into her already full arms and seeming to ignore the fact that she was pulling two suitcases.

"Don't forget your grandfather," she heard her mother whisper even before she could set down her luggage. "Hi, grandpa," Meg said as she made her way over to his chair and bent down to kiss him. "You've lost too much weight," her grandfather replied abruptly. "You've got to put a little meat on your bones." Meg bit her tongue and tried to ignore his remark, turning back to Tim, who had obviously been waiting to show her his second-grade accomplishments. He took her hand and pulled her over to a large box full of papers and artwork. He picked up the top paper, waving it in front of her and began to explain in great detail just how it ended up among his treasures.

"Not now, honey," Meg said as she gently put the paper back into the box. "You have a lot of papers there! We'll have plenty of time to look at them later. Right now I have to get settled in." "You don't like my papers?" Tim placed the lid firmly back on his box and lowered his head, avoiding her eyes. "Go ahead and pout if you want to," Meg replied as she picked up her suitcase and headed for her bedroom. "I am not looking at your papers right now. I need to take care of my things."

Meg opened her bedroom door. She could feel a strange sensation in the pit of her stomach as she looked around the room that had been entirely hers just a few months before. The bed had been moved, and her stuffed animal collection was nowhere in sight. Worse, the room had been repainted; there were only a few telltale signs along the wooden trim that the harsh white walls had once been peach, her favorite color. Meg could tell her mother was standing behind her, watching her intently.

"Well, how do you like it?" her mother asked as she passed Meg and went on in to adjust a picture on the opposite wall.

"I hate it," Meg replied as she dropped her bags. "This was my room. How could you ruin it without even letting me know?"

"Meg, really," her mother began. "I know this room was yours, but it is part of our house and we have to live here, too. It's different, but I'm sure you'll get used to it. Now, it's not a big deal. I'm fixing dinner and we should be ready to eat as soon as you've settled in. Cheer up—we've all been looking forward to seeing you and I want everything to go smoothly." She smiled and squeezed Meg's shoulder as she left the room, closing the door gently behind her.

There was still a lump in her throat as Meg stood looking around her room in disbelief. Cheer up? How could she cheer up? Just then the door flew open and Tim bounded in, fully recovered from their previous encounter.

"Ready yet?" Tim climbed on her bed and began jumping up and down. "Are you ready to see my pictures? Ready? Ready?" He chanted loudly, rhythmically, as the bed sagged down under his weight and then rose up again.

"No, Tim, I'm not ready," Meg managed a smile as she picked Tim up off her bed. "It's almost time for dinner though. Why don't you see if you can go help Mom in the kitchen?"

"Why don't you want to see my pictures?" Tim persisted. "I've been waiting to show them to you for a long time and now you're here and you don't want to see them."

"Tim," Meg felt completely out of control as her voice quivered and she became visibly upset, "I never said I did not want to see your pictures. I said not now. Not now. Do you understand? Soon. Not now. That's it. Go help Mom." She ushered him forcefully through the door and closed it tightly behind him. She needed a few minutes to herself or she felt she would explode.

Twenty minutes later dinner was on the table, and Meg felt ready to venture out once again. As everyone took their seats, Meg noticed that her grandfather was absent. "Where's grandpa?" Meg asked.

"He's coming. Be patient," her mother replied as she placed her napkin on her lap.

For some reason Meg couldn't help taking offense at her mother's remark. Just because she wanted to know where he was didn't imply that she was impatient. As she was pondering the incident, the sound of her father's voice brought her sharply back to the present.

"So, how's school going, Meggy?"

"Fine," Meg replied.

"We haven't seen you in three months. What's 'fine'?" her father probed.

"Fine means just fine. I like my classes a lot, especially anthropology," Meg offered. After a pause she continued, "It's really interesting to see how different cultures develop. We were studying African tribes . . ."

"There he is!" Meg's mother sounded relieved as she stood to help her father take his place at the table. "Okay, everyone, we can start! Ken, why don't you say the blessing?"

Meg closed her eyes, almost grateful for the moment of peace. She could tell Tim was making faces across the table from her, trying to get her attention without their mother catching him. She knew, too, that Ken hated to say the blessing and was surprised that he acknowledged the request with a short but appropriate passage.

"Couldn't hear a word," Meg's grandfather said as he lifted his head. "You've got to speak up, boy. I remember when I used to say the blessing, there was no doubt about what was said. Young people are in too much of a hurry nowadays to even give thanks for their food."

"Thank you, Ken," Meg's mother sighed as she passed the salad. "It's so good to have all of us together. Meg, we're so glad you decided to come home instead of going off with your roommate—is it Sandra? How is she, anyway? Didn't you tell us she has some sort of medical problem?"

"It's Sara. She goes into the hospital for tests as soon as she gets back from Bermuda. No one has been able to figure out what's wrong with her yet, although she's been very sick and out of school quite a lot this term."

"Honey, pass the salad dressing to your grandfather," Meg's mother pointed to the bottle next to Larry. "I love that dressing. You can only get it around here at Todd's Market. Have you seen it anywhere on campus, Meg?"

"No," Meg replied. She suddenly had a strange feeling that she no longer belonged to this family. She loved them all, but somehow being home made her feel uncomfortable and alienated. When the meal ended Meg went back to her room and

sat on her bed for a long time. Then she opened the door and called to Tim. "Time to look at those papers," she said as she pulled him over and gave him a big hug. He grinned and darted off to find his box.

LISTENING RELATIONSHIPS

Remember that listening requirements are determined by your purpose and context. Therefore, every listening relationship, requires a slightly different balance of listening insights, knowledge, and behaviors. Now that you understand the components of the HURIER model, you can apply your skills to a variety of listening relationships. Four contexts that foster different types of listening relationships are presented in this chapter. You will be introduced to listening in the family, listening in educational environments, listening in helping relationships, and listening in organizations. What will become readily apparent is that there many similarities in the listening competencies required to navigate through the wide range of contexts you will encounter.

Each relationship discussed in this chapter is introduced with a box that suggests a particular listening strategy. That is, boxed information indicates the extent to which each of the six components of the HURIER model is relevant to listening effectiveness in that situation. Keep in mind that there is more to listening than developing an appropriate strategy. The LAW of listening reminds us that listening requires willingness as well as ability. Knowing what listening behaviors to emphasize is the first step; effort, practice, and a sincere desire to improve your personal effectiveness is also essential.

RELATIONSHIPS IN THE FAMILY

Your most intense emotions are expressed toward those closest to you—members of your family. When you are personally involved, it is easy to become overly sensitive. Child ego state behavior emerges; you may shout, pout, become defensive, and feel sorry for yourself.

The home tends to be the place where you let down your defenses and take out frustrations. It is likely the "safest" of your many environments, and so there is a tendency to strike out at those closest to you. Venting anger and hurt feelings on supportive family members, rather than on those who caused the problem, can be risky. Children are often the victims of displacement. Violence and suicide among children and the number of run-aways are all on the rise.

> What listening challenges do you confront with members of your family? Whose responsibility is it to reduce them?

Empathic listening, as you know, is particularly appropriate when emotions are involved. Only after family members have an opportunity to express their true feelings can they realistically consider the facts at hand, propose solutions, and evaluate the best course of action. Conflicts in opinion that arise from healthy discussion and debate illustrate respect for differing points of view and provide a safe forum in which all family members can develop their listening competence.

How do you communicate when you feel misjudged, unfairly treated, or unappreciated? You can begin by influencing your family environment—by consistently practicing your listening skills. When you listen, you demonstrate both caring and a commitment to problem solving. Through your willingness to listen, you demonstrate to family members that you care about your relationships with them as people.

Today, an increasing number of households have an additional consideration—they have opened their home to a grandparent. With three generations under one roof, the number of potential conflicts is multiplied. There is, as you might guess, no magic solution for such complexity. Human relations are dynamic, constantly changing forces that require your continuing attention and nurturing. Never think of yourself as a passive victim of your family's current habits. By changing *your* behavior, you have the potential to make a significant positive impact on the way your family members listen and interact. Here we review the most essential ingredients for effective listening among family members.

Listening to Your Partner or Spouse

Strategy: Listening to Your Partner or Spouse	
H	Moderate
U	High
R	Moderate
I	High
E	Low
R	____

Developing skills that foster authentic and intimate relationships takes time and practice. If there is one consistent message the media projects with regard to lasting relationships, it's that effective communication is the most important factor in maintaining and developing this bond.

The demographics of the family in the United States are changing; more women and mothers are in the workforce than ever before. Increased financial security and dual careers often require tradeoffs. Perhaps the most acutely felt loss is quality family time. Catching and capitalizing on opportunities to listen to family members becomes essential as schedules quickly fill. Relationships take time and effort not only to develop, but to maintain.

Continuous listening is essential to nurturing a changing relationship. There is no more appropriate context for personal disclosure than in the family, especially between partners. One way in which relationships can be analyzed is with regard to the type of information that is shared. Powell (1969) suggests that effective listeners discriminate among clichés, facts, opinions and judgments, and feelings so that they can interact with their partners in appropriate ways (Box 9.1).

Level 1: Clichés.   Your partner comes home from work and you mumble automatically, "Hi, how was your day?" Level 1 communication, or clichés, constitutes the daily give-and-take situations where the verbal interaction serves simply to recognize the other person's presence. Often, we don't really hear what is said because we are relying on our habitual scripts.

> How does technology affect your ability to move relationships to a new level? How about culture?

Level 2: Facts.   Level 2 centers around messages about other people, ideas, and events. Facts are exchanged as you work cooperatively with your partner or simply pass time. This type of dialogue does not encourage disclosure, nor does it facilitate the development of a healthier relationship. As a listener, understanding plays a much greater role than interpretation or evaluation.

Level 3: Opinions and judgments.   Here, you and your partner begin to move toward more open, relational communication. Sprinkled with the facts are glimpses of what your partner thinks about the topics you're discussing. When you demonstrate behavioral empathy, continued sharing is encouraged. If, however, you appear disinterested or critical, communication may quickly move back to an earlier level.

Level 4: Feelings.   Efforts to articulate feelings often bring people closer together. Powell believes, "If I really want you to know who I am, I must tell you about my stomach (gut level feelings) as well as my head" (p. 50). The acceptance of feelings—through emphatic listening—is prerequisite to

---

BOX 9.1

POWELL'S LEVELS OF DISCLOSURE

Clichés	*Facts*	*Opinions*	*Feelings*
Hi, how's it going?	Did you hear, we got a new text in astronomy.	Joe should get more help on his calculus.	It makes me angry when we're given an exam right before vacation.
Good to see you, Sue.	Sally has a 92 average.	It should be fun. They're both really nice people.	I'm upset and confused about the grade I received.
Hey, what's up?	My paper is due on Tuesday.	He's arrogant and hasn't been fair at all.	I feel really stupid when you go off and leave me.

deeper, more meaningful communication and stronger relationships. The healthiest intimate relationships are characterized by reciprocity and a high degree of disclosure and trust.

The Skills of Listening to Your Partner

1. When you talk with your partner, determine your level of communication. Do the two of you stay on facts most of the time, or does more disclosure frequently take place?
2. Set aside time to talk when the two of you are alone. Minimize distractions at other times (go for a short walk, retreat to the study, chat in the kitchen).
3. Work at listening. Family members all too often take each other for granted. The only way to maintain and improve a relationship is to give it the attention and energy it deserves.
4. Be assertive and direct about your needs and feelings. Creating a climate of strategy rather than spontaneity, or sending subtle nonverbal cues hoping they will be recognized, puts unnecessary stress on a relationship.
5. Provide frequent, unsolicited, positive feedback.
6. If you and your partner know each other well, it is often tempting to make assumptions as you communicate. Although a sort of shorthand dialogue can be special, it can also create misunderstandings and pave the way for future problems. Be sure that you accurately understand what your partner means by restating ideas and asking questions.
7. Whenever you feel upset, hurt, or angry, you know immediately that your listening ability is impaired. Postpone any discussion until after you have had an opportunity to work off some of the negative feelings that will only block future communication.
8. If your partner has had a bad day or just needs to let off steam, lend an ear. Never discount the significance of a strongly felt problem. Use your empathic listening skills; paraphrase, reflecting both content and feelings. Provide support and be as generous as you can with your time.

Listening to Children

Strategy: Listening to Children	
H	High
U	High
R	Moderate
I	High
E	Low
R	_____

There is an approach to raising responsible children called Parent Effectiveness Training (Gordon, 1975). It's not just for parents; rather, it's a useful philosophy about how to treat children so that they will develop into responsible, caring adults. Children need to be heard. Yet, the average family with teenagers spends only fifteen minutes each day communicating face-to-face, and much of this time is devoted to discussing routine concerns—what's for dinner, who needs a ride to evening activities, and so on (Barbour, 1981).

Young children do a great deal of talking. They are interested in exploring all aspects of their environment and sharing these discoveries with friends and family. The quantity and repetitiveness of their verbalizations, however, may tempt you to fake attention. Assuming that the child doesn't know the difference, many adults provide minimal reinforcers while allowing themselves to be distracted by other concerns.

When you model effective listening behaviors, children are likely to develop these skills at an earlier age. This proficiency can significantly benefit a young person's learning. Your active listening can also help a young person work out problems and make decisions. Your brief questions and support provide her with an opportunity to explore feelings and consequences. It is easy to lose touch with the child's world, since very often she sees things from an entirely different point of view. In fact, the family unit influences her world view in more ways than you realize. One author reports a study where small children were shown a picture of the Mona Lisa and asked, "Why is she smiling?" Their private perceptions were revealed in the following responses:

> How might you help a child understand the importance of listening?

> "She backed the car out of the garage without scraping it."
> "Her husband was washing the dishes, and she had nothing to do."
> "She was cold, and someone turned on the heat."
> "They have a nice family and a good baby."

Through listening, you also get to know this person better at a critical stage in his or her development. As she grows and other options—school events, computer-related activities, friends—become more attractive, you will have established a solid foundation on which to build your relationship into the future. That alone may be enough to justify the time spent.

Here are some suggestions for improving communication with young family members.

The Skills of Listening to Children

1. Follow the rules of constructive feedback. Focus on the child's behavior rather than making judgmental statements about the child herself. When you say, "Sam, you are so sloppy," you communicate a very different message than if

you were to say, "Sam, you have to slow down when you carry a full glass of juice."

2. Children need to understand consequences. When you listen, try to determine whether or not the child realizes why a particular action is acceptable or unacceptable, wise or unwise. Help her to see the consequences of her behavior. "Sue, I don't like it when you use my school supplies without asking me. I look for something and I can't find it." These responses provide clarifying information which the child can use in making future decisions.

3. Do not fake attention. If you are tired or upset and cannot concentrate, tell the child about the feelings you are experiencing and how they prevent you from being a good listener, just as you would handle the situation with an adult. Arrange to get together at another time. Use this approach, however, only when you absolutely cannot listen.

4. Try to avoid giving advice, making evaluations, or criticizing a child unnecessarily. It prevents her from expressing her true thoughts and forces her to constantly monitor what she says in light of your anticipated reactions. Rather than changing key attitudes and orientations, it simply turns a spontaneous child into a strategic planner.

5. Consider nonverbal factors. Listen to the child's voice and observe her nonverbal cues. In this way you will catch glimpses of what is important to her, what conflicts she is experiencing, what uncertainties or insecurities she feels.

6. Remember that a child's mood and situational factors influence her as much as they do adults. Is she tired? Has she had a difficult day? Has she been sick? Has she had a new experience? Is she upset or anxious?

7. Designing appropriate environments is as important when listening to children as when listening to adults. How about taking her to a place where the two of you can be alone to share some quiet time? Is the TV turned up, or is there loud music playing? Are there other children running around, other adults talking? If so, chances are your encounter will not be as meaningful as it could be.

8. Sit down with the child. Give her your undivided attention and let her know her ideas and thoughts are valued.

9. Express frequent, unconditional positive regard for a child. Let her know that she is loved and appreciated because she is a unique, special person in her own right—not because she brushed her teeth without being reminded or picked up the puzzle or helped carry in the groceries. Express specific, positive feelings just before she goes to bed. Leaving a child with a thought such as, "Sue, I really enjoyed our walk together this afternoon," provides her with a comforting, reassuring thought to take with her to sleep.

Listening to the Elderly

```
Strategy: Listening to the Elderly
        H      High
        U      High
        R      Moderate
        I      High
        E      Low
        R      _____
```

People are living longer. Those over sixty-five comprise one of the fastest growing segments of the U.S. population. Unfortunately, the elderly often have an awkward position in the extended family. Many families are opting—either because of cost or conscience—to bring their elderly parents into their own homes. This arrangement creates a new set of concerns, since new role relationships need to be established, new habits formed, and new interaction patterns facilitated.

Listening to the elderly is not always easy. Their speech is slower paced, their thoughts may be less well organized, and their conversation is sprinkled with redundancies. As a consequence of the aging process, many people lose their flexibility; they do not organize incoming information as readily as they used to (Box 9.2). Since there are wide variations and individual differences, you're safest to assume that if an elderly person's hearing is normal, his listening is likely to be impaired only by a slight decrease in his ability to store and retrieve information. If

■ ■ ■ ■ ■

BOX 9.2

MEMORY AND AGING

Some memory concerns associated with the elderly include:

1. Concentration is more difficult. Distractions have a stronger impact as individuals age. Consequently, it may be important for both communicators to seek situations where distractions can be minimized.

2. Recall takes more time and requires a greater number of memory cues. All information processing systems work more slowly as a person ages. It takes more time for information to be stored and retrieved.

In order to recall information, older people require more memory cues, or bits of related information that help them remember a particular item.

3. Memorization strategies become more difficult to use. If information is not stored properly, it will never be as readily available as if appropriate memory strategies were used at the time the information was received. The more slowly information is received, the more likely it will be that older individuals can apply techniques that will make recall easier.

you live with or interact regularly with an older person, the following skills will help to improve your relationship.

The Skills of Listening to the Elderly

1. Recognize that talking to an elderly person may take more time. If you need an answer in a hurry, try asking "closed" rather than "open" questions, or design your queries in an either–or format. You cannot expect a quick response to a question such as "What would you like to do tonight?" Asking a more direct question, such as, "Would you like to take a ride after lunch?" or "Would you like to take a ride after lunch, or would you rather go look for that book you were talking about?" are less stressful and provide you with more concrete information.

2. Your attitudes are communicated to an elderly person in the same way that they are communicated to other family members. As an older person begins to participate less in the mainstream of family life, however, it is often necessary for you to focus his attention before speaking to him. Using his name, for example, or standing in front of him when you speak will let him know that he will be involved in the next encounter.

3. Let the older person know that she is important. Rather than shouting a question from across the room, stand next to the person whenever you can. Folks who have trouble hearing will appreciate the ability to see you as you speak with them.

4. Don't be reluctant to verbalize your feelings. Practice your assertive skills. Let an elderly person know if you feel he is violating your rights, but also let him know that he is a valued member of the family.

5. Ask questions. Take the time to be interested in what an older person is doing and thinking. Put yourself in the role of listener as much of the time as possible. Share when it seems appropriate, but otherwise develop the attitude that you will gain more by listening than by speaking.

6. Provide support. Recognize the older person's accomplishments and reinforce the little things that he or she does. Help him to feel loved and valued by allowing him to share in the family's chores and pleasures.

EDUCATIONAL RELATIONSHIPS

You learn by listening. Although the majority of your educational opportunities occur within the formal school structure, your education doesn't stop when you graduate nor do you, as a student, necessarily learn the most important things within the classroom. Organizations, in particular, have recognized the importance of continuous, life-long learning and professional development. Consequently, you now hear about learning organizations, businesses that value change and continually develop their employees through such strategies as training seminars, guest speakers, on-the-job training, and coaching. Distance technologies are making it possible for you to learn anything from anywhere you are in the world. In all educational contexts, your listening skills are critical to your success.

Listening in the Classroom

Strategy: Listening in the Classroom	
H	High
U	High
R	High
I	Moderate
E	Moderate/High
R	_____

Listening is the main channel of communication between teachers and students. Yet, as you know from your own experiences, until very recently, listening was the most neglected of the four language arts skills. Think of all the teachers who kept talking while none of the students were listening—or who might have listened more when students had something to say.

When Wolff assessed the extent to which listening was offered in higher education, she discovered that the number of colleges providing listening instruction had gone from 14 percent to over 60 percent in just ten years (Wolff & Marsnik, 1992). At the turn of the century, it was increasing still further. Twenty years ago, the Association of American Colleges made improved listening skills an important component of their call for increased literacy. Yet, teaching listening to college students may be too late. As one study indicated, first graders listen to considerably more of what their teachers say than do high school students (Geeting & Geeting, 1976). It seems that rather than learning to listen *effectively,* school children learn to listen *selectively.*

> How could students facilitate a classroom environment that encourages effective listening? How about teachers?

Perhaps, however, the problem isn't all simply lack of instruction. As Geeting and Geeting (1976) point out, students in traditional classrooms listen largely because it's the rule. Poor attitudes toward listening are developed when communication is distorted in classroom settings. Classroom environments are often unrealistic listening arenas. Students are required to overcome numerous distractions and to listen for long periods of time in uncomfortable seats. Teachers who believe that they are the only ones who have something useful to say not only prevent healthy communication from taking place, they also affect children's perceptions of listening as well.

Much of the educational listening you do is necessarily in presentational settings and, increasingly, will be facilitated through distance technologies (Daniels & Rubin, 1998; Pedersen-Pietersen, 1999; Rea, Hager, & Rooney, 1999). Your ability to hear, understand, interpret, evaluate, and remember what is said depends in large measure on your motivation. The good news is that there are ways that you and other students can work to create a classroom environment in which listening is practiced and valued.

The Skills of Listening in the Classroom

1. Apply the transactional analysis model (see Chapter 8) to your classroom listening. Whenever you are in your Child ego state, listening because you have to rather than because you see the immediate or potential value of the information presented, you will sacrifice effectiveness. Ask yourself how, as a listener, can I make the information relevant and useful?
2. Strive to create two-way communication, even in large classes. Ask questions when appropriate. Stay mentally involved.
3. Listen carefully to the responses your classmates make; comment on them or ask probing questions if the meaning isn't clear to you. Address questions and make responses to other students rather than just to the teacher, especially during class discussions.
4. Take responsibility for sitting where it's easy to listen and participate. Suggest alternative classroom arrangements if you believe they would encourage more effective communication.
5. Think of your instructor as a person with his or her own interests, prejudices, and beliefs. This will help you express your ideas effectively and interpret what you hear.
6. Share responsibility with the instructor for classroom management. Don't allow one of your peers to dominate at the expense of others.

Listening to Presentations

The classroom setting is only one of many formal occasions where you learn from listening. Almost every day you hear speeches and presentations designed to educate or persuade. As a listener, keep the speaker's concerns in mind regardless of the specific occasion. Considering your partner's viewpoint will help you improve your listening effectiveness.

Presenters in formal, large group speaking situations have a difficult task. Not only must the message be understood by many different people, but it is necessarily one-way. This makes it even more important that the speaker's ideas be well organized, or he risks losing at least some of his audience long before he is finished. Given these challenges, most speakers become anxious. The presenter is concerned about holding your interest and attention; he is concerned that he will not remember what he planned to say; he is worried about what you will think of his speaking ability.

Even if he has been effective, it is difficult for him to accurately judge the impact his ideas have had on you. In large groups, he may not even see many of the faces in front of him. Few listeners will respond in ways that let him know that his message has been understood. He realizes that his delivery is very important in this context and that he will have to vary his voice, incorporate visual aids, and appear relaxed and confident in order to project a credible, poised image. He needs your help.

Remember that you and the speaker, no matter how remote he may seem, are partners in the communication event. Your task as a listener is to support the speaker as he works to accomplish his goals (Box 9.3). Active, attentive listening facilitates this process and builds rapport (Barker, Johnson, & Watson, 1991). Think of your listening responsibility as equal to your partner's, no matter what the context.

Here are some suggestions you can apply when listening in presentational contexts. Almost all of them apply to classroom listening as well.

The Skills of Listening to Presentations

1. Prepare to listen. Find out as much as you can about the speaker, the topic, and the speech occasion. Take a few moments immediately before the presentation to think about your own experience with the topic and your interests in that area.
2. Whenever possible, meet the speaker. Personalize your listening relationship.
3. Minimize distractions by sitting close to the front of the room and looking directly at the speaker. Use the vocalized listening technique.

■ ■ ■ ■ ■

BOX 9.3

QUESTIONS TO ASK WHEN LISTENING TO PRESENTATIONS

Concerning the **communicator**:

- How does she view me as a listener?
- How does she think I see her?
- What is her purpose?
- Does she have any underlying or hidden purposes?

Concerning the **content-message**:

- Are the ideas expressed clearly?
- Are the ideas well organized?
- Is the logic and reasoning sound?
- Is there valid and sufficient support?
- What emotions or values is the message targeting?

Concerning **feedback**:

- Is my feedback helpful and appropriate?
- Is my feedback sufficient?
- Is my feedback honest?

Concerning your **listening**:

- What internal distractions am I experiencing?
- What external distractions am I experiencing?
- What could I be doing to listen more effectively?

4. Decide whether or not to take notes. If you do, select the most appropriate note-taking system for the particular situation.

5. Regardless of whether or not you take notes, listen for main ideas as well as facts. Jot down any questions you might want to ask later. Think critically about what you have heard.

6. Determine the speaker's purpose: exactly what does he want to happen as a result of his presentation?

7. Analyze the speaker's credibility. What did you know about him before he spoke? Is he in a position to talk on this subject, to this group? Observe him throughout the speech situation to determine his attitudes and prejudices.

8. Analyze the speaker's logic and reasoning. Make sure all generalizations are supported. Try to recognize and identify any logical fallacies.

9. Analyze the speaker's use of evidence. Is it recent? Does it come from reliable sources?

10. Focus on the speaker's meaning as well as on the details that may be presented visually; don't allow a glitzy powerpoint presentation or colorful slides to distract from your responsibility to objectively analyze the speaker's credibility and argument.

11. Don't be misled by emotional appeals. Although they add interest and variety, make sure that you identify the values that have been targeted and attempt to minimize the influence of irrational appeals on your thinking.

12. Listen intentionally to new and difficult material.

Listening to Feedback and Evaluation

Strategy: Listening to Feedback and Evaluation	
H	High
U	High
R	High
I	High
E	Moderate/High
R	_____

In school and in the workplace, you learn by listening to feedback from your teacher, coach, supervisor, or mentor. Few contexts provide as rich an opportunity to learn and to develop your skills as one-to-one coaching conversations which are specifically designed to improve your current performance.

Coaching has become an essential tool as classrooms and boardrooms become more diverse. Students must be assisted on the basis of their individual backgrounds and unique needs. This process now continues into the workplace. Rapid and constant change has necessitated that everyone become "lifelong learners." This process is facilitated through coaching.

Listening to feedback and evaluation, as you know, isn't always easy. You have learned the rules of constructive feedback, the essentials of supportive communication, and assertive skills to help you handle negative feedback. In coaching contexts, you can put many of these ideas into practice.

Avoiding defensiveness is your most important challenge. You need to understand thoroughly how your coach sees your behavior and learn as much as possible about how she believes you can improve. Only when you have listened effectively to the feedback your teacher or supervisor provides are you in a position to discuss alternative viewpoints.

The suggestions provided below will help you get off to a good start as you participate in coaching conversations. Later, the skills of coaching are discussed as supervisors strive to improve employees' performance on the job.

The Skills of Listening When Being Coached

1. Listen carefully for differences in perceptions between your understanding of the situation and your coach's. Do you agree on the nature of the problem? Do you have specific criteria and standards that can be used to discuss how you are progressing?

2. Relax. It is difficult to remember anything when you are anxious—especially if you are anxious about whether or not you will be able to remember the information. Take a deep breath. Talk to yourself. Do whatever you need to in order to control your mental and physical response.

3. Determine whether you are hearing opinions or facts. If you believe the information is largely subjective, ask for specifics. Be sure you understand exactly what led your teacher or coach to her conclusions. Unless you know precisely what it is you are doing, it is almost impossible to make any meaningful changes in your behavior.

4. Listen with an open mind; don't refute or defend until you are sure you understand what your coach means. Try to see your behavior from your teacher's point of view.

5. If you agree with your coach's criticism, try using the assertive technique of negative inquiry. Ask what recommendations she has for change. Obtain as much information as possible that will help you modify your current performance.

6. If you disagree with your coach's criticism, *first acknowledge that you understand what she is saying*. Then, explain how you look at things differently. If, for example, your coach believes you should speak up more in class, discuss your viewpoint. Explain that you feel uncomfortable taking up class time asking questions you know you could answer on your own. Be prepared to negotiate perceptions. If you truly disagree with what you have heard, you need to speak up.

7. Interrupt only if you need clarification. Avoid interruptions caused by strong emotional involvement.

8. Make a plan for constructive change. You must come away from this conversation with the information necessary to improve your performance.

9. Restate any agreements that are made or goals that are set. A paraphrase gives your coach immediate feedback concerning whether or not she has been clear, and allows her to explain any points that may not have been interpreted accurately.

10. Ask to be evaluated or checked again within a short period of time so you can ensure that your understanding was correct and that your performance has improved.

HELPING RELATIONSHIPS

While the purpose of educational relationships such as coaching is to facilitate the acquisition of new knowledge or the development of skills, the purpose of the helping relationship is to provide emotional support and guidance to someone in need of assistance. You cannot always anticipate when you will find yourself in a helping relationship.

Some helping contexts, such as the counseling interview, are planned and formal. In these instances, help is provided by a trained, professional counselor. In other cases, the need for help arises spontaneously. A friend gets back a failing exam or receives a devastating phone call. You're right there, but do you know what to do? You are suddenly in the helping role because your friend has defined your relationship as helper–helpee (Arnold, 1991). Although in most situations your support will be appropriate and sufficient,

> Do you believe that the act of listening itself is therapeutic? Why?

it is important to be aware of your limitations. Next, you are introduced to both the formal counseling encounter as well as helping situations in which your empathic listening skills are sufficient.

Listening in the Counseling Interview

A distinguishing feature of the counseling interview is that its first concern is with the development of trust and the nature of the relationship itself. Next, the counselor identifies and assesses the problem while simultaneously encouraging her client to share his feelings. The final stage is problem solving and collaborative; when effective, it provides a sense of empowerment for the counselee.

The counselor's unique relationship with her client will greatly influence the outcomes of the interview. Its success will, of course, be affected by both the quality of the counselor's listening skills and her general interpersonal competence. Listening responses such as reflecting, confronting, interpreting, and empathizing may be particularly appropriate as the counselor seeks to help her client. Other responses, however, may block efforts to facilitate authentic communication (Box 9.4).

■ ■ ■ ■ ■

BOX 9.4

RESPONSES TO AVOID

Clichés

Inappropriate clichés are often worse than not responding at all. They create distance between people, particularly if the individual had hoped for some honest information.

Ignoring

This often means the listener is trying to avoid a confrontation. To simply say nothing or change the subject after listening leaves the speaker frustrated. It is better to disagree, let a person know that you didn't understand, anything (almost!) is better than no response at all.

Advice

You may feel that giving advice is helpful. In reality, however, it puts you in the higher status position. Nothing is worse than getting unwanted or unsolicited advice. Be careful that you don't express your "help-

fulness" by telling people what *you* think they should do without giving them an opportunity to take responsibility for their own actions.

Blaming

Avoid a preoccupation with finding fault. Take a positive approach whenever possible and focus on problem-solving. Generate solutions to conflict and focus on constructive action. Blaming quickly creates defensiveness.

Joking

It's good to have a sense of humor, but joking about serious matters can frustrate your colleagues. Try to face conflicts and other matters squarely. There are times when being serious is most appropriate, and it is important to be able to recognize these times.

Since many of the same skills used by a counselor are relevant to the spontaneous helping situations in which you are likely to find yourself, they have been combined in the following section.

Listening to a Friend in Trouble

Strategy: Listening to a Friend in Trouble	
H	Moderate
U	High
R	Moderate
I	High
E	Moderate
R	_____

The majority of interactions with your friends are positive and enjoyable. In any relationship, however, there are times when you are called upon to lend emotional support and guidance. The way in which you provide this encouragement may determine whether your friend moves out of depression, anger, and anxiety or whether the situation escalates to the point where professional help is required. Your role as a listener in this situation is critical.

Your relationships with classmates and friends can be either casual or intimate; the development of a relationship on this continuum can be facilitated by the type of response you chose to make (Arnold, 1991). The appropriateness of the response is always determined by your goal—whether your intent is to gather information (task orientation) or to project concern and empathy (relationship orientation). Arnold presents a useful framework for assessing the appropriateness of your efforts by proposing four different types of response (Box 9.5).

When listening to someone with a problem, one choice is to give a "same subject" response. This encourages the flow of conversation on the topic at hand. A "minimal response" does not add substance to the discussion, but demonstrates involvement through such reinforcers as head nods and "uh huh." A "tangential response" is less helpful. Instead of staying with the subject of concern to the speaker, the listener moves the conversation to a related issue. Finally, "different responses" are least supportive. Rather than demonstrating interest in the speaker's problem, the listener changes the subject entirely. As you might imagine, in helping relationships your goal is to increase the percentage of same and minimal responses while decreasing the number of tangential and different responses.

Listening to friends with disabilities may also require special skills. Phipps (1993) notes that listeners often have difficulty focusing on the messages of differently-abled people. Until listeners have "made sense" of the situation, it is difficult to accurately interpret the speaker's meaning. Phipps describes the case of a person whose disability was at first misunderstood. Not realizing she had multiple sclerosis, listeners described her as "acting drunk" and "out of control." Once the disability was identified, however, the interpretations, and subsequently the listening responses, changed dramatically. No longer distracted by the atypical speaker variables and able at last to assign common meanings to the situation, listeners almost immediately began to provide encouragement and positive reinforcement.

In all helping relationships it is essential to maintain mutual respect and empathy with your partner so that you can assess the usefulness of your interventions. Remember, too, that empathy is a shared commitment; your partner must be equally engaged in the encounter.

■ ■ ■ ■ ■ ▬▬▬▬▬▬▬▬▬▬▬▬▬▬▬▬▬▬▬▬▬▬▬▬▬▬▬▬▬▬▬▬

BOX 9.5

DETERMINING A HELPFUL RESPONSE

Goal: Project empathy and concern
Response: *Highly Appropriate*   *Inappropriate*

| Same subject | Minimal | Tangential | Different |

The Skills of Listening to a Friend in Trouble

1. Make sure you are sincerely willing to help. This is not a time to fake empathy.
2. Maintain respect and an unconditional positive regard for the other person.
3. Rusk and Gerner (1972) suggest that you are most helpful if you demonstrate calm confidence which is likely to reduce any anxiety your partner may be experiencing.
4. Open with broad statements that allow your partner to determine the specific direction of conversation. If the person is emotional, allow ample time for him to talk out his feelings.
5. Use minimal reinforcers and silence to communicate your interest and support. Attending behavior is extremely important in this context.
6. Pay close attention to nonverbal cues. Your perceived empathy depends largely on your interpretation of these behaviors.
7. Make sure your nonverbal cues do not project an attitude of superiority. Minimize any status differences, demonstrate behavioral empathy. Practice your self-monitoring skills, paying attention to how your behavior affects your partner.
8. Listen for both information and feelings to determine the specific problem and its scope.
9. Discuss alternatives. Try to prevent your partner from making a hasty decision. Plan a course of action and participate in goal setting.
10. The environment you create has a significant influence on the person's willingness to share information. Make sure you're on neutral ground and not in a setting that is uncomfortable for the counselee.
11. Take your time. Make sure the person is not just touching the surface of the issue. Allow sufficient time for him to get to what may be his real agenda.
12. Encourage the person to check with you at a specified time to make sure that the situation is improving.

Listening as a Patient

Strategy: Listening as a Patient	
H	Moderate
U	High
R	High
I	Moderate
E	High
R	_____

Much attention has been paid to the quality of listening in health-care relationships. In most cases, however, focus has been on the provider's listening behavior. All we know for certain is that, generally, patients are dissatisfied with the communication accompanying their health-care experiences, both with regard to the amount of information provided and the manner in which it is communicated (Ray & Bostrom, 1990;

Zimmerman & Arnold, 1990). In addition to professional expertise, patients seek empathy, concern, and friendliness from their providers. Too often, patients must be satisfied with a detached, objective presentation of information delivered with little accompanying explanation and no apparent regard for the individuals' sensitivities.

Relatively little research has been done to guide patients who must understand and follow directions to facilitate their medical care. To ensure effective health care and maintenance, you must completely understand all relevant aspects of your illness and remember accurately the directions you are given regarding treatment (Ley, 1983; Bush, 1985). In potentially stressful, occasionally embarrassing situations, this task is not always simple.

Two of the variables that influence patient–doctor relationships and make communication problematic are status and time. The physician's role has traditionally been one of high status, causing many patients to feel uncomfortable and powerless. The perception that the physician's time is more valuable than yours as a patient often begins in the waiting room, where you may spend as much as an hour reading magazines before being called into an inner office. Even then, the array of support staff that first attend to your routine care makes it clear that the doctor only has time for the most immediate, most essential, aspects of your treatment.

To ensure respect in the health-care relationship, the appropriate exercise of assertive skills and a high level of listening competence are required. The more control you take for managing your health-care experience, the more likely you are to find it satisfying and helpful. You will find that the guidelines presented for students and employees in coaching relationships are similar to the ones that follow, and might be helpful for you to review. The doctor–patient relationship, however, remains somewhat unique and has therefore been addressed as a distinct context.

The Skills of Listening as a Patient

1. Perception check whenever you want to confirm your understanding. Don't assume that you will put the pieces together at another time, or that with more information things will become clearer.
2. Ask probing questions. Don't worry about wasting the doctor's time if you have a relevant question that is important to you. Make sure you get answers to all of your questions.
3. Write down important information so you won't forget it and so there is no chance of misunderstandings.
4. Insist that the doctor focus on the interaction when giving you directions or advice. If he asks a question while engaged in some other activity, wait until he has turned to you before you begin speaking. Your confidence that he has heard what you have to say is essential, and it's difficult to feel valued when there is no eye contact or rapport.
5. Effective health-care relationships are two-way. If your provider does not respond to your efforts to create a collaborative relationship, consider exploring alternatives.

ORGANIZATIONAL RELATIONSHIPS

There is no question that effective communication is key to success in organizations, and that listening ranks among the most critical communication skills (Hunt & Cusella, 1983; Sypher, Bostrom, & Seibert, 1989; Seibert, 1990; Wolvin & Coakley, 1991; Wheless, 1998; Shugart, 2000).

From the moment you enter an organization, your listening plays a key role in determining the quality of your worklife and the effectiveness of your professional efforts. Recall that new employees make sense of their environment by paying attention to the right things. Through listening, you learn the expectations your manager has of you as well as the unique meanings of common terms like "office party," "time off," "getting to work early," or "team player." The ease with which you are oriented and integrated in a new setting depends largely upon your skill as a listener (Brownell & Jameson, 1996). Hearing and understanding the views of colleagues in other departments is often particularly problematic (Box 9.6).

> What verbal and nonverbal cues might you use as a new employee to "define the situation"?

In addition, as organizational members are bombarded with information from a wide range of sources, effective listening skill is more essential than ever before in helping you determine what is useful, appropriate, or important. In fact, recent studies of organizational leaders (Brownell, 1993) suggest that as individuals move up in the company the need for effective listening increases. As you become members of global organizations and as technology links you with your counterparts around the world, listening skills become the foundation of both business relationships and effective business practice.

Just as poor listening is costly in your personal encounters, the consequences of not listening well in global business environments are equally significant. Practitioners and researchers alike emphasize the importance of developing listening skills. With increased competence comes a variety of key benefits to the organization, including financial savings, greater efficiency and productivity, increased morale, and more satisfied customers.

BOX 9.6

LISTENING ACROSS DEPARTMENTS

Problems are created by:
1. Different perceptions and priorities
2. Different vocabularies
3. Lack of information-sharing
4. Competitiveness among departments

Different organizational contexts require sightly different listening skills and strategies. The following sections introduce you to some of the most common organizational listening relationships.

Listening to Employees

Strategy: Listening to Employees

H	Moderate
U	High
R	Moderate
I	High
E	Moderate/High
R	_____

Employees, in general, are dissatisfied with their managers' listening behavior. Numerous studies have concluded that, in the employee's opinion, listening is one of the most needed management competencies (Husband, Cooper, & Monsour, 1988; Lobdell, Sonoda, & Arnold, 1993). It also appears that managers consistently overestimate their own listening competence, creating significant discrepancies between their self-perceptions and the ratings given to them by members of their staff (Brownell, 1990). If organizations are to be successful, listening must begin at the top.

As a leader, one of your key responsibilities is decision-making. Although many tasks can be delegated, when it comes to crucial choices you are often the person to gather information, weigh alternatives, and set the plan of action. Wise decisions can only be made, however, when information from all relevant sources is considered and when each individual feels free to express his opinions and viewpoints openly and honestly. If those you supervise are well informed and communicate their ideas clearly, you have the best possible opportunity to choose wisely among alternatives.

Eisenberg and Goodall (1995) emphasize that leadership is really a relationship between leaders and employees. Developing this relationship depends upon effective listening behavior. Sensitive, empathic leaders provide the kind of environment that encourages high performance. Current research suggests that women's transformational leadership styles, where emphasis is placed on facilitative rather than directive skills, encourage a range of positive outcomes including employee trust and commitment. While a supportive, open climate encourages individuals to communicate in both directions and contributes significantly to organizational effectiveness (Brownell, 1994a), highly competitive environments block communication and undermine morale and team cooperation.

By following a few simple guidelines, you will find that your behavior can directly lead to a freer flow of information, better decisions, and a more supportive communication climate.

The Skills of Listening to Employees

1. Listen to a number of individuals who represent different points of view before making your decision. Remember that each person's perspective is likely to bias the way in which he interprets the facts. Listen to individuals privately as well as in small groups.

2. Ask probing questions. Draw out employees to determine if there is any information that is being omitted or distorted.

3. Avoid making immediate judgments. Keep each discussion as objective and as factual as possible. Do not give individuals the impression that there are certain things you want to hear, or they may become selective in what they tell you.

4. Ask your staff for their opinions to see how they would resolve a dilemma. Give them hypothetical situations and try to use them as resources to check the consequences of various courses of action.

5. Record all information or ask for it in writing from your sources. Make sure your group represents various points of view.

6. Neutralize the environment so that your respondents are able to relax. Let them know that you really care what they think. Minimize status differences.

7. Hold a brainstorming session if creative ideas are necessary.

8. Apply a proven problem-solving method to your information. After you have listened well, a decision still may be difficult to make.

If you were a manager interested in coaching employees, how would you encourage them to listen?

Coaching Your Employees. In today's organization, leaders have taken on yet another important responsibility—that of educating and training their employees through on-the-job coaching. Coaching is the ongoing process of assessing performance and providing constructive feedback for the purpose of clarifying standards and motivating change. Coaching develops greater individual competence by:

1. analyzing the reasons why unsatisfactory performance occurred;
2. engaging in face-to-face conversations to address the problem;
3. monitoring and supporting efforts toward performance goals;
4. providing constructive feedback.

In a coaching relationship, who has most responsibility for ensuring success—the manager or the employee?

Whether in educational settings or in work organizations, coaching is aimed at developing a specific individual's potential. In this regard, coaches begin by valuing the unique contributions and strengths of each organizational member. The effective coach creates a collaborative relationship in which the person who is being coached recognizes the importance of the desired outcomes and actively participates in the goal-setting process. Much of your effectiveness, as you know from reading in Chapter 8, depends on your ability to create a supportive communication climate in which your employee feels free to express her opinions and concerns (Box 9.7). Cultural differences may provide additional challenges as you identify opportunities for those with unique perspectives to enrich the organizational environment.

In sports, coaches develop players' skills and techniques; their success is based on how the team performs. In organizations of all types, your ultimate effectiveness depends upon your employees' performance. Consequently, your most essential task is to assess and support your employees so that they will know exactly how they are doing and where they need to improve. Think of it this way. The last thing you should do before firing an employee is to look in the mirror and say to yourself, "You know what? You failed."

The Skills of Listening as a Coach

1. Make sure the employee has enough lead time to prepare for the coaching session and to get her own ideas clear.
2. Consider the setting to make sure that all aspects of the listening environment encourage honest and open information sharing.
3. Listen for attitudes that may provide an explanation for more observable behaviors. Is the person performing poorly because she thinks the task is unimportant? Because she doesn't think anyone appreciates her efforts? Or because she doesn't get along well with a colleague and avoids asking him for the necessary information and support?
4. Allow the person to talk as much—or as little—as she needs to. Your role as listener will let her know that you are interested in her views and personal goals. Again, a supportive climate encourages problem solving; a defensive environment quickly becomes an arena in which the prize is saving face.
5. Manage the conversation, but make sure you listen more than you speak. Interrupt as little as possible.

■ ■ ■ ■ ■ ▬▬▬▬▬▬▬▬▬▬▬▬▬▬▬▬▬▬▬▬▬▬▬▬▬

BOX 9.7

DEVELOP A SUPPORTIVE COMMUNICATION CLIMATE

Defensive Approach	*Supportive Approach*
Blame centered	Problem centered
Attitude of certainty	Attitude of provisionalism
Indifference	Empathy
You Language	*I* language

Listening to Supervisors

Strategy: Listening to Supervisors	
H	Moderate
U	High
R	High
I	Moderate
E	Moderate
R	_____

Your supervisor decides how much responsibility to delegate based on her perceptions of your competence. If she believes that you are capable and trustworthy, your professional opportunities are likely to increase. You have good reason to pay attention to what your supervisor thinks and to develop a positive and professional relationship.

Remember that effective listeners not only learn new skills and move up the career ladder more quickly than their peers (Brownell, 1994b), they also learn how organizational members interpret various aspects of their environment. The additional advantage of having developed a greater number of shared meanings enables them to behave appropriately in a wide range of situations, from negotiating a business deal to entertaining an international guest to participating in noon hour workouts. If you are interested in advancing in your career, there is no more important skill to practice and develop than listening.

Certain types of listening situations are particularly common to the supervisor-employee role relationship; in each case, there is potential for misunderstandings to occur (Box 9.8). Perhaps the most troublesome context you will encounter as an employee is listening to directions and explanations. In organizations, the costs of ineffective listening can be high; misunderstandings account for millions of lost dollars annually. Through effective listening you can create an environment of trust and efficiency.

■ ■ ■ ■ ■ ▬▬▬▬▬▬▬▬▬▬

BOX 9.8

LISTENING TO YOUR SUPERVISOR

Problems are created by:

1. Filtering and distortion (individual's unique perceptions)
2. Hearing too much or too little information
3. Lack of skill in listening
4. Overreliance on oral communication for communicating details
5. Inappropriate timing of communication

The Skills of Listening to Supervisors: Following Directions

1. Pay attention to what your supervisor says. Relax, and try not to let your mind wander.
2. Ask questions and perception check as soon as you are uncertain or confused. Don't assume you will be able to make sense of the directions later.
3. Whenever possible, gather your questions together and ask them all at one time. Constant interruptions, even for legitimate questions, distract the other person and make both of you less efficient.
4. Take notes if appropriate.
5. Use your memory techniques. Practice whenever you get a chance so that you will notice progress within a few weeks. It takes at least twenty-one days to form any new habit, such as the effective application of long-term memory strategies.
6. Provide feedback to your supervisor; let her know that you listened.

Listening in Small Groups and Teams

Groups are one of the most valuable organizational resources. If used effectively

Strategy: Listening in Small Groups and Teams	
H	Moderate
U	High
R	Moderate
I	High
E	High
R	_____

and led by a skilled facilitator, a group is an indispensable managerial tool. Working effectively in groups is seldom easy. When individuals come together, particularly around emotion-laden topics, the group process often goes astray. Emphasis moves to the fulfillment of individual interests and agendas rather than the exploration of ideas. Conflicts may be managed poorly. The consequence is that the original group goals become lost or misdirected.

Hunt and Cusella (1983) report that individuals from the Fortune 500 companies they studied ranked "listening during meetings" the most problematic listening context. Performance appraisals ranked second and superior–subordinate communications third. When participants of another study group were asked,

> With regard to listening, what specific member behaviors have distinguished the high-performing groups that you have been in from the poorly performing ones?

"What is wrong with meetings?" their replies included (1) they're boring, (2) we get off the track, (3) the same few people do all the talking, (4) there's too much griping, (5) items drag on and on, (6) some people won't talk, and (7) the leader does all the talking. Only a skilled listener is able to recognize when a group strays from its task or when an individual is being blocked from expressing his ideas.

In addition, the complexities of diverse organizational environments create even more challenges for group leaders as they assess each person's potential contribution to the team. Attitudes and norms regarding group communication vary significantly from one culture to the next. Some individuals may look at problem-solving discussions as opportunities to brainstorm, but others will find it difficult to speak up unless their ideas are well formulated and reflect the thoughtful consideration of all options. Although some enjoy the social opportunities that teams provide, others are high-task, anxious to make decisions, and move on.

In addition to recognizing individual differences, group facilitators have responsibility for two separate but interrelated functions. They must focus on accomplishing the task at hand and, simultaneously, they need to address the relationship aspect of group communication. Task functions are those behaviors which help the group in its problem-solving activities. When the leader or other group members provide information, summarize, ask or give opinions, or clarify information, task functions are being performed. These functions are emergent; that is, if the designated group leader does not perform the necessary tasks, you must assume these functions to ensure that the group progresses smoothly. Team building, or relationship roles, include such behaviors as giving praise, compromising, or encouraging participation from all members. These functions promote positive attitudes and group cohesiveness and can be performed by any member. Only by listening carefully can you recognize appropriate opportunities to fulfill task and relationship functions.

In their theory of situational leadership, Hershey and Blanchard (1984) describe an effective leader as an effective listener—someone who listens to the group and determines its stage of development. From this information, the leader then knows the amount of direction (task-related behavior) or support (relationship-building behavior) to provide (Box 9.9). Groups in the earliest stage require a good deal of direction, while those going through stages 2 and 3 require increasing amounts of support. High-performing teams, those in the fourth stage of development, require almost no leader intervention.

With the globalization of business, there has been an increasing need for teams to accomplish their work with the aid of distance technologies. Computer-mediated communication (CMC) has become the norm in many large companies where tasks must be coordinated across cultural boundaries. One recent study (Walther, 1996) suggests that, although CMC fosters less personal interaction than unmediated communication, it may enhance the task-oriented functions of equalizing participation, coordinating, and so forth.

> In what ways do you personalize your on-line communications?

What is particularly interesting, however, is the notion that, over time, individuals using mediated communication begin to personalize this inherently impersonal medium. Longstanding partners report emotionally rewarding exchanges; they are driven to develop social relationships in spite of the lack of tradi-

BOX 9.9

BLANCHARD'S STAGES OF GROUP DEVELOPMENT

Stage 1 Orientation Leader Behavior: Directing (High Directive–Low Supportive)
Set realistic and attainable goals
Clarify tasks and relationships
Give feedback on performance and group dynamics

Stage 2 Dissatisfaction Leader Behavior: Coaching

Directive
Redefine goals and expectations
Provide vision
Facilitate interdependence

Supportive
Actively listen
Accept and understand differences

Build supportive relationships
Manage conflict

Stage 3 Resolution Leader Behavior: Supporting (Low Directive–High Supportive)
Involve group in setting goals and standards
Involve group in decision-making
Actively listen

Stage 4 Production Leader Behavior: Delegating (Low Directive–Low Supportive)
Share information
Link to the larger organization

tional nonverbal cues. In addition, researchers discovered that, in the absence of face-to-face cues, subtle cues such as word choice or the length of the message take on more than normal meaning (Olaniran, 1994; Spears & Lea, 1994). Communicators also are likely to engage in "overattribution"; that is, such things as misspellings or typographical errors will cause them to develop stereotypical impressions of their partners without recognizing that they are forming these opinions on very limited information. A similar study of interactive video found that, although the group task was accomplished as successfully using video as with face-to-face communication, member behaviors were perceived and interpreted very differently (Storck & Sproull, 1995).

While we will address the impact of technology on listening in Chapter 10, its specific application to group communication undoubtedly will continue to expand and evolve. This development should be of significance as you consider exactly what it means to "listen" in this new business environment, and as you prepare yourself to engage in new forms of interaction.

Although effective group leadership and process deserve more attention than is possible here, the listening skills most important to effective face-to-face group interaction merit your consideration and review. The ability to manage and motivate teams will become one of the key competencies that distinguishes future leaders.

The Skills of Listening to Facilitate Group Tasks

1. The amount of structure a group needs is dependent upon the members' skills, maturity, and degree of interest in the task. Listen to determine how much or how little control the group needs from you in order to achieve optimum results.
2. Listen for members who take off on tangents and distract their colleagues. Turn the discussion back to the topic at hand.
3. Listen for indications of what group participants need and behave accordingly. If at first the group flounders, step in. If the group is highly motivated and involved, you need to exert far less control.
4. Provide feedback to group members. Focus on the person's objective and help him get his point across to other members, whether or not you agree with him.
5. Help all group members by providing constructive feedback. Remember the essential characteristics of a nonthreatening response; it is descriptive not evaluative. Maintain a problem-solving orientation. Keep the focus on understanding the facts, ideas, and opinions presented, not on who's "right" and who's "wrong."
6. Ask probing questions that will stimulate both creative and critical thinking. Listen for what the individual does not say—draw him out. Ask participants to repeat their ideas if you don't believe everyone heard their response.
7. Don't interrupt unless you feel the person is interfering with the group's process.

The Skills of Listening to Facilitate Group Relationships

1. Encourage an attitude of acceptance and open-mindedness through your own responses to participants' contributions. Provide both nonverbal and verbal reinforcement; let the person know that you understand and acknowledge what he says whether you agree or not. Confirming responses appropriate for this situation include:

   - direct acknowledgment
   - agreement (when true)
   - supportive or reassuring response
   - clarifying response
   - expression of positive feelings about what was said

2. Notice when an individual does not participate. Draw him in by asking a general question with many possible answers.
3. Reduce status differences through position at the table.
4. Discourage individuals who are critical of other suggestions or who interrupt and ooververbalize. You may need to be assertive in such instances and say something like, "Your ideas have been helpful, but you are so quick to speak up that Mary and Jo haven't been able to share their views. I'd like to hear from them."

5. Allow yourself and others to be spontaneous in their contributions. The group needs some energy and excitement to perform optimally.
6. Encourage moderate and appropriate humor.
7. Stress teamwork. Encourage participants to think in terms of *we* rather than *I*. Provide meaningful group incentives and rewards.
8. Be patient, kind, and flexible, and recognize cultural differences that affect levels of participation.
9. Listen carefully to identify potential conflicts before they escalate. Remember, disagreement is healthy if handled constructively. Focus the discussion on ideas, not individual personalities.
10. Make sure that the meeting room is appropriate and encourages all individuals to participate in the group process. Chairs should be comfortable, and all participants must be able to see one another easily.

Listening to Rumor

A rumor is a message that is passed orally from one person to the next without "se-

Strategy: Listening to Rumor	
H	Moderate
U	High
R	Moderate
I	Moderate
E	High
R	_____

cure standards of evidence" present. Rumors are informal; that is, they are not part of the information organizational members intentionally communicate in meetings or memos. Rather, rumors flow through an organization's informal communication channels, moving from one person to the next according to friendships and social groups.

Rumors are often so ambiguous that those who pass them along must reconstruct some of the meaning and interpret the vague or ambiguous portions in a way that makes the most sense (Box 9.10). A rumor is usually temporary; it deals primarily with a situation that is difficult or impossible to verify. Initiators of rumors are generally not experts on the subject. An individual starts a rumor when there is a high demand for information that has not been received through formal or official channels (Brownell, 1993). Layoffs, promotions, dismissals, or any major organizational change are all likely to stimulate rumors as employees seek information on the subject.

> What symbolic functions (such as defining power and influence and establishing social networks) might rumors play in an organization?

BOX 9.10

PASS IT ALONG

Colonel communicates to Major: At 9 o'clock tomorrow, there will be an eclipse of the sun, something which does not occur every day. Get the men to fall out in the company street in their fatigues so that they will see this rare phenomenon, and I will then explain it to them. Now, in the case of rain, we will not be able to see anything, of course, so, then, take the men to the gym.

Major passes message to Captain: By order of the Colonel tomorrow at 9 o'clock, there will be an eclipse of the sun. If it rains, you will not be able to see it from the company street, so, then, in fatigues, the eclipse of the sun will take place in the gym, something which does not occur every day.

The Captain then said to the Lieutenant: By order of the Colonel in fatigues tomorrow at 9 o'clock in the morning, the inauguration of the eclipse of the sun will take place in the gym. The colonel will give the order if it should rain, something which does not occur every day.

The Lieutenant then told the Sergeant: Tomorrow at 9, the Colonel, in fatigues, will eclipse the sun in the gym, as it occurs every day if it's a nice day. If it rains, then, this occurs in the company street.

The Sergeant then instructed the Corporal: Tomorrow at 9, the eclipse of the Colonel in fatigues will take place because of the sun. If it rains in the gym, something which does not take place every day, you will fall out in the company street.

Finally, one Private said to another: Tomorrow, if it rains, it looks as if the sun will eclipse the colonel in the gym. It's a shame this does not occur every day.

Source: Reprinted with permission of Macmillan Publishing from *Understanding Communication in Business and the Professions* by Abne M. Eisenberg, Copyright 1978 by Abne M. Eisenberg.

Are rumors unavoidable?

Rumors are not necessarily false. In fact, most employees believe that there is at least some truth in the statement they are passing along. There are at least three changes that take place in the information as it moves from one person to the next (Allport & Postman, 1947):

1. *Leveling:* rumors tend to become shorter and more concise
2. *Sharpening:* a limited number of details are retained, due to each listener's selective perceptions
3. *Assimilation:* rumors become more internally consistent as people add their own elements in order to make better "sense" of the information

Rumors are unavoidable. If listeners are wise and use caution both in responding to and passing along information, rumors need not become a negative influence on a group or organization. Indeed, rumor may indicate that informal information channels are active and are efficiently linking together members in various parts of an organization.

When you receive information that has not been or cannot be verified, your most appropriate response is to recognize it as rumor and to apply your critical listening skills.

The Skills of Listening to Rumor

1. Determine whether the information is based on inference or on facts.
2. Determine the source of the information—where did the rumor originate?
3. Assess what motives might have inspired the rumor.
4. Determine the scope of the rumor. Does it affect one person, a department, or the entire organization?
5. Conduct, if necessary, a systematic search to uncover evidence that either will prove or disprove the critical elements in the rumor. You may bring it to the attention of those who might confirm or refute its validity.
6. Work with the grapevine, not against it. Share as much information as possible as early as possible. Ask those in a position to know if your information is accurate. Make sure key information sources have the story straight.

SUMMARY

Listening is prerequisite to the development and maintenance of healthy relationships whether at home, in school, or in the workplace. Effective listeners realize that each purpose and context requires a slightly different combination of skills, and adjust their listening behavior to the special needs of each situation they confront.

Although family members are often taken for granted, it is within this environment that your strongest relationships can be developed. Listening to a partner, a child, or an older family member requires a commitment of time and energy. Listening openly and nonjudgmentally is often most difficult when you are affected by your partner's opinions and attitudes. The home is one of the most neglected listening environments.

Listening in educational settings requires both the ability to listen in large lecture settings as well as the skills of listening to constructive feedback. Skills developed in listening comprehension are essential as you listen to understand the ideas presented in educational settings. Increasingly, however, one-on-one coaching situations are supplementing classroom instruction. Particularly in the workplace, lifelong learning opportunities are provided as supervisors coach employees on a regular basis. In this context, you have opportunities to practice and improve your assertive listening behavior.

The skills of empathic listening are particularly appropriate in helping situations where a friend or family member needs your support. You may also find yourself listening as a patient and using your listening skills to get the information you require from medical practitioners.

Finally, organizational environments provide a rich array of listening opportunities. Regardless of your specific role, you will find yourself listening in formal and informal communication settings. You listen to your supervisor and to your employees, to information through the grapevine, and in groups. The development of effective listening behaviors has a profound impact on all aspects of your work life.

APPLICATIONS

> Application 1: Listen to Members of Your Family
> Application 2: Listen in Educational Relationships and Presentations
> Application 3: Listen in Helping Relationships
> Application 4: Listen in Organizational Contexts

Application 1: Listen to Members of Your Family

The most important listening contexts are often the most neglected. It's easy to take family members for granted; yet, most families provide enduring and meaningful support for your growth and development. Listening in the family provides the foundation upon which other relationships are based. It offers a safe environment in which to share and learn.

Activities

1. What messages did you get from your family members about the importance of listening while you were growing up? What were your family's "norms" with regard to listening practices?

2. How much time do you spend listening to children? Seek out opportunities to listen to and interact with children. How can you help them to become better listeners?

3. How many opportunities do you have to listen to the elderly? If older family members are not living near you, there are many volunteer organizations that put you in touch with the elderly. Spend some time listening to people who may have a lot to offer, but who have few opportunities to share their experiences.

4. How often do you listen with patience and sincere concern to members of your family? The family is often the group in which children are the most egocentric. If you find that much of your communication is self-centered, deliberately take time to listen and pursue topics of interest to your parents, siblings, and other family members. Next time you are home with members of your family, talk with them about how they perceive one another's listening behavior.

5. Analyze your relationships with three of your family members according to Powell's levels of communication. Do you tend to disclose more or less than other members of your family? Under what circumstances do you disclose?

6. Look at the list below. Put a check in front of those topics you would discuss with almost anyone. Put an X in front of those you would discuss with family members. Do your results tell you anything about your relationships in your family?

_____a.   your hobbies, how you like to spend your time
_____b.   your favorite foods, your chief dislikes in food and beverages
_____c.   your preferences in music
_____d.   your educational background
_____e.   the places you have traveled, your reactions to those places
_____f.   aspects of your daily work that satisfy and bother you
_____g.   the educational and family background of your parents
_____h.   your personal views on politics, foreign and domestic policy
_____i.   your personal religious views
_____j.   your personal goals for the next five years
_____k.   your present financial position: income, debts, savings
_____l.   habits of yours which bother you a great deal
_____m.   characteristics of yourself in which you take pride
_____n.   your usual ways of dealing with depression, anxiety, setbacks
_____o.   the circumstances under which you become depressed, or are hurt
_____p.   the ways in which you feel you are unreasonable or immature
_____q.   the actions you have most regretted taking in your life
_____r.   what you regard as the mistakes your parents made in raising you
_____s.   the worries you experience in regard to your health
_____t.   the aspects of your body you are most pleased or displeased with

Count the number of check marks and Xs, and compare your score to the following scale.

Check marks:	0–15	= extremely low risk-taker
	6–10	= low risk-taker
	11–15	= moderate risk-taker
	over 15	= high risk-taker
"X" marks	over 9	= low risk-taker
	6–9	= moderate risk-taker
	0–5	= high risk-taker

What level of disclosure is required to answer each of the statements? Is level of disclosure the only factor that influences the degree of risk involved? Does the nature of the topic also determine what is appropriate to discuss? Support your position.

Group Activities

Form a small group of four to six people. You may want to keep the same group for all activities, or you may find it more interesting to change groups so that you get to hear the opinions and ideas of a greater number of your classmates.

1. Brainstorm ideas that would help any family develop a culture of listening. What rules, routines, or practices might encourage better listening? When all ideas have been presented, review each in turn and determine which ones have the most merit. Share them with the rest of the class.

2. Develop a list of obstacles that may interfere with effective listening in each of the following situations:

   a. Father listening to teenage son's summer plans
   b. Son listening to mother describe her upcoming hectic weekend
   c. Brother listening to sister's concerns about an important dance
   d. Mother listening to young daughter naming all of her stuffed animals

3. Identify a time when you were young that a family member's listening or not listening had a significant impact on you. Describe the situation to members of your group. Discuss the effects of listening on an individual's relationships, trust, and self-esteem.

4. Take turns going around to each member of your group. The first person gives a cliché, the next person states a fact, the third person gives an opinion, and the last person describes his feelings. Try, if you can, to relate all statements to the same topic. Keep going around the circle until everyone has had a chance to try all four types of statements. Check your group members to make sure each statement is correct.

5. What level of disclosure is appropriate for the following relationships? Identify each direction; in other words, the level a supervisor uses in talking with her subordinate may not be the same as the employee in talking with her supervisor.

   supervisor–subordinate
   parent–child
   student–teacher
   doctor–client
   husband-wife

   Are all relationships reciprocal? Under what circumstances would one party be likely to disclose at a different level? What are the implications for a relationship that is imbalanced in terms of level of disclosure?

Application 2: Listen in Educational Relationships and Presentations

As was emphasized in your reading, it is common to think of educational relationships as only those that take place in classroom environments. More and more often, however, work organizations are assuming a role in employees' continuing education. In establishing a learning environment, such strategies as coaching and mentoring are being used to personalize the educational process. As older workers change careers, it is even more important to think in terms of how lifelong learning is facilitated through educational relationships. The exercises below will make you more conscious of the variety of ways in which you learn.

Activities

1. What types of external and internal distractions do you notice most during classroom listening? What could you do to overcome some of these obstacles?

2. Rate yourself as a classroom listener on a scale of 1 (poor) to 5 (excellent). What are your listening strengths in the classroom? What elements of the situation motivate you to listen?

3. Choose the instructor you have most difficulty listening to and make a list of the things you believe most interfere with effective classroom listening. Examine each item and determine if it is something over which you have control. Are you prepared? Interested? Seated in the right place? Do you take notes? Make an action plan to reduce the distractions that interfere with effective listening in that class.

4. Have you belonged to an athletic team? What coaching skills did you find most effective? Do you have an academic mentor or coach? How can you apply the suggestions made for listening in the coaching relationship to your situation?

5. Select one of your lecture classes and work at behaving like a good listener. Maintain eye contact, nod, take notes when appropriate, practice various strategies to maintain attention. After the class period, reflect on your experience. Did you gain more than usual from the class? Are you tired? What factors prevent you from putting this much energy into the class during every session?

6. How do you respond when you are given negative feedback—when your instructor talks with you about problems you are having? Are you satisfied with your response? If not, what might you do to create a more collaborative relationship?

Group Activities

Form a small group of four to six people. You may want to keep the same group for all activities, or you may find it more interesting to change groups so that you get to hear the opinions and ideas of a greater number of your classmates.

1. Discuss the nature and quality of listening in this class. Is communication one-way? Two-way? Do you have any suggestions for ways in which your listening could be improved?

2. What changes could be made to ensure that students take more responsibility for their learning at your college or university? Brainstorm ideas and share them with other groups. Why do you suppose that the educational process operates the way it does— with teachers doing most of the talking and students doing most of the listening? What are the advantages and disadvantages? What are the costs and benefits of making changes in the system?

3. Take notes in class for several days. At the end of the designated period, compare the various sets of notes. What do the notes tell you about your listening behavior? How do your notes compare to those of your classmates?

4. Discuss the way in which the classroom environment affects your listening behavior. Where do you sit? What are the chairs like? What is the temperature? Are there windows? Summarize your perceptions, and then ask your instructor to respond to the same questions. Compare students' perspectives to your instructor's. Are there differences? As a team, prepare a list of changes that might be made to improve the classroom environment.

Application 3: Listen in Helping Relationships

It feels good to be able to help someone who needs support. Too often, listeners have good intentions but the nature of their response is inappropriate and does not contribute to helping their partner problem-solve or recover from an emotional trauma. By participating in the following activities, you will gain greater understanding of the nature of the helping relationship as you receive feedback on your empathic listening skills.

Activities

1. Often, personal style contributes to your effectiveness in empathic listening situations. What personal traits contribute to your effectiveness? Which ones work against your ability to listen openly to another person's concerns?

2. We have emphasized the importance of having a sincere interest in your partner's welfare in order to be effective in empathic listening situations. What would you do if someone you actively dislike came to talk with you about a personal problem and asked for your help? What experiences have you had where you were not personally interested in the problems that were being shared? What did you do? Would you handle it the same way again?

3. The next time you go to a doctor's, practice some of the suggestions for listening in the doctor–patient relationship. Note which strategies you applied and indicate how effective each was in giving you more control over your health care. What was your doctor's reaction to your behavior?

Group Activities

Read each passage below and the four possible responses that follow it. As you read, imagine a good friend is speaking to you. The same person is talking to you in each of these helping situations. In every case, you will be listening to someone with a problem.

Decide how likely you would be to make each of the four responses. Rank order the statements, assigning 4 points to your most probable response, 3 to the next most likely, then 2 points and 1 point to the responses you would be least likely to choose. The more points you assign to a statement, the more likely you would be to respond in that way.

a. I never know what's going on at work. My supervisor doesn't tell me how I'm doing, even when I ask. Every day I come in and try my best, but nothing happens. I never hear, "Good job!" or "Glad to see everything's in on time." I'd just like, for once, to be sure where I stand.

_____ 1. How would you like Joe to act?
_____ 2. You're upset by the lack of feedback Joe gives you.
_____ 3. Look, just tell him this thing's bothering you! He's a good guy, he'll understand.
_____ 4. You must be alienating him somehow.

b. I've been here at school almost a month, and do you know what? You're the only friend I have. It's not that I don't like the other students here. It's that I find it really hard to start conversations. Several people in my classes say hello, but I'd feel much better if someone would just stop for a few minutes and talk with me instead of always seeming in such a hurry all the time.

_____ 1. Why do you think it is that no one has gone out of their way to talk with you?
_____ 2. You're just shy, that's all.
_____ 3. Why don't you join some clubs or take a course? That's the way to meet people.
_____ 4. You feel isolated in this new environment.

c. This job has really got me down. I thought I'd be good at it, but little problems drive me crazy. I go home at night and can't seem to get them off my mind. None of my coworkers do their job as well as I know I could, and it kills me to stand around and watch them mess up. I sure need the money, but I'm thinking that quitting may be the only solution.

_____ 1. What do you think you'd like to do?
_____ 2. You really feel frustrated with your job right now.
_____ 3. What you need is a decent vacation so you can sort things out.
_____ 4. Hey, the buck stops with you. If your people aren't doing a good job, who's to blame?

d. There are just no rewards to working hard. I get in early—sometimes I even leave the dorm before anyone else is up. I go to the library and work steady until I can't see straight. Then I run around all day, going to classes, then back to the library. And for what?

_____ 1. It's something that comes with being a student. You have to get used to it.
_____ 2. Why don't you try working a 10-hour day. See what happens.
_____ 3. You feel unappreciated and overworked.
_____ 4. What would you like to change about your life?

e. I need more money, that's all there is to it. I used to think that material things didn't matter, that I could get by on almost nothing. Well, I've learned! It takes money for every single thing you need in the world. Those that have it survive. Those that don't, just don't make it.

_____ 1. It sounds like money has become very important to you.
_____ 2. You haven't got anything to complain about. You're much better off than a lot of people I know.
_____ 3. What would you do with more money.
_____ 4. I think you should reevaluate your position and needs.

Answer Key

a. 1. Question
2. Paraphrase
3. Advice
4. Evaluative/Judgmental

b. 1. Question
2. Evaluative/Judgmental
3. Advice
4. Paraphrase

c. 1. Question
    2. Paraphrase
    3. Advice
    4. Evaluative/Judgmental

d. 1. Evaluative/Judgmental
    2. Advice
    3. Paraphrase
    4. Question

e. 1. Paraphrase
    2. Evaluative/Judgmental
    3. Question
    4. Advice

Add up the number of points you assigned to each of the four different types of response-paraphrase, judgmental, advice, and question.

P = _____   E = _____   A = _____   Q = _____

Questions

Discuss your findings with other members of your group. How are your response styles similar or different?

Consider the following questions:

1. What types of response did you consistently make?
2. What effect would your particular response style have on a person who is having a problem?
3. How would you rate yourself as a listener in helping situations?

Application 4: Listen in Organizational Contexts

Organizational contexts provide numerous listening challenges. The elements of status, role relationships, personal agendas, and job responsibilities all contribute to creating a complex and often unpredictable environment. The better your listening skills are when you enter an organization, the more successful you will be in carrying out both task and relationship functions. It is helpful to give thought to the special listening behaviors each setting requires.

Activities

1. Identify a past job experience. Who in that organization was a good listener? What characteristics did this person demonstrate? What impact did their behavior have on you or on others?

2. What are some of the obstacles to effective listening that you've had to overcome in the places you've worked? In other words, why might you not listen as well as you'd like to when you're on the job? Use any job—part-time, volunteer, or other.

3. When you're working in a group, do other members listen to you? Pay attention to your behavior during the group activities in this class. Note instances where someone

listens well, and examples of poor listening. Keep a record and share your observations at an appropriate time.

4. Make a list of guidelines for when the following "channels" are most appropriate:

    ▪ Catching someone in person
    ▪ Calling a meeting
    ▪ Writing a memo
    ▪ Calling on the phone
    ▪ Sending electronic mail

    Discuss the advantages and disadvantages of each type of situation with regard to effective communication.

5. How have work organizations taken over the responsibility for educating employees? In addition to the traditional training and development function, what other ways do organizations educate employees? Talk with friends who work in large companies.

Group Activities

Form a small group of four to six people. You may want to keep the same group for all activities, or you may find it more interesting to change groups so that you get to hear the opinions and ideas of a greater number of your classmates.

1. Given what you know about the potential listening problems associated with each type of communication network, what practices would you recommend to improve listening effectiveness organization-wide?

    a. Upward
    b. Downward
    c. Horizontal
    d. Grapevine (informal)

2. Coaching Role-Plays
    Each of the following four scenarios is designed to allow you to put into practice what you have learned about listening in the coaching process from both the employee's and coach's perspectives. Each scenario presents an employee performance situation. The situation is first explained, then the perspectives of both the coach and the employee are provided.

    Based on the scenario, take turns playing the roles of manager and employee. You may want to first role-play a situation in which one or neither of the participants listens well. After discussing the problems that were created by ineffective listening, you can role-play a second time, demonstrating the principles of effective listening.

    Observers provide feedback to both participants using questions on the *Observer Checklist: Coaching Role-Plays* at the end of the scenarios. Observers, however, should feel free to add their own observations.

Scenario 1

Situation.   Linda Chou is a new receptionist at a busy downtown office. She started work only two weeks ago following a week of orientation. Lily Thomson is the office manager and personally supervised Linda's orientation and training. She was satisfied with Linda's performance during training, but has kept an eye on her, particularly during peak hours. For the past week, Lily has noticed that Linda sometimes hesitates to greet customers with a warm smile as she was asked to do. In fact, many times Linda doesn't even look at the customer when he comes up to her desk. In addition, she often speaks too softly and avoids dealing with the problems and questions that arise.

Manager's Perspective.   It has always been a company policy for the receptionist to greet customers with a warm smile and a friendly hello. Linda appears almost indifferent when customers enter. Therefore, Lily felt the need to coach Linda on this point. She believed that Linda's performance was probably a result of her adjustment to the working environment.

Employee's Perspective.   Linda was brought up in a traditional Asian family. She has always been taught that it is inappropriate for a lady to smile or to look directly at a man. Speaking too loudly is considered rude and inappropriate. Consequently, Linda feels uncomfortable greeting customers the way Lily suggested, particularly since she did not have to do so when she worked in a similar position in Hong Kong.

Scenario 2

Situation.   John Kelley is an assistant manager in the food and beverage department of a New York hotel. He has worked in the hotel for four years and has received good performance ratings from his supervisors. He often works late in the evenings and sometimes comes in on days off to finish urgent business.

Shawn Alexander is the food and beverage manager, and has taken John under his wing since he joined the department three months ago. He is aware of John's industriousness and is pleased with his performance. However, he noticed that John has been late in coming to work for the past two weeks, sometimes by as much as half an hour. Although John puts in more than his share of total hours each week, he also leaves early and without notice on a regular basis.

Manager's Perspective.   Shawn is extremely pleased with John's work performance. However, to be fair to the other punctual employees, he feels he has to talk to John about his tardiness. Strict guidelines have been set to govern when employees need to report to work. Shawn is also concerned that John may be getting too lax in his working attitude, which creates morale problems. When Shawn mentioned something to him one other time about his tardiness, John didn't take the comment seriously.

Employee's Perspective.   John has been under a great deal of stress lately to meet the deadline on several important projects. He has been bringing work home in order to be with his infant daughter, Kara, and staying up late to finish it. As a result, he has overslept several times in the past two weeks. In addition, his wife is taking late afternoon classes and on several occasions he has had to leave work in order to take care of Kara. He doesn't feel as if his work has suffered at all. In fact, he often feels like he does twice as much as his colleagues.

Scenario 3

Situation.   Jane White is an older, very opinionated clerk in the personnel department. She has been with the same publishing company for fifteen years. In line with the company's new policy of job enrichment, she is assigned a new duty—preparing the budget for the personnel department. Fred Puck, the human resource manager, was previously in charge of the budget. As a result, it is his responsibility to train Jane in her new task which may account for up to 30 percent of her job responsibility.

Manager's Perspective. Fred is an ardent supporter of the job-enrichment policy and welcomed the chance to teach his staff some managerial tasks and skills. He is therefore positive about the entire coaching process. In fact, he doesn't really see that coaching is all that big a deal. All he has to do is tell Jane a few things and she should be all set.

Employee's Perspective. Jane has worked in the company for over fifteen years and has extensive experience in other publishing companies. Over the years she has grown comfortable with her routine duties and has herself trained numerous employees. The idea of learning a new skill makes Jane feel very uncomfortable and defensive. Secretly, she is concerned that she might fail and embarrass herself in front of Fred who, although twenty years younger than she, is her supervisor.

Scenario 4

Situation. Kevin Pollack has worked for six months in sales and marketing. He has just delivered a presentation to approximately ten senior managers at the client's firm. While the managers discuss the presentation with their associates, Kevin speaks to his direct supervisor, Gertrude Stacks, who was with him. This is an important contract and Gertrude is worried.

Manager's Perspective. Gertrude has extensive experience in sales and marketing, having worked in three different companies over a seven-year period. She is especially skilled in giving presentations. She always imagined that Kevin had great potential in sales and marketing. However, she was not at all pleased with his recent performance and feels that his presentation skills need polishing. In her opinion, his fidgeting with a pen and random movements made him look nervous, and there was no question that he spoke too rapidly. Kevin also has a very informal style of delivery which, for important occasions like this one, Gertrude believes is inappropriate. Realizing how sensitive Kevin is about criticism, Gertrude approaches her task with some reservation.

Employee's Perspective. Kevin feels very confident about his presentation. Although he has delivered only a few in this job so far, he believes he is really a gifted speaker. In fact, his philosophy is that speaking comes naturally. Kevin is particularly pleased to think that he gets very personal with his listeners and establishes a close rapport with his clients. He is particularly proud of himself for taking on this tough group, and believes that there's no one else in the company who could do a better job.

Observer Checklist: Coaching Role-Plays

As Observer, check the functions that you hear the Manager and Employee performing in the role-play. Add additional items or comments as required.

1 = no, did not observe
2 = adequate
3 = yes, did a good job
4 = couldn't tell, can't say

Manager Behavior

_____ a. Did the manager create a supportive climate for coaching?
_____ b. Did the manager make the performance problem clear?
_____ c. Did the manager listen carefully to the employee?
_____ d. Did the manager collaboratively establish performance goals?
_____ e. Did the manager follow the rules of constructive feedback?
_____ f. Did the manager project a positive, caring attitude?

Employee Behavior

_____ a. Did the employee restate or otherwise clarify her understanding of pe-
formance expectations?
_____ b. Did the employee perception-check?
_____ c. Did the employee remain objective, not defensive?
_____ d. Did the employee participate in the goal-setting process?
_____ e. Did the employee demonstrate effective assertive skills?
_____ f. Did the employee project a positive, involved attitude?

Comment on the Manager's listening behavior:
Comment on the Employee's listening behavior:

3. Below are descriptions of listening situations that might arise in handling telephone calls. Determine the most appropriate way to respond to the caller, and role-play the situation. After each dialogue, discuss the effectiveness of your listening behavior and how it affected the outcome of the call.

Situation 1.   You work as a receptionist in a hospital. An older woman calls to find out where she should go for X-rays. She is hard of hearing, and you sense she will have difficulty following directions, but you must communicate the following:

- Park across the road, and make sure to bring your ticket into the hospital to get it stamped
- Come in through the main door, and turn left at the gift shop
- Take the elevator to the second floor
- Go down the hall and turn right at the second intersection
- X-ray is three doors down on the left
- Make sure to check in with the receptionist and get your parking card stamped

Situation 2.   A good friend from home calls you at work just to chat. You are very busy—right in the middle of a major accounting project—and you do not have the time to spend on the telephone. She is obviously in the mood to talk, and determined to "get your ear."

4. As a group, prepare in writing a set of instructions for someone to put on a coat. Assume this person knows nothing about coats—collar, lapel, lining, belt, pockets, buttons. Each group takes turns reading its directions to an individual who will follow them *exactly* as they are presented. The individual who is reading should have his back to the person performing. The speaker cannot add information that was not written down, and the listener can do only what he is instructed to do. Were the directions complete? What assumptions were made about what the listener "knew"?

5. As a group, create a short message (three or four sentences) that incorporates several words that sound the same or have similar meanings. When all groups have finished, begin the "rumor" by whispering it to a person in one of the other groups. (Be sure you have it written down!) That person, in turn, whispers it to the individual next to him and so on until everyone in that group has had a turn. Ask the last person to say what he heard out loud. Did the rumor survive? What changes, if any, occurred?

6. Discuss some of the rumors you have heard recently. How do they affect morale and interpersonal relations? How should you handle a rumor when you hear one?

7. Do you believe that good leaders are good listeners? Generate a list of four well-known leaders from any type of organization. How does each demonstrate effective listening?

8. You frequently hear that successful service organizations "listen" to their customers. Just what does that mean? In what ways would the following types of organizations demonstrate that they listen?

   - Hotels
   - Restaurants
   - Airlines
   - Insurance companies
   - Computer companies
   - Grocery stores

LISTENING IN GROUPS: SHORT CASES

Case 1.   You are the leader of a highly creative, committed project group. Unfortunately, two members, Sally and Jeff, consistently voice their opinions and reactions in ways that inhibit participation by other members. In fact, you feel certain that at least three of the other four members of the group would contribute many more ideas if they weren't so afraid of being openly criticized. It is particularly troublesome because both Sally and Jeff are bright, capable students whose opinions you value, but they certainly don't do any listening at all.

   You have joked casually about their behavior hoping that Sally or Jeff would get the hint, but so far nothing has happened. You are frustrated because it seems as if interest in the project and involvement among the members of your group is decreasing. You want to do a good job, but you don't know where to begin in your search for a solution.

   a. Clarify the problem as you see it.
   b. Role-play the situation as described. Discuss the instances of poor listening that are evident and the effect Sally and Jeff have on the group.
   c. As group leader, what would you do to create a more supportive climate?
   d. Role-play the situation a second time, putting some of your suggestions into practice. What was the result?

Case 2.   Your group has been working together all semester. Generally, members are motivated and sincerely concerned about doing a good job on their projects. The main problem you've had as the official group leader has been the strong emotional involvement members seem to feel about all the comments of other participants and about the decisions that are made. These emotional responses have made it particularly difficult for team members to be objective in their decision-making. Rather than viewing problems in perspective and exploring potential solutions, team members become defensive and upset whenever they think some change will affect their work, interfere with their personal plans, or give them more to do than other members. This focus on personal issues blocks listening and makes effective communication—and effective problem solving—almost impossible.

Recently, your group missed a deadline for the submission of a rough draft of the final paper. Rather than exploring the problem and its potential causes, members immediately began to blame each other. As group leader, you were frustrated by the constant accusations and defensiveness.

a. Clarify the problem as you understand it.
b. Role-play the situation as described. Discuss the instances of poor listening that are evident.
c. As group leader, what would you do to create a more supportive climate?
d. Role-play the situation a second time, putting some of your suggestions into practice. What was the result?

HOME FOR THE HOLIDAYS: CASE QUESTIONS

1. Identify two instances of ineffective listening demonstrated by Meg's mother. Role-play each example, illustrating the situation described in the case and then again, incorporating the strategies you would recommend Meg use to encourage more effective communication.

2. Role-play the dialogue between Meg and her mother when Meg enters her room and discovers it has been repainted and refurnished. How did Meg respond? How could she have encouraged her mother to listen to what she was feeling?

3. Was Meg's father really interested in what she was doing at school? Discuss the incident when he asked her to tell him more about what she was doing. Was he listening? What should Meg have done?

4. What listening problems were evident when Meg's grandfather communicated with members of the family? Did other family members respond in positive ways?

5. Discuss Meg's mother's interactions in terms of Transactional Analysis. How does this analysis help you understand her listening behavior?

6. How did Meg handle Tim's need for attention? Did she listen effectively? Did she respond appropriately? Why or why not?

7. Do you believe Meg was honest and open in her communication with her family? What factors affected her decisions about *what* to communicate?

8. How did different points of view and personal interests affect each family member's ability to listen effectively?

9. What overall strategies could Meg use to make her visits home more satisfying? Are the listening challenges described in the case inevitable, or can they be reduced? Develop a comprehensive plan that Meg could implement when she returns home for spring break. How could Meg improve her listening skills and attitudes?

BIBLIOGRAPHY

Allport, G. W., & Postman, L. (1947). *The psychology of rumor.* New York: Holt.

Arnold, W. E. (1991). Listening in the helping professions. In D. Borisoff and M. Purdy (Eds.), *Listening in Everyday Life: A Personal and Professional Approach,* pp. 264–283. Lanham, MD: University Press of America.

Barbour, J. (1981). Lines of communication. *The Evening Sun,* 37–38. (From Suzanne Fornaciaai, *How to talk to kids about drugs.* New York: Doubleday. p. B-1.)

Barker, L., Johnson, P., & Watson, K. (1991). The role of listening in managing interpersonal and group conflict. In D. Borisoff and M. Purdy (Eds.), *Listening in Everyday Life: A Personal and Professional Approach,* pp. 59–86. Lanham, MD: University Press of America.

Brownell, J. (1990). Perceptions of effective listeners: A management study. *Journal of Business Communication, 27*(4), 401–416.

Brownell, J. (1993). Communicating with credibility: The gender gap. *The Cornell Hotel & Restaurant Administration Quarterly, 34*(2), 51–61.

Brownell, J. (1994a). Relational listening: Fostering effective communication practices in diverse organizational environments. *Hospitality and Tourism Educator, 6*(4), 11–16.

Brownell, J. (1994b). Managerial listening and career development in the hospitality industry. *Journal of the International Listening Association, 8,* 31–49.

Brownell, J., & Jameson, D. (1996). Getting quality out on the street: A case of show tell. *Cornell Hotel & Restaurant Administration Quarterly, 37*(1), 28–33.

Bush, D. (1985). Gender and nonverbal expressiveness in patient recall of health information. *Journal of Applied Communication Research, 13*(2), 103–117.

Daniels, S., & Rubin, D. (1998). 'Virtual' courses are real dilemma. *ENR, 241*(18), 10.

Eisenberg, E. M., & Goodall, H. L., Jr. (1995). *Organizational communication: Balancing creativity and constraint.* New York: St. Martin's Press.

Geeting, B., & Geeting, C. (1976). *How to listen assertively.* San Francisco, CA: International Society for General Semantics.

Gordon, T. (1975). *P. E. T.: Parent effectiveness training.* New York: New American Library.

Hershey, P., & Blanchard, K. (1984). *Management of organizational behavior: Utilizing human resources.* Englewood Cliffs, NJ: Prentice Hall.

Hunt, G., & Cusella, L. (1983). A field study of listening needs in organizations. *Communication Education, 32*(4), 393–401.

Husband, R. L., Cooper, L. O., & Monsour, W. M. (1988). Factors underlying supervisor's perceptions of their own listening behavior. *Journal of the International Listening Association, 2,* 97–112.

Ley, P. (1983). Patient's understanding and recall in clinical communication failure. In D. Pendleton and J. Hasler (Eds.), *Doctor–Patient Communication,* pp. 89–97. London: Academic Press.

Lobdell, C. L., Sonoda, K. T., & Arnold, W. E. (1993). The influence of perceived supervisor listening behavior on employee commitment. *Journal of the International Listening Association, 7,* 92–110.

Olaniran, B. A. (1994). Group performance in computer-mediated and face-to-face communication media. *Management Communication Quarterly, 7,* 256–282.

Pedersen-Pietersen, L. (1999). Reworking education in a virtual schoolhouse, *New York Times, Late Edition,* (3), 13.

Phipps, T. C. (1993). Listen with your heart: Listening to people with disabilities. *Journal of the International Listening Association,* special issue, 8–16.

Powell, J. (1969). *Why am I afraid to tell you who I am?* Los Angeles: Argus Publishers.

Ray, E. B., & Bostrom, R. N. (1990). Listening to medical messages: The relationship of physician gender, patient gender, and seriousness of illness on short and long term recall. In R. N. Bostrom (Ed.), *Listening Behavior: Measurement & Application,* pp. 128–143. New York: The Guilford Press.

Rea, A., Hager, B., & Rooney, P. (1999). Communication and technology: Building bridges across the chasm. *Business Communication Quarterly, 62*(2), 92–96.

Rusk, T., & Gerner, R. (1972). A study of the process of emergency psychotherapy. *American Journal of Psychiatry, 128,* 882–886.

Seibert, J. H. (1990). Listening in the organizational context. In R. N. Bostrom (Ed.), *Listening Behavior: Measurement & Application,* pp. 118–127. New York: The Guilford Press.

Shugart, A. (2000). Is anyone listening? *Computer Technology Review, 20*(3), 6–11.

Spears, R., & Lea, M. (1994). Panacea or panopticon? The hidden power in computer-mediated communication. *Communication Research, 21*(1), 427–459.

Storck, J., & Sproull, L. (1995). Through a glass darkly: What do people learn in videoconferences? *Human Communication Research, 22*(2), 197.

Sypher, B. D., Bostrom, R. N., & Seibert, J. H. (1989). Listening, communication abilities, and success at work. *The Journal of Business Communication, 26*(4), 293–303.

Walther, J. (1996). Computer-mediated communication: Impersonal, interpersonal, and hyperpersonal interaction. *Communication Research. 23*(1), 3–11.

Wheless, B. (1998). Is anybody listening? *Business and Economic Review, 44*(2), 9–12.

Wolff, F. I., & Marsnik, N. C. (1992). *Perceptive listening.* Fort Worth, TX: Harcourt, Brace, Jovanovich.

Wolvin, A., & Coakley, C. W. (1991). Listening in the educational environment. In D. Borisoff and M. Purdy (Eds.), *Listening in Everyday Life: A Personal and Professional Approach,* pp. 162–200. Lanham, MD: University Press of America.

Zimmerman, R., & Arnold, W. E. (1990). Physicians' and patients' perceptions of actual versus ideal physician communications & listening behaviors. *Journal of the International Listening Association, 4,* 143–164.

CHAPTER 10

LISTENING CHALLENGES

There is no worse lie than the truth misunderstood.
—WILLIAM JAMES

OUTLINE

CHAPTER OBJECTIVES

After completing this chapter, you will:

Become more aware of:
- the challenge of listening to the media
- the challenge of listening in high-technology environments
- the challenge of listening globally
- the challenge of listening across gender
- the challenge of ethical listening

Better understand:

- the influence listening to the media has on individuals
- the ways in which computers and other technology affect listening and relationships
- cultural differences and their impact on listening
- gender-linked differences in verbal and nonverbal communication
- gender-linked stereotypes and their consequences
- the ethical responsibilities of listeners

Develop skills in:

- analyzing the impact of mediated messages
- analyzing the impact of technology on relationships and decision-making
- applying third culture concepts
- cognitive, behavioral, and perceived empathy when listening across cultures
- recognizing and reducing gender stereotypes
- effective cross-gender communication
- ethical listening

CASE: GENDER AND COMMUNICATION AT THE FORTUNE

The Fortune Hotel, one of several well-established, small but exclusive properties in Chicago, has a long tradition of quality and service. Fortune's culture is strong; over forty percent of its salaried employees have been with the organization for more than ten years. Jordi Secall, general manager, has made several significant changes. One of the most striking was to hire two women managers, Sylvia Thorz and Brigitte Westbrook. In doing so, the Fortune's long-standing tradition of an all-male management team was permanently disrupted.

Sylvia, the Food and Beverage Manager, was soft-spoken and somewhat shy; yet, she had proven to be a very capable manager. Brigitte was hired as Assistant Manager of Marketing for Fortune, having earned an MBA from Dartmouth and having spent two years at Lever Brothers, Inc., in their Marketing Department. She had a reputation as a troublemaker and "bitch." Her behavior seemed to strengthen the opinion both her male and female colleagues shared; women make excellent employees in housekeeping or on the waitstaff, but keep them out of upper-level management.

One of the strongest aspects of Fortune's culture was its Tuesday morning meetings. As the nine-member management team convened, the sound of jokes and good-natured bantering could be heard down the hall. "Hey, Steve," Jeff Car, the reservations manager, said as he grabbed the arm of the Fortune's new director of finance. "Listen to this." As Jeff turned around he saw Sylvia taking a seat across the room. "Well, maybe I'd better wait on that one. We don't want to offend any of our colleagues—right Sylvia?" The two men laughed as they went back to the table. Sylvia caught Brigitte's eye and she shook her head. She could tell it was going to be one of those days, and began fidgeting with her bracelet.

"You have met the better-looking members of our team, haven't you?" Jeff said as he motioned to the women at the table. "Yes," Steve nodded. "I've had the pleasure." "Well, we'll fill you in on what really goes on around here when we hit the 19th hole next Saturday! These girls may look. . . ." Jeff was stopped abruptly by the loud thump of Jordi's hand hitting the table as he brought the group to order.

The meeting was a long one, as usual, drawn out by discussions that wandered from the main issue and by the fact that Jordi, although a solid businessperson, was not a particularly good discussion leader. After over an hour of reports and various debates, Jordi pushed back his chair.

"All right gentlemen," Jordi began. "I know this has been long, but I think we've about come to the end." He looked down at his agenda. "Hold it," he said with emphasis, "I almost forgot. We've got one last agenda item. It's a problem that Sylvia is having with several of her employees. Sylvia, why don't you explain your problem to the rest of us?"

Sylvia could feel herself becoming angry, not only at the way Jordi was presenting her situation to the rest of the management team, but also because both times in the past when she had proposed a discussion topic, it had been put at the very end of Jordi's agenda. In spite of her anger, she took a deep breath, smiled, and began.

"You all know Karen Duncan, one of our most loyal employees. She came in to talk with me last week about a concern she has with the way our guests have been treating the barmaids. Ever since the staff began wearing, ah, those new uniforms, verbal abuse—which they always had to put up with to some extent—has drastically increased. They're just, ah, I don't think they're appropriate. Last week a guest, um, actually pulled Mary Sanders onto his lap and wouldn't let her up. I guess she was really frightened and refused to work the late night shift again."

"Anyway, the employees, well, the employees attribute some of the problem to their new uniforms. They think the short, low-cut uniforms invite suggestive comments and more aggressive behavior. And, well," Sylvia looked down at the table but continued, "Karen even suggested that, um, a couple of the F & B assistant managers were giving the women a hard time. So," she rushed on, "I've been asked to discuss this with you and, um, see if we can't propose some action plan."

"I wish I had problems like that," Jeff commented. "All those cute girls down at the bar won't have anything to do with me—heaven knows I've tried!"

"Okay, okay, guys," Jordi said as he raised his hand to quiet the group. "Sylvia needs help, and the least we can do is make some suggestions."

"If you want my opinion," Tony said as he leaned back in his chair, "it's the way the girls act toward the guests, not the uniforms. If they want to be treated like

professionals, they need to act like professionals. I've seen them strutting around down there in the bar myself. What do they expect? They're dealing with men who are away from home, who have been working hard all day. Those barmaids are just what the doctor ordered."

"In fact," Tony continued, leaning forward in his chair, "Remember Marge? Well, she was one of our best barmaids. Used to sit on the table and laugh at all the bad jokes. When her customers were ready to leave, she'd give them this pink note that said, 'Hurry back now.' She knew how to increase business."

Brigitte had been silent, listening to the conversation. She could see that Sylvia was about to cry—or leave the room—and wondered what she could say that would help. She raised her hand. Jordi seemed to look past her as he took suggestions from two more managers. Finally Brigitte had had enough. "Jordi," she said with irritation, "I know you don't care what I think, but I've been trying to present my opinion and I wondered if you could be quiet and listen."

"Right on, Brigitte," Mark said with a grin. "Go for it."

"You men are so insensitive," Brigitte replied indignantly. "What is the matter with you? Sylvia has brought up a legitimate problem and you guys just think it's funny. What does it take to get your serious attention?"

"More coffee!" Tony said as he stood up. "And more time. I think we've had enough for one meeting. Tell you what, Sylvia. I'll sleep on it (there were a few isolated chuckles from the group) and let you know what I think next week."

Others quickly agreed that the meeting had gone on too long already, and Jordi offered no resistance. "Fine," Jordi said in closing. "See you next Tuesday."

Sylvia and Brigitte walked out of the room together. Although they had seemed anxious to adjourn, most of the others stood around and shared reactions to the recent Lakers versus Knicks game. The women wondered if they would always be made to feel as if they were the "new kids on the block." "Guess the old boys are enjoying themselves," Brigitte remarked. Both women knew well that, in addition to informal sessions at work, the Fortune tradition was golf on Saturdays, bowling Thursday nights, racquetball during noon hours—there was a whole world from which they were excluded.

Upset by the events of the meeting and annoyed to discover that no one was really in any hurry to get back to work, Sylvia and Brigitte headed for Brigitte's office so they could talk in private.

THE CHALLENGE OF LISTENING TO THE MEDIA

It's likely that you or your friends have, at one point in your lives, spent a considerable amount of time listening to the media. Whether you choose it or not, the media is such a pervasive influence in most western cultures that it's important to think seriously about

> How does it make you feel to know that everyone in the world might be watching the same event simultaneously?

how it affects your listening. In fact, in some instances the media may be listening to you. Electronic billboards can now monitor radiation leakage from your car antenna (Emling, 2003; Barrios, 2003). This information is then used to determine which radio station you are listening to so that billboards might target their advertisements to the most popular stations' demographic.

When electronic media were first introduced on a widespread basis, theorists like McLuhan (1964) spoke of a new global village, of individuals from different parts of the world unified through a common, shared experience—participation in a media event. He further proposed that the media had an impact on other dimensions of human communication, particularly on information processing. The change from print (cold) media to the television (hot) medium was a transition from rational, private, and analytical modes of handling information to a stimulus that demanded immediate involvement and attention. Americans went from linear processing to a more holistic engagement with the electronic medium (Cerulo, Ruane, & Chavko, 1992; Willey, 1998).

Television and its impact on individuals and culture has fascinated, and worried, the U.S. public for almost half a century. Does programming influence attitudes and behavior? Are children predisposed to more violent, aggressive acts after viewing cartoon characters handling disagreements by clubbing their enemies on the head or pushing them over a waterfall? Do young people learn what life is like vicariously, through the screen in their living room?

> Do you believe that TV programming reflects culture or shapes culture?

We do know that TV can be watched mindlessly. Since viewers depend on cognitive schema to understand situations and events, the mental processing needed to make sense of television plots, which rely on stereotypical situations, becomes almost automatic. There is little demand for thinking or problem-solving; the majority of television listening has a very minor evaluative component.

While predictable schema make following media plots a simple matter, researchers have also suggested that children develop many of their schema from television viewing. They argue that a young person's only knowledge of many situations and relationships is gained through their media exposure. What does an urban child know of jungles, Native Americans, or spaceships? Because it may be a child's only source of information on a wide range of topics, television influences and reinforces notions about what the world is like and how to handle conflicts, solve problems, or act in a wide range of situations. For the thousands who watch over thirty hours of television each week, it may be their primary means of socialization, shaping their perceptions of the world they cannot experience firsthand.

> What schema have you developed from watching TV?

Many television shows also make use of music to create an auditory "set" that influences how other visual images are perceived (Shatzer, 1990). Variables such as tempo, rhythm, and harmony influence your affective response; music not only affects your mood, but your attitude as well. Studies conducted with various types of background music found that fast and appealing music resulted in greater exposure to programming (Liu, 1976; Wakshlag, Reitz, & Zillmann, 1982).

The passive manner in which people view television makes it possible to engage in a variety of other activities while partially attending to the television screen. Israel and Robinson (1972), for instance, found that people frequently do housework, eat, study, and talk while in front of the television. Their attention, scholars discovered, is primarily auditory rather than visual. In fact, after years of research, no conclusive evidence exists to support the contention that your comprehension improves if you receive both visual and verbal stimuli simultaneously (Bostrom & Searle, 1990).

If we turn to radio listening, you might agree that it, too, has increasingly become a solitary venture, carried on while the listener is engaged in other activities. You are most likely to listen to the radio in the car, or through earphones when jogging or studying. The NOLAD concept, which stands for nonlistening attention demand, accurately describes much of radio listening.

To counter the NOLAD effect, disc jockeys strive to project their personalities so that you will feel involved, comfortable, and responsive. Frequently, you have opportunities to interact with these media hosts through call-in and talk shows. You can win prizes, have your birthday announced, and ask questions on selected discussion topics. Even radio drama has been revived in some locations, providing opportunities for you to use your imagination as did people in the 1940s and 1950s when shows like "The Lone Ranger" and "The Shadow" captured listeners' imaginations in the United States.

Television and radio news are also powerful arenas. To a large extent, the U.S. media serve as a cognitive filter for millions of people. In selecting news stories and video coverage, television reporters have tremendous influence over the public's impression of what is important. Clearly, no coverage can be completely objective; your impressions of what is important to know and how you should think about what happened are shaped by the media. Newscasters have already filtered and interpreted events before bringing them to you. With little opportunity to discover the original source, the public is often left wondering how closely the media presentation matches the real event, and how many key ideas, however dull, were left on the editing room floor.

> If the media serves as a gatekeeper of information, do you think it helps to bring people from different cultures together or to keep them apart?

The potential impact of the electronic media has led educators to advocate developing receivership skills, the knowledge and awareness that enables you to effectively analyze media messages.

Suggestions for Listening to the Media

Is mindless listening such a bad thing? It would not be difficult for you to argue that the media serves a useful function by providing programming that doesn't require your undivided attention, that provides an opportunity for you to relax as well as to learn or to be entertained. Effective media listeners, however, are aware of the potential influence of the media and make conscious decisions about their media use.

Because media listening is often so enjoyable, it is easy to forget that not all media listening is for entertainment. Problems arise when the distinction between entertainment and education is blurred. Perhaps the best example is the television news, where it is clear that visual stimulation as well as social significance is a criterion for prime-time airing. How interesting would it be for you to hear legislators discussing a vital financial issue? Compare watching eight men in grey suits sitting around a table with scenes from a fire, from a protest march, or from a war zone.

In addition to providing appreciative listening opportunities, then, the media also requires you to be alert for occasions when critical listening skills may be equally as appropriate. Especially when young people are involved, you might take a more active role in assessing the listening experience.

For example, if you have been watching a situation comedy with your niece, encourage her to discuss her perceptions with you. Ask for the child's opinions about the events that took place, about how characters were feeling, about how they approached problem-solving and how they responded to various situations. Perhaps the show was about a 12-year-old whose mother won't let her go to a skating party. You might ask such questions as: Why did Sally's mother refuse to let her go skating with her friends? Why did Sally talk back to her mother? Was that a good way to handle her frustration? What would you have done if you were Sally? Remember, children learn and mimic responses they are exposed to in the media. Socialization through the media may not always be desirable, but you can turn these listening experiences into opportunities to educate if you are alert to the ways in which schemas are developed and reinforced.

Consider, too, how television watching influences your relationships and your lifestyle. What would you be doing during those times that you are watching television? What activities are scheduled in relationship to particular programs? At home, how does television viewing affect the interaction among family members? At school, how does it affect when you eat or study? Some theorists have even suggested that the traditional functions of family and friends are now being performed by media (Walther, 1996; Willey, 1998).

The power of the media on listeners is both direct and indirect. Skilled listeners are aware of the ways in which television and radio may potentially influence patterns of thinking and behaving, and respond in appropriate ways to what they hear.

THE CHALLENGE OF LISTENING IN HIGH-TECHNOLOGY ENVIRONMENTS

Technology has become not only pervasive but also essential to our daily routines. A recent survey by Auvi Technologies, for instance, found that most summer vacationers between the ages of twenty-two and thirty-two were more likely to pack an

MP3 player than aspirin or other pain relievers (Brady, 2004). The rapid developments in information technology not only make life more pleasurable but continue to redefine the process of communication itself. This new environment is interactive, asynchronous, and rapid. Participants have a high degree of control over the communication process, and those who use the system determine its content. No longer a linear model, technology—like the Internet—makes it possible to send messages simultaneously, to transmit to any number of receivers, and to access, delete, forward, or save information at will (Hills, 1992; Louhils-Salminen, 1999; Hulnick, 2000).

Human communication relies on your ability to select information from a large field of options and interpret it in many different ways. As you know, the meaning of a message shifts depending upon your perceptual filters and interpretations; nonverbal communication also plays a vital role in establishing meaning (O'Connell, 1988). Contrast this largely subjective process with high-technology environments where information is explicit and predictable and where digital language leaves no room for perceptual differences.

> In what ways are machines *better* listeners than humans? Under what circumstances would you rather listen to a machine than a person?

Voice itself is now produced through technology as computers translate data into sounds with variations in pitch, rhythm, and volume (Roush, 2003). Voice-activated software allows users to speak into a computer and to receive a vocal response. These and similar technological advances have created new forms of listening. Marketers, for instance, are using interactive voice-to-voice call centers for remote real-time contact (Ruyter & Wetzels, 2000).

Beyond differences in the nature and characteristics of messages is the power of technology to deliver vast quantities of information worldwide. As we have repeatedly emphasized, the impact of the knowledge economy cannot be underestimated. In a recent book, Tapscott, Ticoll, and Lowy (2000) discuss how the Internet has connected customers, suppliers, and the work force in ways that dramatically change traditional roles. They emphasize that in this new knowledge-based economy attention is the most valuable commodity. When bombarded with unrelated messages, how do you know what is important? How do you know what information to trust?

> Do you think the pace of the information explosion will continue to increase? What are the probable consequences with regard to communication effectiveness?

The sheer volume of data now available through some form of technology makes listening stressful. Your range of choices increases as data is gathered from all parts of the world and transmitted to your home or office. Human wisdom and insight is increasingly difficult to achieve or even recognize. A number of theorists warn that the "human factors gap," the difference between the information processing capacities of humans and the machines they create, results in negative consequences. Exposure to the sheer volume of information, much of which cannot be processed, serves to reduce an individual's listening effectiveness. There is no question that technology has an impact not only on the volume of messages received but on human relationships as well. When your interaction is with a terminal, you can't see your partner's posture or hear the anxiety in her voice. This affective dimension, as you know, is essential to developing trust and creating shared meanings. Messages regarding feelings and values decrease or disappear in high technology environments. A note left in a computer file cannot compare to casual conversation over coffee. Yet, a number of researchers suggest that interpersonal dimensions have not disappeared, it's just that the very means through which they are developed and maintained has changed dramatically (Storck & Sproull, 1995). One of the more radical thoughts is that we are actually bonding to machines as technology becomes the medium through which you and your friends accumulate experience, increase knowledge, and continue human contacts (Brown, 2002).

How does technology affect your personal relationships? How do you make judgments regarding the ethical nature of electronic messages?

Even group dynamics are radically altered by the introduction of technology for group discussion and decision making (Willey, 1998). Participants "hear" messages that are no longer connected to specific sources; status and personality variables are obscured as participants consider the validity and value of responses that appear anonymously on their computer screens. Although some individuals begin to "speak" more loudly when they cannot be identified, the way in which their ideas and feelings are heard is qualitatively different from the way they are perceived in face-to-face encounters. The trade-offs apparent in a mediated environment are clear; messages become less personal as communicators express their views more directly and more rapidly.

In spite of much controversy, there remain many researchers who believe that the technological transformation of the workplace will lead to a higher value being placed on interpersonal skills, trust, and relationships (Walther, 1996), and many agree that there will always be an important qualitative difference between being "plugged in" and actually connecting (Gunn, 2003, p. 13). As Hulnick (2000) suggests, while technology has made it possible for you to do business on the other side of the globe with individuals that you may never meet, the key point is that "people do business, not machines" (p. 33). Clearly, those who are prepared for the changes technology brings will enjoy a tremendous advantage in navigating tomorrow's workplace.

Perhaps the most profound impact of technology on human relationships and human development is its ability to create a truly global community. Distance technologies applied to education bring students or businesspeople together in real-time, interactive contexts—from anywhere in the world (Trevino & Webster, 1992; Walther, 1996). Web-based relationship management is truly global, linking persons from any neighborhood at any time. As our use of technology becomes increasingly pervasive and sophisticated, its implications for globalization and cross-cultural "listening" become one of the most significant realities of the twenty-first century.

Suggestions for Listening in High-Technology Environments

Technology is here to stay; developing the attitudes and skills needed to use the medium effectively is time well spent. Your first task may be to put technology into perspective and to resist the tendency to allow the keyboard to replace the majority of your human interactions. Continuously ask yourself if interfacing with your computer is replacing, rather than supplementing, face-to-face time with your colleagues and friends.

Respect technology for what it can do, but recognize its limitations. When you hear that a colleague's grandfather passed away, it's easy to e-mail a quick note of condolence. How does the impact of the electronic message compare with stopping by your co-worker's office to share your sympathy?

You may also feel overwhelmed by the amount of information available on line. Listening to hundreds of different voices from various sources can be a difficult and stressful task. Realize that you cannot do justice to every message. Remember, again, that just because someone speaks doesn't mean you are obligated to listen. Yet, be careful not to be overly selective. Your tendency may be to consider only those messages from the people you trust, or those whom you find easiest to understand. To be fair and objective, you need to expose yourself to a variety of viewpoints and to strive not for the easiest, but for the best, solution.

THE CHALLENGE OF GLOBAL LISTENING

"Listening enables individuals to span the gulfs in understanding and viewpoint among different groups. The speaker can try hard to reach out to listeners and speak their language, but listeners can also work at expanding themselves, and going out toward the speaker . . ." (Purdy, 1991, p. 63).

To some extent, all interactions involve cross-cultural communication since no two people share the same background and past experiences that shape their perceptions and values. Dodd (1987) suggests that listening is appropriately identified as cross-cultural when communication outcomes are clearly influenced by cultural differences. Recall the Sapir–Whorf hypothesis, which holds that language and thought are intimately interrelated. While the language you use influences the way you frame or think about your

> How will globalization influence our thinking about and definitions of cross-cultural listening?

experiences, the events and ideas that are valued in your culture are reflected in the vocabulary and structure of the language. Whenever communicators' native languages vary, therefore, complications are almost certain to arise in communicating and understanding intended meanings.

Among the many dimensions of culture that affect your listening, the following are perhaps most apparent:

- values and beliefs
- nonverbal systems
- behavioral norms

Value differences affect listening at the most fundamental level. One important value difference to keep in mind is that, whereas many people in the United States are speaker centered, listening is valued over speaking in several other cultures. While the majority of the U.S. population views listening as a passive activity, individuals in other cultures have grown up viewing the listening role as active and involving. In some Eastern cultures, nature and many physical objects are personified so that one listens to the mountains, the flowers, the snow, as well as to human speakers.

> What are the communication implications for a culture that is speaker-centered versus a culture that is listening-centered?

Cultural value differences have a profound impact on what is important to each person and, subsequently, on what he hears and how that information is interpreted. There are significant cultural differences in the value cultures place on the importance and nature of work, social events, formal education, and many other activities (Box 10.1). While people in the United States tend to believe that they are in control of their affairs, members of other cultures explain many more events in terms of fate. These biases affect decision making and other key processes, making shared understanding and negotiation problematic.

As you know, nonverbal systems and behavioral norms are learned and vary, sometimes dramatically, from one culture to the next. When two communicators share a good deal of knowledge and experience, it is often unnecessary for them to express their ideas fully and explicitly. These interactions, as you may recall from

---

BOX 10.1

CULTURAL DIFFERENCES IN VALUES

United States Values	*Values of Other Cultures*
Personal contol	Fate
Change	Tradition and stability
Action, proactive	Being, peace
Informality	Formality
Materialism	Spiritualism

Chapter 6, have been termed highly contexted. For example, you might sigh heavily as you say to your housemate, "Guess I'll go to Mann and hit the books tonight." Knowing that you have an exam in Asian studies, recalling that you didn't do particularly well on the last quiz, knowing that Mann is a library, understanding that "hit the books" meant to study, and recognizing your frustration from the tone of your voice, she would be able to put your message into a fairly rich context to derive its full meaning.

In other situations, where listeners have few shared experiences from which to draw in interpreting messages, communication is low context; in other words, little information is provided by the context and so communicators must be explicit. Repeating the situation above, your meaning might only be clear in a low context situation if you said something like, "I haven't been doing well in Asian studies and I have an exam tomorrow. I'm feeling nervous about it so I'm going down to the library to do some studying tonight."

Recall that cultures themselves can be classified into either high or low context depending upon the extent to which cultural norms prompt individuals to be explicit or indirect in their communications. In low context cultures, like the German and Scandinavian, individuals provide a large number of explicit indicators by which to determine meaning. In high context cultures, members see such elaboration as a waste of time and depend heavily on individuals' shared experiences to interpret cues in a similar fashion. Examples of high context cultures include Asian, Arabic, and Latin American. An outsider, as you can imagine, has greatest difficulty when communication indicators are not only foreign but also implicit. The more aware you are of culture-related differences, the better able you will be to respond in ways that encourage understanding and goodwill.

In addition to skills in listening comprehension, empathy is also required for effective cross-cultural communication. Our earlier focus on the production or co-creation of meanings is particularly relevant when we consider its implications for creating empathy in diverse environments. We have always assumed that empathy was facilitated by similarities between communicators and hindered or blocked by major differences in values, attitudes, and beliefs. Those with similar backgrounds, what we refer to as having a high

> Is it possible to have empathy with someone when you do not share any common experiences?

degree of homophile, are thought to have much greater potential for empathic communication than those whose world views are different. Obviously, the more similar your experiences, the *easier* it is for you to empathize with someone (Figure 10.1).

Our relational view of communication provides a framework within which to understand how individuals with very dissimilar backgrounds can engage in meaningful, satisfying interactions. This framework has been called the third culture concept. The approach suggests that similarities between you and your partner are not essential in order for you to empathize with one another. What is required is a great deal of effort and the willingness to create a third dimension, a unique view somewhat different from that held by either of you (Brownell, 1994). When effective, partici-

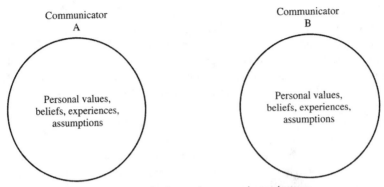

Without common backgrounds, communicators have no
shared experience and no common understandings

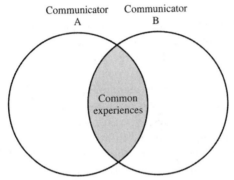

Communication is effective to the extent that
communicators' backgrounds overlap

FIGURE 10.1

pants in the encounter do not "exchange" or "transmit" messages, but rather co-create meanings through the negotiation of their separate understandings (Figure 10.2).

> What does it mean to you when you hear people comment that success and survival in the future will require effective "knowledge management"?

When we move our lens to a more macro level, the concept of cross-cultural communication—individuals from one culture sharing meanings with individuals from another culture—is dwarfed by the impact of technology and the subsequent globalization that it has facilitated. As discussed in the previous section, our ability to increase the reach of information worldwide has changed the very nature and scope of communication activity. Rather than taking place in restaurants and living rooms, communication among nations occurs on line. Videoconferencing brings experts from throughout the world into the class-

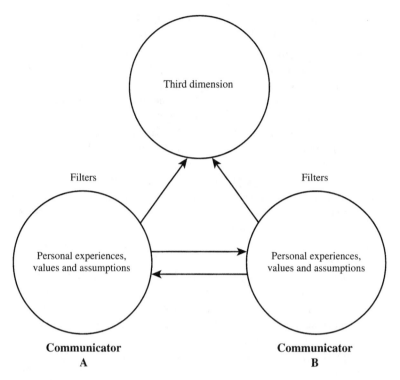

FIGURE 10.2   Creating a Third Dimension

room; interactive, Web-based communication serves as a powerful means of creating and sharing information among individuals separated by millions of miles.

Where will it lead? No one knows for sure. What we do know is that the future will require rethinking the ways in which we "do business," both individually and collectively. When the world is all about managing information, the skills of listening—attending to the right messages, paying attention to context as well as content, critically evaluating information, and making an informed response—will be a strong competitive advantage (Geddie, 1999; Stringer & Lusardo, 2001).

Suggestions for Effective Global Listening

Nishida (1985) proposes that the most effective cross-cultural listeners have a high tolerance for ambiguity. They can see many points of view, and remain open-minded when confronted with information that contradicts their previously held beliefs. In fact, each of the principles of clear thinking discussed in Chapter 8 is particularly relevant to cross-cultural listening contexts.

Not only do vocabulary and thought processes differ among cultures, not all languages include the same kinds of sounds. Some are characterized by clicks and whistles. At its most basic level, cross-cultural listening requires concentration and focus as you become more familiar with the speech patterns of an unfamiliar language. In these instances, discriminative listening is particularly important. Listening in cross-cultural contexts takes greater attention and concentration than it does when interacting with members of your own language community.

Effective cross-cultural listeners recognize differences in nonverbal systems and do not make assumptions about what various behaviors mean. In other words, apply the rules of low context cultures to be sure that your interpretations are accurate. If someone is late for a meeting, it may be that her perceptions of time are different from yours and that she had no intention of appearing rude or causing hard feelings. If a classmate stands so close that you feel uncomfortable, it's likely because his perception of appropriate distance is different from yours. Even regulators, used to monitor the flow of conversation, vary from one culture to the next.

In such instances, make your reactions to these differences explicit or elaborated (Thomlison, 1991) so that the person realizes how you are interpreting her behaviors. If, for instance, you were having a group meeting and one of your members constantly arrives late, you may eventually determine that it is because of her cultural background and perceptions of time. Even though explained, the behavior is still disruptive and has a negative impact on the group. You might therefore determine that the cultural differences in perceptions of time need to be discussed so that an explicit agreement regarding appropriate behavior can be reached. In other words, when diversity is valued, the group develops its own norms to accommodate the needs of all its members.

Cross-cultural listening requires patience and kindness. When listening to those who are unfamiliar with your language or your point of view, be willing to make mistakes. The effective cross-cultural listener maintains an attitude of acceptance and open-mindedness, listening not only to accomplish a specific task but also to learn and to appreciate other ways of seeing the world. Increased awareness and understanding of cultural differences can reduce the level of uncertainty you experience in the communication process. When you are more confident about the communication choices you make, your chances of developing positive relationships and encouraging productive outcomes are increased.

THE CHALLENGE OF LISTENING BETWEEN GENDERS

Communication creates gender, just as it creates other realities. It is through your communication that you learn what it means, within a particular culture, to be male or female. You may have Indian friends, for instance, who grew up with very different assumptions and expectations about their sex role and responsibilities.

Gender itself is a significant variable in influencing your perceptions; men and women simply perceive and experience the world in different ways. What is responsible for these perceptual differences? One explanation might be that, from their earliest years, boys and girls have different social experiences that subsequently influence the way they see and interpret events. Regardless of the culture, virtually without exception, boys and girls are reinforced and recognized for different sorts of behavior (Tannen, 1990).

In the United States, little boys play competitive games in hierarchical groups and tell stories and jokes; girls play games in which everyone gets a turn and winning and losing are much less important. While girls who are pretty and well dressed may receive attention, boys are more often rewarded for their athletic accomplishments. Talk among young women establishes connections; listening to young girls and listening to young boys are two very different experiences. Consciously or unconsciously, each gender is provided with different types of stimuli and sent different messages about what is valued or appropriate.

Some critics believe that sex-role stereotyping is introduced to children through fairy tales, in which the woman is typically helpless and beautiful and is saved by a prince who takes control of the situation and rescues her from danger. Although such messages are changing in ways that de-emphasize the role of gender, numerous expectations and myths remain that are largely based on preconceived notions and sex-related stereotypes (Borisoff & Merrill, 1991; Marsnik, 1993; DeVoe, 1999).

Because attributing certain characteristics to one gender or another is likely to produce behavior that is based on stereotypes, rather than on individual talents and abilities, it is important to develop a culture in which expectations are not gender linked. As Liza Dolittle noted in the well-known story of her transformation from uneducated urchin to a well-mannered woman, "I'll always be a flower girl to Professor Higgins, because he treats me like a flower girl and always will." Those who treat her like a lady, however, empower her to behave in a more appropriate and productive manner.

Although perceptions of behavior are often confused with actual behavior, the truth is that our perceptions are our reality. What we believe is what is true: our beliefs influence our subsequent attitudes and behavior. The fact that our language perpetuates many of these perceived differences between the sexes is troublesome. If you examine the connotative meanings of adjectives used to describe men and women, you will conclude that male and female behaviors are not only different, but that they are associated with power or powerlessness, confidence or uncertainty, competence or ineffectiveness (Box 10.2). The words we use influence our judgments and make change difficult at best. In North America, for instance, women nag, bitch, fuss, or are scatterbrained. They're emotional and tentative. Men remind, complain, are exacting, and are sometimes forgetful. They're confident and firm.

If all of this seems exaggerated to you, there also are undisputable differences between men's and women's communication styles that perpetuate this stereotyp-

---

BOX 10.2

GENDER-RELATED TRAITS: TRUTH OR MYTH?

Which characteristics are associated with American men? With American women? Which are neutral? Do any of these characteristics have positive or negative connotations?

Picky	Nurturing	Emotional
Strong	Shy	Credible
Assertive	Insecure	Flexible
Giddy	Loud	Understanding
Sensitive	Decisive	Objective
Certain	Direct	Careful

---

ing. If we compare a woman's communication behavior with a man's, the origin of some of these perceptions becomes apparent. The next sections describe gender-related differences in verbal and nonverbal communication.

Verbal Differences in Gender Communication

In what ways are you an exception to common gender stereotypes?

Verbally, women's speech is often characterized by elements that create the impression of powerlessness and uncertainty (Box 10.3). When they speak, women often use "tag" questions. Instead of saying, "That report is due on Wednesday," a woman is likely to say, "That report is due Wednesday, isn't it?" This tag pro-

---

BOX 10.3

GENDER DIFFERENCES IN THE SPEECH OF NORTH AMERICAN MEN AND WOMEN

- women use more qualifiers
- women use tag questions
- women speak with an upward inflection
- female voices are higher, softer
- men tend to overlay women's speech
- men interrupt women more than women interrupt men

- men tell stories; women ask questions
- the content of women's speech is more personal; women talk about their feelings more readily than do men
- men state ideas more directly
- men use profanity more frequently
- women wait for a sign of interest before continuing

jects a lack of confidence and a need to secure agreement and confirmation (Tannen, 1990; Leeds, 1991; Carr-Ruffino, 1993).

Women also qualify statements and use disclaimers more frequently than men. They are more likely to preface their statements with, "I'm not entirely sure, but . . ." or "This probably sounds outrageous, but . . ." Although similar qualifiers can be used to encourage a supportive climate, in other contexts qualifiers communicate uncertainty and weaken the communicator's credibility. Look at the difference between "It's time to go" and "Well, I guess it's time to go now, isn't it?" When making requests or presenting negative information, women appear less confident than men when their statements are indirect or qualified. In addition, women interrupt men less frequently than men interrupt women. In general, both genders appear to listen more carefully to men than to women (Emmert, Emmert, & Brandt, 1993).

Nonverbal Differences in Gender Communication

We know that nonverbal communication is, to some extent, culturally determined; nevertheless, gender differences in nonverbal behavior are also apparent (Box 10.4). In mixed company, women are more likely to look away when speaking and maintain steady eye contact only when listening. Smiling, often interpreted as submissive behavior, is much more typical of women. Women tend to reveal emotions to a greater extent than men—there is more "leakage" in their facial expressions. Men also appear to touch women more than women touch them, and to require more space for their interactions. The sweeping, forceful gestures men use project confidence and assertion, especially when compared to a woman's tendency to use smaller movements and to limit the amount of space she occupies.

Another nonverbal element that adds to the perception that women are less confident than men is the pitch and volume of the female voice. As discussed in Chapter 9, assertive skill requires a forceful delivery. Women tend, because of the size of their vocal cords and larynx, to have a higher pitch. This can put them at a disadvantage, particularly in group settings where perceived credibility is essential.

■ ■ ■ ■ ■

BOX 10.4

GENDER DIFFERENCES IN NONVERBAL COMMUNICATION

- men display a more relaxed posture
- men tend to take up more physical space
- eye contact varies with gender
- women use more facial expressions and emotional displays

- women are more likely to pay attention to nonverbal cues
- women smile more frequently
- men use more forceful gestures
- women have softer, higher voices

In addition, women's voices tend to be softer than men's. Although volume can be increased with practice, many women do not recognize the importance of their voice in communicating credibility and confidence.

Gender-related listening tendencies have also been identified. Due to their stronger nonverbal cues and their focus on the relationship aspect of communication, women are often perceived as more empathic than men by both men and women (Bassili, 1979; Emmert, Emmert, & Brandt, 1993; Solomon, 1998; Richardson, 1999). Yet, men score better than do women on tests for factual comprehension and recall from lecture material. Borisoff and Merrill (1991) suggest that men and women have different listening expectations and needs which may account for their different competencies. While women are interested in the way their partner is feeling, men often perceive fact-related messages, particularly in the workplace, as more significant.

The topics men and women choose to listen to are also different. While men frequently engage in conversations about sports events, stock market reports, and fishing trips, women are more likely to be discussing relationships, personal experiences, or health-related topics. This gender-based selective attention further distinguishes listening behavior between the two groups. In addition, men tend to engage in other activities while listening; women are more likely to focus their complete attention on the speaker (Marsnik, 1993). This may be why over two-thirds of the women in Hite's (1987) study on women and love, when asked what their partner did that created the most frustration for them, responded, "He doesn't listen."

> In what cultures does a large gap exist between the communication behaviors of men and women? In which cultures is there less of a difference?

What does all of this mean for the listener? It means that in order to communicate effectively, men and women alike must recognize that there are indeed differences in verbal and nonverbal behaviors. The stereotyped perceptions we perpetuate, even through our language, color our attitudes and shape our subsequent behavior. While specific gender differences may vary from one culture to the next, men and women everywhere display sex-linked communication behavior. Although the situation is continuously improving, at this point many women throughout the world still appear to experience, or perceive, a sex-linked disadvantage communicating with men, particularly in the workplace.

Suggestions for Effective Cross-Gender Listening

The behaviors that make it difficult for women to gain credibility and authority in a male-dominated environment can be modified and changed. Communication styles are largely learned, and can therefore be replaced by more effective behaviors. In addition, our notions regarding effective leadership are increasingly characterized by behaviors typically associated with women's communication. Those who earn the respect of their colleagues and who foster a healthy, productive workplace do so by listening, guiding, mentoring, and coaching. Images of leadership as power and control have been replaced by a profile of the most effective leader as one who develops employees and facilitates interaction around key issues. While speaking has been associated with status in the past, listening has become the critical management competence of the twenty-first century.

As a listener, there is much you can do to ensure that all communication participants are viewed with equal respect and judged as unique people rather than representatives of their gender. The first technique is to apply the general semantic principle of indexing. Remember that male manager 1 is not necessarily at all similar to male manager 2 or manager 3; neither is female manager 1 identical to female manager 2. Don't make judgments about an individual until you have had an opportunity to meet the person firsthand and observe him or her in a variety of contexts.

Cultivate a nonsexist vocabulary. Pay special attention to the language you use to describe gender-linked behavior. Avoid overreacting to the connotative meanings of the words used. Be sensitive to how your vocabulary and images may be affecting others. Develop sensitivity to the ways in which even common expressions sexualize the conversation: low blow, on target, playing hardball, all elicit images of masculinity.

Analyze your own nonverbal communication cues. Make sure that your behaviors are appropriate and neither intimidating or too timid. Remember that the speaker is responding in large measure to you. While women may find it beneficial to monitor their nonverbal cues and develop assertive skills, men can encourage women's participation by using more pauses in their speech, interrupting less, and creating supportive environments in which women feel free to speak out.

Bring your biases and stereotypes to the surface. Ignoring or denying them isn't a solution. When you recognize the basis for your reactions, you will be in a much better position to control your response and work with any insights that develop. As stereotypes fade, and as our perceptions of effective male and female role relationships change, communication between men and women will become increasingly effective.

THE CHALLENGE OF ETHICAL LISTENING

Every communication event has an ethical dimension. Ethical issues focus on value judgments concerning the degree of right and wrong, good and bad, in human conduct. As a listener, your task is to determine whether communication should take place and, if so, at what level of disclosure. Just because someone is willing to tell, does that obligate you to listen? Clampitt (1991), for one, believes that in the very act of listening you take a moral stand. Ethical listeners must consider all aspects of their choices—not only what to listen to, but also to whom, where, and when.

> What is meant by the statement, "Every communication event has an ethical dimension"? Do you agree?

Suppose, for instance, that you are aware a rumor is circulating about one of your group members. You know the rumor is unsubstantiated; it was originated and perpetuated by an old girlfriend who has reason to distort the truth. When she stops you after class and whispers, "I have to talk with you about Jason. When can we get together?" What do you say?

> Is it typical for you to listen with "reasoned skepticism"?

Since we view listeners as bearing mutual responsibility with their partners for the outcome of communication events, it is only reasonable that listeners share in the ethical responsibility as well. Larson (1989) points to two ways in which, as a listener, you can become a more active participant in the process of ensuring ethical communication. One way is to maintain reasoned skepticism, and the other is to provide the communicator with appropriate feedback.

Reasoned skepticism is a mental viewpoint, a healthy curiosity that encourages questions and probing. Ethical listeners prepare themselves for the task of objectively evaluating what they hear by following the principles outlined in Chapter 7. Think of the numerous immature, superficial, and misleading judgments that are made every day by those who have not taken their listening responsibility seriously. In fact, relying on your immediate response or intuition may cause you to distort the intended meaning. Often, it is only by distancing yourself from the emotionalism of the event that you can make wise choices.

Appropriate feedback is also critical. The nature of your response affects the outcome of the encounter. Feedback, as you know, can be verbal or nonverbal, oral or written, immediate or delayed. The important element is that it be an honest reflection of your judgment or position so that your partner receives the information he needs to make further decisions. If you sacrifice honesty to avoid an uncomfortable or possibly even a conflict situation, you are making a significant ethical choice. Neither does remaining silent disengage you from your ethical responsibility; in fact, remaining silent is often in itself a critical ethical decision.

Technology has created additional ethical dilemmas because it allows for access to information that was unavailable in the past. Imagine the decisions regarding confidentiality that must be made daily by executives in companies that depend on detailed market analysis for their financial success. What mailing lists should not be sold? What health-related information should be kept confidential?

> What fears do you have regarding the effect of new technologies on norms of ethical behavior?

Employees are also confronted with ethical choices in their daily activities (anonymous, 1999; Baker, 1998; Stevens & Brownell, 2000). In one recent study conducted by International Communications Research, nearly half of all American workers admitted to engaging in at least one unethical act as the result of technology in the workplace. Behaviors included such things as listening in to private conversations or using company equipment for personal business (1999).

As you are confronted with more information and greater options and as you interact with those whose values and world views are different from your own, ethical dilemmas will increase. It is never too early to consider your personal values and how you can respond most ethically in a world of conflicting and often competing social and business practices.

> What steps can you take to become a more ethical listener?

Suggestions for Ethical Listening

It is commonly believed that a failure in ethics is less excusable than an error in performance. This may be because ethics reflects on your character. Ethical communicators are characterized by their discretion and judgment. They ensure that information is relevant and accurate. They time communications appropriately and are fair in making decisions.

Discretion is the intuitive ability to discern what is and is not intrusive or injurious and to use this understanding and compassion in responding to the day-to-day situations that arise. Ethical listeners focus on the purpose at hand and do not consider irrelevant information; they strive for accuracy in understanding and appropriate timing in their encounters. Ethical listeners ask themselves, would I want this done to me? The wisdom of a particular course of action must be judged on the basis of its final impact or outcome as well as on the communicator's motives. Good intentions, in daily interactions, are only half of the picture.

Whether as a member of a family, a school, a club, or a work organization, you act as part of a larger community. Clampitt (1991) addresses this relationship by identifying three ethical dimensions that he believes constitute a useful model. An ethical framework, in his words, is created and sustained by "individuals of personal integrity, operating in a culture of principle and governed by conscientious policies" (p. 283). As a listener, then, you begin by developing your personal ethical framework and behaving in ways that are consistent with your beliefs. If each person acts with integrity, the development of an ethical culture and the implementation of fair practices within that culture are likely to follow.

SUMMARY

In the United States, many people spend a large percentage of their time listening to the media. Consequently, the influence of the media on your attitudes, values, and behavior has been a topic of increasing concern. Understanding how to listen to the media and how to evaluate its content is essential. Perhaps of even more consequence, the technological revolution has ushered in such a pervasive transformation in the way we think about information, commerce, and business generally that it has affected all aspects of human communication. Recognizing the impact that technology has on your listening behavior is helpful in making wise decisions about what, where, when, and how to communicate.

Your listening is also affected by other variables, the most significant of which is culture. As technology makes true globalization possible, you will find yourself communicating regularly with individuals from other parts of the world who have different backgrounds, experiences, and languages. Understanding how to listen effectively when participants have different perspectives and world views will be a key competency for success. On a somewhat more focused scale, gender differences also create challenges for effective communication. Men and women develop different communication styles, and these styles subsequently influence the perceptions of their messages. Gender, like culture, affects individuals' attitudes and viewpoints and requires that participants practice effective listening to bridge gaps created by these differences.

Finally, listeners have an ethical responsibility in all their communication encounters. Listening is not a passive activity; as a listener, you choose what to listen to and what to do with what you hear. The careful consideration of your responsibilities in this regard will help you to perform tasks and build relationships that are healthy and productive.

APPLICATIONS

Application 1: Meet the Challenges of Listening to the Media and Listening in High-Technology Environments
Application 2: Meet the Challenge of Global Listening
Application 3: Meet the Challenge of Listening across Gender
Application 4: Meet the Challenge of Ethical Listening

Application 1: Meet the Challenges of Listening to the Media and Listening in High-Technology Environments

You are a member of the media generation. It may be difficult for you to imagine a time without television or computers or the advanced technology that allows you to see glimpses of the moon and receive events as they happen on the other side of the world. The changes that have come so rapidly, and that will continue with increasing frequency, are having a profound impact on the nature of human communication generally and your listening practices in particular.

Activities

1. How much time do you spend listening to the media each week? How do you make choices about what to listen to? What percent of your media listening time falls into each of the following categories:

    Television   *Radio*
    Entertainment_____   Entertainment_____

News_____   News_____
Education_____   Education_____

2. Do you engage in other activities while listening to the television? How does that affect your listening? Does it matter?

3. What kinds of media listening do you do for relaxation and enjoyment? If these sources were not available to you, what do you think you would be doing instead? In other words, what impact does listening to the media have on your activities?

Group Activities

Form a small group of four to six people. You may want to keep the same group for all activities, or you may find it more interesting to change groups so that you get to hear the opinions and ideas of a greater number of your classmates.

1. How does music influence your perceptions of television programming? Discuss some of the best known themes and how they create an auditory "set" for each show. Plan creative combinations of themes that would be totally inappropriate backdrops for certain programs. What effect would that have on the listener?

2. Do you believe that television violence is harmful to children? In other words, do you believe that children who listen to harsh language and verbal aggression are more likely to demonstrate these behaviors?

3. Brainstorm a list of phrases that originated on television or radio programs but which have become part of the common vocabulary in the United States. Do the same for advertisements. For example, Nike's "Just do it" has become a well-known expression.

4. Do you agree that television news provides listeners with "pseudo-events," stories that are visually interesting but which may not be legitimately newsworthy (or at least not as newsworthy as other stories)? As critical listeners, what might you do to reduce this tendency?

5. How do the media affect choices in political campaigns? You might research the Kennedy versus Nixon debates of 1960, which were the first to be televised. How were listeners influenced in this situation? As a critical listener, what can you do to ensure that the judgments you make are not manipulated by the media?

6. Generate a list of the schema, the "routines" or "common understandings" about the way things are done that have been created or reinforced by the media. For instance, the media portray certain images of the way family members relate to one another and the roles each member plays.

7. It has been suggested that the media perpetuate stereotypes. Do you agree? Can you think of examples from the media of how stereotypes have been reinforced for the following groups:

women   truck drivers   teenagers
African Americans maids   salespersons

8. Read the following passages from Sue and John, two recent college graduates who are at their first jobs. For each one, discuss the main issues and then recommend a course

of action. In both cases, the employee needs to have someone listen to the problem he or she is experiencing.

Sue:
I took a new job several months ago. I love the atmosphere and the people in the office. A portion of my work requires that I use some complicated computer systems. I have discovered that technology really scares me, and I'm consequently not doing very well at all. I've had a lot of training—probably more than anyone else in my department, but I continually make mistakes. My boss, although she's tried to be patient, is becoming increasingly angry and skeptical of my ability. It looks like things are going downhill quickly. What should I do?

John:
I love my job and when I first started working here the people were all very friendly. Now, however, I'm beginning to feel isolated. We all have electronic mail that is used for all sorts of purposes. Because this is so convenient, no one ever calls or stops to talk in the halls. It seems as if I can go all day long without a conversation; everything is communicated over the computer system. I have a lot of questions, but I have few opportunities to talk with anyone. What should I do?

Application 2: Meet the Challenge of Global Listening

The world is getting smaller. The global village that seemed so far away now describes your own community, your school, your organization. Understanding the values and expectations of those who are different from you is critical if you are to be an effective listener in this environment. Your housemate, your supervisor, or your team member may have very different assumptions and beliefs due to their cultural backgrounds. Recognizing the impact of these differences is the first step to sharing meanings across cultures.

Activities

1. A statement is made in your text that people in the United States value speaking over listening. Do you agree? In what ways is this true?

2. Do you have a high or low tolerance for ambiguity? How did you come to this conclusion? How does this tendency potentially affect your cross-cultural listening?

3. Have you traveled to foreign countries? What differences in communication were most striking to you?

Group Activities

Form a small group of four to six people. You may want to keep the same group for all activities, or you may find it more interesting to change groups so that you get to hear the opinions and ideas of a greater number of your classmates.

1. Generate an example of a high context interaction you might have with your friends or classmates. Role-play the situation for the rest of the class. Discuss what aspects of the

situation were indirect. Role-play the same situation, this time making all of your intentions explicit. Discuss the differences and the ways in which misunderstandings can result when you are not familiar with the indirect cues of a culture.

2. Discuss the challenges involved in listening to someone from a foreign country. Generate a list of the problems that have arisen for members of your group. Select several of the most significant problems and brainstorm possible solutions. Share these with the rest of the class.

3. A culture's values, beliefs, and attitudes are often expressed through the advice members of the culture provide to one another. Imagine that you have been appointed the new "Mr./Ms. Advice," a columnist known for providing commonsense insights to people who are uncertain about how to handle a particular situation. Respond to the following in a way *that reflects your own cultural background*. Provide enough information for the reader to clearly understand your viewpoint. If few cultures are represented within your class, solicit opinions from non-U.S. friends outside of class and be prepared to share their views.

   a. My teacher never listens to me. Last week he gave me back a paper with the grade of "C–." I went in to explain why I had done poorly and to ask if I could rewrite the paper. He didn't even sit down to talk with me. He just waited for me to finish and then said, "Study harder next time." What should I do? *Discouraged*

   b. I'm the only female in our engineering seminar. Sometimes, especially when everyone is trying to impress our teacher, I feel that none of the others are really listening to me. I have a hard time expressing my ideas under such competitive circumstances, and 40 percent of our grade is based on participation. What do you suggest? *Ignored*

   c. I'm in love with a wonderful woman (I'm 20, she's 28). We want to marry, but there's a problem. My parents oppose the marriage not only because she is older than I am, but because she has two young children and is of a different religion. I am a very religious person myself—it's a very important part of my life. She and I respect each other's beliefs and feel that we could raise her children, and any others we might have together, to appreciate both. I do hate to go against my parents' wishes because I am afraid they would not speak to me if I married her. They don't listen to my arguments at all—to them, it's not an issue that requires discussion. What should I do? *In love*

4. Read the situation below and, as a group, generate several recommendations for Mary. Share your conclusions with the rest of the class, and determine the best alternative.

   Situation: You are manager at a resort property in Asia where women are just beginning to be accepted in leadership positions. You have just promoted Mrs. Mary Frank, who has been with your company for three years, to Front Desk Manager. Although she is very capable, she has experienced repeated problems with guests who ask to speak with the manager and, upon discovering the manager is a woman, insist on speaking with a man. Yesterday she burst through your office door in tears, complaining that "no one listens to her" and that she finds it impossible to work in a culture where women have such low status. What do you do?

5. How diverse is your college or university? Your class? Respond to the following questions.

   a. How are the following groups represented within the student body? administration?

Black	Elderly
Hispanic	Disabled
Women	Other cultural groups

   b. How are the following groups represented among your school's faculty and administration?

Black	Elderly
Hispanic	Disabled
Women	Other cultural groups

6. Cultural differences have a profound effect on listening in organizations. Discuss the following situations with members of your group and decide what should be done to improve listening effectiveness in each case.

   a. You work in a hotel that has recently hired a large number of Hispanic housekeepers. Almost 65 percent of the housekeeping staff, in fact, are non-native speakers. Very few read at more than a first- or second-grade level, and listening comprehension is creating major problems. Rooms are not ready on schedule, directions are misunderstood, and procedures are ignored. This problem is affecting not only relationships and efficiency within the housekeeping department, but perceptions of service in the property as well.

   b. In an effort to recruit minorities, your university hired an Arab supervisor for the kitchen of one of your student dining halls. Immediately, the human resources department began receiving complaints from employees who felt that they were being harassed. The Arab supervisor stood very close to his employees and maintained what one woman described as "extremely intense" eye contact. He frequently touched the waitstaff as the women passed through the kitchen with dishes, and constantly touched both male and female cooks when he spoke with them. As a consequence, his employees (many of whom were students) were so uncomfortable they found it impossible to listen to him. Misunderstandings increased and the atmosphere was tense.

Application 3: Meet the Challenge of Listening across Gender

Understanding the influence of gender on listening will become increasingly important as men and women assume a variety of new roles. Studying and working closely together provides opportunities to better understand and appreciate similarities as well as differences.

There is little question that traditional communication styles have created stereotypes and gender-linked images that both men and women are working to reduce. By valuing differences and by analyzing your own communication, you will be in a better position to move beyond any obstacles gender may present to hearing and responding appropriately to each communicator.

Activities

1. Consider the extent to which you project the stereotypical male or female communication characteristics. Does this affect your cross-gender communication?

2. Do you notice that you listen differently to your male and female friends? In what ways?

3. What gender-linked messages did you receive when you were young about how boys and girls should behave?

Group Activities

Form a small group of four to six people. You may want to keep the same group for all activities, or you may find it more interesting to change groups so that you get to hear the opinions and ideas of a greater number of your classmates.

1. Divide your group into men and women. The men then brainstorm all of the stereotypes associated with women, and the women will do the same for men. Each group creates a list. After 10 minutes, the women begin by choosing one adjective and sharing it with the men. The men have an opportunity to respond in terms of whether or not they think it is accurate and how they feel it either harms or helps their personal and professional relationships with women.

   After each group has shared several stereotypes, all participants discuss how well each group listened to the other.

2. Look at the list of topics below and determine which topics are gender-linked. Indicate whether you think the topic is of interest largely to M (men) or W (women) or whether it is N (neutral). Compare the results of your group with other groups. Discuss why you think many topics are gender-linked, and how that affects listening behavior. Consider whether any of your conclusions are culturally based. Add topics to the list.

Guns	Horses	Mechanics
Babies	Farming	Feminine Hygiene
Baseball	Stock Market	Abortion

3. Role-play the meeting at the Fortune the way in which it was described in the case. Then, role-play it a second time, experimenting with different ways Sylvia might have handled the situation. How do Sylvia's choices affect her credibility? How do they influence the extent to which others listen to her?

4. Choose one of the following topics. Spend some time researching the subject and prepare a 15-minute presentation for your class. End your presentation by responding to the following question: "How does this affect listening?" Save time to discuss the issues that arise.

   ### Topics

   a. Differences in men's and women's oral communication.
   b. Differences in men's and women's nonverbal communication.
   c. Differences in the ways girls and boys are socialized in the United States.

    d. Gender-linked challenges faced by women on the job.

    e. Gender-linked challenges faced by men on the job.

5. Choose a fairy tale with which your group members are familiar and examine the listening behavior of the characters. Are there any gender-linked tendencies? Are women listened to as much as men? What changes would need to be made in order for both genders to be portrayed as equal in credibility and competence?

6. Brainstorm a list of suggestions for more effective cross-gender listening. How do groups of all men differ from groups of all women in their communication? Do you believe there are any differences in how these two groups solve problems, resolve conflicts, or make decisions?

Application 4: Meet the Challenge of Ethical Listening

As a listener, you share responsibility with your partner for the communication encounter. This implies that ethical concerns are also shared. As a listener, you have choices; you participate actively in determining the outcomes of each exchange. You therefore have an obligation to consider the ethical dimensions of all communication situations and to anticipate what your ethical response might be if confronted with an ethical dilemma.

    As you come together with individuals whose backgrounds and beliefs are different from your own, and as you join and move up in highly competitive organizations, the need for a thoughtful listening response is even more critical.

Activities

1. Do you believe that listeners share in their partner's ethical responsibility? Explain.

2. As a listener, what values do you believe are important to:

    a. a student

    b. a teacher

    c. a parent

    How do these values have the potential to corrupt each group—that is, tempt individuals to make choices that may not be ethical? For instance, students value grades. How might this influence their behavior?

3. Keep an ethical journal for two weeks. Note any instances where you were confronted with an ethical dilemma as a listener, and explain how you reacted.

Group Activities

Form a small group of four to six people. You may want to keep the same group for all activities, or you may find it more interesting to change groups so that you get to hear the opinions and ideas of a greater number of your classmates.

1. Does your school have an ethical code? If so, examine it and make sure everyone in your group understands and agrees on its purpose. How does it relate to your respon-

sibilities as a listener? Who knows about the code? How could it better serve its purpose in your college or university?

2. Identify a recent event that has generated a significant ethical dilemma. You might get ideas from the newspaper or news magazines. What are the various sides of the issue? What position do you take as a listener?

3. What ethical dilemmas have you experienced as a student (refer to exercise 3 above, if you chose to keep a journal)? Discuss the situation with members of your group. Do you all hold similar views?

4. Discuss your responses to the following ethical dilemmas. First, decide what the person in each situation should do. Then, having listened to each situation, what do you believe would be your ethical responsibility?

   a. A close friend tells you the following: About six months ago I began bartending at a local club. Everything was fine for a while, but at our last employee meeting the owner complained that we were losing too much money and told us we could help to "fix" things by adjusting the way we made the drinks. I just discovered from my manager that what he meant was that we were to put less alcohol into the drink than what was required. I just don't feel this is right, but now the manager is watching me carefully as I make the drinks and I know I'll be fired if I don't change. I really need this job—the money is excellent and the people are friendly. It would be almost impossible to find another job this good without relocating. What should I do?

   b. A classmate pulls you aside in the hall and says: Dr. Jones just told us about a rally that is going on in the quad tomorrow at the same time as our next class. Although he'll be here, he encouraged us to attend the rally if we wanted to instead of going to class since he felt it was for a good cause. So, let's skip class and go get that computer we've been trying to find the time to buy. He'll never know the difference.

   c. Your housemate comes in with a bag full of food: My job at Jim's Cafe isn't so bad after all. You know I don't get paid very much. Well, it seems everyone takes home food at the end of their shift. I'm not sure whether this is enough for both of us tonight, but I've got fifteen of those great corn muffins and enough turkey to make ten sandwiches!

GENDER AND COMMUNICATION AT THE FORTUNE: CASE QUESTIONS

1. What stereotypical communication behaviors were demonstrated by both the men and the women at the Fortune?

2. What communication behaviors did Sylvia exhibit that prevented her from establishing credibility at the meeting? Suppose one of the men decided to mentor Sylvia. What advice might he give her?

3. What specific listening challenges did Sylvia and Brigitte experience in the situation?

4. What "meaning" did the men share? The women? Describe what you learned about how employees "defined the situation" at the Fortune.

5. Role-play the meeting as it is described in your text. Discuss the problems you recognize, particularly with regard to:

- individual differences in perception and focus of attention
- interpreting messages
- evaluating messages
- responding to messages

Now, coach Sylvia and Brigitte with regard to how you believe they might handle the situation more effectively.

Role-play the meeting a second time. Discuss the outcome.

6. Would you say that Sylvia was being harassed? Do you suspect that different members of the group would have different meanings for the word *harassment*? Explain these differences in terms of what you now know about listener-defined meanings.

7. Imagine you are the Director of Training and Development for the Fortune. What type of seminars would you recommend for all employees? Assume that you decided to devote eight hours to listening training. Which components of the HURIER model would you emphasize? Why?

BIBLIOGRAPHY

Anonymous. (1999). New technology strains ethics, *USA Today, 127*(2649), 4.

Baker, L. W. (1998). Communication ethics in an age of diversity. *Public Relations Review, 24*(2), 254–255.

Barrios, J. (2003, December 14). The 3rd annual year in ideas: Billboards that know you. *New York Times Magazine,* 54.

Bassili, J. (1979). Emotion recognition: The role of facial movements and the relative importance of upper and lower areas of the face. *Journal of Personality and Social Psychology, 37,* 2049–2058.

Borisoff, D., & Merrill, L. (1991). Gender issues and listening. In D. Borisoff and M. Purdy (Eds.), *Listening in Everyday Life: A Personal and Professional Approach,* pp. 59–85. New York: University Press of America.

Bostrom, R. N., & Searle, D. B. (1990). Encoding, media, affect, and gender. In R. Bostrom (Ed.), *Listening Behavior: Measurement & Application,* pp. 25–41. New York: The Guilford Press.

Brady, K. T. (2004 June 24). Tech gadgets high on list of travelers' things to pack. *St. Charles County Business Record.* Wentzville, 1.

Brown, A. (2002, September). Listening to the Luddites. *USA Today, 131*(2688), 26–28.

Brownell, J. (1994). Relational listening: Fostering effective communication practices in diverse organizational environments. *Hospitality & Tourism Educator, 6*(4), 11–16.

Carr-Ruffino, N. (1993). *The promotable woman.* Belmont, CA: Wadsworth Publishing Company.

Cerulo, K., Ruane, J., & Chavko, M. (1992). Technological ties that bind: Media-generated primary groups. *Communication Research, 19*(1), 109–118.

Clampitt, (1991). *Communicating for managerial effectiveness.* Newbury Park, CA: Sage Publishers.

DeVoe, D. (1999). Gender issues range from salary disparities to harassment. *InfoWorld, 21*(44), 78–79.

Dodd, C. H. (1987). *Dynamics of intercultural communication.* Dubuque, IA: Wm. C. Brown.

Emling, S. (2003, February 16). Digital billboards change sales pitch to match audience. *Knight Ridder Tribune Business News.* Washington, 1.

Emmert, P., Emmert, V., & Brandt, J. (1993). An analysis of male-female differences on the listening practices feedback report. *Journal of the International Listening Association,* special issue, 43–55.

Geddie, T. (1999). Moving communication across cultures. *Communication World, 16*(5), 37–41.

Gunn, B. (2003). Confident listening. *Strategic Finance, 85*(4), 13.

Hills, B. (1992). Interpersonal effects in computer-mediated interaction: A relational perspective. *Communication Research, 19*(1), 52–55.

Hite, S. (1987). *Women and love.* New York: Alfred Knopf.

Hulnick, G. (2000). Doing business virtually. *Communication World, 17*(3), 33–36.

Larson, C. U. (1989). *Persuasion: Reception and responsibility.* Belmont, CA: Wadsworth Publishers.

Leeds, D. (1991). *Powerspeak.* New York: Berkley Books.

Liu, A. (1976). Cross-modality set effect on the perception of ambiguous pictures. *Bulletin of the Psychonomic Society, 7,* 331–333.

Louhils-Salminen, L. (1999) "Was there life before them?": Fax and e-mail in business communication. *Journal of Language for International Business, 10*(1), 24–42.

Marsnik, N. (1993). The impact of gender on communication. *Journal of the International Listening Association,* special issue, 32–42.

McLuhan, M. (1964). *Understanding media.* New York: Signet.

Nishida, H. (1985). Japanese intercultural communication competence and cross-cultural adjustment. *International Journal of Intercultural Relations, 9*(3), 247–269.

O'Connell, S. E. (1988). Human communication in the high tech office. In G. M. Goldhaber and G. A. Barnett (Eds.), *Handbook of Organizational Communication,* pp. 473–482. Norwood, NJ: Ablex Publishing.

Purdy, M. (1991). Listening and community: The role of listening in community formation. *Journal of the International Listening Association, 5,* 51–67.

Richardson, H. L. (1999). Women lead in style. *Transportation & Distribution, 40*(4), 78–82.

Roush, W. (2003). Listening to data. *Technology Review, 106*(9), 26.

Ruyter, K., & Wetzels, M. (2000). The impact of perceived listening behavior in voice-to-voice service encounters. *Journal of Service Research, 2*(3), 276–284.

Shatzer, M. J. (1990). Listening and the mass media. In R. N. Bostrom (Ed.), *Listening Behavior: Measurement & Application,* pp. 177–193. New York: The Guilford Press.

Solomon, C. M. (1998). Women are still undervalued: Bridge the parity gap. *Workforce, 77*(5), 78–86.

Stevens, B., & Brownell, J. (2000). Ethics: Communicating standards and influencing behavior. *Cornell Hotel & Restaurant Administration Quarterly, 40*(1), 39–43.

Storck, J., & Sproull, L. (1995). Through a glass darkly: What do people learn in videoconferences? *Human Communication Research, 22*(2), 197.

Stringer, D., & Lusardo, L. (2001). Bridging cultural gaps in mediation. *Dispute Resolution Journal, 56*(3), 29–39.

Tannen, D. (1990). *You just don't understand: Men and women in conversation.* New York: William Morrow.

Tapscott, D., Ticoll, D., & Lowy, A. (2000). *Digital capital: Harnessing the power of business webs.* Boston: Harvard Business School Press.

Thomlison, T. D. (1991). Intercultural listening. In D. Borisoff and M. Purdy (Eds.), *Listening in everyday life: A personal and professional approach.* New York: University Press of America.

Trevino, Klebe, L., & Webster, J. (1992). Flow in computer-mediated communication: Electronic mail and voice mail evaluation and impacts. *Communication Research, 19*(5), 539–547.

Wakshlag, J., Reitz, R., & Zillmann, D. (1982). Selective exposure to and acquisition of information from educational television programs as a function of appeal and tempo of background music. *Journal of Educational Psychology, 74,* 666–677.

Walther, J. (1996). Computer-mediated communication: Impersonal, interpersonal, and hyperpersonal interaction. *Communication Research, 23*(1), 3–11.

Willey, S. (1998). Civic journalism in practice: Case studies in the art of listening. *Newspaper Research Journal, 19*(1), 16–29.

NAME INDEX

SUBJECT INDEX